HARVARD

HARVARD

Through Change and Through Storm

By E. J. KAHN, JR.

W · W · NORTON  & COMPANY · INC ·
NEW YORK

*For the ten thousand sons of Harvard,
and especially for those among them
who are also mine.*

Preface

ON APRIL 9, 1969, as I was walking through Harvard Yard, a few hours after some students who had forcibly occupied the main administration building had been forcibly removed, I ran into Stanley Hoffman, the social scientist, who before that day was over would further enlarge his already formidable reputation as Harvard's Voice of Reason. Professor Hoffman had little time for chitchat. "You harbinger of disasters!" he said to me, and rushed off to some meeting or other.

The epithet was really quite unmerited, and almost unreasonable. True, I had been visible around Harvard during some tense moments, but I was so far from being a harbinger that I usually got to the scene of dramatic events after they were over. Had I suspected on April 9 that disaster was imminent I'd have arrived sooner. But the fact was that I was as certain as I could be, after more than a year's close scrutiny of Harvard, that what had happened at Berkeley, Columbia, and San Francisco State could never happen *there*.

This is not to say that I was surprised to have Harvard involved with worldwide student unrest. When I attended Harvard, in the nineteen-thirties, the boldest of the radical Americans of my generation were, I suppose, those who fought for the Loyalists in Spain. The next boldest were those who stayed home and worked, either overtly or covertly, for the Communist Party. I had one classmate who many of us suspected of being a bona fide, card-carrying Communist, but we could never be quite sure. I guess he was, all right; writing a brief autobiography for a class report published twenty-five years after our graduation, he said that his principal occupation was being executive secretary of the Communist Party of a New England state. I see him every now and then walking through Harvard Square. He looks middle-aged, conservative, and irrelevant.

My chief undergraduate memory of this paragon of consistency harks back to the Scottsboro case. Late one night, he burst into a suite I shared and cried, "We've got to send a telegram to the Governor of Alabama!" That was a good example of how students then expressed militancy. My roommates and I were the sort of people he would naturally seek help from, because we were on the next highest level of campus activism. We were liberals. He wanted our signatures to pad his telegram, and our money to pay for it.

We often joined forces with Communists, either because it seemed like the better of two evils or because we just wanted to *do* something. For a while, for instance, I helped edit a weekly paper that was started up by some Communist types who called themselves—can my memory be this precise?—the Greater Boston Student Committee for Peace and Freedom. I was one of a number of undergraduates who cared about journalism, had had a falling-out with the *Crimson*, and, lacking a Harvard outlet for our special energies, gladly worked for the left-wing sheet.

Its editor-in-chief was a non-Harvard student, a Party-line functionary whom we called the Dictator. He didn't seem to mind. He insisted on approving the contents of the paper before it went to press. The rest of us would escort him to our printing plant and, explaining that there was no time to run off proofs, hand him columns of type, which had to be read upside down and backward. He hadn't mastered the knack, but was too vain to admit it, so he would let just about anything we wanted to publish go unchallenged. Not that there was anything particularly daring about our output. We spent most of our time attacking the right-wing press, which nobody around Cambridge took very seriously in the first place; we were kicking a dead Hearst.

I had entered Harvard in the fall of 1933, at the same time that James Bryant Conant became president. I hadn't been there long when, with a few hundred other students, all of us knowing beyond the shadow of a doubt exactly what we were up to, I stood on the steps of the Widener Library, raised my right arm, and recited the Oxford Pledge. I thus committed myself irrevocably never to serve in any war for any reason. Five years or so afterward, I raised the arm again, took a further oath, and embarked on a four-and-a-half-year stint in the Army.

I almost didn't finish Harvard. When a junior, I resolved to spend the next year going around the world with a friend from Princeton. My family demurred (families *could* demur then), I backed down, and my place on the junket was taken by a Harvard classmate who never bothered to return to college. While I was writing a thesis in Cambridge, during my senior year, he was lolling in Tahiti. Neither my thesis nor his Tahitian had any lasting impact on our respective lives. He went on, once he had inexplicably returned to civilization, to become president of one of the world's largest advertising agencies, and I cannot remember what my thesis was about. It must have had something to do with Greek and English literature, because that was my field of concentration.

Concentration was, in my case, the wrong word. I took four years of Greek at Harvard, and at the end of it all was less conversant with the language than when I'd matriculated. I am not proud of this. *Mea culpa.* That isn't even Greek. The sad truth is that I don't retain enough Greek to flagellate myself in it. Some of my classmates could not understand why I thought it was hilariously funny that, at our twenty-fifth reunion, I should have been elected to honorary membership in the Harvard chapter of Phi Beta Kappa.

I have been a moderately loyal Harvard alumnus ever since, in a conventional way—a football game once yearly, on the average; a modest yearly contribution, too, except when I forget. I never attended a class reunion until I had been out of college a quarter of a century. By that time I had been detached from my classmates so long that I couldn't find anyone whom I positively remembered ever talking to as an undergraduate. It didn't matter; the men I fell in with at our twenty-fifth were congenial, and since then we've all been pretending that we knew each other all along.

Curiously, the longer I have been out of Harvard, the fonder I have grown of the old place. I must have talked about it a good deal at home. When my first two sons got old enough to go to college, both applied to Harvard, and both, to my delight as well as theirs, were admitted. Their accounts of life around the Yard stirred my curiosity, so, in the fall of 1967, I decided to spend a year at Harvard. It was very pleasant. The maître d'hôtel in one Cambridge restaurant once addressed me as "Professor." A number of my classmates were around, occupying impressive positions, and thanks to their intercessions and introductions I soon found myself equipped with a library card, Faculty Club privileges, a Harvard Coop membership, and an honorary association with Dunster House, where my oldest son lived. His brother and he tolerated my presence; Harvard is big enough so that we did not keep falling over each other, and small enough so that our paths would now and then cross. Occasionally, one of the boys would even have me to lunch at his club.

After I had been hanging around Cambridge for a while, people who knew that I was gathering material for a book about Harvard would keep asking me, "What aspect of the place are you going to cover?" The question was flattering to Harvard, implying as it did that the University was far too complex for any one person to contemplate covering it *in toto*. My answer, which never fully satisfied me, usually was to the effect that I was hoping to do an impressionistic study of what Harvard has become, with emphasis on those aspects of Harvard's past and present that had nothing necessarily in common beyond that I found them interesting. I had thought from the outset that a phrase from the old Harvard anthem—"through change and through storm"—might make an appropriate subtitle for a book covering so much chronological ground. I had no idea then, of course, how much change and storm Harvard would undergo. Harvard has had to survive much turmoil of late, and in the months and perhaps years immediately ahead may be confronted with a good deal more. I happen to believe that Harvard will survive that, too. I believe also that if it does not, much of what has been most valuable in the intellectual life of mankind will have died with it.

E. J. K.

Truro, Mass.
1 September 1969

HARVARD

"But surely it is a strange sort of logic to use in a university community in the light of all that has been learned through the centuries that because in one's own eyes one's aims are 'noble,' the means used to achieve them, however inconsiderate and injurious they may be to others, are thereby justified."
—Nathan M. Pusey to the annual meeting of the Associated Harvard Alumni, June 12, 1969.

i

HARVARD is an old university, dating back to 1636. Its movers and shakers—those, at any rate, beyond undergraduate age—sometimes think of it in terms of centuries. If Harvard survives until the year 2636—and despite its recent convulsions its chances seem as promising as those of any other twentieth-century American institution—chroniclers of its first thousand years may find it handy, and accurate, to divide its history into three equal parts, and to say that the first phase ended, with a loud and un-Harvard-like bang, after the first 333 years, in the tumultuous spring of 1969.

April 9, 1969, was the pivotal day. That was the day that crimson blood defiled the Harvard Yard. The prevailing mood there that day, once the waves of dismay and anger had passed, was one of sadness. There was disbelief, too, but to a lesser degree; on many other campuses, belief had long since been suspended, if not shattered. Nonetheless, Harvard had been, and probably still was, and might even continue to be, something special—the quintessential university, the very symbol of higher—

nay, highest—learning. One junior faculty member, standing in the Yard at noon that day, twenty-four hours after the Students for a Democratic Society had occupied University Hall, rudely expelling the deans who worked there, and seven hours after the police had even more rudely expelled the students, said sadly, "Some of us are suffering today from the kind of hangover that comes only from overindulgence in *hubris*." He went on: "It's all so irrational. It's surrealistic. A photographer who loves Harvard was roughed up first by the demonstrators and then by the cops. After that, he couldn't focus his camera because he was crying. A dean who told me about this started crying, too. And the mere telling about it is putting me in tears." The banner of the university whose motto is "Truth" was being carried by, as it were, a crying drunk. *In vino, Veritas.*

There were those in Cambridge that bleak spring day who were saying, not without hindsight, that Harvard had been overdue for trouble; it had been lucky too long; it was too prominent, too inviting a target to be further spared. But not even the editors of the *Crimson*, the campus daily, students who were presumably closer to the undergraduate pulse than most mortals, and in whose ranks stood quite a few first-rank Harvard activists, were exactly oracular. Less than a month before the university cracked open, several of the editors helped form a somewhat larksome "Conspiracy Against Harvard Education." The idea was that education should be a liberating, free-wheeling, do-whatever-you-like experience. "And so in April we are going to hold a Festival of Life," the Conspirators publicly announced in March. For a few days in April, during the strike that followed the bust, there was a strangely festive air to Harvard. There were rock concerts and light shows galore, and a great deal of plain, carefree *mingling;* but the conspiracy died aborning.

There had been more substantial hints of action in the *Crimson.* Late in March, President Nathan M. Pusey had attended a meeting of the Student-Faculty Advisory Council. The prickly issue of the Reserve Officers Training Corps was on the agenda—

as in what campus meeting of that year was it not? An intrusion by S.D.S. was not scheduled, but it happened anyway. The S.D.S. invaders, not surprisingly, were dissatisfied with Mr. Pusey's attitude toward R.O.T.C. (There was probably nothing he could have done, at that point in history, to mollify his adversaries, short of self-immolation.) The president's stance, one militant told the *Crimson*, "represents the type of rigidity which breeds confrontation."

The incubation period took two weeks. But even when the seeds of disruption had germinated and were ripe, it was hard for some Harvard officials, no matter how much they might normally be amenable to empiricism, to believe what they saw and heard. S.D.S. was muttering about taking over a building, but threat-making was, after all, a principal S.D.S. line of business. Asked for his views on a possible occupation, Franklin L. Ford, the dean of the Faculty of Arts and Sciences, said, "I have never heard of anyone seizing a building here, so I have no particular comment to make now." (He had never had to use a bullhorn before, either, in the exercise of his decanal functions, but he would very soon be doing that.)

There were few people at Harvard who thought that what did happen would happen, or could happen. Indeed, at an evening meeting on April 8, S.D.S. had voted three times *not* to occupy. But its leaders had swiftly called for a meeting at noon the next day to reconsider, and even as that session was getting under way the more militant members of S.D.S. were moving into University Hall. These were students affiliated with the all-out-revolutionary Progressive Labor Party. They were Maoist-oriented, didn't give a hoot for parliamentary procedures, and sometimes rather grandiosely referred to themselves as the academic portion of a Worker-Student Alliance. (The only workers the Harvard group established any detectable connection with were those well-known idealists the Teamsters Union; by way of demonstrating their solidarity with some striking Teamsters, the Harvard S.D.S. intercepted some laundry trucks and—quite uncommon for dedicated conspirators—aired a good deal of dirty linen in public.)

The invaders of University Hall were well prepared. They had chains and padlocks and placards reading, "Fight Capitalists—Running Dogs" and "Put Your Body Where Your Head Is." They had legal-aid lawyers' phone numbers inked on the backs of their hands. They had the building's regular tenants hustled out within the hour. The evictions were executed without personal injury, except to pride. It was, in a way, Revolution Harvard Style: at 3:00 P.M., with S.D.S. securely inside University Hall and at the same time being burned in effigy just outside, the tower bells of the Memorial Church close by began sonorously pealing, and from the open window of a freshman dorm a few yards farther on came the weird contrapuntal blare of Bach's Fourth Brandenburg Concerto.

S.D.S. had earlier made known its demands, which, like many student demands, were non-negotiable. The main one was that Harvard abolish R.O.T.C. The administration had already stripped the Corps of its academic standing and its instructors of their professorial rank; but the faculty had voted, by a ten-to-one ratio, *not* to abolish R.O.T.C. The S.D.S. apparently didn't really care one way or the other. It was not the issue that mattered but the event. By mid-afternoon, the S.D.S. had the situation well in hand. Its occupation was reasonably orderly. At one point, there must have been at least four hundred students inside University Hall, perhaps half of them observers. Early on, the participating students voted against doing willful damage to the building, and against smoking marijuana while inside. By solemn ukase, they desegregated the rest rooms; these were used interchangeably by males and females. Oh, the boldness of youth! Some filing cabinets were moved around, to serve as barricades, and the contents of a few of them were inspected. (Two days later, the *Old Mole*, the sprightliest of a number of underground journals hawked around Harvard Square, began publishing documents that were purported to reveal unsavory connections between the University and the C.I.A., but which actually disclosed little more than that

Harvard administrators, not unlike human beings everywhere, do not always in ostensibly confidential personal correspondence state exactly the same views that they pronounce in public utterances.) Finding a batch of blank identification cards for freshman proctors, a few students at once conferred proctorial status upon themselves; others, aware that Ivy League acceptances were about to be mailed to high school seniors, whiled away the hours by typing on Harvard letterheads warm notes to young men around the country, congratulating them on their admission as freshmen the following fall. (One observer reported that, near as he could make out, the S.D.S. group, which had long been celebrated for its zealousness in communicating, had simultaneously put to use every typewriter in University Hall—a building amply endowed with stenographic equipment.) Still others typed stencils, and one mimeograph machine churned forth a manifesto that concluded, "This is the first action of many to build a strong anti-imperialist movement in this country."

From time to time, during that afternoon and evening, the occupiers held a more or less formal meeting in the spacious faculty room, from which they voted to bar the faculty; they would communicate with it and with the administration, they further voted, only by public statements. Their friends outside provided them with food and bedding. Other friends, and spectators, milled around outside, in a blaze of television lights. One camera crew, it developed, was filming background scenes for a movie about a fictitious campus revolt. "Here we are in front of Jenkins Hall at Metropolitan University," an actor impersonating a television commentator was saying. "The atmosphere here is like a carnival."

Elsewhere in the Yard, other students were meeting, hoping to reach a moderate consensus that might forestall trouble. The Student-Faculty Advisory Council was represented, along with the Harvard Undergraduate Council and the Harvard Policy Committee; a member of a student film-making group stopped by to request, should this ad hoc gathering issue a statement, that his outfit be listed as a co-sponsor. "We need the publicity," he explained.

The deans were meeting, too—the big ones, representing the University's diffuse faculties, gathered nervously at President Pusey's residence; the littler ones, hierarchically subordinate, gathered at the Faculty Club library. There was a good deal of confusion among them. "The kids were much better organized than we were," one assistant dean said later.

Eventually, many of the two hundred or so students who remained inside University Hall went to sleep. Quite a few of them, as the night dragged on, expected no trouble. They were wrong. With the blessing of the senior deans, but without consulting the faculty, the administration had already resolved to have the students routed out at five in the morning. The decision, Fred L. Glimp, then dean of Harvard College, would say afterward, was "one of a lot of miserable options." The administration believed that the longer it waited the greater the chances were of violence, and the greater the probable interference with its orderly functioning, because of the loss, duplication, or mutilation of crucial documents. Somehow, the administration also entertained the hope—all but incredible in the light of recent history—that it was possible to throw college students and municipal policemen together without inviting, as it were, a chemical reaction that would blow out the walls of a laboratory.

At 4:00 A.M., some four hundred police were within striking distance of the Yard. To summon other students to the scene, fire alarms were set off—presumably by S.D.S.—throughout the Harvard community. The students inside University Hall had been told by Dean Ford, over a bullhorn, within a short time of their taking the building over, that if they didn't clear out in fifteen minutes they'd be liable to charges of criminal trespass. Now, at 4:55 A.M., Dean Glimp used a bullhorn to warn them that they had just five minutes to get out with impunity. Evidently, hardly anyone inside heard him.

At 5:00 A.M., the police moved in. There were two kinds—

dark-blue shirts and light-blue shirts. The dark-blues were municipal police; their job was to clear students off the four flights of
steps leading into University Hall. The light-blues were state police; their job was to get the students inside the building out. It
was generally conceded that the dark-blues were the least disciplined and the most brutal. As they converged on the steps, clubs
in hand, a few students within the building leaped from windows
and ran to freedom. "My roommate tried that but couldn't run
fast enough," one student said afterward. "He was too fat. His father didn't like his being arrested one bit. His father's company
puts up a lot of Harvard buildings, and I'll bet that from now on
most of them fall down."

There was little else to jest about. Many of the wounds suffered that morning were as much psychological as physical, but
all the same, boys and girls were getting clubbed. One student in a
wheelchair was hit. "I had to leave," a Radcliffe girl said. "I
thought it was too voyeuristic to stick around and watch students
bare their skulls to nightsticks."

One hundred and eighty-six young men and women were
bundled into police vans and taken off to jail. Some forty were injured. So were some policemen; a couple of them were treated for
bites. The cops were gone by 6:15. The Yard was littered with
trash and rutted by police vehicles. Buildings and Grounds personnel moved swiftly into University Hall to tidy it up. All
morning long, students milled about in the Yard, in a daze com-
pounded of sleeplessness and shock. "Whatever I think about seizing buildings," one of them said, "and I don't think much of it, I
keep reminding myself that human beings perform these acts, not
three guys whose initials are S, D, and S." Some classes went on as
scheduled. One resolutely anti-S.D.S. student reacted to the occasion by attending a course he hadn't been to in three months.

At 11:00 A.M., while the students who had been arrested were
being arraigned and, in most instances, released on their own re-
cognizance, between fifteen hundred and two thousand moderate
students assembled in the Memorial Church. How strange to see a

college church so crowded! There were students perched atop the reredos. One of the undergraduate moderators of the meeting invited those present to turn to and reflect on Hymn 256 in the hymnals on hand: "O God of earth and altar/ Bow down and hear our cry./ Our earthly rulers falter./ Our people drift and die."

Professor Stanley H. Hoffman, the social scientist, got up to speak on behalf of rationality. "This is the only university we've got," he said. "It could be improved. It can be improved. But it cannot be destroyed." He was loudly cheered. He advocated changes in Harvard's decision-making processes, but warned against changing the processes so much that the will of a minority should prevail. "No university can function if the minority insists on winning all the time," he said. More cheers.

The students began debating what course of action they should take. They finally decided on a three-day strike, and they passed a number of resolutions—among others, condemning the administration for unnecessarily summoning the police, condemning the police for their brutality, and calling for the resignation of President Pusey if he didn't meet student demands. "This is the most impressive and most exciting thing I've seen in four years at Harvard," a Radcliffe girl said. "It's the first time that moderates have dealt with radicals on their own terms. There's no longer a murky atmosphere here. The way the moderates have reacted is electrifying."

A resolution to condemn S.D.S. was tabled. Nevertheless, some of the S.D.S. people who had gotten out of jail had hastened to the church and were already crying "Foul!" They said that the administration had purposely delayed their release so they couldn't get to the church in time to vote. The meeting broke up at 2:00 P.M., amid ringing, responsible cries of, "Clean the church! Clean the church!"

Outside, a girl screamed, "Bail money!" into the ear of Dr. Chase Peterson, the dean of admissions of Harvard College. Dr. Peterson looked haggard. Even in halcyon years, the first week in

April is a nightmarish time for college admissions officials. The girl didn't know who he was. He just happened to have a mature ear. When she yelled into it, he winced. "Women shouldn't be allowed to talk in public," he said, not ill-naturedly. A boy in the junior class, who had a campus-wide reputation for not having missed a demonstration of any size since his matriculation at Harvard, slunk by. He seemed crestfallen. "My alarm clock didn't go off," he said. "I slept through the bust. I've lost my honor."

The Yard was still full of clusters of disputants. Graduate students from the Business School and Medical School had drifted over to see what was going on. A Divinity School student came by and asked no one in particular if it was all right for a lady organist to practice in the church, between meetings, for an imminent recital. Two S.D.S. members ripped an orange sign off a tree. "Hey, that's my sign!" shouted a student. "You wrote that?" said one of the rippers scornfully. "Yeats did," said the sign's owner, even more scornfully. "The ceremony of innocence is drowned," the sign read. "The best lack all conviction, while the worst are full of passionate intensity." The S.D.S. men shrugged and yielded up the sign.

A hundred yards away, a Western Union messenger carrying a sheaf of telegrams entered Massachusetts Hall, where President Pusey's office was. "The alumni are overreacting already," a student said. He looked serious. "Would you like to hear the views of an ordinary middle-of-the-road student?" he asked a bystander. He proceeded to give his views: "I have always been incensed by the moral arrogance of the S.D.S., but I'm afraid that this morning they scored a brilliant victory. Because of the administration's response to their totally unwarranted action, the issue, God help us, is no longer what S.D.S. did. The issue is cracked heads. It puts moderates like me in an uncomfortable position. I won't absolve S.D.S. of any responsibility, and I won't support any strike, but I'll sign all the petitions in the world to disapprove of calling in the cops that way. Most of all, I am deeply concerned about the future of Harvard University."

So were eighty or so older men and women who got together in Sever Hall, a classroom building, for an impromptu faculty meeting. George Wald was there, and James D. Watson, and John Kenneth Galbraith, and everybody was sitting facing a blackboard on which someone had chalked "on strike." "For Heaven's sake, let's reject, or let's repudiate, but whatever we do let's do anything but deplore," a voice implored. Those present agreed that the sense of their meeting was that they repudiated the occupation of University Hall, the eviction of the deans, the calling of the police, and the failure to inform the faculty that the police were being called.

The meeting broke up. Professor Wald fell into conversation with an undergraduate, who filled him in on the turbulent events of dawn. "The exasperations have been building up," Wald said, "and there may be still more blowups. The faculty is going to have to yell its head off to avoid them."

What had triggered the Harvard explosion in the first place? How could so many intelligent people have been so cocksurely convinced—despite Berkeley, despite Columbia, despite Chicago—that Harvard would never be hit? There was, of course, plain myopia: the inability of one generation to perceive the extent of the restiveness and bitterness that gripped another, and the inability, too, to realize how many students were no longer willing to subscribe to, among other splintering yardsticks, their elders' version of accountability. It is quite possible that precisely the same factors that caused people to believe it wouldn't happen at Harvard made it inevitable that it would happen.

Harvard's preeminence was supposed to have been its shield, but may instead have been its Achilles' heel. Harvard was supposed to have been so great and strong that it could stand above the battle—an unassailable fortress dominating the academic arena. But simply because Harvard was Harvard, because it was Number 1, Harvard was probably doomed. With S.D.S. cadres shooting down college administrations right and left, it would have been a terrible loss of face for S.D.S. at Harvard—probably the smartest

S.D.S. group anywhere on earth—if Harvard had got off scot-free.

Professor Seymour Martin Lipset, who came to Harvard by way of Berkeley, has said, "In a sense, as Harvard goes, so go the other universities in America." Even after S.D.S. moved into University Hall, Harvard had some choice about where it might go. Harvard chose to call in the cops, and, as President Pusey put it two months afterward, "the roof fell in." But when this happened, Harvard was merely continuing to play its conventional leadership role. Delivering the principal address at the literary exercises of the Harvard chapter of Phi Beta Kappa in June, 1969, Senator Eugene McCarthy said, "Harvard takes up both error and truth in advance of other places." There are times when even Harvard would be happy to let somebody else set the pace.

The strike that followed the bust was fairly successful. Most classes were held, many students abstained from attending, and where the educational process was pursued in its old-fashioned guise there were a few attempts to interfere with it. "In the middle of the strike, I was giving a course that met at 10:10 A.M., and I thought it might be disrupted," said Assistant Professor James C. Thomson, Jr. "The session went off without incident. At 11:05, as I was gathering up my notes, a young man wearing a T-shirt and a red armband and with every outward indication of being potentially disruptive rushed in and asked me, in non-negotiable tones, 'Is this History 171B?' I said it was, or, rather, had been. 'But you're supposed to meet at 11:10,' he said. 'No, 10:10,' I said. 'We always meet at 10:10.' He was downcast. He had failed to accomplish his mission. It was my first sense that there was a chink in their armor—an inadequate knowledge of time."

The strike was useful in another sense. It gave everyone time to cool off and to reflect. It was a time of year when mushrooms grow, and committees sprang up like them. For a while, there were committees that consisted of representatives of other committees that had been established by different authorities to explore the same areas. Conspicuous among the new groups was a sixty-eight-man advisory committee set up by Mr. Pusey, with which, its ponderousness notwithstanding, he proposed to consult before acting in future crises.

While Harvard licked its wounds, analyzed its past, argued its present, and very gingerly contemplated its immediate future, society's antediluvian institutions did their thing. Specifically, the courts brought to trial the University Hall interlopers who'd been arraigned. Harvard had threatened them with arrest, Harvard had brought in the cops to arrest them, and Harvard, in Harvard's sometimes quixotic way, had then asked to have the charges against them dismissed. But the judge, a Harvard man himself, had demurred. Ultimately, most of the defendants were fined twenty dollars, for trespassing.

Meanwhile, the Faculty of Arts and Sciences had created a special committee to determine how, if at all, Harvard itself should discipline the University Hall demonstrators, and also to draw up guidelines for future disciplinary situations. The committee consisted of ten faculty members and five students—the first time in Harvard's history that students had passed judgment on the behavior of their peers—and it became known as the Committee of Fifteen. S.D.S. called it illegitimate. Its recommendations to the faculty, made on the eve of Commencement, struck many people as being remarkably lenient. More than one hundred of the students identified as having taken part in the University Hall occupation were merely warned against repeating such behavior. For only three students, whose actions were thought to be especially intolerable, was dismissal advocated. Over 90 per cent of the faculty who voted on the recommendations for punishment, and on the proposed guidelines, voted in favor of them. The faculty, it seemed, was prepared to take a stand. It was saying to the students, in effect: "We are the ultimate arbiters of permissible behavior. We are prepared to let you go quite far—much further than many of us could have imagined ourselves condoning just a few weeks back—but in a community of rational men and women there must always be a point when enough is enough."

When the rumor spread that during the Commencement exercises some students might attempt to storm the platform where the chief administrative officers of the University would be assembled, a number of faculty members made a difficult but important decision: they were going to interpose their bodies between the students and their targets. To get to the administration, the students would literally have had to climb over the bodies of their professors—professors, what was more, accoutered in full academic regalia. That particular confrontation, happily for Harvard, did not come to pass.

As S.D.S. had predictably not liked the Committee of Fifteen, so did it not like its report. S.D.S. had demanded amnesty for all concerned. "This repression against us will not keep us from coming back even stronger next fall!" some of the radicals warned in an ominous letter to the *Crimson*. (They appended the sweeping indictment that "only militant action can be effective in fighting the violence and exploitation perpetrated by the Harvard Corporation on working people in Cambridge and throughout the world.") Now that it had been demonstrated that at Harvard, as elsewhere, the students not only could but would adopt disruptive tactics, no one would go so far out on a limb as to predict that, come fall, the militants would not make another move, perhaps one calculated to shut down the entire university. The mere fact that there could be serious speculation about such a possibility showed how much a Harvard student had evolved from the pusillanimous individual who a century before had sometimes been punished for shouting to a friend from the third floor of a dormitory. Still, the old Harvard had not entirely vanished. A senior who messed up his final exam in a Chaucer course in 1969 was given a failing grade for the year and couldn't graduate with his class; there was no public outcry about the relevancy of the course or the rightness of the action. And around the country, there were as usual thousands of high-school seniors bemoaning the fact that Harvard had not room enough to take them as its sons.

"O relic and type of our ancestors' worth
That has long kept their memory warm,
First flower of their wilderness! Star of their night!
Calm rising through change and through storm!"
—From *"Fair Harvard," by the Rev. Samuel Gilman, 1811*

ii

Shortly before midnight, on Friday, April 12, 1968, three weary men from Cambridge, Massachusetts, drove across the Charles River into Boston, dragged three mail sacks into an all-night postal annex at South Station, and, impressed with the gravity of their mission, made rather a ceremony of presenting their burden to a clerk. The clerk was unimpressed and dumped the sacks onto a pile of other sacks, which for all his visitors could tell contained junk mail. Thus ignominiously culminated seven weeks of intense, delicate, sometimes quarrelsome, and often frustrating work: the selection of 1,375 young men who when they opened their mail on Monday would learn that they had been admitted to Harvard College and could accordingly climb aboard what is widely—if no longer universally—conceded to be a surefire catapult to glory. The sacks also contained letters of rejection to 5,208 other young men who on Monday would have to face up to the prospect of no bouncier a springboard to a full, rich life than, say, Yale.

Until fairly recently, it was just about as easy to get into Harvard as any other college. With what ruefulness must the present-day college advisors and parents of high-school seniors in New

York City, not to mention the seniors themselves, reflect that between 1737 and 1790, at the start of which stretch Harvard had already completed a century of existence, not a single New York boy bothered to apply! (Of course, Harvard was then a long way off; the Eastern Shuttle had not begun to operate; and as late as the early nineteenth century it took John Quincy Adams, traveling the few miles between his home at Quincy, Massachusetts, and Cambridge to attend a meeting of the Harvard Board of Overseers, a whole day for the round trip.) Even as recently as the Depression years of the early nineteen-thirties, Harvard had no significant surplus of what it calls academically qualified applicants—young men, that is, who if they get in are reasonably certain not to flunk out; the first class for which there were more acceptable aspirants than there was space was the class of 1936. Before that, almost anybody with a modicum of intelligence and the tuition money could make Harvard. Thus, today, for anyone over fifty-five to brag of being a Harvard man may be indicative more of a state of mind than of a mind.

Up to 1880, however, when President Charles William Eliot prevailed after an eleven-year struggle with his faculty and governing boards, there had been one requirement for admission that tended to confine a Harvard education to the socially and economically privileged—a knowledge of Greek. Since it was a rare public school that taught the language, nearly all Harvard students came from private-school backgrounds. Today, 60 per cent of Harvard undergraduates come from public schools. If an institution can be thought of as sentient, Harvard has learned over its 333 years that progress in education, while it must always be pursued apace, can sometimes be attained only at glacial speed; and that in achieving desirable goals, institutions, like people, cannot hope to please everybody. Thus, for Eliot to do away with the Greek was clearly to strike a blow for democracy, but only at the cost of slighting the folks who'd invented it.

Like Athens in its heyday, Harvard is an enclave of wealth and tradition. Much of the former has been given, and much of the latter sustained, by Harvard sons following in the footsteps of their fathers, grandfathers, and, in the case of a few old and patrilineal New England families like the Cheevers and Saltonstalls, ancestors of almost astronomical great-greatness. (There was a Henry Saltonstall in Harvard's very first class to graduate, that of 1642, and eighteen succeeding Saltonstalls had gone through Harvard by the end of the nineteenth century. A latter-day Saltonstall, fittingly, was in University Hall at dawn on April 9, 1969.) Up to the Second World War, at least one-quarter of all Harvard freshmen were Harvard sons. Any familial tie to Harvard is judiciously noted by its Admissions people. ("Don't sit next to his uncle at a football game," one said to another when a certain's boy's name came up. "One of these days they'll have to take the apoplectic old bastard out on a stretcher.") But the son of a man who was first in his class at the Harvard Law School or the son of a Radcliffe summa cum laude has less going for him, genetically, than the son of a Harvard College dropout.

Now that so comparatively few boys who hope to go to Harvard can be accommodated, what to do about Harvard sons—there are fifty thousand living alumni of the College, though some of course are beyond breeding age—is a matter of increasing concern to Harvard. The authors of a 1960 faculty-committee report on admissions, while arguing that "some degree, probably a quite substantial degree, of family continuity is vital to any college," conceded that they were exploring "a torrid zone," and the area is not likely to cool off under any foreseeable circumstances.

Often it is the fathers who get more heated than the sons. When he was thirteen, one member of the Harvard class of 1969 made a deal with *his* father. The father would choose the boy's prep school, and the boy, at the appropriate time, would choose his college. At eighteen, the boy had no doubt that he wanted to go to Harvard and that he could. His marks were excellent, his school record was studded with extracurricular jewels, and his father and his paternal grandfather were both Harvard graduates of loyalty, distinction, and generosity. Indeed, the boy was so certain of making Harvard that he applied nowhere else. But to raise his father's temperature a little, he hinted at home that he was considering Yale and a few other spots. He even made a trip to California, ostensibly to inspect Stanford. It was the kind of teasing in which Harvard families occasionally indulge.

Of 250 Harvard sons who sought admission in the class of 1955, only sixteen were turned down. While Harvard today has room for only 20 per cent of all applicants, it makes room for 40 per cent of Harvard sons who apply. (Yale is currently turning down two-thirds of its old grads' progeny.) At a recent meeting in Cambridge of Harvard alumni who help the Admissions staff interview candidates around the country, the assemblage was told by a resident administrator that though the rejection rate for Harvard sons was more likely to rise than fall, the following year's freshman class would nonetheless contain, as usual, between 250 and 300 boys conceived by Harvard sperm. "How do you identify Harvard sperm?" called out one young alumnus, anticipating a Harvard joke. "Slightly pink," shot back an older man, providing it.

For the first three hundred years or so of Harvard, the nature of its undergraduate body was determined by its applicants—most of them being Harvard sons, non-Harvard-sired Bostonians, New England prep-school graduates, or boys from big-city high schools in the Northeast. It was so simple and routine a matter to put together each new freshman class that even after the Second World War the College could get by with an Admissions staff of one not terribly hard-pressed administrator and one part-time assistant. Today, Harvard has a full-time Admissions staff two dozen strong. Some of the people who work at Harvard are, all things considered, comparatively relaxed a good deal of the time; the exceptions are those few who concentrate on getting individuals in and out of the place—the squeezers and easers, as they're called. In deciding what kind of a freshman class they want, the harried squeezers follow guidelines that were first hesitantly propounded in the nineteen-forties, when James Bryant Conant was president of the University, and that have been energetically implemented under his successor, Nathan Marsh Pusey. Mr. Conant thought that Harvard undergraduates were too much of the same cut; he wanted Harvard to be a truly national institution. And so, with the diffidence and clumsiness of any tyro angler, Harvard began to cast a countrywide net for the best students it could catch, and began taking in—Harvard sons excepted—those boys who had the highest school marks and the highest College Board grades.

Harvard was soon drenched with brilliance. But this tended to produce a new and unsettling kind of homogeneity: Harvard seemed to be attracting a disproportionate share of young men who, while of uncommon intellect, were something less than well rounded. Some were unstable, and some were effete. The balance between brain and brawn that most universities aspire to was demonstrably askew. Soon after Mr. Pusey took office, in the fall of 1953, he had a nasty shock. Harvard went to New Haven for its annual football game with Yale, and Yale won, 54–0. Harvard alumni mouths went so dry that day they could scarcely bring themselves to sing, "With Crimson in triumph flashing. . . ." Pusey retained some powers of speech. Leaving the scene of the massacre, he muttered grimly to a companion, "I don't want this to happen again." It has not happened again; Harvard's worst loss to Yale since then was by the tolerable score of 39–6.

The dean of admissions during much of Harvard's restructuring of its undergraduate body was Wilbur J. Bender, who retired in 1960 to run a Boston philanthropic organization called the Permanent Charity Fund. Like many old Harvard hands, Bender continued, until his death in March, 1969, to have much to do with Harvard. He lived in Cambridge, and he often pondered fund-raising appeals from Harvard students, who he thought made far better presentations, all things considered, than most professional social workers. (One Harvard undergraduate, for instance, who lived in California, singlehandedly arranged—

with Bender's blessing and support—for six low-income Negroes from Texas to attend a junior college on the West Coast.) Anything in Boston called a Permanent Charity Fund is the sort of outfit one would expect to be run by a character out of Marquand. Bender, though, like many other persons who have lately had a big share in shaping and reshaping Harvard, was not himself shaped in the conventional New England mold. He was born in Indiana, into a family of such humble means that it took him seven years to get through Harvard. He had to keep dropping out to help support six siblings. He finally graduated in 1929, taught history for a while, served in the Navy, returned to Harvard as an administrator, and became dean of the College.

When Bender switched to Admissions, he set out at once—in a polite, Harvard way, with no aspersions cast—to demolish the criteria of a predecessor in that job who had construed it as his mission to attract to Harvard "as many as possible of the very rich and the very bright." Conant's goal of a national college, Bender felt, did not mean that Harvard should precisely reflect the national level of intellectuality, but he saw no reason why the undergraduates should not relate socially and economically to the rest of the country. What Bender wanted was "a good mix"—a term that college admissions people now use as incessantly as if they were in the wholesale baked-goods business.

Within a couple of years after Bender had taken over Admissions, the number of incoming freshmen whose fathers were dues-paying trade unionists had quadrupled. To help him find students who had more to them than mere intelligence or wealth, Bender recruited a corps of alumni who agreed to prowl around backwater schools and search for hidden talent, both brainy and brawny. Some of the senior scientists on the Harvard faculty were dismayed by this approach. In their view, Harvard could best serve its educational function by reaching out for the top 1 per cent, or even one-half of 1 per cent, of the country's most able scholars. The scientists' idea of a good mix was something in a test tube, and if every Harvard undergraduate spent all his days and nights in a chemistry lab and never learned where the football stadium was, so much the better.

But Bender won out—the fact that Conant was on his side and was a chemist himself did not hurt any—and in striving to broaden and diversify Harvard College, he was abetted by a number of gifted administrators. Notable among these was John U. Monro, who was to become dean of the College himself and who in 1967 voluntarily left that prestigious and comfortable post to assume the directorship of freshman studies at Miles College, a small, all-Negro, unendowed, and scrambling rural academy outside Birmingham, Alabama. Monro had always been something of a maverick. Raised in Andover, Massachusetts, he attended Phillips Academy as a day student on scholarship. In the spring of his senior year at Harvard, he left the prestigious and comfortable presidency of the Harvard *Crimson,* the undergraduate daily, to edit a short-lived but lively rival paper. He threw himself into the losing cause so unflaggingly that he failed to graduate with his class. (Harvard has a ceremonial president's chair, and so does the *Crimson,* with nameplates on it for all who have occupied it; at Monro's defection, a bar sinister was slapped across his name and is still there.)

After getting his degree in 1935, a year late, Monro did a hitch as a journalist and another as a naval officer. Then he came back to Harvard, as director of veterans' affairs, when the campus was swarming with men studying under the G.I. Bill. (Years after the war, an aldermanic candidate in a Chicago election tried to blunt the edge of an opponent's ugly charge that he was a Harvard man by explaining that he had merely been there at a time when a patriotic homecoming soldier had no recourse but to go wherever he could.) Monro got along well with the vets, in part because he didn't look or act much like a conventional Harvard man. He had thick black eyebrows that marched across his forehead in a nearly unbroken, emphatic line, and he once observed that while twenty-one of thirty Harvard men serving on the University's governing boards had as undergraduates belonged to social clubs, he had not only not been a club man but had even worn black shoes.

Monro was an outspoken dean. Provoked one time by a *Crimson* editorial that seemed to equate freedom of sexual intercourse with freedom of speech and religion, he issued a statement in which he deplored the possibility of "wild parties" on Harvard premises. It might have occurred to an ex-journalist that the Hearst paper in Boston would react with a headline like the one it did concoct: HARVARD BARES WILD PARTIES. Harvard hadn't actually bared anything beyond Monro's words, and their author was further discomfited when some of the students under his jurisdiction took to grumbling that they wished somebody had told them where the wild parties were before they were exposed. (Monro later disclosed that one of his most refreshing experiences as a dean had been when a junior stopped by his office one day and lectured him for an hour on sex.) Monro was a popular dean, and a hardworking one; it was said of him admiringly that he knew more undergraduates by their first names than any other Harvard eminence. David Riesman is generally thought to have succeeded to that distinction, though the sociologist modestly disclaims the honor; anyway, he points out, it is difficult to know young people these days by anything *but* their first names, because of their penchant for rarely introducing themselves in more extended fashion.

Monro was an innovative and compassionate administrator. It was largely he who convinced Harvard that scholarship aid should be based principally on financial need, and not on academic standing. (It was Harvard, too, in 1952, that instituted the now widespread practice of helping students by granting them loans along with scholarships.) Monro was the guiding spirit behind a student-employment program, and although Harvard generally encourages its students to live and board in dormitories, he arranged for two old apartment houses belonging to the University to be converted into cooperatives, where needy students could keep house and do their own cooking for considerably less than they would otherwise have had to spend. As a foretoken of his interest in Negro education, it was Monro, further, who, at a time when other colleges were gingerly beckoning to middle- or upper-class Negroes, had Harvard reach into the ghettos to pluck forth students to whom neither Harvard nor any other first-rate college had earlier shown much hospitality. Monro also gave Harvard its first Negro dean.

The liberal establishment is not without its ironies. After a Massachusetts Fair Employment Practices law was passed in 1948, universities in that state were no longer supposed to require applicants for admission to submit photographs. The obvious purpose was to protect individuals from being turned aside because their pictures disclosed their race. Alas, the law went into effect not long before Harvard, and other places, began *seeking* Negroes, and now the colleges couldn't single out those very applicants in whose favor they wanted to discriminate. Had the F.E.P.C. come into being a year before it did, Harvard might never have obtained an administrator who was to succeed Monro as dean of the College and who before that put in seven years as dean of admissions. This was Fred L. Glimp, who, like his predecessor Dean Bender a generation earlier, was a comparatively disadvantaged white man. Glimp, who also succeeded Bender, in the summer of 1969, as head of the Permanent Charity Fund, had an American Indian ancestor a few generations back. A college administrator at Berkeley once remarked enviously that Harvard's comparatively late exposure to insurrectionist minority groups was probably attributable to its sheer luck in having a red man for a dean.

A native of rural Idaho and the son of an Okie who never got beyond ninth grade, Glimp finished high school at Boise during the Second World War and enlisted in the Army. After three years in service, he decided to go to college, and picked Harvard because, although he knew literally nothing else about it, he had liked the descriptions of it in a book about Oliver Wendell Holmes. As the story is now told in Cambridge, Glimp's application, photo attached, came across Monro's desk when there was exactly one opening left in the student body, and the Idaho boy got the spot because Monro's secretary thought he looked nice. (He didn't look Indian.) If it hadn't been for the picture, Glimp likes to say these days, he might well now be an Idaho potato farmer. (There must have been moments, during the S.D.S. take-over of his office in the spring of 1969, when he wished he were just that.) Glimp's academic performance more than justified Monro's secretary's romanticism. He got his degree magna cum laude, made Phi Beta Kappa, spent a year at Cambridge, England, on a fellowship, earned a Harvard Ph.D. in economics, married a Radcliffe girl, and, in the eyes of some of his academic associates, achieved his greatest educational honor, in the winter of 1969, by being elected, despite the handicap of his Harvard deanship, to the Belmont, Massachusetts, School Committee.

Like his predecessor, Glimp had a wide acquaintance among the current crop of undergraduates. He *should* have known many of them; as dean of admissions, he admitted many of them. Hitch-hiking a ride to his home in Belmont during a New England bliz-zard in November, 1967, Glimp began chatting with a young man who picked him up. They had never laid eyes on each other before, and the driver had no idea who his passenger was. But after the driver had disclosed only the sketchiest autobiographical data, Glimp identified him—a fellow from Iowa who had sailed safely through Admissions six years earlier, one of about thirty thousand applicants Glimp had dealt with over that period.

Glimp was struggling through the storm on foot because he had invited some undergraduates to dinner and was determined to receive them. He couldn't hope to entertain all of the forty-eight hundred students in the College, but his wife and he now and then would ask a half dozen or so over and ply them with roast beef and wine. Glimp nearly missed his first such dinner, which was held on a date memorable in recent Harvard history—Octo-ber 27, 1967. That was the day some students held a Dow Chemi-cal Company recruiter captive for seven hours in a Chemistry building. The fall term, Glimp's first as dean of the College, was only a few weeks old, and suddenly he had a major crisis to deal with—a crisis that, he was subsequently to reflect, was his responsibility in more ways than one. "When the demonstration began," he said later, "I was just about the only person around who didn't have the easy excuse of being able to say, 'Jesus, who let *these* guys into Harvard?' These guys, whatever they might be up to on the twenty-seventh, had once looked awfully good to somebody in Admissions, and that somebody, I couldn't help reminding myself, was me."

When Glimp resigned as dean of the College, Harvard had a whole class that he *hadn't* admitted. "I still felt new at the job," he said, "but as far as the freshmen were concerned, I could have had it for a hundred years. I was the old dean who was there when they got there." Glimp's abrupt abdication from a once-vaunted deanship he actually held only a couple of years was unquestionably influenced by the painful events of April, though the Permanent Charity Fund had made overtures to him some time before that. He was a marked man on several counts. It was he who had given the largely unheard warning that the police were about to crash into University Hall. It was he who had the chairmanship of a committee, unpopular with many students, that had tried to work out a rapprochement between Harvard and the R.O.T.C.

What was more, the Dean of Harvard College has in some respects an unrewarding job. He has no faculty directly under him, but at the same time, he is responsible for more students— nearly five thousand of them—than any dean other than his immediate superior, the dean of the Faculty of Arts and Sciences. And the students he has are the undergraduates, a varied and volatile bunch. Within a few minutes one day in June, 1969, for instance, Glimp had to cope with a desperately unhappy and disoriented freshman whom Harvard had plucked from a black ghetto and who had flunked four courses, and with a brilliant senior who was highly ambitious (he already had founded his own financial firm, which specialized in raising venture capital for oil investments) and was convinced that bureaucratic mismanagement at Harvard had robbed him of a summa cum laude he deserved and left him with a mere magna with highest honors.

Glimp genuinely liked students. It was sometimes thought that his failing was that he tried too hard to be agreeable to them. Three days after the April bust, he spent four hours at the Freshman Union, standing on a chair, the only administration spokesman in a sea of disgruntled students. "I was trying to get a discussion going as to where we should proceed from there, and I was telling the students, 'You guys have to use your critical faculties as never before,'" Glimp said later. "From my point of view, I had a good forensic afternoon. From the point of view of the students, I'm afraid I was being evasive and too detached. In the whole four hours, only one guy stood up for me, and he was from the Medical School. For weeks afterward, when I walked around the Yard, I felt strange. The guys who had thrown me out of my office didn't respond at all to my presence. It was sort of the way I always responded, back home in Belmont, to Robert Welch, except that I was minimally civil."

It has long been Harvard's contention that admissions could be handled only on an extremely personal basis, but now that applications have passed the eight-thousand mark each year, some administrators are wondering if at least the initial culling could not be done by computers. Some medical schools are already using them to help place their graduates as hospital internes. The medical students give preferential ratings to hospitals. The hospitals give preferential ratings to students. The data are fed into a machine. An individual remains in contention for his most wished-for hospital until its available spaces have been filled by people it wants more than it wants him; a hospital remains in contention until an individual is accepted by a place he'd rather be at. If something of the sort could be worked out for college admissions, it might save some time.

Meanwhile, however, admissions remains, at best, a very inexact science. Any group selecting Harvard freshmen, Dean Bender once said, should base its judgments on "experience, study, contemplation, hunch, prayer, and shrewd practical observation of changing conditions and the impact of its decisions, always having a sense of Harvard's ancient roots and of the desirability of getting from here to there in a real, not a test-tube, world, without blowing up the laboratory in the process." Dean Glimp, for his part, said that when he was in charge of Admissions, "One of the things that helped me and others take a gamble on a guy who seemed pretty un-Harvard was that he resembled me."

Glimp came to look unimpeachably Harvard—tweedy, graying crewcut, an air of insouciant solemnity—and he gave at least some of the credit to a kind of osmosis. "The New England tradition comes right out at you through the walls," he said. "The fact that Harvard is where it is has a lot to do with the effect it has on people." When he took over Admissions in 1960, though, his most challenging task was to disabuse quite a few Americans who still felt that the stereotype of a Harvard undergraduate was a genius who was either effeminate, aristocratic, snobbish, radical, or some combination of all. (Long hair had yet to come.) Glimp accomplished his mission in part by ranging far and wide across the country, trying to convince people that what they thought was Harvard really wasn't. "The best way to get people to stop believing in mythology is to go right to them and cornball them," he said. He had some deft cooperating cornballers on his staff—a North Dakota man, for instance, who had the confidence-inspiring, un-Harvard nickname of Fargo Fats.

One of Glimp's most piquant contributions to the annals of Harvard admissions was a phrase. In the late nineteen-forties and early fifties, the College was inundated with students who throughout high school had ranked at the head of their class. Now, it stood to reason that with twelve hundred boys in a Harvard freshman class, not all of them could rank first. Not all, indeed, no matter how intelligent or industrious, could rank in the upper half. The grim statistical truth was that some were bound to end up in the bottom quarter. That didn't bother Harvard—three-fourths of all whose undergraduates now get their degrees with honors—but it bothered some students, and it was even more vexing to their grade-conscious parents and their home-town high-school principals. At vacation time, boys whose local papers had trumpeted their entrance into Harvard would be asked on returning home if they were still in the academic van, and if they had to confess that they weren't, people looked at them askance, and they themselves not infrequently lapsed into pathetic funks.

That did bother Harvard. Its admissions people decided that inasmuch as *somebody* had to be in the lower depths of every class, they would search for boys who if they ended up there could accept that fate with equanimity and even cheerfulness. The phrase Glimp coined was designed to describe this special group—"the happy bottom quarter." (David Riesman, thinking along similar lines, once proposed that Harvard hire some mani-festly stupid professors. Their presence, he argued, would be a boon to students who might otherwise suffer from a sense of in-tellectual inferiority. The inevitable answer to the suggestion was that Harvard had already done precisely that, and certain faculty members' names were quickly bandied about in evidence.)

Not everybody near the bottom of a Harvard class is happy nowadays, especially if he plans to apply to a competitive gradu-ate school. The college population, though—to the delight of the resident psychiatrists, who have enough to cope with as it is—does now include a generous smattering of individuals who, if they get a few C's or even D's, don't go into tailspins. That they are at Harvard at all still surprises outsiders unacquainted with the happy-bottom-quarter philosophy. Not long ago, a high-strung, top-of-the-heap student from a Midwest state university met a relaxed young man who gave every appearance of never being a candidate for a Nobel Prize, and asked him where he went to college. Harvard, was the reply. "How'd you ever get in?" the brain asked. "Harvard *likes* people like me," his acquaintance answered happily.

If Harvard University has been the role model for higher education in America, and Harvard College the bedrock core of the University (some would hold these propositions debatable, but few would deny that they're statable), then the man who has the most to say about who enters the College is a man to reckon with. The quality of the finished products that any college turns out is significantly influenced, after all—although some faculty members might demur—by the quality of the raw material it takes in. Accordingly, when Fred Glimp took over from John Monro as dean of the College in 1967, the choice of Glimp's successor in Admissions was a matter of deep concern in Cambridge —all the more so considering that applications were increasing at the rate of six hundred a year.

Upon learning that the new dean of admissions, Chase N. Peterson, was a Mormon physician, a lot of Harvard people thought Harvard must be kidding. An abstemious endocrinologist from Utah as keeper of the holy gates! Chase Peterson as Harvard's St. Peter! An examination of the doctor's curriculum vitae brought some relief. He had gone to both Harvard College and Harvard Medical School. As an undergraduate, he had played on the varsity tennis and squash teams. He had been a member of the Porcellian, Harvard's snootiest social club. He had been elected first marshal of the class of 1952, which meant that in his senior year he had won his class's only popularity contest. Moreover, he had a reassuring educational lineage. His father, the son of a Danish immigrant who worked as a lumberman in Oregon, had been president of Utah State University for thirty years.

Chase Peterson had been contendedly practicing and teaching medicine in Salt Lake City for five years, and had no idea Harvard was considering him for any job. But Harvard keeps an eye on its sons. The doctor, like some twelve hundred other alumni, had been interviewing admissions candidates in his home state. He had scrutinized a couple of dozen Utah prospects annually, and some of the ones he had recommended had turned out remarkably well. There were four seniors in the class of 1968, for instance, who were there in large part because he had sponsored them. One had become first marshal of Phi Beta Kappa. The second had taken time off to be a missionary in Japan. The third had helped some farmers in East Africa organize a cooperative. And the fourth—although prior to college he had never touched an oar —had become captain of the varsity crew that represented the United States in the 1968 Olympics. *There* was a good mix if Harvard had ever seen one; in an area where intuition rated high, Dr. Peterson's hunches were clearly worth betting on. ("There is a bell that rings in your ear when you hear about a truly fine boy," he says.)

So, Dean Glimp, who had never met Peterson, phoned his Salt Lake City office one day and asked if he had a couple of minutes to chat about a possible post that was a little out of his line, but that he might find challenging. Peterson had been thinking for some time about changing his life; he had got about as far as he could in private practice in Utah. He had become increasingly interested in social problems, such as broadening the distribution of medical care, and the Harvard environment seemed a promising one in which to pursue that bent. When Glimp called, the doctor wrapped a blanket around a patient on his examining table and heard him out. Two months later, Peterson agreed to take the job.

The doctor has since concluded that a medical background can be helpful in admissions work. "We have to reject many excellent candidates, and this causes a lot of pain," he has said. "I don't know what kind of streak I need to live with it, but I suppose the suffering in medicine was good training." Sometimes he startles his colleagues by discussing candidates in terminology to which they have not previously been exposed. "This boy strikes me as potentially too alloplastic," he said one day. An alloplastic, he had to stop to explain, is someone who wants the rest of the world reshaped, but not himself. "I'm leery of the opposite type,

45

too, the out-and-out autoplastic," the doctor went on. "I think our boys should have a healthy bit of both in them." His colleagues blinked. The people around Harvard who don't work closely with Peterson still find it hard to believe that a physician is running college admissions. The Harvard Medical School not long ago issued a news release about the formation of a committee to explore ways and means of recruiting more Negroes. The release put a "Dr." before every name except that of Dr. Peterson.

Freshman advisor: "In August, you have the hippies around with their smelly feet, and in early September the football players with theirs, and then—whango!—there they are—the freshmen—all twelve hundred of them—the whole purpose of this university—and it's thrilling!"

iii

I T H A S B E C O M E fashionable of late in some educational circles to downgrade Harvard and accuse it of, among other things, living off its reputation. Fair Harvard, it is argued, spends too much time looking at a mirror and exclaiming, "Who's the fairest of them all?" The president of another university said, not long ago, "The trouble with Harvard is that it still thinks it's leading the pack, but if took the trouble to look over its shoulder it'd realize there's nobody back there following." Educators of that stripe whooped with delight—or came as close to whooping as college presidents can—when in 1966 the *New York Times* gave front-page coverage to a report of the American Council on Education that seemed to substantiate their viewpoint.

The Council had surveyed the graduate schools of 106 universities, and had evaluated them according to five broad fields of instruction—humanities, social sciences, physical sciences, biological sciences, and engineering. The University of California at Berkeley had been acclaimed "the best-balanced distinguished university," with Harvard the runner-up. ("We may only be second best, but we try harder," said the *Crimson*.) On close inspection, Berkeley's preeminence seemed a mite tainted. In four of the five fields, Harvard had outranked Berkeley. In the fifth field, engineering, Harvard hadn't been given any rating at all, for the very good reason that Harvard doesn't *have* a graduate school of engineering. It is difficult to win a pentathlon by competing in only four events.

Berkeley is very self-conscious about its alleged competitiveness with Harvard, and sometimes calls itself "the Cambridge of the West." (Harvard calls Cambridge, England, "the other Cambridge.") Geography is a subject not much taught any more in America—Harvard dropped it as a separate course of study not long after dropping veterinary medicine—and Californians sometimes tend to get confused about Harvard. A Ph.D. from out there attended a summer seminar at the Buffalo campus of the State University of New York, and on returning to California reported to some of his academic colleagues that Governor Nelson Rockefeller was hoping to transform the Buffalo institution into "the Harvard of the East." Berkeley, good as it is, is considered by scholars who have worked both coasts to be a far more parochial place than Harvard; one Harvard professor says that whenever he gets tired and wants a rest he takes a term off and spends it at Berkeley. Subsequent to the student revolution at Berkeley in 1964, a number of faculty members there, including the vice-chancellor, fled that beleaguered campus—sometimes they call themselves the White Berkeleyans—and sought refuge at Harvard. They found it, at least until 1969, at which point some of them ruefully confessed to feeling like those few soldiers of the Second World War who earned the right to wear ribbons attesting to their having seen combat service in both the European and Pacific Theaters of Operation.

It is as senseless in a way to compare good universities as it is to compare good restaurants. The quality of an academic course may change from time to time as strikingly as that of a culinary one; the migration of a single key professor, like that of a chef de cuisine, may shore up a creaky academic department or cause a robust one to sag. Perhaps the data that come out of admissions offices over the years are as useful as any yardsticks for measuring the relative standing of institutions of higher learning. In the 1967–1968 academic year, among high-school seniors who applied to both Berkeley and Harvard, Harvard rejected 122 boys whom Berkeley accepted. Not a single student accepted by Harvard was rejected by Berkeley. (Berkeley, to be sure, has more room, with seventeen thousand undergraduates compared to Harvard's forty-eight hundred—six thousand counting Radcliffe.)

Inasmuch as most high-school seniors apply to more than one college and most of the good students win multiple acceptances, every college admits more of them than it expects to receive. M.I.T. calculates that 59 per cent of the boys it admits will actually turn up, and thus sends out 1,600 acceptances for 900 places. Columbia figures that only 61 per cent of those it accepts will attend, Brown has a 67 per cent rate, and Yale's is 70 per cent. Far and away the highest figure in the country is Harvard's. In 1968, rightly expecting an 87-per-cent turn-up rate, it accepted only 1,375 boys for a class of 1,200. In the spring of 1969, though, anticipating a turn-up rate of only 85.7 per cent, it accepted 1,400; the reasoning was that Yale could be expected to do a little better than usual, that year, vis-à-vis Harvard, because it had embarked on coeducation.

Up to then, as far as Harvard was concerned, Yale had been pretty much in Berkeley's boat. Over the five previous years, of all the young men who had applied to both Harvard and Yale and had been accepted by both, 85 per cent had elected to attend Harvard. The balance was tipped a mite further in Harvard's favor in 1967, when a Yale sophomore transferred to Harvard. Harvard is not ordinarily receptive to transfers. About a thousand students a year who've begun their college education elsewhere attempt to switch to Harvard, but only twenty-five or so succeed. One of those who failed recently was a Boston University undergraduate who, feeling he wasn't making much headway through conventional channels, took ads in the *Crimson* and printed handbills to plead his case. After the Columbia riots in the spring of

1968, the Harvard admissions office had quite a few phone calls and telegrams from Columbia students who hoped to transfer. The Columbia men were too late in any event; the disturbances occurred two weeks after the Harvard admissions people had mailed out their sacks of acceptances. Even if the timing had been better, it was unlikely that many, if any, of the Columbia defectors would have been welcome; if the students involved were the sort of people Harvard would like, Harvard felt, they should stay where they were because Columbia needed them more.

After the Admissions people had made their selections in the spring of 1968, the *Crimson* pronounced the incoming freshman class "the brightest" in Harvard's history. That may well have been true, but Admissions would have been equally satisfied with some other superlative—perhaps "most interesting." The sort of person who makes their eyes light up and their votes affirmative is a New Mexico boy (good for geographical mix) who has spent the previous summer apprenticed to a violin-maker. An astronomer who worked exclusively underground would unquestionably appeal to them, all the more so if he was also a shortstop who could move to his left. An academic prodigy from the Bronx will always get consideration, but he does not warm Harvard hearts as does one of eleven children of a migrant farmworker, or the Crown Prince of Tonga, especially if this royal personage turns out, as one recently did, to be both captain and coach of the rugby team. Some months ago, a high-school senior told his college advisor, "This year, Harvard is going to take a math-oriented Chinese who plays the violin, and it's going to be me." He was right. Harvard is aware, though, that to wax romantic about the unorthodox can have its own built-in dangers. It is constantly on the alert to make sure that all that glitters is also gold.

The college still accepts some boys who merely have glittering academic records. Harvard's problem is that it could easily fill its freshman class with unadulterated brains. An authentic genius, when spotted, will always be admitted. But there are few geniuses and many boys who achieve top scores on admissions tests. In the spring of 1968, for instance, there were 105 applicants with the highest possible grade—an 800—in their verbal College Board exams, and 206 with 800's in their math exams. Only 55 per cent of the former group—a little better than the 40-per-cent average for Harvard sons—got in, and only 41 per cent of the latter. Four boys applied from the same high school in Atlanta. One was admitted. The three who didn't make it had ten 800 scores among them. There were only the 1,375 acceptances, but there were more than 1,400 applicants whose College Board grades averaged over 740. Forty per cent of the entire group of applicants had had calculus, a subject that few secondary schools taught a generation ago. But as the violin-playing, math-oriented Oriental correctly guessed, Harvard is apt to look less fondly nowadays at an uninspired mathematical whiz than at a kid who while floundering in algebra is widely read and has built a church with his own hands. "The most desired applicant," Dr. Peterson has said, "is still a boy with honesty, imagination, generosity, and discipline in a strong mind."

Of course, paragons turn up who seem to excel at everything: a boy was recently admitted who not only got 800 in all his College Boards and edited his school yearbook (practically everybody who currently applies to Harvard seems to have edited *something*, not to mention playing the clarinet), but also made a telescope. Other recent favorites of the Harvard admissions people have included the youthful producer of an animated film on the dissection of a frog, the son of a Hungarian freedom fighter now in Montana (doubly good for geographical mix) who was an Eagle Scout, president of his high-school class (almost everybody seems to have been *that*, too), and, for icing on his particular cake, state tennis champion.

Sometimes the admissions staff feels unqualified to assess an individual's accomplishments and solicits help from experts on the Harvard faculty. Thus, when young poets submit their work, the poems are apt to be turned over to Professor Theodore Morrison for a critical reading. Then there was a New Jersey boy who, though he stood a paltry thirtieth in a class of 110, had composed a chorale. Harvard asked him to send in the score, and when he did, passed it along to G. Wallace Woodworth, the director emeritus of the Glee Club. Professor Woodworth reported back that while the work might be difficult to sing, it showed considerable imagination. The boy was admitted.

"Harvard hasn't yet reached the point," McGeorge Bundy said a decade ago, when he was dean of the Faculty of Arts and Sciences, "of refusing admission to a boy simply because he is intelligent." Some current members of that faculty, particularly in the physical sciences, have been grumbling lately that the college is coming dangerously close to reaching that point. "Admissions people tend to reproduce their own kind," one Harvard physicist said recently. "Put a bunch of us scientists in there and we'd reproduce ours. We get marvelous undergraduates, mind you, by and large. They make the damn place jump. But it would be nice if the Admissions people paid a little bit more attention to students' grades, instead of to synthetic leadership. Every letter of recommendation that comes in about a boy harps on his leadership. Let a kid come along who's done an outstanding job in chemistry but who is only a mediocre pianist and is rather inarticulate and was never even elected *vice*-president of his class, and he's in a tough way. He'll probably get passed over in favor of some debater. I sat in on Admissions for a while, and I never knew there were so many desirable debaters in the United States."

Harvard does still take in scientists, of course. Indeed, with so much emphasis on science in the high schools, a large proportion of the number-one-in-the-class students are science-minded. Joel R. Kramer, who was elected president of the *Crimson* in 1968, was pleasantly surprised to be admitted to Harvard, because while in a Queens high school he had specialized in literature and had graduated only second—a scientist was ahead of him—in a class of twelve hundred. "It wasn't until I got to Harvard that I realized you didn't have to be a scientist to be a man," Kramer said.

Creating a freshman class at Harvard is not unlike fitting together a jigsaw puzzle—when one already knows what the finished picture should look like. Harvard wants its undergraduate body to have a little bit of everything. Should the orchestra find itself short of flute players one year, it is a good year for flutists to aim at Harvard. "A couple of years ago, I casually mentioned French horns to a friend of mine in Admissions," the director of the Harvard Band said not long ago, "and the following fall we had nine in the Freshman class. Maybe it was a coincidence, but before that we hadn't had any French horns at all two years in a row." Of course, the French horn players all had other attributes. "We look for triple-threat people," one Admissions man says. "My ideal is a running guard who is also a National Honor Society president and plays first board in the Chess Club." Dr. Peterson's demands are less specific. "What *I* look for," he says, "is guys who have a particular talent that'll allow them to put a hook down into Harvard and catch hold of it. A guy has to have one special thing." Most Harvard undergraduates would be inclined to agree with him. "You meet people here and you wonder to yourself, 'How did *this* guy get in? Where's *his* touch of greatness?'" a member of the class of 1968 said shortly before his graduation. "And then if you really look for it you find it."

There are all sorts of myths about Harvard admissions quotas. Some of the Negroes at Harvard contend, erroneously, that Harvard always admits at least one boy from a particular high school in Athens, Greece. There is no quota for Greeks and none for Negroes. Briefly, in 1925, under President A. Lawrence Lowell, the number of Jewish students was limited, but under alumni pressure Harvard abandoned that scheme. It took the rest of the place a little longer to see the light. The English department, in the late nineteen-twenties, declined to hire a young poet, who had graduated summa cum laude from Harvard College and who later won the Pulitzer Prize, because he was Jewish; and the *Crimson*, for the same reason, turned down a man who later became president of the Harvard Board of Overseers. Now perhaps 30 per cent of the students are Jewish, and one hears tales—they have an apocryphal ring to them—of a Cabot or a Lowell being turned down in favor of a Cohen or a Lowenstein, and of the loser's family complaining, "Just as I always thought; Harvard is pro-Semitic."

Most applicants get interviewed. Each full-time member of the Admissions staff has an area assigned to him—it may be southern Connecticut, or several far-western states lumped together—and visits it during the fall. One staff man, L. Fred Jewett, had a tight schedule that permitted him only one day at Ottumwa, Iowa. (Jewett has the reputation of being partial to athletes. This is quite true, but he also has unimpeachable intellectual credentials; he is corresponding secretary of the Harvard chapter of Phi Beta Kappa.) The day was November 11th, and the high school where he would normally have conducted interviews was closed for the holiday. Jewett phoned ahead from Des Moines that he'd be glad to see prospects at an Ottumwa motel where he'd be spending the night. It was one of those motels that have marquees that carry messages—Rotary is lunching, optometrists are convening, and the like. As Jewett drove up to his Ottumwa destination, he saw, in giant letters, FRED JEWETT HARVARD ADMISSIONS TODAY. He did, as a result, get a few out-of-the-ordinary interviewees, but then Harvard is always looking for the unexpected.

The Admissions men, moreover, like those from other colleges, make annual pilgrimages to schools that have consistently furnished Harvard with substantial numbers of students; in his first year on the job, Dr. Peterson led a five-man team to Andover, where over a two-day stretch they talked to 148 boys. Soon after these interviews 31 Andover boys received the good news that Harvard had given them an "A rating"—that was, they were assured of a place, barring some catastrophe, such as failing to get an Andover diploma. A "B rating" is supposed to indicate to a boy that he will still have a chance when the final decisions are made the following spring, and a "C rating" that he had better look elsewhere. Eighteen Andover students who were given "B's" were ultimately admitted; of 49 Andover boys taken altogether, 42 matriculated. Harvard, Yale, and Princeton used to give these early ratings to students from about seventy-five schools. Yale and Princeton have dropped the practice, but Harvard has clung to it, though by now at only forty-two schools in the northeast—both private and public—that provide large numbers of applicants every year. It gives A ratings each fall to about 250 boys in all, which in a sense simplifies the Admissions staff's job in the spring, inasmuch as there are fewer boys to pick, but in another sense complicates it, since there are fewer spots to fill.

The alumni who help out by interviewing candidates in their local areas work with varying degrees of intensity and efficiency. There is one lawyer in Iowa who closes his office for two weeks in the fall when "Harvard time" comes around, and who spends that time beating the high-school bushes for likely prospects. Some of these proselyting alumni have an old-fashioned view of higher education; one of them, for instance, to the dismay of the Harvard administration, persists in referring to all colleges outside the Ivy League as "slopover schools." A few of them, as is perhaps inevitable when alumni get involved in recruiting, are especially on the alert for football players, to whom they refer among themselves as "horses." They refer to themselves as "alums." (There are subversives in all walks of life. One alumni recruiter recently confided to an outside acquaintance, when no other alum was listening, "I'm on a private committee to do away entirely with intercollegiate athletics.") A particularly prestigious alum these days is one who persuaded a fleet halfback horse to come to Harvard although four or five dozen other places, Notre Dame and Southern California among them, were bidding spiritedly for his patronage. It did not hurt Harvard's case at all that, while the halfback was at a school football practice one afternoon, Robert F. Kennedy '48 just happened to stop by and put in a good word for his alma mater.

Harvard cares quite seriously about attracting a decent number of athletes. Prowess on the playing fields is, in Dr. Peterson's phrase, "a significant extracurricular talent." He once told a meeting of alums, "We accept the notion that the special athlete-scholar demands top proselyting attention," and he added that his medical background had given him a personal bias in favor of a coordinated union of muscle, bone, and the central nervous system. (Radcliffe does not have a football team, but some of the academic purists among its girls complain that *their* Admissions people always seem to be looking for topflight cheerleader types). Although Harvard coaches are not allowed to initiate contact with a student before he applies, as a rule, when an exceptional athlete applies, Admissions tips off the coach of his principal sport; this gives the coach a chance to look over the boy and at the same time, should he have applications in elsewhere, to put in a plug for Harvard. On learning, however, that a boy who had twice won the men's squash championship of India had applied to Harvard and nowhere else, Admissions gleefully slapped an "A" on his dossier and solicitously kept the whole business secret; they thought it would be nice, come April, to surprise the squash coach. Harvard will not take an athlete who isn't also a respectable student—two first-string players on its 1967 varsity football team won Rhodes scholarships—and those recruiting alums who want to make sure their horses have heads sometimes engage in peculiar proselyting. One group of them cross-examined a fullback so aggressively that he was reduced to tears. He finally went elsewhere and spent several years retributively ripping holes in the Harvard line.

Some of the horses whom Harvard does corral prove disappointing; there was an all-state tackle who after reaching Cambridge got interested in a medical career and never even went out for football. But Harvard keeps trying, although it will probably never catch up with Dartmouth, which is reported to play footsie annually with some three thousand football players.

The Harvard Admissions office functions on a year-round

basis, but its most frenetic weeks are those between mid-February and notification time in April. By then, every applicant has his own thick folder. It would be thicker were it not for computers. A good deal of the information about each contender has been reduced electronically to a single line on a data-printout sheet—his school rank, his College Board scores; his ratings from his school principal and two of his teachers; an assessment of his extracurricular and athletic achievements and potentialities; his Harvard-son status, if any; and a few other random bits of information. Among these is his standing on something called a Predicted Rank List.

One of the shadowy figures in the Harvard administrative hierarchy is a man named Dean K. Whitla, a native of Nebraska who probably has more titles than anyone else on the Cambridge scene. At last count he was Lecturer on Education, Director of the Office of Tests, Associate Director of Admissions in Harvard College, Member of the Faculty of Arts and Sciences, Member of the Board of Freshman Advisers, and Acting Allston Burr Senior Tutor in Lowell House. Because of Whitla's Christian name, he is also sometimes erroneously thought to be a dean; because he works closely with Harvard's titular deans, he has become known among them informally as the Deans' Dean.

Basically, Whitla is the chief statistician for the Faculty of Arts and Sciences. He has specialized in studying admissions. Not long ago, for instance, with the help of a computer, Whitla did a study of 48,881 candidates for admission to forty-three colleges over a ten-year period. It is he who makes the important guess each year—what percentage of those admitted will come. If he guesses 86 per cent and the figure turns out to be 88, he receives reproachful looks, and it has even been suggested that he board the excess bodies at his home.

Whitla also handles the Predicted Rank List. Each candidate, based on his academic achievements in high school, is assigned a figure supposed to be suggestive of his academic performance at Harvard. The very best rating (it would go to a fellow who had been first in a public high school class of one thousand and had all 800's on his college boards) is 1.4; the worst is 7. As a rule, Harvard admits 90 per cent of the applicants to whom Whitla and his computer assign a PRL—as this measurement is called for short—of 1.9 or better; as a concomitant rule, nobody with a PRL of 6 or worse is seriously considered.

A shining exception in Harvard admissions lore, whose case is cited whenever the college officials are tempted to follow the computer's judgments over their own hunches, is a young man with a dismayingly high PRL, Eugene Kinasewich, who was admitted notwithstanding and became an assistant dean of the College. He got in largely because he was a superlative ice-hockey player—a native of Edmonton, Alberta, who could skate as soon as he could walk and who might have followed one of his older brothers into professional hockey if Harvard hadn't made him aim at higher goals. After a discouraging start in college—admitted because of his hockey prowess, he was for a while declared ineligible because he had taken expense money while playing in an Edmonton league—he graduated magna cum laude and won a traveling fellowship, under the singular but agreeable terms of which he had to spend a year in Western Europe but couldn't engage in any formal academic program. Kinasewich took his skates along and played hockey in, among other cultural centers, Geneva, Innsbruck, Turin, and Milan. At Harvard, where square pegs are rarely put in round holes, he eventually became the dean in charge of fellowships, and also the assistant coach of the hockey team. And very shortly after that—as if by way of demonstrating that to be a college administrator these days is not always a prelude to disaster—he was appointed president of the Western Hockey League.

By mid-February, each applicant's dossier, containing the raw material about him, much of which ultimately gets computerized, has been carefully read by at least three individuals—members of the Admissions office, or faculty members, or both. Then the full-time Admissions people begin meeting. They convene six and a half days a week for seven weeks, usually starting their deliberations at 9:30 in the morning and often not quitting until midnight. An orange-juice cooler and a coffee machine sustain them throughout their ordeal. People drift in and out of their sessions; there are twenty-three faculty members on the Admissions committee, and they stop by when they have a few free hours.

The Admissions people follow a system of advocacy. "We're always looking for reasons to take boys, not to turn them down," Dr. Peterson says. Each Admissions staff man has an area of his own, usually the one he has visited in person, and he puts the case for (or, sometimes, regretfully, against) each applicant on his list. By this time, some of the advocates know some of their applicants quite well. When a boy from Oregon comes up for discussion, for instance, the Admissions man handling that state not only may be familiar with the boy's achievements and personality but may recall having visited his home out there and sampled some cookies his sister baked. The advocacy system has a few built-in dangers. The lightness of a well-remembered cookie may turn out to be a factor in Admissions. One Admissions staff man's hobby is birdwatching. Every other year or so, an applicant mentions that as *his* hobby, and the Harvard birdwatcher is apt to urge that he be admitted for that reason alone. Like any other applicant, the student would still need a majority vote based on other reasons.

The assembled judges begin with the West Coast and work their way east. Every applicant has had to submit an essay. "What choice have you recently made that you consider important?" was one recently suggested topic; others have been "Whom do you consider the greatest man in the twentieth century?," and, for the prospective Class of 1972, "What is the most crucial global issue your generation is likely to face? Why do you feel this way and can you envision any solutions to this problem?" If someone in the meeting room remembers a student's essay as particularly striking, it may be passed around or read aloud.

Letters of recommendation from friends and politicians are

noted, but are not taken too seriously. (A United States senator once told a Harvard dean of admissions that he was obliged now and then to write on behalf of a constituent's son but that the dean should ignore his testimonials; if there was a boy he *really* fancied, he'd give the dean a ring.) Letters from school principals and teachers are studied with care, and sometimes innocent boys suffer cruelly from the ineptness of their sponsors. On being confronted for the thousandth time with some such eulogy as "one of those rare superior human beings," Harvard Admissions men groan. Such phrases as "an ideal foundation on which to build a mathematical edifice" or "a textbook picture of a cerebratonic individual with mild sociophobia" may strike their authors as having just the right touch, but they strike Harvard as awful. Sometimes the schools' earnest attempts to present a boy in the best possible light produce dark Harvard antiphonies: "Any further attempt to describe him would be simply a chronicle of superlatives" ("*A nice kid, but I saw little to separate him from the herd*"); "Steadfast, loyal, true . . . never guilty of not doing his homework" ("*Hmm, a goody-goody*"); "I have no hesitation in giving him an enthusiastic recommendation; he will no doubt make a substantial contribution to any college he attends" ("*That's about as bad a counseling opinion as you can get*").

It usually takes about three weeks for the Admissions men to make their first boy-by-boy cross-country trek. At the end of that journey, some seven hundred boys, the obvious standouts, will have had a red "A" (for "Accepted") penciled on their computer line, and nearly five thousand have earned a black "R" (for "Rejected"). A number of individuals in each category will have a dot or an asterisk alongside their letter; they are still in limbo. At that point, the advocates often put in a phone call to a boy's school, to seek further information about him that may get him in or drop him out. There are twenty-five hundred cases still pending, and less than seven hundred vacancies left. And the horrible thing about it is that just about *any* seven hundred boys selected from the twenty-five hundred would probably be as good as any other seven hundred.

The going gets harder and harder. After six weeks of practically non-stop evaluation and comparison, the Admissions people are growing numb. Their patience is wearing thin, and they turn snappish. "It's been some time since we've taken a boy from East Central High," the advocate for one midwestern metropolis may say, "and the alumni have worked hard. Now, this guy writes a nice essay about a lake and has two cousins at Harvard, for whatever that's worth."

The advocate looks around the room, pleadingly, but receives no encouragement. He begins to wish he had not quite so icily rebuffed the advocate for the southwest a week earlier, when that chap was pushing a cellist who had designed a supermarket in his spare time.

The southwest advocate speaks up. "Look, we took a boy from *West* Central High last year," he says.

Nobody has a good word for East Central.

"I guess we've got to sweep this school again," says Dr. Peterson, with a sigh. "He seems like a nice kid, but he's just not unusual enough."

As the final days drag on, the Admissions men are gloomily aware that, in spite of the hardheartedness that is thrust upon them, they have nonetheless given A's to more boys than they can ultimately accept. So they grimly go into what they call a lopping session, changing A's to R's, throwing out of Harvard boys who, though they will never know it, were briefly in. "We'll never get a better kid from Springfield than this one," says Dr. Peterson, sadly picking up a black pencil, "but this one isn't good enough." Lop.

But wait—someone down the table has heard that the boy had a summer job as a nailer in a wooden-box factory! It is enough to stay his execution. Unlop and reconsider. "You can get a whiplash from all this bending over forwards and backwards and forwards again," murmurs Dr. Peterson clinically.

To break the tension, two other Admissions men begin tossing around a squash ball. They stop when somebody's orange juice gets spilled all over southeastern Connecticut. On and on the harassed, conscientious men proceed. "No boy from this high school has *ever* attended Harvard," is the gambit the Texas advocate elects to use. "This one will be the first!"

"Will he?" asks Peterson bleakly, "I'm not sure he's got anything here that says 'Don't take me,' but I don't see anything either that says he's any different from the people we reject."

Texas subsides.

The next boy up for grabs is editor of his school paper, captain of the football team, editor of the yearbook, president of the student council, star of the dramatic club, stands fourth in a class of 210, has College-Board scores well in the upper 600's, is president of his church's youth group, and, to cap it all, is the son of a truckdriver. He cannot miss.

Or can he? For a moment, it looks as though he may be kissed to death by over-advocacy. "Look," one Admissions man says in a near-snarl, "I don't want to hear any more about this guy. He sounds pretty good, and he isn't going to sound any better."

The advocate hastily shuts up, and the boy gets in.

The next boy has far less impressive credentials, and his father is merely a businessman, but he shines in his advocate's memory because when a schoolmate was injured on the eve of an important track meet, he gallantly volunteered to enter the high hurdles, though he had never before confronted even a low hurdle. What was more, he ran cross-country for the fun of it. "Anybody who runs cross-country just because he likes to *has* to be a special breed," the advocate argues.

A colleague snorts; surely Harvard demands more than that; why should they take a chance? To the advocate's surprise, Peterson rallies to his cause. "Look," says the doctor, "if some of the guys we pick don't blow it, then we haven't been gambling on the right kind of guys. And if a couple don't really blossom, then we won't have been gambling right, either."

Peterson is willing to take some real gambles. A handful of the Negroes Harvard has been admitting lately—109 acceptances for the fall of 1969, with, Yale or no Yale, a probable turn-up rate of 87 per cent—have looked risky by old-fashioned Admissions standards (though no riskier than a considerably larger number of whites). Among forty-two Negroes who entered in the fall of 1968 was a twenty-three-year-old man who had spent the two previous years working on drug prevention in Harlem—in collaboration with a recent Harvard graduate who discerned in him a lively potential and became his personal advocate. The student's College Board scores were unimpressive, but inconsequential; he had been tested when he was seventeen, and a narcotics addict himself. He did excellently as a Harvard freshman. Another black student, though, whose test grades were superior, had to be suspended for a year for gross academic deficiencies at Harvard; the fact that he was seen, during the April troubles, walking around with a meat cleaver probably didn't help him any.

The very last Admissions meeting takes place on Sunday, April 7. When the bone-tired men convene that morning, they have 1,380 A candidates—6 over the target of 1,374 that the Deans' Dean has originally decreed. Six more lops will be sad, but manageable. But then a new argument breaks out. Certain areas, perhaps southern New Hampshire, perhaps greater St. Louis—who can remember exactly afterwards?—have been slighted; certain categories, perhaps oboeists, lacrosse goalies, biochemists, alto singers, or Harvard sons, have been neglected. The men riffle afresh through their well-thumbed rosters, and award thirty more A's.

Now thirty-six A's must be withdrawn. As this painful lopping begins, the wails and groans of outraged advocates rattle the room. At 11:30 P.M., the A list is down to 1,375. Nobody will budge an inch on dropping one single more boy, and Peterson hasn't the heart to make an arbitrary decision. Whitla be hanged! They will admit thirteen hundred and seventy-five, and hope that their acceptance rate is only 86.9 per cent.

A few minutes later, Dr. Peterson serves champagne all around (he himself has ginger ale), and the tedious business of preparing nearly eight thousand individual notifications is ready to begin.

Harvard tries manfully to keep its records straight, but every few years, nonetheless, a boy who should have got a letter of rejection inadvertently gets one of acceptance instead. Harvard honors its admissions, naturally, even mistaken ones. Mr. Whitla, out of curiosity more than anything else, once followed the undergraduate career of a student who had been rejected out of hand when his name first came up—even his own advocate had urged his non-admission—because he seemed like a run-of-the-mill boy who would probably be a C-average student and accomplish nothing spectacular. (He didn't even look good for the debating team.) That was precisely what the boy did do during his four years at Harvard, but he had a very good time and made a lot of firm friends. His high-school guidance counselor hasn't been able to figure out to this day why boys who were clearly his superior haven't made Harvard.

The notifications had to be mailed late the following Saturday night because Harvard and the other seven Ivy League colleges have agreed (as have Radcliffe and its six Sister colleges) to try to get the fateful word to all their applicants on the 15th of April—a day that, as the competitiveness of college admissions has increased, has in many households produced far more elation and far more despair than the 25th of December. In the case of candidates outside New England, Harvard uses airmail stamps. The postage bill for the three weighty sacks came to nine hundred dollars. With an endowment that is very conservatively reckoned at over a billion dollars, and an annual operating budget of well over 150 million, Harvard could afford it.

*A professor in the humanities, at the Faculty Club:
"In a community devoted to free inquiry and free expression, you
can never be sure who, rightly or wrongly, will be the next to
cry 'Eureka!' In a corporation, you'd have to shout it up through
channels, and it might be muffled by the time it surfaced. Here,
every cry must be heard and must be greeted with respect."*

iv

IN 1961, EIGHT YEARS AFTER Nathan Pusey became president of Harvard and twenty-seven years after he had first trod its ancient paths, he told an alumni group that he was not sure what the University *was*. His uncertainty was not unique. Many people have tried to analyze Harvard, and few have succeeded. Dean Peterson calls it "an intellectual activity organized as an academic community." William L. Marbury, the senior member of its chief governing body, the Corporation, speaks of "the immense variety of its activities and its people, and the lack of a definable character that covers the spectrum of its activities," adding vaguely, "It is a place where almost anybody can find an opportunity to develop whatever abilities he has in an atmosphere of minimum interference," and concluding helplessly, "There are no adjectives or apothegms to summarize it." Professor Arthur E. Sutherland, the chronicler of the Harvard Law School, has likened the entire University to the United States Supreme Court. Both, he said, are august intellectual institutions that pride themselves on their freedom from outside pressure, and that as a result often attract outside hostility.

The novelist Benjamin DeMott, formerly of the Harvard English department and now at Amherst, once likened Harvard, from an American viewpoint, to the continent of Europe. "Either you've been there or you haven't," he said. Other appraisers of Harvard have compared it to a tiny part of Europe—specifically, to the Vatican. Members of the Corporation, among whose responsibilities is the selection of Harvard's president, have compared themselves to the College of Cardinals.

No president of Harvard is known to have invested himself publicly with Papal stature, but the analogy has its points. Harvard has traditionally operated like a small, powerful, and subjectively infallible political entity with a worldwide constituency. Like any self-respecting government, Harvard has its own protocol office, and it even issues passports of a sort—ornately inscribed documents on fine bond paper watermarked with the Harvard *Veritas* seal. These are called "dazzlers" and are given to Harvard officials traveling abroad, for the purpose of stupefying cabinet ministers or sheiks or anyone else they may consort with. When Dean Glimp rushed to Mexico in 1968 to cheer on Harvard's Olympic crew, there wasn't time to prepare a dazzler for him. Instead, he merely carried a to-whom-it-may-concern letter, on plain paper, from the secretary of the Corporation, attesting to Mr. Glimp's authenticity and enumerating his degrees. Austere though it was, the letter, possibly because it contained scholarly flourishes like the word *ibid.*, got him waved through gates against which ordinary citizens were flinging themselves in vain.

It is one of Harvard's special problems that it has long been conscious of being a superpower—king, as it were, of the academic mountain. A newspaperman from Manila, while spending a year at Harvard as a Nieman Fellow, wrote in the *Philippine Herald* that "Harvard belongs to the world." There are those who think, though, that Harvard thinks the world belongs to Harvard—or that the world *is* Harvard. On some campuses, there is an almost discernible dividing line, in faculty circles, between localism and cosmopolitanism. The locals are those men who focus their attention on the university itself and who feel there aren't enough faculty meetings. The cosmopolitans are those who gaze afar and think the faculty meets entirely too often. At most universities, most of the better faculty people, or at any rate the more prestigious, are the cosmopolitans.

It is not so at Harvard. The faculty men whose opinions carry weight think that the sophisticated world is wherever they are; they are known among sociologists as local cosmopolitans. They are like the legendary Parisians who always think in terms of Paris no matter where in France they may be. Dr. Stanley H. King, a Harvard psychologist who has devoted the better part of the last decade to studying the institution, has said, "Harvard is the most cosmopolitan provincial village on earth."

A professor who left Cambridge to take a fling at a new and offbeat business said afterward, "When I spoke from Harvard I was ten feet tall. Now, instead of the sure prestige of Harvard, I find people saying I'm a crackpot." (If he had stayed around Cambridge until 1969, he might have felt only seven or eight feet tall.) One Harvard undergraduate who is by no means a snob, on returning from a vacation during which he had been reunited with some high-school classmates, told a friend, "The ones who went to Yale are satisfied with it, and they defend it, as I guess one should who goes to Yale. I don't waste time on such arguments. As far as I'm concerned, there's Harvard and then there are all those other places." Adam Yarmolinsky, a Harvard College-Yale Law School product who now teaches law at Harvard, recently observed, "Harvard may not be superior, but it's supreme." Harvard reminds Yarmolinsky— who, though he had never taught anything anywhere, was appointed a full professor at the Law School after a Washington stint in the Kennedy administration—of the old definition of a lady: a woman who is treated as one whether or not she has any innate ladylike traits. People let themselves be unnecessarily intimidated by Harvard. A lecturer from the perfectly respectable Boston Museum of Fine Arts, after looking at a not terribly fancy art-teaching device at the Fogg Art Museum in Cambridge, said, "It's all right for Harvard, but it's too high-class for us."

According to McGeorge Bundy, another Yale-Harvard-Washington drifter who from 1954 to 1960 was dean of Harvard's Faculty of Arts and Sciences, "Harvard has a serene awareness of its own importance. One of its virtues is that it doesn't have to go around all the time saying it's nearly as good as Harvard. Harvard has a special sense of quality. By extraordinary good fortune and management, it also has a style of living and a sense of purpose. There are moments of pressure, to be sure. But more than in most of life there is freedom to do your best and openness of judgment as to what is the right way—a plurality of criteria and purposes. You don't have to push somebody down to get yourself up."

If a professor's appeal to students can be measured by the number of them who sign up for his lectures, then the most popular member of the Harvard Faculty of Arts and Sciences has lately been the playwright William Alfred, who gives a course on tragic drama with an enrollment of 945. (In the Age of Relevance, he won high marks among his students by requiring in a mid-year exam an essay on *Bonnie and Clyde*.) Alfred goes a bit beyond Bundy and says that one of the distinctive aspects of Harvard is that there you *have* to do your best, or suffer from the tough and not always open judgment of your colleagues. "Harvard demands so much of you that you come to fear that if you ever went anywhere else you'd turn into a slob," Alfred says. "I happen to have an enormous untapped reservoir of sloth, and for me Harvard is a kind of living conscience."

There are other members of the Cambridge academic community, however, who feel that some professors figure they have it made once they achieve tenure at Harvard, and that they then lapse, if not into slothfulness, at least into smugness. One M.I.T. professor turned down a chance to move to Harvard largely because he feared that if he went there he wouldn't work hard enough to salve *his* conscience. M.I.T. is a topnotch institution and would be towering in most locales; in Cambridge, its faculty members sometimes refer to themselves as being two miles down the river—two miles down from *what* being implicit. It was perhaps characteristic of one difference between the two institutions that when an ambitious and mischievous student named Winshall —whose parents had perhaps contributed to his unusual pattern of behavior by christening him Walter—simultaneously went through the Harvard Law School and the M.I.T. Graduate School of Arts and Sciences without telling either place he was leading a double life and completed his scholastic requirements at both, M.I.T. granted him the degree he had earned but Harvard withheld its official recognition of his accomplishment, on the ground that he had somehow played unfair.

The president of M.I.T., Howard W. Johnson, not long ago spoke at a Cambridge lunch and said afterward that, as he was introduced and identified, he could tell which ladies in his audience were Harvard ladies from their facial expressions—tolerant and mildly superior. It is worse across the Charles River, in Boston, where the stories about grandes dames and Harvard are legion. There is, for example, the tale about the Beacon Hill dowager who, asked what college her grandson was attending, replied, "He doesn't go to college; he goes to Brown."

After traveling to New Haven for the Yale-Harvard game in the fall of 1892, George Santayana wrote, "We feel that Yale is at once most similar and most opposite to Harvard, that she is not only a rival in those things, such as athletics, which are common to both colleges, but at the same time an embodiment of what is most hostile to our spirit." Sixty-odd years later, the Harvard University administration did not think it had much in common, athletic contests excepted, with Yale or the rest of the Ivy League. At Yale, where there are four thousand undergraduates out of a total student population of eighty-four hundred, the College looms largest in the academic scheme of things. At Harvard, the College is in some people's eyes the heart of the whole University structure, but out of a student population of fifteen thousand only six thousand (including twelve hundred Radcliffe girls) are under-graduates. The places that Harvard University officials feel most akin to educationally are Berkeley, Michigan, and Wisconsin, against none of which it competes, fortunately, in football.

But a certain traditional bond of kinship continues to perme-ate the Ivy League, within which Harvard unabashedly considers itself the paterfamilias. Yale is a kind of daughter, Princeton a grandchild, or stepgrandchild, and Dartmouth a country cousin, several times removed. Radcliffe girls tend to voice the harshest verdicts on the rest of the clan. One Cliffie remarked, "I think the Ivy League is really irrelevant. Yale boys are ill at ease, and seem so young, and Princeton is even worse. Dartmouth is impossible, of course, but at least it's aware of it. And then there are those other weird places."

Men have uttered gentler judgments. When President Ken-nedy was made an honorary doctor of laws at Yale in 1962, he said, "Now I have the better part of two worlds—a Harvard edu-cation and a Yale degree." (For a politician, he was curiously remiss; he could have added that he had initially matriculated at Princeton.) The two worlds have many differences. Thornton Wilder, a Yale graduate, once stumbled into and spent a rollick-ing evening with a Harvard group celebrating a class reunion; it is hard to imagine a Harvard man reversing the situation. In Cam-bridge, these days, Yale is treated benignly enough; after all, Kingman Brewster used to be a professor at the Harvard Law School.

And there are many other Yale alumni who, like McGeorge Bundy, have occupied respectable and respected positions at Harvard. "Some of Harvard's most precious gifts come from New Haven," the presiding officer at a Cambridge ceremonial function said while introducing Archibald MacLeish, who went to Yale and taught at Harvard. Teasing Yale is not a sport peculiar to Harvard men. MacLeish himself has compared a Yale man's visiting Harvard to an earth man's visiting the moon. To be sure, he made the comparison in Cambridge, not New Haven. Another

Yale man, Zeph Stewart, a professor of Greek and Latin who is also master of Lowell House at Harvard, has been on the faculty there since 1953, and has thoroughly enjoyed the experience. "It's nice to be a Yale man at Harvard," he says. "People treat you as a sort of pleasant pet to have around." Academic traffic does not move one way only; the research for Kenneth Keniston's widely read book *The Uncommitted: Alienated Youth in American Society* was done while the psychiatrist was at Harvard. By the time the book came out, he was at Yale. This may have accounted for the color scheme on his dust jacket, which depicted fifteen heads of conventional youths and one alienated head. The fifteen heads, facing right, were blue and the odd one, facing left, was crimson.

Yale and Harvard have many high-level links. Dean George P. Baker of the Harvard Business School went to Yale; his father was the famous Theatre Workshop man who left Harvard for Yale in 1925 after a disagreement with President A. Lawrence Lowell over a new theater. Dean Theodore R. Sizer of the Harvard Graduate School of Education also went to Yale; *his* father was curator of the Yale Art Gallery. Harvard and Yale collaborated on two art shows in the fall of 1967, the Yale Gallery lending some of its prize exhibits to Harvard's Fogg Art Museum, and the Fogg reciprocating. The swap was not entirely successful; Fogg restores its paintings under natural light and Yale under artificial light, which made some of the works look odd when transplanted. But the exchange did give the then director of the Fogg, Professor John P. Coolidge, a chance to reflect in some catalogue notes that "Yale and Harvard seem to their intimates as different as Jonathan and David and to everybody else as indistinguishable as Pollux and Castor."

The shuttling of graduate students and more advanced academic types between Cambridge and New Haven is not exceptional. The transfer of an undergraduate from Yale to Harvard in the fall of 1967 was. The oldest Harvard Admissions hands cannot remember any comparable instance, and can remember no instance at all of any undergraduate's switching from Harvard to Yale. The student in question, Marc Strassman, was a California public-school graduate who had been turned down by Harvard when he first applied. "I wasn't surprised," he said later. "After all, I was just a run-of-the-mill high-school valedictorian." So he had gone to Yale (though, he insists, he secretly rooted for Harvard at The Game), where he had started off studying political science, since he was entertaining the notion of some day becoming President of the United States.

Strassman, however, found the political climate of New Haven a bit tepid for his taste, and there were other aspects of the environment that distressed him. There is a statue of Theodore Dwight Woolsey, the one-time president of Yale, on the Yale campus. One night, the unhappy Strassman saw, with distaste, a drunken Yalie and his girl climbing on the statue. Two nights later, he was visiting Cambridge. His heart leapt up when he strolled into the Harvard Yard and there beheld, sedately sitting at the base of John Harvard's statue, a Harvard boy with a guitar and a Radcliffe girl, singing folk songs.

A passing tribute to their relative decorum led to further conversation, and presently they invited him to a party being given at Phillips Brooks House, the Harvard undergraduate social-welfare center, for some patients from a nearby mental hospital. "I'd been to social mixers at New Haven where they bused in these girls from Smith and Vassar like so many exhibits in a cattle show," Strassman said, "and the Brooks House party struck me by contrast as a really splendid mixer, if a bit surrealistic. I had a very nice chat with a crazy woman and I knew after that that I could only be happy at Harvard." Harvard, however, he realized, wouldn't let him transfer just because he was miserable, eccentric, or ambitious; he got in by convincing a number of Harvard faculty members that a course of study he wanted to pursue in his last two undergraduate years was unavailable at Yale.

The rivalry between Harvard and Yale goes way back. It can be said to have started, in a sense, when an Englishman named

Edward Hopkins crossed the Atlantic in 1637 on the same ship that carried John Harvard. Hopkins' wife had been born a Yale; Elihu Yale was her nephew. On Hopkins' death, in 1657, much of his estate was earmarked for "public ends" in the United States, and there was considerable wrangling in London courts over its distribution. In 1710, Harvard won out, but as a sop to New Haven, some money was allocated for the establishment there of the Hopkins Grammar School. If Yale had been in existence at the time, Harvard might have come out second best; after all, John Harvard had only been an ocean-crossing acquaintance, and blood is thicker than water.

The rivalry crops up in unexpected ways. Nobody knew that the resignation of a president of Harvard, in 1773, had been caused by his impregnation of a maidservant in his house until the naughty truth was revealed, nearly two centuries later, in the publication of a Yale man's diary. Some Yale men thought that the disclosure was fair retaliation for the just previously published assertion, by a Harvard undergraduate, that Harvard was the only place in the world where nobody was impressed by the simple fact that a person went to Harvard.

It is in athletics, of course, that the vestigial competition between the two academies is most evident, and most rampant. (John W. M. Whiting, a professor of social anthropology at Harvard with two Yale degrees, never goes to the Harvard-Yale game, because he can't make up his mind whom to root for. Zeph Stewart does attend, and sits on the Yale side, mainly because a Yale College graduate can get better tickets than a full professor at Harvard who also presides over a house. He is non-partisan.) Anachronistic though it may seem, around Cambridge, nowadays, one still sometimes hears snatches of conversation like that between a middle-aged man and woman at the 1968 Harvard-Yale football game, miraculously tied in the last hysterical seconds by an underdog Harvard, 29–29, after both teams had gone into it undefeated—a situation that engendered excitement that itself seemed somewhat anachronistic. The woman confessed to her escort—one of those Harvard alumni spectators who is capable, given good field position and a blanket to sit on, of running amok—that she had never gotten drunk until she went to a Harvard-Yale game, when she was fifteen. Which side had she been sitting on? he asked. The Yale side, she said. "Thank God," said the Harvard man.

Poor Yale! There are times when it must feel especially sorry for itself. Yale was well ahead of Harvard in modifying the rules governing the presence of women in men's living quarters. Yale led Harvard by several weeks in downgrading the status of R.O.T.C. on campus. But when Harvard does something, even though it may not be especially novel, it is news. It was thus right after the Second World War, when Harvard got most of the credit for instituting courses in general education, even though Chicago and Columbia had done most of the spadework in the field. Thus, too, when Yale authorized an Afro-American Studies program in December, 1968, the action created little stir outside of New Haven. When, a month afterward, Harvard followed suit, its decision was deemed worthy of front-page coverage and editorial-page acclaim in the *New York Times*. After acknowledging that Yale had indeed set the pace, the editorial justified its timeliness by calling attention to "Harvard's leading position in American scholarship and academic administration." Although, to be sure, James Reston of the *Times* once identified Daniel Patrick Moynihan, then director of the Harvard-M.I.T. Joint Center for Urban Studies and a full professor on the Harvard faculty before he joined the Nixon administration, as simply "of M.I.T.," a social headline in that newspaper went A HARVARD MAN AND MISS STUART MARRIED IN R.I. The bridegroom, though enrolled in the Harvard Business School, was a graduate of Yale.

THE SNOBBISHNESS that is often attributed to Harvard is not entirely Harvard's fault. Among the educated, Harvard is often the butt of the same kind of joke that, among the uneducated, involves Brooklyn. After the Harvard melee of April,

1969, there was a spate of new jokes, some of them not very funny; George Jessel, for instance, said that if he had his choice of visiting Harvard or Vietnam, he'd pick Vietnam, because it was safer. The plain word *Harvard* may not have charisma, but it has cachet. Publishers of textbooks dote on volumes to which they can append a Harvard identification tag. One publisher crowingly told a Harvard professor that he had a volume on American history in the works, written collaboratively by three professors from Berkeley, Chicago, and Harvard. "You can't beat that!" he exulted. He never mentioned the contents of the book. The headline of an engagement story on the *New York Times* society page referred to the bride-to-be as "of Harvard." The text said she came from Delaware and had attended Colby College; her only itemized Harvard connection was that she was employed in the charter-flights division of the Harvard Student Agencies.

Harvard publications take Harvard eminence less seriously. Reviewing a joint concert of the Harvard and Princeton Glee Clubs, the *Crimson* said, "There they were: the Glee Club grads, the Princetonians up for the game, the dates of the boys on stage, all there to remind themselves how terrific it is to go to an Ivy League school. We may not be quite ready for the jet set, but we are ever the Golden Race." And, mocking Harvard magnificence, the *Crimson* headlined an account of a solar eclipse UNIVERSITY TAKES LOOK AT SUN. Undergraduate humor at Harvard is often no better than that at any other youthful hangout, but there can be nice touches; a weekly called the *Harvard Student Calendar* started off its entry for December 16 with "Before anything else, celebrate Beethoven's Birthday. One of the world's few Good Guys."

Like many other high-class American institutions, Harvard is no longer an aristocracy, but a meritocracy. Even so, there is a prevailing aura of elitism. Some of the most proletarian-minded members of the faculty are sometimes the quickest to brag to their colleagues that they have the son of this or that renowned banker or statesman or musician in one of their classes. And even the brashest undergraduates are apt to find themselves impressed, if not overpowered, by the sheer solidity of Harvard's reputation. One junior who was devoting most of his time to trying to undermine some of Harvard's entrenched and, he thought, encrusted, practices paused to remark, "It's difficult to come out and say that three hundred years of ivy are all wrong."

A no less radical sophomore who had entered Harvard with advanced standing, and thus had the option of finishing in three or four years and of aligning himself with either of two graduating classes, was asked by an acquaintance which one he had decided to join. He mentioned one, and, asked why he had chosen it, said it was really very simple. "The guys in it are the guys I want to spend my twenty-fifth reunion with," he said. Whatever alterations he was seeking as an undergraduate to impose on Harvard, he clearly did not want the place to topple.

When Robert Hutchins was president of the University of Chicago, he would sometimes say that it was a hell of a poor university but the best there was. Harvard spokesmen don't much discuss its relative luster, in jest or seriousness. They take it for granted. They would regard it as rude and pushy—however accurate it might also be—to exclaim, as Buddha did when he sprang newborn from his mother's hip, "I am the first and the best!" The first American college Harvard unarguably is; there was a fifty-seven-year gap between its founding in 1636 and that of William and Mary. (Nowadays, American colleges spring from the body politic at the rate of one a week.) In nearly all observable respects, Harvard has changed since 1636—as what has not?—but it has not changed, or at any rate hopes it has not, in its reverence for and pursuit of excellence.

Harvard has Puritan origins, and it was the Puritan tradition to shun the second-rate. Mere cobbler or candlestick-maker a man might be, but if he was the best cobbler or candlestick-maker around, nobody could fault him. Harvard is suspicious of the second-rate, the sleazy, and the adequate. Take, to cite a small example, its athletic office. The office has a public-relations staff, which sends out releases to newspapers, as do the comparable staffs of other universities. But Harvard issues its releases single-spaced. For one thing, this saves on paper costs, and Harvard, for all its resources, is a place that stands second to none in the sport of pinching pennies. For another, the practice makes it difficult for papers to use Harvard releases word-for-word; most lino-typers shy away from single-spaced copy. Harvard sports re-leases, or so their creators theorize, have to be rewritten before they can be used. This is what Harvard wants. Harvard believes that everybody—even the hardpressed and undermanned sports departments of small New England weeklies—should be encour-aged not to run handouts but to think and to write for them-selves.

The best American educational institution Harvard may also well be—the best in the world, perhaps—but there have always been plenty of dissenters from this viewpoint, not inconspicuous among them Harvard men, whom Harvard has tried to teach, for one thing, to embrace skepticism, or at least tolerate it. In the spring of 1968, a committee of seven senior Harvard professors issued a report on some aspects of the University, in the course of which they asserted, probably not without wincing, "For a half-century, Harvard was believed by many to occupy a unique posi-tion in the American system of higher education; and that posi-tion no longer seems as secure as it once did." It was less than a half century ago—in 1934—that President A. Lawrence Lowell said in his Commencement address that of the members of the National Academy of Sciences affiliated with higher education, Harvard could claim forty, or twice as many as Chicago and Columbia combined and twenty-four more than Yale. "Take not a straw too seriously, yet it may indicate the breeze," Lowell said.

The winds of change have been blowing ever since, but not so strongly that Harvard cannot still muster comparable statistics. Through 1968, seventy-seven United States scientists had won the Nobel Prize. Fourteen had been at Harvard when they did the work that was thus honored. Columbia was the runner-up, with nine. True, at that time Harvard had only seven Nobel laureates actually on its faculty, one less than Berkeley, a West-Coast edge that Richard Nixon stressed in the waning moments of his successful presidential campaign. He lost Massachusetts' fourteen electoral votes the next day, but he also won California's forty. (After that, he felt safe, in his Inaugural Address, to quote two men with strong Harvard connections—Archibald MacLeish and Franklin D. Roosevelt.) Professors now at Harvard have been awarded the Nobel prize six times in the last eight years, and while the University is naturally pleased by this, it does not put them on pedestals. It does not even always formally congratulate them. It refrains from making too much fuss because, it reasons, there are only a few disciplines in which men are eligible for the Nobel Prize, so why single them out for further acclaim at home when there are in the family so many scholars of equal or perhaps even greater eminence in other disciplines?

President Lowell was not invariably modest about Harvard's relative weight on the scale of human affairs. It was during his administration that a Harvard functionary uttered the memorable line, "The President is in Washington to see Mr. Wilson." Harvard men have become so inured to that kind of attitude toward chief executives that when in the fall of 1967 the *Harvard Alumni Bulletin* referred to Lyndon Johnson simply as "the President," a few readers were confused; to them, in the context of that publication, the phrase should have been reserved exclusively for Nathan Pusey.

Echoes of the Lowell attitude can still be heard in Cambridge. After delivering a tirade against something Lyndon Johnson had or hadn't done at a cocktail party, a Harvard elder was chided by a fellow guest for his belligerence; after all, he was reminded, Mr. Johnson was president of the United States. "Well, I'm professor of history and literature at Harvard and I don't behave like that," was the retort. At another social gathering, a lady who heard that a graduate student was doing his doctoral dissertation on American politics in the eighteen-seventies said she couldn't remember who was president then. "Charles William Eliot, of course," snapped an eavesdropping professor's wife.

President Lowell never earned a Ph.D., and though he accumulated the usual flock of honorary degrees, he insisted on being called "Mister." Lowell left the bulk of his estate to Harvard's select Society of Fellows, which he founded to encourage and facilitate graduate study on the part of scholars—McGeorge Bundy and Arthur Schlesinger, Jr., came to be among them—who were not especially interested in going through the formalities of obtaining a doctorate. James B. Conant and Nathan M. Pusey both held Ph.D.'s, but following Lowell's stance it was Harvard custom for them always to be addressed as "Mr. Conant" and "Mr. Pusey." While Bundy was the dean of Arts and Sciences, he was walking across the Yard one morning with an associate who expressed concern that the previous week a Boston paper had wrongly identified a Harvard instructor as a professor. "Don't worry about those little things," said Bundy, looking worried. "This morning the *Herald* called Mr. Pusey 'Doctor.'"

Newcomers to Cambridge sometimes find Harvard's stratospheric self-evaluation irritating. Not long after a full professor transferred from Berkeley to Cambridge, his wife was told by a colleague's wife, "Now that your husband has finally made it to Harvard, it must be a great thrill for both of you." "What did you think he was before—a shoeshine boy?" the emigrée replied. Most people who have been at Harvard for any length of time find it difficult, though, not to develop a special feeling toward the place. "If you have ever made this University your home," Mr. Bundy said after seven years away from it, "there is a sense in which you never leave it, wherever you go or whatever you do." An undergraduate from California who spent much of his college career criticizing Harvard, often in savage terms, reflected mournfully on the eve of his graduation, "People keep arguing with me that Harvard is the best school in the country, and the awful thing is that it may be. For all I dislike about this place, I can see myself at a future reunion being *nostalgic* about it."

Harvard's impact on the people who rub against it has even affected some members of S.D.S., who are generally not impressed by traditions. In the course of the campus upheavals at Cambridge in the spring of 1969, a leading student militant said he was thinking of contributing his annals of anarchy to the Harvard Archives. During the seizure of University Hall, when somebody painted an obscenity on a wall of Dean Glimp's office, somebody else Scotch-Taped a note alongside it saying: "Dear Sir, We apologize for whoever did this. This vandalism was not a purpose of our protest." At Columbia, a year earlier, some S.D.S. students had scuffed up their president's desk; when a Harvard S.D.S. man was asked if he and his allies had ever contemplated any similar action, he replied, "Good God, no. Mr. Pusey's desk was used by Mr. Eliot." He went on to further reveal, in a most curious fashion, his private view of Harvard as *sui generis*. "The Harvard faculty is something real special," he said. "It's hard to have a happy, relaxed homosexual relationship with a Harvard professor, because all the time you're aware that he isn't an ordinary professor—he's a *Harvard* professor. It would be quite different at Columbia."

Harvard men credit Harvard with all sorts of improbable achievements. During a discussion of summer jobs, one undergraduate said he'd heard that a certain Cape Cod restaurant was on the downgrade. A companion disagreed. "It was slipping for a while," he explained, "but that was before they had Harvard waiters." The Harvard mystique extends beyond human beings. Reminiscing about a summer job *she'd* had, which involved a psychological experiment with pigeons, a Radcliffe girl said things hadn't worked out according to plan. "Being Harvard pigeons, the birds were too damned bright and kept chewing up the wires the scientists were using," she said.

Professor Stanley Hoffman: "Harvard activity is a conspiracy against giving you any time to write or even to think."

ν

PEOPLE LIKE TO HANG AROUND Harvard. The University Health Services have an arrangement with the National Institute of Mental Health whereby young psychiatrists spend two years working in Cambridge. A couple of doctors have stayed on an extra year at their own expense, simply because they find the patients so fascinating.

There is an ailment, endemic to Cambridge, called the Harvard disease. There are two common symptoms. Individuals who have known Cambridge but are not there suffer acute pangs of wanting to be there. Individuals in Cambridge pale at the prospect of going elsewhere, no matter how fetching the bait may be that's dangled before them. Edward S. Mason, for instance, the economist and public-administration specialist, had been at Harvard for forty-six years when he retired in 1969. (To mark his twenty-fifth anniversary, the University gave him a Harvard chair with a testimonial brass plate, a token bestowed on all quarter-century employees, regardless of academic stature.) Professor Mason had several times had attractive offers from other campuses, but he had turned them all down out of hand. "I was terribly happy at Harvard," he said. "I was never even slightly tempted to leave."

Professor Jerome S. Bruner, the psychologist who wrote *The Process of Education*, the Harvard University Press's all-time best-seller, has diagnosed a side effect of the Harvard disease.

"Everybody here who's afflicted with it feels that he has to do something special," he says. "This can lead to intolerance and smugness. If there's one guy here, and another guy elsewhere who's equally good in their field, the one here is apt to feel that because the other one isn't here he *can't* be as good."

Bruner, another twenty-five year man and anniversary-chair recipient, has several specialties. Scientists—social as well as physical—must these days often raise the funds for their own research projects; among his colleagues, Bruner is regarded, not without envy, as a master solicitor. In the patchwork quilt that is Harvard, he runs a small but colorful square called the Center for Cognitive Studies. It is considered highly unusual because it dares to explore a field that most psychologists ignore—the behavior of normally functioning human beings.

To get the Center rolling, in 1960, Bruner almost singlehandedly raised a quarter of a million dollars from the Carnegie Corporation; when that source dried up, he turned to the National Institute of Mental Health and the National Science Foundation, which have lately been granting him, between them, half a million annually. This has enabled him to invite thirty post-doctoral behavioral scientists a year to share his facilities. Bruner also wangled a used but perfectly operable computer from the Air Force (later, he was chairman of a faculty committee that recommended Harvard's complete severance of relations with R.O.T.C.), with the help of which one of his post-doctorals, a Japanese psychologist who was interested in testing intelligence and behavioral discrimination, devised an experiment involving a fungus-fuelled robot theoretically dispatched to an asteroid to mine uranium.

Bruner himself has been concentrating on earthbound children. In 1964, Harvard gave him a year off so he could devise and supervise a curriculum for fifth-grade students, based on his prior research into youthful thought processes. "I found that it was a hell of a lot harder teaching fifth-grade children in Newton than Harvard undergraduates," he said afterward. Lately, Bruner has been working mostly with infants; the elevators at William James Hall, the behavioral-sciences building in which he presides over a floor-and-a-half enclave, now and then resemble a pediatric ward. Some young women are so eager to have their babies take passive part in Harvard research that they volunteer for his program as soon as they learn they're pregnant.

Bruner's pair of open-handed national agencies not long ago bought him a portable laboratory—a van fitted out to his specifications—that he could take around to housing projects, where he measured the relationship between hand and eye movements of stay-at-home infants. The psychologist planned at first to drive the truck himself but found this too challenging. So he enlisted a laboratory technician with a flair for large rigs. It all worked out nicely; if, after the two men lumbered to their destination, the delicate instruments in the rear needed calibration, the technician could hop around back and attend to them. "We have marvelous facilities here," Bruner says, "and moreover, we're privileged people because of our associates. A while ago, I wanted to measure the flow of blood inside a baby's body, and with a couple of phone calls I got onto a guy in Biology who knew absolutely everything about that. At Harvard, you feel that you're part of the 'we happy few.' "

Bruner's sentiments have been echoed by, among others, one of the most redoubtable figures of Harvard's modern history and Harvard's own house historian, Samuel Eliot Morison. Now a professor emeritus, Morison is also a retired Navy admiral. Around Harvard, he is known as *the* admiral. (After a brisk early-morning canter, Morison, who turned eighty in 1966, often materializes at Harvard in riding habit, and is thus sometimes taken by impressionable freshmen for a retired cavalry general. He could still, if he chose, use the facilities of the final club he joined as an undergraduate over sixty years ago, and a tankard with his name on it awaits his pleasure there, but he rarely drops in any more. "They're a little too awed by me," he says.) "Working at Harvard is great because there are so many specialists around," Professor Morison said. "If I want to know anything about the Azores, I just call Frank Rogers [professor of romance languages and literature]. If I want to know about American Indians, I call John Brew [Peabody Professor of American Archaeology and Ethnology, and director of the Peabody Museum]. If I want to know about botany, I call Paul Mangelsdorf [Fisher Professor of Natural History, emeritus, former chairman of the Institute for Research in Experimental and Applied Botany, etc., etc.]."

Morison not infrequently finds himself making such inquiries —when he is not answering ones from professors or ordinary human beings seeking to tap *his* rich lode of information— because as an historian he is anything but retired or emeritus. His principal place of work at Harvard is a cubicle in the stacks of the massive Widener Library. Having a Widener office is prestigious. But there are only 105 offices in the building, and there are 375 tenured professors and associate professors on the Faculty of Arts and Sciences. The top floor is generally considered most desirable (the Admiral, though on a lower deck, prefers his spot because it is all but engulfed by Widener's American-history stacks), and up there perch such Harvard luminaries as the classicist Mason Hammond and the historians Paul H. Buck, Oscar Handlin, and Robert Lee Wolff. Handlin shares his chamber with an outsize bright-red piece of abstract sculpture; a student gave it to him, and although it is hard to circumambulate, he hasn't the heart to get rid of it.

The late Werner W. Jaeger, the professor of classics, was reportedly lured to Harvard from Chicago in 1939 solely because President Conant made him the unprecedented offer of *three* top-floor rooms in Widener. These precious quarters are usually doled out, one to a person, on a basis of strict seniority. Erik H. Erikson, though, got one as soon as he joined the Harvard faculty, in 1960, when the discoverer of the identity crisis was fifty-nine and, in terms of Harvard longevity, an infant. Dean Bundy brilliantly solved the delicate problem of slipping Erikson into Widener. Bundy asked him if he had ever been at Harvard before. Erikson recalled having given a lecture at the Medical School somewhere around 1934. "Splendid!" cried Bundy. "We'll put you on the seniority list as if you'd *been* here since 1934."

Professors are supposed to vacate their Widener offices no later than five years after they become emeritus. No one would dream, however, of dislodging a man like Morison, and anybody who dared to dream about it would no more dare to suggest it to him than would an ensign keelhaul an admiral at sea. Morison has occupied his office since 1931, and from it he has launched an armada of books. (His latest, and twenty-fifth, is a revision of his first—a biography of Harrison Gray Otis, one of his great-great-grandfathers, that he wrote as a Ph.D. dissertation in 1913.) One cannot write about Harvard without rewriting Morison. He was official historian for Harvard's tercentenary celebration in 1936, and at that time produced his classic *Three Centuries of Harvard*, which in subsequent Harvard University Press catalogues has been listed right after *Three Centuries of Harpsichord Making*.

Morison has devoted two whole volumes to Harvard in the seventeenth century, when the place was, in effect, little more than a finishing school for presumptive ministers. (The first presiding officer was a mean man named Nathaniel Eaton, who stole money and beat a tutor almost to death; Harvard is proud of its traditions and its early leaders, but it hardly ever talks about the scoundrelly Eaton.) Up to 1700, Harvard graduated only 543 students—an average of less than eight a year—half of whom became clergymen. Boys entered at thirteen or fourteen, in many instances, and the sole requirement for an A.B. degree was to translate the Old and New Testaments from English into passable Latin.

Perhaps because there were so few graduates in those early days, in the mid-nineteenth century one of Harvard's bravest sons embarked on one of the most strenuous of literary enterprises. This was John Langdon Sibley, who aspired to write a biography of every graduate of Harvard College, beginning with the first class, that of 1642. A native of Maine, Sibley graduated from Harvard in 1825, and eventually came back as librarian. It was not much of a job, and the library wasn't much, either. Today, Harvard has one of the world's truly noble libraries, but in the mid-nineteenth century a Harvard president, abetted by an abutting architect, rebuked Sibley for installing some new shelves he needed; the two inspectors thought these were aesthetically displeasing. "For what was the library built—for books or for looks?" Sibley spunkily retorted.

Sibley thought big. Though he had limited acquisition funds, it was his ambition to procure one copy of each book ever published, and at every opportunity he would badger alumni to help make his wish come true. A bachelor, he mothered his books. At dusk one evening, an acquaintance saw him walking across the Yard, a volume under his arm, and asked where he was bound. "This is the only book that's not in the library tonight," Sibley said, "and I'm putting it back."

Sibley's most grandiose thoughts centered on his biographies, which became known as "Sibley's Harvard Graduates." The University was not especially keen on the project. President Eliot, under whom Sibley served as librarian for sixteen years, was so unsympathetic that when Sibley died he vengefully willed his publication rights not to the Harvard University Press but to a grateful Massachusetts Historical Society. The Press has done all right notwithstanding. Although it publishes no standard textbooks, it sells more books—some eight hundred thousand a year —than any other university press. It makes money (being part of Harvard and thus tax-exempt), but it is less interested in profits than scholarship. Of the 2,500 books in its catalogue, fewer than one-fifth sell more than 350 copies a year. Nine-tenths of the orders the Press gets are for a single copy of a single book. Some of its ventures would depress a commercial publisher. When the first of a series of volumes entitled *Scripta Mongolica*, printed in Mongolian, was issued in 1956, there was no chance of a substantial domestic sale, inasmuch as there were only nine individuals in the country who were known to be able to read the language. But enough people learned Mongolian from Volume One so that by the time the Press brought out Volume Two it had a potential American readership of fifty. Last year, the Press brought out Volume Six, and on the basis of its intelligence about the advance of Mongolian studies boldly ordered a first printing of fifteen hundred.

In his lifetime, Sibley was undaunted by Harvard's indifference. By the time he died, in 1886, at eighty-one, he had got through the class of 1689. Sibley had a high opinion of Harvard men in general and of nearly everyone he wrote up in particular. In a preface to his first volume, he was able to state proudly, "More than two centuries had passed since the College was established, yet I found but one graduate who had been executed as a malefactor, and he was a victim of the witchcraft delusion; and but one who had been sent to a state penitentiary, and this was for passing counterfeit money." He did not have to come to grips, though he obviously knew about him, with Dr. John W. Webster, of the class of 1811, who in 1850 was hanged for murdering Dr. George Parkman, of the class of 1809, while both were on the faculty of the Harvard Medical School. Harvard record-keepers other than Sibley handled that awkward situation as tactfully as they could. The minutes of the appropriate Medical School faculty meeting simply stated that Dr. Webster was no longer around, that his professional associates "regretfully took note of action by the civil authorities," and that they had voted to fill the vacancy that existed "in Dr. Webster's absence." Ever since, it has been accepted as a basic truth, at a University with the motto "*Veritas*," that Dr. Webster was Harvard's most egregious malefactor. In the precedent-shattering year of 1969, a Harvard Medical School professor and a Massachusetts judge announced that they were collaborating on a book to prove that Dr. Webster was innocent.

On the death of a chronicler as single-minded and dedicated as Sibley was, one might expect his quixotic venture to come to a halt. Not at Harvard. More than forty years after Sibley's death, a new librarian emerged to pick up and rekindle his heavy torch. This was a graduate in the class of 1926, Clifford K. Shipton, who got interested in Harvard history while serving as Professor Morison's assistant during the tercentenary celebration, and who became known as the Harvard Plutarch.

Shipton deserved the accolade. At last count, taking up where Sibley left off, he had completed 1,900 biographies of Harvard men totalling 2,700,000 words, some of them delightfully lively. In the very first paragraph of his biography of Benjamin Wadsworth, Harvard's eighth president (Wadsworth House, a 1726 frame building that still stands in the Harvard Yard, was the home of nine Harvard presidents), Shipton reminds the world of President Wadsworth's flat assertion that the atom couldn't be split, and later lets it be known that the old educator once bought a Negro wench as a slave. Shipton's Sibleyan biographies have lately occupied much of the reading-for-pleasure time of, among others, Don K. Price, the dean of Harvard's John Fitzgerald Kennedy School of Government. Price was glad to learn that in the eighteenth century Harvard students took precedence, in college affairs, according to the status of their fathers, and that fathers in government rated higher than fathers in business.

The indefatigable Shipton's last completed collection of biographies took him through the class of 1763. The end of the long journey is still over the horizon, but it is finite. Beginning with the class of 1830, most graduates have favored Harvard with autobiographies. So the class of 1829 is the last one on the agenda. Shipton, who was sixty-three years old in 1969, had high hopes of getting through the American Revolution in his lifetime, and was unperturbed by the prospect that he might never reach the nineteenth century. "As far as I'm concerned, the eighteenth century is a much more comfortable place to be," he said. "Harvard has grown at such an appalling rate that I have difficulty finding my way around its recent history. But when I go back a couple of hundred years I feel at home."

Casting their minds over centuries, in either direction, does not frighten Harvard men. When Dr. Roger I. Lee, a Boston physician who served on the Harvard Corporation for twenty-three years, died in 1965, he willed to the University an elegant eighteenth-century secretary. He asked that it be placed in the oldest building in the Yard, Massachusetts Hall, which was built in 1720. President Pusey and a few of his chief assistants now have offices there. The antique was installed in the office of L. Gard Wiggins, Harvard's administrative vice-president. "I expect it will be in somebody's office at Harvard three hundred years from now," Wiggins says matter-of-factly.

"THE JUSTIFICATION of a university," Alfred North Whitehead said in 1928, when he was a philosophy professor at Harvard, "is that it preserves the connection between knowledge and the zest of life, by uniting the young and the old in the imaginative consideration of learning." Uniting the young and old— bridging the generation gap, as a philosopher might have phrased it forty years after Whitehead—is still very much the concern of any university. The methods of accomplishing this have, of course, been radically transformed. Harvard, once it stopped being a production line for ministers, began to think that its main function was to acquaint its students with the historical traditions of Western civilization. Now, many students leap into its midst confidently omniscient and expect it to help them forge new dimensions for uncircumscribed civilization.

President Pusey has spoken of the obligation of the university to "take young men and women into the varied and explosive world of knowledge." But many present-day students have little patience with or trust in what their elders construe to be knowledge, though they do admire variety and explosiveness. They are more interested in societal than intellectual problems, and so are many of their instructors. Paul M. Doty, Jr., for instance, the Harvard professor of chemistry, almost literally never talked to anybody except a scientist during his first ten post-graduate years of research and teaching. He had always assumed he was an introvert, like the great scientists whose biographies used to constitute the bulk of his non-technical reading. Then in the late nineteen-fifties he got interested in politics and social problems; in the last few years, he has spent close to half his time preoccupied with matters like Vietnam and arms control, and not long ago he was astonished to reflect that fully half his friends were non-scientists.

In the early nineteen-sixties Mr. Doty was chairman of a committee of the Faculty of Arts and Sciences that was supposed to examine Harvard's program of General Education and recommend changes, if any seemed advisable. The program had begun just after the Second World War. The idea behind it was to make every undergraduate take at least one broad course in the humanities, the social sciences, and the natural sciences. The idea behind *that* was to wrench the natural scientist out of the narrow world in which he sometimes tended to immure himself. The scientists had taken very well to the non-scientific requirements of the Gen. Ed. program—much more so, all in all, than the humanists had to the scientific requirements. The Doty Committee tried, in substance, to make sure that more non-scientists got thoroughly exposed to science. But its recommendations were turned down. Non-scientists on the faculty voted against them because they didn't want to see students forced into science courses; scientists voted against them because they didn't want to teach grumpy students who had been forced upon them.

As universities and the people who flesh them have plunged ever more deeply into the affairs of the outside world, the ivory tower, that once vaulting, gleaming symbol of intellectual separatism, is rapidly diminishing in size and luster. In his 1969 Baccalaureate Address to the graduating seniors—to those few, at any rate, who bothered to attend—President Pusey said, a trifle sadly, that the ivory tower "has by now been all but toppled." It is still possible in academic communities, though, to find individuals who are by nature and inclination ivory-towerish—those contented, lonely scholars whose thing is to keep their noses out of other people's business and close to their own grindstones. At Harvard, for one, there is Richard E. Schultes, the economic botanist, who was recently appointed curator of the Botanical Museum. For him, science is still just about everything.

Schultes is not without his lighthearted side; he was delighted when a fellow scholar named a newly discovered variety of cockroach after him—*Schultesia romundiana*—and he carries a snapshot of the creature in his wallet. He does not believe, however, that serious students should be diverted from their principal business by beating their breasts over California grapepickers or beating the bushes for Congressional candidates. He himself reads no newspapers or nonscientific journals, and he never looks at television; he keeps more or less abreast of current affairs by turning on his car radio twice daily while commuting between his home and his office, a seven-minute ride. A professorial associate of his at Harvard, the biologist Carroll Williams, is unsparing of his time when academicians are involved. Nearly every day, he has his graduate students in for tea. But he also has an unlisted phone; time spent with students is one thing, time wasted on anyone who might chance to call him is another.

Schultes is a paragon of scholarly devotion. A member of the Harvard class of 1937, he planned as an undergraduate to take up medicine. But he fell in with a professor of botany with the apt name of Oakes Ames, and under Ames' guidance wrote an honors thesis on some Mexican hallucinogenic mushrooms. Schultes was hooked, in a scholarly way. He subsequently spent a total of sixteen and a half years ferreting out narcotic plants in the backwater jungles of the Amazon. Harvard's collection of plant specimens includes fifty thousand South American ones brought home by Schultes. Not all are narcotic; three of them, for instance, are relatives of the jack-in-the-pulpit that, when chewed, serve effectively as contraceptives.

For the better part of ten years, the only buffers between nature and Schultes were two Indians and a fifteen-foot canoe. At one stretch, he chewed coca daily for eight years. It dulls hunger pangs. In the summer of 1967, he was lucky enough to be able to classify a numbing snuff used during their big annual feast by one of South America's few surviving tribes of cannibals. But Schultes' thirty-year devotion to narcotic plants brought him a kind of notoriety that he finds upsetting. He became very big on the drug scene. Non-botanists, such as legislators and social scientists, began pestering him for learned opinions on various drugs (he happens to believe that there is no scientific foundation for saying marijuana is either harmful or harmless), and this distracted him from his work.

Schultes' dilemma, and that of other scholars like him who are being wrenched out of the routines they espouse, was alluded to in 1968 by a committee of senior Harvard professors. Reporting on an examination they had made of some aspects of faculty life at the University, they wrote, almost wistfully, "Today a little more academic isolation might be welcome." Over the years, of course, many university professors had participated energetically in public affairs. But they had done so mainly as individuals. Then, more and more universities—Harvard among them—were faced with troubling questions: Should they, as *institutions,* become actively engaged in contemporary social issues? Was that their obligation, or was it, rather, to train their students how to do so as informedly, effectively, and compassionately as possible? Assuming that the world needed changing, was it the function of a place like Harvard to help its students change the world, or merely to try to teach them how to?

Harvard's answer, which many of its students soon showed they found unacceptable, was that it would be misleading for the university to speak out on all issues. For, in a group of many able minds with many attitudes and convictions, what voice should it use? The voice of the majority, if a majority viewpoint could in fact be ascertained? What then would become of the minority, in a sanctum of free thought and expression? Would every dissenting opinion have to be appended to each Harvard verdict? The Supreme Court can generate no more than nine different opinions on any single issue. Harvard could produce thousands. Harvard argued that its scholars, senior and junior, should joust on their own in the public arena; as an institution, it would observe, and to be sure often also root, from the sidelines. It would harbor its strengths—its knowledge and skills and resources—largely for the instructional role it has played, with polished proficiency, over so many years, and that it thought it stood a pretty fair chance of playing again to the distant edge of the intellectual horizon.

As far back as 1909, President Lowell was saying that it was the function of an American college to take the inherently social animal that was man and develop his powers as a social being. What influence Harvard could have on society should be exerted, its chief policy-makers contended, not through their efforts but through those of the constituency whose attitudes they helped to shape. By thus acting through students rather than with them, one militant undergraduate said grumpily, "Harvard gets to wallow in the mud of conflict without getting soiled." Some members of the administration shared this viewpoint. "Harvard won't grab the ball and run with it," one of them said, "because that's not the way that Harvard works."

In the convulsive world of modern higher education, the way that Harvard chose to work was to stand steady, or as steady as any establishment could stand with the earth trembling underfoot and the sky crackling with thunderstorms. At times of stress, Harvard found its own sheer durability comforting, and fell back on the long view. Discussing the state of liberalism in the spring of 1967, Franklin L. Ford, a historian before he became dean of the Faculty of Arts and Sciences, said, "As these things go, in terms of centuries, modern rightism and leftism alike are recent, transient formations. The liberal attitude toward education is somewhat older, being part of our legacy from the eighteenth century. Harvard University is older still. Having come to accept the dispassionate, individualistic value system of true liberalism,

Harvard and institutions like it will not be stampeded . . . even in the noisy nineteen-sixties."

The following year, Ford said, "You can take the view that Harvard is as good as it is because it is old and stable and doesn't have to keep up with the times, or the view that it's so good because it has always not only kept up but kept ahead." It was nonetheless becoming increasingly hard for Harvard—though nowhere near as hard, probably, as for less deeply rooted institutions—to maintain its equanimity and its equilibrium at a time of moral siege. It was what happened to Dean Ford during the 1969 student takeover, when he was ordered out of his own office, that as much as any other single incident probably infuriated the Harvard hierarchy and triggered its firm response. Administrators are often thought to be dispensable these days on campuses, but Professor Ford was not basically an administrator; he was a distinguished scholar. Harvard did not lightly take the laying of hands on the McLean Professor of Ancient and Modern History. At the same time, Harvard students did not lightly take the summoning of the police. It required less than one hour of police presence on the campus to convert into a self-avowed flaming radical an undergraduate who for more than two years had served as chairman of the policy committee for Harvard's Young Republicans.

Before that, the pressures had been gradually building. In 1968, Professor Jerome Alan Cohen, a Sinologist on the Harvard Law School faculty, wondered if the Maoist slogan "Politics Takes Command" was not beginning to be as applicable to Cambridge as it was to Peking—where Chinese students and their teachers were throwing so much of themselves into non-academic matters that they hardly had the chance or strength to open a book, or at any rate a textbook. (Over on Taiwan, when it came to that, a seventeen-year-old student displeased at being disciplined chopped his teacher's head off.) What with the war in Vietnam, the draft, race relations, the presidential elections, and the assassinations, the 1967–1968 academic year was one in which—no matter how much Harvard might try to maintain its institutional detachment—Harvard people were concerned with off-campus matters to a phenomenal degree.

It was a concern that, though at first relatively orderly, was nearly as disruptive to the conventional operations of a university as any number of sit-ins, lie-ins, love-ins, or teach-ins. In a single week, a not particularly unusual one, another Law School professor felt obliged to sandwich in his prescribed duties as well as he could while also conferring on Vietnam with Herman Kahn, counseling the Urban Affairs Planning Committee of the Boston Bar Association, working on a book about the impact of the military establishment on American life, attending an afternoon meeting in New York on urban education, dining with Senator Edward M. Kennedy that same night in Cambridge to discuss crime-control legislation, delivering an address in Maine on foreign aid and military spending, preparing a paper about federal grants for various urban programs, and writing an analysis of the report of the National Advisory Commission on Civil Disorders.

A few ivory-tower men aside, Harvard became politicized as never before. Senator Eugene McCarthy's campaign was launched in Cambridge, with much University assistance (his own daughter dropped out of Radcliffe to help him, and a *Crimson* reporter joined his ranks full time in retaliation for the paper's endorsement of Robert Kennedy). When John Kenneth Galbraith returned to Cambridge after a March weekend in Milwaukee campaigning for McCarthy, the students in his Social Sciences 134 course expected him to begin his regular Tuesday-morning lecture with an up-to-date commentary on the campaign, and he did not disappoint them. It was no accident that Senator Fulbright concluded his Foreign Relations Committee hearings on Vietnam (during which Secretary of State Rusk, after months of evasiveness, finally testified over network television) by reading an anti-administration letter from five members of the Harvard faculty. Fulbright's office had asked for the letter.

Harvard has long taken an indulgent view of the political involvements of its faculty, and of its students, too. Harvard has a profound commitment to tolerance—it was granting degrees to heathens two hundred years before one could get a degree in England without being an Anglican—and to liberalism. Undergraduates of New Left persuasion sometimes seem resentful of Harvard's credentials. "The trouble with this place is that the liberal structure has reached its height here," one of them complained not long ago. In the days that some Harvard administrators now look back on almost with nostalgia, the University's liberal bent came mostly under fire not from the New Left but from the Old Right, and whenever the Old Right can make itself heard these days, Harvard is seldom ignored. The New Right has little use for it, either, when it comes to that.

It is probably inevitable that a university that President Pusey has described as a "free association of free men" should be periodically attacked for espousing freedom. Early in the First World War, there was on the faculty a German-born psychologist, Hugo Münsterberg, who made no secret of his support for his fatherland. An Englishman who had briefly attended Harvard at the end of the nineteenth century (he was thrown out for, in those simple days, having a girl in his room) wrote to Cambridge that he had once had Harvard down in his will for two million pounds but now wanted his name stricken from his class records "until the faculty has the grace to kick that ass Münsterberg out."

There is no evidence that the Englishman ever had that kind of money or really meant to leave it to Harvard, but Münsterberg, reluctant to do the University out of an even hallucinatory ten-million-dollar bequest, which would have been Harvard's biggest up to then, offered to resign. Harvard wouldn't hear of it, and President Lowell, in his next annual report, reiterated the University's devotion to freedom of thought and went on to say that "knowledge can advance, or at least can advance most rapidly, only by means of an unfettered search for truth on the part of those who devote their lives to seeking it in their respective fields, and by complete freedom in imparting to their pupils the truth that they may have found." In 1933, Mr. Lowell, preparing to step down as president in favor of Mr. Conant, again dwelt on the endlessness of the search for truth. "This is a relay race," said Lowell, who was a track man in his youth. "It has been going on for a long time, and I pass the flag to him."

Lowell is perhaps best remembered outside of Harvard for his role in the Sacco-Vanzetti case, when as chairman of a commission appointed by the governor of Massachusetts he concluded that the two men had been fairly sentenced to death ("the hangman of Harvard," Heywood Broun, Harvard '10, promptly called him), but some of Lowell's less-remembered achievements were of a quite different sort. During the Boston police strike of 1919, which launched Calvin Coolidge into national prominence, Harold Laski, then on the Harvard faculty, sided with the strikers. This was then a very radical thing to do. Harvard was concurrently embarking on its first major drive for endowment funds. A number of wealthy alumni said they wouldn't contribute unless Laski was fired, and the Harvard Board of Overseers demanded that they have a chance to question the Englishman on his political views. Lowell promptly announced that "if the Overseers ask for Laski's resignation, they will get mine." The Overseers subsided.

The following year, Professor Zechariah Chafee, Jr., of the Harvard Law School, a long-time devotee of civil liberties, wrote an article supporting three people who had been convicted under the Espionage Act of 1918 for putting out leaflets attacking the United States' sending troops to Russia to thwart the Bolsheviks. An overseer named Austin Fox insisted that the University investigate Chafee and, while Harvard was at it, the whole Law School faculty. A hearing was held at the Harvard Club in Boston; it became known as "The Trial at the Harvard Club." The jury consisted of an overseers-sponsored committee to visit the Law School. On the fateful day, to the surprise of many on hand, Chafee's counsel proved to be Abbot Lawrence Lowell. (It was the president's habit also to turn up in real courtrooms to support undergraduates in trouble with the police.) Lowell explained that "there are few creatures so low that they will not defend their young," and went on, punning about Mr. Fox, to talk about a man who had raised game birds and had once seen a hen "protect its whole brood with success against a fox." The committee voted not to discipline Chafee, who in later dedicating a book to Lowell said that "so long as he was President no one could breathe the air of Harvard and not be free." Sacco and Vanzetti, of course, were not Harvard men.

"There is no better explanation for the inflationary disruption of our economy than that no man ever remembers his gambling losses—only his winnings. This makes many people think that there is a good deal more money around than there actually is, and they spend every illusory bit of it. And so, in their own disruptive activities, does it go with students. They have simply closed their eyes to the old-fashioned concept that life consists of both give and take."

—An assistant professor at Harvard who in the old days would have been proud to call himself a liberal.

vi

CONSIDERING THE ATTACKS on freedom that Germany has mounted in the twentieth century, it is not surprising that Germans, in one way or another, have played a part in Harvard's defense of freedom. President Conant's report to his class of 1914 on the occasion of their twenty-fifth reunion in 1939 said, *inter alia*, "And when I come to think of it, through the last twenty-five years of my own personal experience the word Germany has kept recurring like a theme song." Organic chemistry, his field, was a German science. (After the Second World War, he resigned from Harvard to become American high commissioner in Germany.) "In the spring of 1933 I was elected president of Harvard University," he went on. "I can hardly blame Germany for that."

As the case of Professor Münsterberg had ruffled Lowell's Harvard in 1915, so, in 1934, was Conant's Harvard to be aroused by another controversial German. There was a *Sturm und Drang* over one of Hitler's henchmen, Ernst F. S. Hanfstaengl, known as "Putsi," who was about to attend *his* twenty-fifth Harvard reunion. Harvard men are sometimes irrationally loyal to their classmates. A Harvard doctor was once called in by a classmate he hardly knew to examine his sick wife. The doctor made a number of suggestions to the husband, who rejected them all. In exasperation, the doctor finally asked the man why, if he hadn't been prepared to take his advice, he'd summoned him in the first place. "Why?" said the man. "Because we're classmates."

In the case of Hanfstaengl, some of his classmates invited him to take a small honorific job at their twenty-fifth reunion. There was a big flap when this became known, and the invitation was withdrawn. Hanfstaengl turned up anyway (a few of the classmates—it is to be hoped they were drunk or spoofing—exchanged Nazi salutes with him), and offered Harvard an annual traveling fellowship to Germany in the amount of a thousand dollars. Conant spurned the gift.

Toward the end of the Conant era, Harvard found itself concerned with still another radical German, though at the opposite end of the political spectrum from Hanfstaengl. This was Gerhard Eisler, a Communist and a professor-designate at the University of Leipzig, who had just been convicted of contempt of Congress in the United States. Eisler was invited to lecture at Harvard early in 1949 by the John Reed Club—a now-defunct student group named in honor of an authentic Harvard-educated radical—and the radio commentator Fulton Lewis, Jr., took exception to the scheduled appearance. Lewis suggested that Harvard, in addition to subverting the youth in its custody, was paying Eisler's way to East Germany.

The whole episode prompted Wilbur J. Bender, then dean of Harvard College, to issue still another statement trying to define Harvard's basic beliefs, in which he said, "The world is full of dangerous ideas, and we are both naive and stupid if we believe that the way to prepare intelligent young men to face the world is to try to protect them from such ideas while they are in college. Four years spent in an insulated nursery will produce gullible innocents, not tough-minded realists who know what they believe because they have faced the enemies of their beliefs. . . . If Harvard students can be corrupted by an Eisler, Harvard College had better shut down as an educational institution. . . ."

Bender was not as impressed by his pronunciamento as were some of his colleagues in Cambridge. "It's easy to take a stand on principle at Harvard," Bender said nineteen years later. "You don't have to worry here, really, about the reactions of politicians and newspapers to what you say or do. Harvard is rich enough and strong enough to do what it feels is right, and weak little colleges are always thanking it for taking the stands it does. That makes it easier for them. The important thing is that Harvard will always back its people on controversial issues." Dean Bender died in March, 1969, just two weeks before Harvard became involved in perhaps the most controversial issue of its history, in which the University could hardly back all its people because they were badly split. Mr. Bender would probably have found it incredible that the Corporation warned that it might have to shut the place down as an educational institution because the students were acting up, and that in this instance the enemies of the beliefs of many of the students were no others than the very members of the Corporation themselves.

When, to go back to 1949, a Maryland lawyer named Frank B. Ober said he wouldn't contribute to a Law School fund-raising campaign because two members of the Harvard faculty had spoken at meetings Ober thought were Communistic, Conant turned over Harvard's defense to the New York lawyer Grenville Clark, then a member of the Harvard Corporation. Clark reminded the Maryland man of some of Harvard's traditions—citing Lowell's defense of Professor Chafee, among other things—and told him, "For whether the policy [of allowing professors their head] gains money or loses it [and he suspected that in the long run Harvard would gain more than it lost], Harvard, in order to *be* Harvard, has to hew to the line."

Then came Senator Joe McCarthy. For him, Harvard was a beautiful target. He thought it was, among other obnoxious things, "a smelly mess." All he had to do was to establish that a few Harvard people were, by his lights, suspect, and that made all Harvard men guilty by Harvard association. (How times have changed! In the spring of 1968, when Pierre E. Trudeau was running for prime minister of Canada, he was accused of leftist leanings because he had gone to Harvard. Trudeau pleaded innocence by association; the Kennedys had gone there too, he said.)

The Senator from Wisconsin was in full cry against Harvard when Nathan Pusey succeeded Conant, in the fall of 1953, and Pusey, fresh from Wisconsin himself, stood up to him reasonably well. When one instructor took the Fifth Amendment, and when Pusey stated mildly that while Harvard deplored the use of the Fifth it didn't regard that as tantamount to an admission of guilt, McCarthy said that the mothers and fathers of America would consider it reprehensible and un-American for Harvard to continue to let Fifth-Amendment Communists educate the sons and daughters of America. Harvard survived that blast and so did the instructor; he became a full professor and the chairman of an important academic department. Pusey has been steadfast in his belief that government interference is a grave and ever-present threat to education. It was characteristic of the prickly paths college presidents must tread these days that within a few weeks of being vilified by his own students for using force against them he was warning congressional committees in Washington of what he considered would be the dire consequences of federal retribution against campus militants.

Over the years, there have been Harvard faculty members with leftist leanings. There were in McCarthy's day, and there still are. One of the gripes of the New Left students at Harvard today is that there aren't enough of them. S.D.S., for instance, demanded in the spring of 1968 that Harvard introduce courses given by Marxist instructors, including one on trade-union organizing. Harvard, however, has listened and responded to these insistent voices. Its Committee on General Education approved for the 1969 spring term a social sciences course on "The American Economy: Conflict and Power," the specific purpose of which was to present to interested students the views of instructors among whom were self-proclaimed Marxists.

Even without the prodding of its radical students, Harvard, like so many universities, has been hospitable to radical attitudes. In 1962, the subsequent chairman of its history department, H. Stuart Hughes, ran in Massachusetts as a third-party candidate for the United States Senate. He was for peace in Vietnam, and for espousing that then way-out viewpoint was—despite a fairly conservative background, including service in the O.S.S. as an Army lieutenant colonel—looked upon as a wildeyed leftist. "I've stayed about where I was in 1962," Professor Hughes said six years later, "and a lot of students and some of the faculty have moved over to the left of me. They don't need me any more."

DURING President Kennedy's administration, Harvard was sometimes called the fourth branch of the government. Bundy, Schlesinger, Galbraith, Cox, Reischauer, Chayes—the roster of these and other names that had been big in Cambridge and became bigger in Washington was impressive. Considering the size of the federal establishment, though, and the understandable inclination of Kennedy to reach out for men of proven intellectual distinction, the migration could hardly be equated, as some of President Kennedy's critics sought to equate it, with a cabal. Richard M. Nixon, in 1968, inducted into his palace guard— along with Harvard professors Daniel P. Moynihan and Henry A. Kissinger—three men from a single advertising agency, but no one accused J. Walter Thompson of trying to dominate the country—any more, that was, than it had been trying all along.

Still, there were non-Harvard people in Washington, in the early nineteen-sixties, who seemed to take the view that anybody remaining in Cambridge was either a Republican or an incompetent or both. There was so much nasty talk about a Harvard invasion of the Capitol that when President Kennedy asked Francis Keppel, Harvard's dean of the Graduate School of Education, to come down and be his commissioner of education, and Keppel found that he needed a first-rate deputy, he resolved to recruit one through Washington channels rather than through his academic community. Everybody he consulted in Washington commended his attitude and concurred in his choice, who, after he had reported for duty, turned out to be a Harvard man, and thus inadvertently contributed, in the eyes of suspicious Harvard-watchers, to the thickening of the plot.

At Harvard, there are both a passionate concern for public affairs and a singularly high level of information. Harvard will probably never take over Washington—almost certainly not during a Republican administration—but there is a special affinity between the two power centers. Scholars on other campuses discuss the processes of federal government, but rarely with the intimacy, or the perspective, that is commonly found in Cambridge. Or, when it comes to that, with the personal experience. There are probably more people at Harvard who have served time in Washington than there are at any other educational institution. It is said in Cambridge that the ex-Washingtonians now on the scene use every excuse they can think of to telephone Mr. Pusey, because they like to hear themselves open a conversation with "Hello, Mr. President."

Many of the same people who, during the Kennedy administration, accused Harvard of trying to take over Washington have, since the President's assassination, accused the Kennedys of trying to take over Harvard. The proposed location in Cambridge of the Kennedy Memorial Library was the first item of alleged evidence in the indictment. Actually, John F. Kennedy had decided on Harvard over a year before his death. It was all well and good from a sentimental viewpoint to have a repository of presidential papers at Abilene, Kansas, but it was not very convenient for scholars—nor, when it came to that, for President

Eisenhower himself when he was working on his own memoirs.

President Kennedy had never really had a hometown, except at Hyannis Port, and he felt that he had caused enough disruption to that placid Cape Cod village without saddling it forever with a bustling institution. Furthermore, the legislation that Congress passed relating to presidential libraries provided for the President concerned to have an office in his library, and Mr. Kennedy, who would have been only fifty-one at the end of a second term, relished the notion of making Harvard his headquarters for a few months each year. (There were even jokes about where his White House staff would fit in—Bundy back as dean of something very important, Sorenson running the Law School, Lawrence O'Brien directing athletics, Kenneth O'Donnell coaching the football team, and so on.) The President had not formally designated Harvard as the site for his library, however, and after his death it was not his family that took the initiative but Mr. Pusey, who successfully urged Cambridge upon Robert Kennedy.

It was Harvard, moreover, that changed the name of its Graduate School of Public Administration—which serves the scholarly needs of mid-career people in civil service, foreign service, and related areas—to the Kennedy School of Government. When people criticized the University for naming a graduate school after a person who hadn't even been a patron of it, Dean Price retorted, "It is, I admit, unusual to name a school for an individual, but then it is unusual to have a Harvard graduate assassinated while serving as president of the United States."

That would seem to have covered that. Then, though, there arose a new complication. The renamed School of Government set up a subsidiary center to which men in government could be invited as fellows to spend a reflective year or two at Harvard, absorbing whatever they chose to draw from the University and at the same time contributing to it whatever they chose to give from their experiences in the non-academic world. Richard E. Neustadt, who had been an adviser to the Truman, Kennedy, and

Johnson administrations, was recruited from Columbia to be assistant dean of the Kennedy School of Government and director of its Institute of Politics. The Institute had glamor. Robert Kennedy was its president, and among its trustees were W. Averell Harriman, C. Douglas Dillon, Lord Harlech, Robert A. Lovett, Senators John S. Cooper and Henry M. Jackson, and the then Mrs. John F. Kennedy. And the Institute had instant difficulties. "When you impose any new institution on Harvard, you're looking for trouble," one veteran of the Cambridge scene has said.

From the start, people began to think of the Institute as a power base for the Kennedy government-in-exile. It wasn't. Neustadt bent so far over backward to avoid its becoming that that he incurred the displeasure of, among others, Arthur Schlesinger, Jr., who had been in on its creation but complained later that he had been left off the Institute's mailing list. (The explanation for that, Neustadt said, was simple; there wasn't any mailing list.) A widely published article by the British journalist Henry Fairlie, implying that the Kennedy family, through the Institute, was trying to take over Harvard, didn't help matters any. The Institute had bad luck in getting under way when it did. It was supposed to be a bridge of sorts between men who theorized about government at Harvard and men who practiced it in Washington, but it began operating at a time when the gulf between those two power centers was as vast as that between the United States and the Soviet Union during the height of the Cold War.

The disenchantment felt in Cambridge toward Washington was made manifest in the fall of 1966, when the Institute invited Secretary of Defense McNamara to spend two days in Cambridge in informal colloquy with the academic community. McNamara was mobbed by students outraged about Vietnam, and he came close to being physically injured. And when, a few months later, a similar invitation was extended to Arthur J. Goldberg, then President Johnson's ambassador to the United Nations, several Harvard officials, fearing a repetition of the McNamara episode or something worse, urged Mr. Goldberg not to accept.

Arguing that if one could not have a free discussion of controversial issues at Harvard things had come to a sorry pass indeed, he accepted notwithstanding. His visit went off without too much trouble, but only after elaborate security arrangements had been made and after the faculty had negotiated with the students most likely to wish to confront him and had set up meticulous ground rules.

The Institute was also plagued, as it still is, by confusion over its name. Officially, it is the Institute of Politics. The word *Kennedy* nowhere appears in the title. But because the Institute is part of the Kennedy School of Government, everybody took to referring to it as the Kennedy Institute of Politics, and some, not at all to Neustadt's amusement, as the Institute of Kennedy Politics. (When Robert Kennedy came to Cambridge early in 1968 to have lunch with its fellows, one of them said to him wryly, "Welcome to your government-in-exile.") For all that has been said and insinuated about the Institute, it has actually had very little impact on the University. Its eight fellows each year (plus random part-time fellows like the prime minister of Singapore) have wandered around the Harvard community all but unnoticed outside their own limited circle, though they have sponsored some non-credit seminars for undergraduates on subjects like campaign management, the role of the press in political campaigns, and the political responsibilities of the medical profession.

The Institute fellows have a pleasant time. They receive fifteen thousand dollars apiece, plus a thirty-six-hundred-dollar housing allowance, and have no responsibilities at all. They have frequent lunches and dinners, with good food and wine and interesting companions; when, for instance, they meet to discuss urban problems, the glamor of Harvard is such that the guests may include the mayors of both Boston and Detroit. Not that the fellows idle the rest of their time away. One of them, Stephen Hess, a journalist with good Republican connections who would soon afterward be on the White House staff himself, spent part of his Harvard time in the spring of 1968 writing a *Ladies Home*

Journal article on "The Courtship of Julie Nixon."

It would not be stretching the truth much to say that nearly all of Harvard, in the post-Kennedy years, has been an institute of politics. Football, sex, and drugs have had their conversational innings, naturally, but the dominant themes of student and faculty discussion, no less naturally, have been Vietnam, the draft, and race relations. Some Harvard anthropologists brought a Zinacanteco Indian back to Cambridge from a field trip to southern Mexico. The Zinacanteco gave some lessons in Tzotzil, his native tongue, and by way of checking his students' pronunciation had them recite a statement he put on a blackboard in Tzotzil, the English translation of which was, "It is very bad that there is a war in Vietnam. They're killing each other too much."

The Zinacanteco was lucky. He was not liable to the draft. Nor did he have to stay at Harvard. Before the escalation of the war in Vietnam, it had become commonplace for as many as 20 per cent of Harvard undergraduates to drop out of college for a while. Now, with the College obliged to notify a draft board when a student left, and the board likely to call him up for service, he no longer had the option of trying to work out whatever problems he might have by, say, taking a year off and working as a stevedore. Instead, he had the dubious choices of staying unhappily at the College, or dodging the draft, or going to Vietnam, or seeking therapeutic help from the psychiatrists at the University Health Services, which for many students could be a frustrating and embarrassing experience. It may be more than mere coincidence that in the early spring of 1969 there were probably not more than two hundred hard-core militants whose disenchantment with the university was strong enough to prod them into rash action—almost precisely the same number of disenchanted students who, except for the draft, would have been taking a year off for one reason or another and would thus have been a very long stone's throw away from University Hall.

And when in 1967 the government took away student deferments from many graduate students, including some who had been awarded traveling fellowships abroad, the whole University structure was shaken. The Law School announced that if any of its students who were earmarked for induction chose instead to go to prison, they'd be readmitted to Harvard after serving their terms. So did the Graduate School of Arts and Sciences. (Law School students who found their courses in Contracts irrelevant flocked to extracurricular seminars given by their professors on such practical subjects as how to defend a client who has received an induction notice and wants to avoid service on the ground that the draft is unconstitutional.) The Department of Government shortened its requirements for an M.A. degree to one year's residence, so that graduate students in that field could more quickly get teaching jobs and draft deferments. One hundred and twenty-four members of the graduating class of 1968 pledged in writing that if called they would not serve. A year later only two were in the Armed Forces. Of the remainder, ten had deferments, thirteen were in medical school, two were ineligible because they were foreign-born; ninety-seven were still honoring their pledge. The University, for its part, had two employees working just about full-time to keep students abreast of Selective Service developments. Harvard prides itself on selecting the right people for the right jobs, and in this instance its choices were perhaps ideal, since neither of its draft experts could have a personal axe to grind, one of them being a man who was 4-F because he stood six-eight, and the other being a spinster.

In race relations, Harvard has come a long way. A fire destroyed its only museum in 1764, and among the treasures of that era that vanished was what Professor Morison has described without embellishment as "a piece of tanned Negro's hide." But whether Harvard has gone far enough in seeking and making accommodations with black America has lately been a cause of much concern to the University. The Latin oration that is a feature of every Harvard Commencement was delivered in 1960 by a Negro senior who said—in translation—"At Harvard, there is no difference between people." Whether or not that was true in 1960, many black students would have hooted at anyone who asserted it as truth in 1968.

In 1968, a survey was taken of the number of Negroes enrolled in Massachusetts institutions of higher learning, and, statistically, Harvard seemed to be above reproach, or at least less liable to it than other places. Negroes comprised .2 per cent of the student body at Boston College, .8 per cent at M.I.T., 2.5 per cent at Radcliffe, 3.1 per cent at Boston University, and 3.6 per cent—the highest percentage of the lot—at Harvard. In 1964, Harvard College had 20 black students. In 1969, it had 174, and it was doing everything it could to attract and hold onto more. By 1970, it expected to have around 270, or nearly 6 per cent. There used to be a possibly fictitious course grade in Cambridge called a "Radcliffe B." It was given, however undeservedly on a strict academic basis, to girls who might otherwise have burst into tears. Now one hears talk of a "Negro A-minus." (A black Radcliffe girl with lachrymose proclivities would seem to have it made.) Harvard does seem to bend over backwards to be nice to the Negroes in its midst, and the black students find this amusing and like to cite anecdotal instances of white overreaction. One black undergraduate reported that at home, when it came to athletics, he had always been considered hopeless; at Harvard, whenever sides were chosen up for informal touch-football games, he would always be picked first.

Another black student had a white roommate. One night, the black student was trying to study, and his roommate had a radio going full blast. The black student asked the white one to turn it off, and got instant compliance. A few nights later, as a sort of behavioral experiment, the black man turned a radio on to maximum volume when his roommate was trying to study, and the white student never uttered a peep of protest.

Throughout the University, Harvard is trying to recruit additional Negroes. The Graduate School of Arts and Sciences, to cite only one of a number of examples, has a $2.5-million five-year program under way. Twenty Negro graduates of Southern

Negro colleges are being brought to Cambridge annually for a year of special study. Then they go off to another graduate school for four years' regular graduate study, with all their expenses underwritten by the program. It is not always easy, however, no matter how good one's intentions, to transmute the disadvantaged into the advantaged. Harvard, for instance, has never had a Negro graduate student in the physical sciences. The simple reason is that to be considered for such study an individual normally needs about ten years of consistently high-class work starting at the age of fifteen, and there are practically no Negroes around with that background.

In the Law School, recuitment proceeds apace, though some of the Negroes who have enrolled have posed unsettling questions. What is the relevance of learning about securities registration or estate planning?, they ask their professors. Of what possible use is that when it comes to dealing with the legal problems confronting a small shopkeeper in a ghetto? Professor Paul A. Freund, one of the senior members of the Law School faculty, once sought to frame a suitable response. "It can't be of much use," he said, "but people who ask questions like that are somewhat shortsighted. A Harvard Law School graduate, whoever he is, ought to know as much about the law as the lawyers he'll be coming up against. In American society, you just can't isolate primitive things like corporations and taxation. Still, it's healthy that students no longer want to learn what Whitehead called 'inert knowledge.' On the other hand, you can't judge education in its entirety by its relevance to Roxbury or Vietnam. When law students raise these points, I don't respect their judgment, but I do respect their motives."

More than a hundred members of the Faculty of Arts and Sciences publicly dissented from both the judgment and motives of some of Harvard's Negroes in the winter of 1969. A visiting lecturer from M.I.T. was starting a course called "An End to Urban Violence," under the auspices of the Graduate School of Design. Several dozen black students moved onto the scene bodily, contending that any course on riot control was bound to have unacceptable racist connotations, and by this show of force they persuaded the lecturer to abandon his course. This fairly clearcut threat to academic freedom was too much for 113 members of the faculty, who wrote an open letter to Mr. Pusey deploring the incident and warning against its becoming precedental.

Pusey was swift to agree with the concerned faculty members, but not swift enough for some Harvard men. One of them wrote to the *New York Times*, saying that when the visiting lecturer was threatened, Mr. Pusey should have followed the example of his predecessor Edward Everett, who in 1848, when a good many white students threatened to quit Harvard if a Negro named Beverly Williams was admitted, had said, "If this boy passes the examinations, he will be admitted; and if the white students choose to withdraw, all the income of the College will be devoted to his education." There were echoes of that statement in a remark made on April 10, 1969, by Professor Daniel Seltzer, during an informal faculty meeting immediately after the police drove the students out of University Hall. The question was whether the faculty should officially endorse a student strike. "The primary purpose of this university is to teach," Mr. Seltzer said. "As long as one single student shows up for any of my classes, I'll teach him." Most of his colleagues who were present nodded approvingly.

Harvard College has had a Negro serving as an assistant dean since 1963. He is Archie Epps III, a Louisianan who went to an all-black college, Talledega, in Alabama, and came to Cambridge to do graduate research. (His field is nineteenth-century American Negro history, but he has also edited a book about Malcolm X.) A few other colleges—Colgate, Cornell, and Princeton, for example—now have Negro deans who are more or less liaison men between their administrations and black undergraduates. Epps was reluctant to take the appointment offered him, suspecting that however his administrative colleagues might regard him, everybody else would regard him as Harvard's showcase Negro and its de facto dean for Negro Affairs.

That was about the way things worked out. Dean Epps, though professionally unqualified and personally averse, often found himself willy-nilly cast in a pseudopsychotherapeutic role. Epps sometimes felt lonely, but he was not unduly discouraged. "I am optimistic about Harvard," he said in the winter of 1968. "As Negroes come along and show their stuff, they'll get jobs here." Not many have, though. Ralph Bunche was once offered a faculty position. He turned it down, apparently because he couldn't find suitable housing in Cambridge. Up to 1969, two black professors with tenure at Harvard weren't even in Cambridge; they were across the Charles River, in Boston, at the Medical School. In the summer of 1969, the Medical School, significantly, further recruited Dr. Alvin F. Toussaint, a black psychiatrist, who had been at Tufts and had a national reputation as a specialist in race relations.

The principal Negro on the Harvard faculty in Cambridge has been a professor of government with a quite evocative name— Martin Luther Kilson. He had no difficulty finding accommodations in Cambridge; his wife—like Dean Epps'—is white and they live in a house that belongs to her family. Kilson is considered by some Negro students at Harvard to be a maverick, because he has expressed reservations about the effectiveness of the black-power movement and insists on considering himself an intellectual, rather than a black intellectual. Professor Kilson's special field of study is West Africa; the Harvard University Press has published a book of his on Sierra Leone. There was some dismay at Harvard when it was revealed that, at a time while the University was trying to bolster its shaky relations with the black world, Kilson would be absent from Harvard during the 1969 spring term to do research on ghetto leadership in Philadelphia. But that was a plan he had made long in advance. Pennsylvania is his home state. His mother's grandfather, a freed slave, settled there before the Civil War. He did return to the scene to cast a concerned, negative vote when the Faculty of Arts and Sciences—shaken by the traumatic effects of the April takeover of University Hall, by the chilling photographs of gun-toting black students at Cornell, and by the fairly well-substantiated information that a dozen or so black students at Harvard had firearms—resolved, for the first time in Harvard's history, to let undergraduates have a say in recommending faculty appointments—specifically, Negro undergraduates and the professors who would be supervising Harvard's newly projected Black Studies program.

Kilson went to Lincoln University, an all-black institution in Pennsylvania, and got both an M.A. and Ph.D. at Harvard. He thinks that Harvard—a few hasty decisions notwithstanding—has done a pretty fair job in handling Negroes and their special problems. Asked not long ago what grade he would give the University in race relations, he said between an A-minus and a B-plus. He was one of the organizers of a new course that Harvard offered on Afro-American history in the fall of 1968, largely in response to the demands of its Negro undergraduates. Kilson had earlier taken the view—a not altogether popular one these days—that in recent years the Harvard curriculum, on the whole, had *not* been neglectful of the black man's participation in and contributions to society. Still earlier, way back in 1962, Kilson had helped found Harvard's Association of African and Afro-American students, which was a bellwether group—the first undergraduate organization of Negro students on any predominantly white campus in the United States. Getting it established at all was something of an achievement, because Harvard frowns officially on segregated groups, and the Association's student leaders didn't want to admit whites to membership. Harvard got around having to invoke its own rules against discrimination simply by closing its eyes to what was taking place—a kind of calculated myopia that has carried the University through many a sticky situation.

The leaders of Afro, as the group came to call itself for short, eventually got to meet regularly with Dean Glimp every other week, even though the organization at times had as few as forty members and never represented more than half of Harvard's black undergraduates. "We had some fairly rough conversations," Glimp would say afterward, "but in private, when things seemed to be getting out of control, I could always say to the blacks, 'I'm too old for you to be talking to like that.' That tactic never worked with S.D.S." One prominent Negro in the College who never formally joined Afro was Thomas S. Williamson, Jr., a 1968 graduate who played varsity football and won a Rhodes Scholarship. Explaining his aloofness from the group, Williamson said, "I didn't have the therapeutic dependence some of the Harvard Negroes had on the ritualistic aspects of the black-nationalist thrust." Williamson, the son of a retired Army officer, was from Piedmont, California, just outside Oakland—a community that, his family excepted, was entirely white. A star athlete at high school, Williamson could have gone to almost any college—he was accepted by Yale, Stanford, and Dartmouth—but picked Harvard and did not regret it.

After Martin Luther King's assassination, Harvard held a memorial service in its Chapel. Williamson was to have been one of the speakers, but at the last minute backed off and instead spoke at a rival, all-black outdoor service that Afro sponsored on the steps of the Chapel. "I got slipped into the bag of separatism," Williamson said a few days afterward. The white community at Harvard reacted to that murder with the same feelings of grief and horror and guilt that typified most communities. The black community reacted with anger and, in at least one instance, with curious exultation. Walking through the Yard, looking at a copy of the *Crimson* that gave the Afro memorial service a bigger play than the University's formal tribute, one black Radcliffe girl exclaimed to another, "It's historic! When have we ever gotten so much coverage!"

The size of its membership notwithstanding, Afro has been highly vocal, and some of its public statements have verged on the extreme. "There is no place for the black man at Harvard" is typical. Privately, Afro's principals are more reserved. Prominent among them has been a member of the class of 1969, Charles J. Hamilton, who made a rather substantial place for himself at Harvard. His freshman year, he ran a jazz program on the College radio station. Later, he wrote for the *Lampoon*, joined the editorial board of the *Crimson*, and became business manager of the *Harvard Journal of Negro Affairs*, a publication of which Dean Epps was also a mainstay. Hamilton had gone to an all-black high school in Pittsburgh. He was president of the student body there. A twin brother went from the same school to Princeton, where he became head of its counterpart of Afro—the Alliance of Black Collegians.

The Harvard Hamilton spent a lot of his time at College reflecting on his relationship to the place. "I had to figure out the terms on which to react to Harvard," he said. "At first, my black classmates and I went through a kind of cultural stripping. We undressed ourselves and put on the garments of Harvard men. In effect, we stopped being black. Then, little by little, we decided not to let Harvard rob us of our identity. We decided that we had to say to ourselves, 'I am a black man first and a Harvard man second.' And in time we came to realize that being black can be an advantage if you want to get some action. Somebody had to shake this place up, and we realized that we could do it."

Hamilton had a good many reservations about Harvard. For all his participation in extracurricular affairs and his membership, moreover, in the Signet Society, an undergraduate club with literary overtones, he often felt socially ill at ease. "A lot of black guys at Harvard still feel you have to prove it to white guys by making out with white girls," he said. "But that's not my music." He was asked to join one of the undergraduate final clubs. He declined at the last minute; he felt that he was being invited only to reinforce the members' lofty conception of their openmindedness. He carried into his senior year the bitter memory of a freshman-year party in his dormitory. One of the organizers of the affair, after rounding up a suitable number of girls from Smith, Mount Holyoke, and a couple of fashionable finishing schools, announced triumphantly, "I finally got somebody for *him*." The somebody was a high-school girl from a black ghetto in Roxbury.

Not that Hamilton found Harvard a social desert. A few months before Martin Luther King, Jr., was assassinated, he went to a party at a faculty man's house. "At one point in the evening," Hamilton recalled, "I found myself standing next to a fireplace explaining the precarious position of the Negro student at Harvard to an audience that included King, Harry Belafonte, George Wald, Seymour Martin Lipset, and David Riesman. All of a sudden I felt very large—to be commanding the attention of these huge men for ten whole minutes. It probably couldn't have happened anywhere else."

In a Harvard Square restaurant, the impact of environment on the senses bluntly asserts itself: "I'll give this onion soup a C-minus."

vii

"THE DAY WHEN Harvard shall stamp a single hard and fast type of character upon her children will be that of her downfall," William James said in a Commencement address at Cambridge, in 1903. "Our undisciplinables are our proudest product. Let us agree together in hoping that the output of them will never cease."

Nowadays, a good many university administrators feel that they could get along nicely with fewer undisciplinables than they have. In the six decades since James's address, and the twenty-seven that preceded it, Harvard's output of undisciplinables has more than measured up to James's hopes, but the University has for the most part harbored them with poise, if not always with pride. Up to the spring of 1969, most people who knew anything about Harvard were convinced that it wouldn't have to come to grips with revolutionaries because it had always been a determinedly evolutionary kind of institution. It was all for change, but in slow, subtle, and, if possible, invisible ways. A case in point was the appearance of a good many of the buildings in its Yard. They looked, to returning alumni, all but exactly as they had looked twenty or forty or eighty years ago. But they were not the same. The exteriors had been meticulously kept intact; the interiors had been gutted and replaced with modern facilities.

Harvard would bend to pressures, they seemed to be saying, but it liked to maintain an unruffled facade.

Harvard's history abounds with student rebelliousness, partly because the institution has shared James's outlook, partly because it has been around so long, and partly because it is where it is. "Resistance to something was the law of New England nature;" wrote Henry Adams in his account of his education; "the boy looked out on the world with the instinct of resistance; for numberless generations his predecessors had viewed the world chiefly as a thing to be reformed, filled with evil forces to be abolished, and they saw no reason to suppose that they had wholly succeeded in the abolition; the duty was unchanged. Boys naturally look on all force as an enemy, and generally find it so, but the New Englander, whether boy or man, in his long struggle with a stingy or hostile universe, had learned to love the pleasure of hatings; his joys were few."

The immediate object of hatred for most college students generally used to be their instructors. Nowadays, of course, the majority of Harvard students don't come from New England, and like students from all over their chief target is not their faculty but society at large. The faculty, indeed, often wants to side with them in the bigger battle. At Harvard, in 1968, Professor George Wald, before his famous speech sympathizing with dissident students, wrote a letter to the *Crimson* putting it on record that if any students were punished for draft resistance, he wanted to share their ordeal to the extent that he could. But proffered faculty hands are not always clasped. When at about the same time Professor Wald tried to take part in the outdoor memorial service that Harvard and Radcliffe Negroes were holding for Martin Luther King, Jr., he was rebuffed; he was white. The black participants, though, out of respect for his stature and his sympathy, did let him sit silently at their feet.

STUDENT-FACULTY RELATIONS ARE one thing on an undergraduate level and quite another in a graduate school, where the majority of students have made a definite intellectual commitment and have become careerists to one degree or another, and where the faculty members, working with that special kind of material, are often preoccupied with searching out satisfactory replacements for themselves in the academic power structure. Graduate students, whose futures depend so heavily on the high opinion of their mentors, sometimes try to be excessively ingratiating to their professors. Learning that one Harvard Law professor's hobby was Oriental art, a student happened to come up with a handsome Chinese scroll to brighten his office. "It got him a master's," the professor told a friend, it is to be hoped in jest. "He'd have got a doctor's if it had been an original."

The Law School—on, to be sure, the initiative of the students rather than the professors—had a student-faculty committee functioning before one was even proposed for the College, and the Graduate School of Education had invited students to sit on its Committee on Academic Policy. In the Law School, moreover, there is a special rapport between the senior and junior citizens because the professors there regard it as a solemn obligation personally to grade every paper submitted in their courses. The College professor who does his own marking is a rare bird indeed, and his colleagues are apt to regard him as dotty. Until recently, David Riesman was such a glaring and glared-at exception. He would read every paper an undergraduate turned in for one of his courses, and it would take him nearly all summer. Now, Riesman looks at only those papers that his section men consider to be of special interest. Even so, he is thought by many undergraduates to have a real affinity for them.

This distresses Riesman. When he was at the University of Chicago, before coming to Harvard in 1958, he likes to say, his wife and he were both working so hard they had precious little time to chat with a Negro couple who ran their household. They were accordingly astonished to hear that their servants were forever telling other people what a splendid relationship they had with their employers. "It made us wonder how wretchedly other people must be treated," Riesman said later. When it comes to faculty relations with undergraduates, the sociologist was further put in mind of the old sociological phrase "tipping the neighborhood." Jews, he said, used to get on comparatively well with Negroes because whereas Irish and Italians would shoot Negroes who moved into their neighborhoods, Jews would just dislike them. "Some of my academic colleagues shoot undergraduates," Riesman says, "so the neighborhood is tipped in the direction of those of us who are merely not entirely unsympathetic."

The accessibility of the Harvard faculty to undergraduates is a moot question. At one S.D.S. rally, a speaker declared, "I think it would be a good idea if students talked to the faculty. As far as I know, this has never been tried." Some members of the Harvard community would regard that statement as outright bosh, others as the revealed truth. Asked whether he thought relations between the two principal groups at the College suffered from a lack of communications, Professor Zeph Stewart, the classicist who is also master of Lowell House, replied, "I feel there could hardly be more." There are Harvard faculty members whose offices are open to students two or three afternoons a week; there are others who demand that appointments be made two or three weeks in advance. An undergraduate bursts into a professor's office, unannounced. "I want to excite you!" the student cries. The professor, who has a visitor, is mildly put out at the intrusion, but asks the student what his problem is. The student, it seems, wants a sponsor for a study project outside of the normal curriculum. "You don't want to excite me, you want to sell me," says the professor; but he sets an hour for the boy to come back the following day.

Often, though by no means always, the most accessible professors are the most eminent ones—the eagles of the faculty, as they are sometimes known. (The lesser lights are canaries.) Before Harlow Shapley's retirement as professor of astronomy in 1956, a diffident freshman called on his faculty advisor one day, to discuss his future. The boy thought he might be interested in astronomy, and wondered what the chances were of meeting an eagle like Professor Shapley. The advisor phoned the astronomer, who said he was sorry, he couldn't see the student that day, but could the boy join him for lunch the next day? The student became an astronomer. "The trouble with Harvard is that too many students assume that the senior faculty is unapproachable," one senior said. "But you can talk to a Reischauer or a Handlin. It makes them feel good, and it makes you feel good, because you're with a nice man who knows more than you do."

Attitudes vary. Professor John Kenneth Galbraith, quite possibly the busiest man at Harvard, spends little time on student tête-à-têtes. "I've never been able to put my mind on anybody else's problems," Galbraith says. "The fact that some student may be exploring the structure of poverty in the United States or the means of financing the Boston Symphony doesn't attract me. I've never been able to give the same standing to someone else's problem that I give to my own." A Harvard faculty member whose own son went through the college recalled dejectedly that the boy's happiest intellectual experience came at the end of his senior year. He had written a dissertation with which he was quite pleased, and a professor whom he had admired, but at a distance, had scribbled "Nice point!" in the margin opposite the student's favorite paragraph. "When my son told me how good that made him feel," the father said afterward, "I couldn't help wondering if in four years he couldn't perhaps have had *two* such uplifting experiences."

Revolt and rejection can be a complicated business. A century ago, when universities, Harvard included, thought it their main mission to pass along revealed truths, students were rising up not only against the nearest and most assailable authority figures, but against the whole concept of doctrinaire absolutism. But now most university establishments have forsaken absolutism and, with sometimes grinding reversal of gears, have embraced relativism. They no longer profess always to know the truth. (Some students resent such admissions of frailty; professors are professors, they feel, and should know all the answers, or at least pretend to.) They seek merely to discover the truth. A few observers of campus dissidence have pointed out an obvious resulting irony: students who revolt before they are exposed to and comprehend the nuances of relativism frequently end up being entrenched absolutists themselves—at about the point where those who hope to help them stood a hundred years ago.

How simple, even simple-minded, the old rebellions now seem! There was the Great Butter Protest of 1766, to resolve which Harvard, then as now dedicated to group inquiry, appointed an ad hoc faculty committee to investigate the students' complaints; seven faculty members condemned the butter out of hand, and four said it was edible, but only in sauces. Two years later, the entire senior class, again fed up with the food, decided to quit and switch to Yale. Then as now, Harvard espoused orderly procedures; the seniors couldn't transfer because Harvard wouldn't give them letters of recommendation. Frustrated, they planted an elm in the Yard that became known as the Rebellion Tree, and from whose limbs Harvard presidents were later hanged in effigy. The Rebellion Tree is gone, but in the area where it stood homecoming alumni still have a Tree Spread on Commencement Day; the ghosts of lynched strawmen dangle over them.

As Harvard students in the nineteen-sixties reacted to the war in Vietnam, so did their prototypes in 1775 react to the Boston Tea Party; that year, the faculty responded to one undergraduate protest by passing the following resolution:

> Since the carrying of Indian teas into the Hall is found to be a Source of uneasiness & grief to many of the students, and as the use of it is disagreeable to the People of this Country in general; & as those who have carried Tea into the Hall declare that the drinking of it in the Hall is a matter of trifling consequence with them; that they be advised not to carry it in for the future, & in this way that

they, as well as the other Students in all ways, discover a disposition to promote harmony, mutual affection, & confidence, so well becoming Members of the same Society: that so peace & happiness may be preserved within the Walls of the College whatever convulsions may unhappily distract the State abroad.

In 1788, some students broke into the College kitchen, melted five dozen pewter plates, and poured the liquid into a bell; others, after dining with an Englishman, returned to the campus at 3:00 A.M. and threatened to burn down the President's house. In 1805, butter was again an issue, this time complemented by bread. In 1807, there was a Rotten Cabbage Rebellion, and a student petition claimed further that the meat was "black, nauseous, and intolerable." A few doughty souls were expelled after offering the President a bowl of maggoty soup, and others were told to their faces, by an administration spokesman, that their behavior was "indecent and unmanly, evincing a disposition to break through all restraints of law and authority, a contempt of all salutory regulations, which if not checked would inevitably make Harvard the nurse of demagogues and disorganizers."

In 1818, some freshmen and sophomores threw bread and butter at each other through the oriels that separated the halves of their dining hall. (The place was called Starvation Hollow.) When four sophomores were rusticated—sent off campus, that is—for a year, Ralph Waldo Emerson and other classmates marched to the Rebellion Tree. One undergraduate, with the arresting name of George Washington Adams, declared, "Gentlemen, we have been commanded, at our peril, not to return to the Rebellion Tree. At our peril, we do return!" Then the protesters plucked twigs from the symbolic tree, to symbolize their unity with the oppressed. There was more food thrown in 1823, and still more in 1834, and indeed the tradition of flinging the stuff about persists at Harvard to this day. When the editors of the *Lampoon*, who think of themselves as the leading campus cut-ups, invite faculty members to black-tie banquets in their ornate clubhouse (some of its walls are covered with rare Delft tiles, a gift of William Randolph Hearst), the hosts furnish their guests with plastic shrouds, to protect their dinner clothes against flying viands. Most *Lampoon* editors have two dinner jackets—one for conventional social events and the other for their own spotty feasts.

Harvard students also traditionally engaged in riots. These usually occurred in the spring and were usually good-natured, unless the Cambridge municipal police got involved. In 1927, after an especially brisk scuffle between students and cops, thirty-five students were actually taken to court and convicted of disturbing the peace and the like; whatever disposition the judge might have had to let them off was eroded when an undergraduate spectator filched his gavel and hid it behind a courtroom radiator. By that time, Harvard presidents had become protective of their young men; President Lowell went to court and personally put up bail for each convicted student, pending appeal of his case. Meanwhile, an enterprising Harvard Square entrepreneur sold a hundred helmets in a single day to other undergraduates preparing for any eventuality.

During the 1952 presidential campaign, Walt Kelly, the creator of Pogo, went to Cambridge to make a speech. The *Crimson* lightheartedly nominated Pogo for President, and distributed three thousand "I Go Pogo" buttons. Kelly was late, and the restless undergraduates awaiting him disengaged a few trolleys from their overhead wires and otherwise irritated the local cops, who arrested twenty-eight of them. They were all ultimately released, but the outside world has a long memory; one of the twenty-eight, who had no other criminal record, had trouble for the next three years getting into the armed forces; he was a dubious risk, he was told, for "moral reasons." Now employed by Harvard, he felt a special twinge of sympathy for the students who were arrested in the spring of 1969. Not getting into the armed forces was hardly likely to vex many of them, he realized;

but he wondered if they would be haunted by police records like his own.

Within its own boundaries, particularly in the Yard, where most freshmen live, Harvard has been hospitable to mass hilarity. Freshmen still now and then break the tedium of study by screaming the rallying-cry "Rinehart!" from their windows, though few now know its derivation. There was a Rinehart, John Brice Gordon Rinehart, a Waynesburg, Pennsylvania, man who enrolled in Harvard as a special student in 1900 and lived in a third-floor room in the Yard. He had a lot of friends, according to the account he gave thirty-six years later, and they used to announce their presence below by yelling at his window. Soon everybody was taking up the cry. Rinehart stories are now legion, including one about a Harvard man in Africa who was about to be kidnapped by some Arabs, screamed "Rinehart!" and was rescued because there happened to be another Harvard man nearby in the French Foreign Legion. Times do not change too much. In 1968, the Yard had a resident who would occasionally emit ear-splitting imitations of Tarzan's mating call.

Among present-day Harvard administrators, the one who had the most to do with undergraduates when they were milling and shoving, and also when they were placid, was Robert B. Watson, the dean of students. He was a kindly man. He exuded old-fashioned goodness. He loved Harvard. He once summarized his occupational philosophy in a phrase that most deans would acclaim, if in certain instances with some trepidation. "We try to do what the students want," Watson said. Toward non-students —non-Harvard-students, that is—Watson and his fellow deans had a quite different attitude. After some young men and women with a Columbia background, calling themselves "Les Enrages," had spent nearly a week trying to disrupt the Harvard campus (they broke up a sociology class by heckling its professor, and they broke up the decorum of Eliot House by staging a nude-in), the Harvard deans had had enough and acted with dispatch. They summoned the municipal police and had the intruders arrested.

(This was a couple of weeks before the police were summoned back to arrest nearly two hundred of Harvard's very own.) Later, the New York underground paper *Rat* ran a special article from Cambridge saying, "Les Enrages of Harvard are individuals who question the American 'spectacular commodity culture' at its control center—Harvard University. Up there on the crimson carpet we challenge the privileged few who are entitled to walk on it. Why not us? We question the concept of the closed university where, sheltered from the real world, the future ruling class is being trained to serve the system; learning to accept the corporate analysis of and solutions to America's and their own problems. . . . We do not distinguish between students and non-students: we are all 'students of life,' some of us happen to be enrolled at Harvard, most of us are not (for obvious reasons)."

Dean Watson was not a *Rat* fancier, and in his mind there was a very clearcut distinction between Harvard students and non-students. For a Dean of Students, there pretty well had to be. To at least some of the students he dealt with, Watson, a onetime Harvard varsity letterman in football and crew and a self-confessed jock, was a guardian angel. He did not believe, for instance, that a Harvard man should be arrested for shoplifting, at least not for the first offense, and it did not hurt a scapegrace's chances of keeping out of trouble that in twenty-two years as a Harvard administrator Watson attained a first-name acquaintance with a hundred or so cops in Cambridge and its immediate environs. To other students, this dean was long an ogre, inasmuch as his office gave out or withheld permits for campus rallies. Watson had some trying altercations with S.D.S., which would sometimes take the position that to apply for a permit would compromise its integrity. "They're trying to convert the Yard into Hyde Park," the Dean remarked gloomily during one unauthorized rally; he didn't do anything to stop it, however.

Watson's job was never easy. Some years ago, he was visited by the mother of a girl whom a Harvard boy had got in trouble. On determining, after some delicate research, that neither party was interested in marriage or abortion, Watson made suitable arrangements for the girl, whose family didn't seem up to it, with an obstetrician, a hospital, and an adoption agency. The grateful girl subsequently offered him a box of candy, which he accepted, and her mother offered him a bottle of whiskey, which —although his nickname is "Booze," he is a teetotaler—he didn't. Some months later, the girl stopped by his office. "Gee, Dean, I'm pregnant again," she said. Watson was not amused, but when he learned that the man in this case was not a Harvard student, he was so relieved that he once again made all the necessary arrangements. No dean could do more.

In the good old days, when Harvard students were merely seeing how many live goldfish they could swallow at a clip or were perplexing their elders by having water-filled paper bags seemingly drop from the windows of a windowless building (the students had propelled the bags with lacrosse sticks from a building several hundred feet away), Watson rather enjoyed his post despite its uncertainties. More recently, though, the dean has been sorely tried. In the fall of 1967, for instance, at the invitation of S.D.S., a hippie musical sextet called the San Francisco Mime Troupe—trumpet, snare drum, tambourine, and a lot of rap—descended on Harvard for a couple of days. They were not exactly a cultural success; in reviewing a performance they put on, the *Crimson* said that the authentic troupe must have been kidnapped by the C.I.A. in Ohio and six inept C.I.A. imposters substituted. The following year, the troupe returned. By then, the *Crimson* had a new set of editors, and the mimers were hailed as "these nice people" who did "groovy things."

Watson felt obliged to summon the mimers to his office, their first time around, after they blockaded the president's doorway, ostensibly so Mr. Pusey would have to walk through their ranks in some symbolic gesture of love. The dean told them it was against Harvard policy for anybody, even for Harvard students, to make the president run a gantlet. Moreover, said Watson, whose only employer other than Harvard had been J. P. Morgan, the mimers were misbehaving on private property. The Californians replied that private property was death, which made that part of the dialogue hard to prolong. If they just wanted a place to congregate, Watson went on patiently, why didn't they sit on the grass in the Yard? This they did, until they got cold and moved on. It later took Watson, as he recalled, forty minutes to clear his office of the aroma of pot. "Honestly, it's getting so difficult these days to be fair," he told a friend. It got more and more difficult from then on. After the April, 1969, disturbance, a student was given a one-year prison sentence (even though Harvard had tried to have the charges against him dropped) for assaulting Dean Watson inside University Hall. And then, when the floor of the Faculty Room began to sag following its seizure by the S.D.S. shock troops, it was the ceiling of Dean Watson's office underneath that was first jarred loose.

For no one has undergraduate behavior been more unpredictable, and more imponderable, of late, than for the university police. Harvard seemed lucky when, in 1962, Dean Watson proposed as chief of the Yard cops, as Harvard's own finest are known, a man whom the dean of admissions would later describe to a group of alumni as a University resource equal to the Widener Library and second only to the best running back in recent Harvard history. The recipient of this uncommon accolade was an uncommon law-enforcement officer named Robert Tonis, who in the Harvard Catalogue had three resonant titles—Director of the University Office of Civil Defense, Security Officer, and Chief of the University Police. The son of an Italian tailor (the family surname evolved from the old-fashioned American practice of calling all Italians "Tony"), Tonis graduated from Dartmouth in 1931, got a law degree from Boston University, and, enchanted by newspaper accounts in the mid-thirties about the downfall of John Dillinger and Bonnie and Clyde, joined the F.B.I. He spent twenty-seven years in its Boston office and ended up in the doghouse because he never solved the Brink's case.

In all that time near Cambridge, Tonis had hardly ever been to Harvard, except once when he unsuccessfully chased a Nazi spy through the University's network of underground steam tunnels. Tonis would later find these handy for preventing George C. Wallace from being chased by Harvard students. They were to prove even handier, in a negative way, for preventing Tonis, on the morning of April 9, 1969, from incurring the wrath of Harvard undergraduates. The University police had never tangled with the students. That fateful morning, ten of his men were leading ten off-campus policemen through a tunnel toward the basement of University Hall. The students inside had barricaded the access area from the tunnel to the building, and by the time the underground force had cleared the obstacles, the Hall had been evacuated. Thus, for Tonis, a possibly awkward confrontation had barely been avoided.

Accepting the Harvard job, Tonis began in a straightforward enough fashion by checking out his men's guns. Nobody had ever fired any of them. One policeman had been carrying the same bullets in his revolver for nine years. The first one he tried to shoot off traveled fifty feet and fluttered to the ground; the second stuck in the barrel. In 1968, one Harvard cop actually fired a gun seriously, wounding a Cambridge youth who tried to run him down with a motorcycle. Such was the reputation by then of the Harvard police that the *Crimson* editorially sided with the cop.

Meanwhile, Tonis had become a raging Harvard buff. An English major at Dartmouth, he resolved in Cambridge to read everything he could about Harvard. He couldn't do that any more than Thomas Wolfe could read his way through the Harvard library, as legend has it he tried to in 1920, but Tonis did his best. (He was terribly hurt when, despite his men's vigilance, some Yale students painted "Beat Harvard" across the eleven stout columns at the main entrance to the Widener Library; to Tonis, it was not a youthful prank but desecration of a shrine.) Tonis audited at least one Harvard course every semester—mostly in

English, history, and music. "This is like coming to Paradise," he said. He has also taught at Harvard, or at any rate has lectured in an expository-writing course. He had done a lot of white-slavery investigating for the F.B.I., and at the suggestion of a poet he'd befriended in Cambridge spoke on "Prostitutes I Have Known." Attendance was flatteringly high, and during a question-and-answer period a couple of Radcliffe girls wanted to know how they could get into the business. Tonis' literary bent puzzled some of his colleagues. One faculty member who saw him going to a poetry reading and assumed a policeman would never do that except for occupational reasons stopped him at the door and asked worriedly what the trouble was inside. Tonis was crestfallen.

Tonis has been a peculiar policeman in many ways. When students began to grow sideburns, he did, too. He would hardly ever wear a uniform, though he had one, and he and his men could be marvelously obtuse at times, being unable to see boys and girls emerging from dormitories together at early hours even when they almost tripped over them. Visitors to his office would sometimes find it preempted by the chief's wife, who used the campus police headquarters to conduct rug-hooking classes for other Harvard wives. He was also a music-lover, having been a violinist in his youth. Invited to conduct a morning chapel service in the Yard, he chose as his subject Harvard's neglect of jazz. Most Wednesday nights, during the academic year, the educational television station in Boston, WGBH, puts on an hour of live jazz. Tonis would almost always go to the studios to listen, usually accompanied by a freshman proctor, W. C. Burriss Young, who was so efficient in helping to quell a potential melee a couple of years ago that Tonis made him an honorary policeman and gave him a gold shield.

Tonis and Young would customarily dine first at the Faculty Club. Half a dozen students who went with them to the television studios would wait in the lobby. A Harvard Police cruiser with a uniformed sergeant at the wheel waited outside. After dinner, Tonis would emerge and round up the students—often as not scruffy-looking ones, the kind many cops would gladly arrest on sight. The students would climb into the police cruiser and the sergeant would drive them to the jazz concert, while Tonis followed along in his own Volkswagen. Afterward, the sergeant would deliver the undergraduates to their dorms. It is not known whether any S.D.S. people took part in these tuneful and amiable excursions.

Curiously, for all its well-known antipathy toward law-enforcement officers, S.D.S. at Harvard never evidenced much anger against the University Police. At one S.D.S. meeting, after the April bust, there was talk about throwing a picket line around University Hall. What if a dean tried to cross it?, someone asked. The consensus was that it would be all right to rough him up. (Some of the April 9 demonstrators were ultimately punished for "mishandling" deans. Not manhandling, but mishandling. Could one infer that Harvard had decided that handling deans was forgivable?) But, someone else asked, what if the dean was escorted by a Yard cop? "Gee, if we rough up one of them it would really upset the student body," an undergraduate remarked.

A sophomore, pigeonholing a junior for the benefit
of a freshman: "She used to be a moderate fanatic, but something
happened to her and now she's an extremist of the middle."

viii

A HARVARD JUNIOR was having lunch with his father at the
Ritz in Boston one spring Sunday in 1968. A woman about the
father's age walked into the dining room. The father grabbed his
son's arm. "My God, you know who *that* is?" the father exclaimed. *"Brenda Frazier!"* "Who's Brenda Frazier?" asked the
son. The father slumped back; the communications gap and the
generation gap had hit him all at once.

In the classrooms of Harvard itself, still another gap is often
discernible—what might be called an information gap. Paul
Freund, the constitutional-law expert, who in addition to his
didactic duties at the Harvard Law School gives a lively and
popular course on law for undergraduates (he is one of a select
half-dozen faculty members to hold the title of University Professor), concludes a discourse on domicile with some light verses
in re Hetty Green and an interstate battle waged over the estate
of her once equally celebrated son, Colonel Edward. Freund finishes and, looking as though he senses gloomily what the response will be, asks if any of his several hundred auditors has
heard of the Greens. Not a hand is raised.

A day or two later, an undergraduate who has skipped a lecture by Edwin O. Reischauer (the former ambassador to Japan is
also a University Professor), asks a friend whether he missed

anything important. "No, he just talked about some island called Okinawa that I think has a million Japanese on it and is under us somehow," is the answer.

There is a valid enough explanation for the information gap. The biggest area of ignorance for many students—those, that is, who are not hooked on television reruns of old documentary films—is that period between the time their history books stop and their personal memories begin. Thus to many undergraduates today Franklin Roosevelt is more fleshless a figure than Benjamin Franklin. There are Harvard students to whom the name James Bryant Conant is meaningless, and when the *Crimson* sent a couple of reporters around to interview Chief Tonis not long ago, they had never heard of the Brink's case. In Europe, a couple of summers ago, the Harvard historian Oscar Handlin ran into an intelligent young Frenchwoman who had never heard of Hitler.

There are gaps about gaps. Handlin took part in a Cambridge debate on Vietnam in the spring of 1968. An undergraduate asked him afterward if he'd mind elaborating on one thing he'd casually alluded to: What in the world was a missile gap?

Some Harvard students, particularly the more radical ones, believe that the gap that most sorely afflicts the place is a curriculum gap. Harvard, they insist, does not offer enough courses dealing with the immediate social problems that concern them. Like many another university, Harvard has lately been reappraising its curriculum and trying to add to it new courses that its students will give high marks for relevance. (Those students, that is, who regard marks as relevant.)

Like the students of many other universities, some at Harvard considered Harvard's progress too poky. At the start of the 1967–1968 academic year, a few of them tried to persuade the Faculty of Arts and Sciences to let them organize and run a credit course themselves—a once-weekly two-hour seminar to be called "Critiques of American Society." For a Harvard course to have official standing, a faculty member with tenure must take responsibility for it. When the students couldn't find an appropriate figurehead, they resourcefully took advantage of a long-standing cross-registration arrangement that Harvard has with M.I.T. It was designed originally to enable Harvard students to take engineering courses at M.I.T. that Harvard didn't offer, and to enable M.I.T. students to take liberal-arts courses at Harvard that M.I.T. didn't offer. The Harvard undergraduates recruited as their sponsor Noam Chomsky, the M.I.T. professor of linguistics who has been in the forefront of political activism. Two hundred Harvard undergraduates enrolled in the seminar. "I've learned more, in the real sense of learning, than in any other course here," one of them said afterward. "I find it awfully interesting, because there's always one fine shade of radicalism pitted against another —something, I guess, like the meetings must have been that Lenin held at the turn of the century." They know more about Lenin than Stalin.

While they were at it, the students who were running the Critiques course decided that each participant in the novel seminar should grade his own term paper. Nothing like that had happened before at Harvard, but there wasn't much Harvard could do about it, inasmuch as M.I.T. was technically in charge of the course and as Harvard honors ancient treaties. Before the start of the 1968–1969 academic year, Harvard, in the best if-you-can't-lick-'em-join-'em tradition, endorsed as a full-fledged course, under its social relations department, a modification of the seminar, in which undergraduates studied social changes in America with unabashedly radical instructors. It was one of the most popular courses of the year.

One new course that Harvard *had* approved, in the fall of 1967, was also proposed by an undergraduate, Marc Strassman, the one who transferred from Yale. He pursued his goal with such entrepreneurial vigor that some of his acquaintances took to calling him Cecil B. de Strassman. As his faculty sponsor, he recruited an assistant professor of sociology, Chad Gordon, who specialized in situational interaction. A Californian who went to U.C.L.A., Gordon personified the younger academic who is reluctant to overinteract with the conventional Harvard situation. "I'm not an Ivy Leaguer in any way and for that reason I intentionally refuse to learn to play squash," he once told a friend. The course over which, at Strassman's urging, he agreed to preside featured discussions on topics like "What would be the implications of a low-rise black housing project in a Polish community?"

At its students' first meeting after the Columbia crisis in the spring of 1968, Columbia was naturally high on the agenda. (The enterprising Strassman wanted to study the Morningside Heights scene at eyeball level but didn't have any funds; with characteristic aplomb and imaginativeness, he telephoned a Michigan outfit called the Society for the Psychological Study of Social Issues and was instantly awarded a forty-dollar research grant: twenty-two dollars for round-trip fare between Boston and New York, fifteen dollars for three days' food, and three dollars for the phone call.) The discussion about Columbia began in routine fashion. Somebody said Columbia *wanted* cops to beat up its students. Somebody else said that it was tough to run a university on the edge of a ghetto, and that after the tumult how would Columbia ever attract bright kids any more, or, when it came to that, contributions? Somebody made an obscene reference to Grayson Kirk, at which a Radcliffe girl laughed the loudest, perhaps by way of demonstrating her worldliness.

A Harvard graduate student who'd gone through college at Columbia was present, and he said that the resident undergraduate body there could pretty much be divided between pukes and jocks; the jocks had been about to beat up the pukes, he went on, when the cops beat up the jocks, which united the student body. He added that while at Columbia he himself had been a jock—"a jock against the war," he added hastily, "but still a jock." What sport?, he was asked. Here the conversation underwent a strange turn. "Lightweight crew," he said. "Best boat in the east!" For a moment, the hot issues of the day were forgotten, and the dialogue took on inflections of an old Jack Oakie Joe-College movie.

"You were a lightweight?" asked a Harvard student. "Maybe you knew my brother. . . ."

ONE MAJOR DIFFERENCE between Harvard and Columbia —between Harvard, for that matter, and places like Berkeley and Chicago—is that whereas these other places have largely separate faculties for their undergraduates and graduate students, the principal Harvard faculty, the Faculty of Arts and Sciences, ministers to both groups. It is this undivided faculty that makes Harvard a university college—an arrangement that a committee of that faculty not long ago hailed, with probably forgivable immodesty, as "the glory of the Harvard system."

When Edward C. Banfield, whose field is urban affairs, came to Harvard from Chicago in 1959, he expected he'd be spending most of his time guiding graduate students in empirical research. A professorial colleague took him to lunch his first day at Cambridge, and told him, "There are only two rules here. You can't ride a bike in the Yard, and you have to teach undergraduates." In eight years at Chicago, Banfield had never met face to face with more than thirty students at a time—graduate students, for the most part, with whom he would hold informal discussions. At Harvard, he found himself lecturing thrice weekly, to a couple of hundred undergraduates. He had to learn how to give lectures. Some professors are contemptuous of them; Banfield's former associates at Chicago used to say that instead of delivering them, their authors might as well just mimeograph them and distribute them.

Banfield disagrees. He thinks the Harvard system is good because it makes professors work harder, if for no other reason than to avoid making fools of themselves before an audience. "With fifteen students, you can start off an hour by saying, 'Well, what are we going to talk about today?'" he says. "With a big class, if you have any self-respect, you can't do that."

Harvard and Columbia are similar in that at both places the radical students are numerically few. Sometimes these angry and outspoken students are described as the tip of an iceberg, but the analogy is imperfect unless one conceives of the bottom of a floe as being made up of different stuff from the top.

Harvard radicals have one thing in common with radicals at other universities. They want to conform to a country-wide conception of American youth, which they visualize as both apocalyptic and apoplectic. And they sometimes seem to want the best of two worlds. It has been said of those at Harvard, for instance, that while they insist on throwing themselves into the lions' den, at the same time they insist that the lions be toothless.

In recent years, the radicals have often been disappointed, not only, for a long time, by the indifference and inertia of their fellow students, but by their own faculty heroes. A case in point at Harvard is that of Martin H. Peretz. A nephew of the famous Yiddish writer Isaac Leib Peretz, and a Brandeis graduate, he took his Ph.D. at Harvard and became an assistant professor in social studies there in 1967. He seemed to have everything going for him. He wore colorful clothes and had a beard. He was brilliant, affable, compassionate, vocal, and under thirty. Nobody so young or so lowly in rank had ever attained such influence and admiration at Harvard. A seminar Peretz gave on the Cold War for 15 freshmen was so popular 140 of them tried to get into it. He probably knew Martin Luther King as well as or better than anyone else at Harvard. He was a key supporter of Senator Eugene McCarthy. He was one of the original financial backers of *Ramparts*. He was one of the founders of the so-called National Conference on New Politics held in Chicago in the summer of 1967.

But then Peretz walked out on that conference, disgusted with the actions and arguments of many of the participants, and the far left turned on him. "A lot of people here don't know what to make of some one like myself," he says. To most of his colleagues on the faculty, he was still a flaming radical. To the hard-core radicals at Harvard who hewed unwaveringly to the S.D.S. line, though, Peretz—who has described himself as an island of non-dogmatic radicalism and has described the S.D.S.

movement as McCarthyism of the left—became a rat fink. The moderates, on the other hand, gave him a rousing ovation, a few hours after the April 9 bust, when he told the concerned group meeting in the Memorial Church that for the first time in ten years' acquaintance with Harvard he felt that the students and faculty, and even a few administrators, were getting together— which struck him as an historic moment both for the university and for the country.

The Harvard chapter of Students for a Democratic Society has around two hundred members out of a student population of fifteen thousand. It is not a hard fraternity to get into. A member, generally speaking, is anyone who considers himself a member. Most Harvard undergraduates have been tolerant of its activities, and many of them would attend its rallies, as much out of curiosity as for any other reason. Most of them used to be put off by its churlishness. When in the winter of 1968 a member of S.D.S. interrupted a lecture by Professor Freund, the legal scholar graciously let the student share his platform. The other students attending the lecture were less kindly disposed. Most of them booed the interloper, and quite a few of them simply got up and walked out on him while he was in mid-rhetoric. Freund was not surprised. "The Harvard community responds to reasonableness and understatement," he said afterward. To make the Harvard community once again responsive to those two admirable and quiet abstractions may be the most challenging educational task the university faces in the immediate future.

The S.D.S. members at Harvard are as tireless as they are strident. They never seem to need sleep. They are apt to organize a rally at dawn and have mimeographed flyers ready before noon. (Instant mimeographing is their forte.) They are also intolerant; one of them spoke disparagingly of a political foe chiefly because of his outward appearance; the enemy wore three-piece suits and smoked cigars. They are cliquey and bristlingly ideological. They are intelligent. They usually get better grades than other students. "Most of these guys are so bright they can get their work done with one hand," one Harvard dean says. They are somewhat schizophrenic; they comfort themselves with the reflection that the further left they go, the more they broaden the middle area of acceptable dissent; but thus in a sense they end up by serving the liberals whom they profess to loathe. They are moralistic and missionary-minded; in another era they might well have been Puritans, and thus those of them at Harvard could be said to fit, in a sense, into the University's ancient mold. Daniel P. Moynihan, who has observed S.D.S. at Harvard with a trained sociological eye, once delivered a similar jab when he prophesied that most of its members would probably end up as civil-service bureaucrats.

They are not without humor. At Christmas time, they serenaded some of the Harvard deans with carols. The tunes were seasonal and familiar, but the words were new: "Preppie boys, corporate joys, Harvard all the way; Oh what fun it is to have your mind reduced to clay. . . ," "Oh come, all ye mindless, conceptless and spineless," and "We three deans of Harvard are/ Fearlessly demanding our car. / We'll stop the riot/ And have peace and quiet./ Bring out the feathers and tar." They like to taunt President Pusey whenever they can. In the annual report that he issued in the spring of 1968, he mentioned "Walter Mittys of the left," a phrase that some of his critics thought was less than felicitous, and the S.D.S. members to whom he was almost certainly referring once or twice followed him across the campus chanting "Walter Mitty! Walter Mitty!"

Now and then Mr. Pusey would dine with a group of undergraduates. When he turned up in 1968 at a gathering of those affiliated with Dudley House, the social center for upperclassmen living off campus, some of the S.D.S. crowd seated themselves en bloc at the center of the room and chatted loudly while he was delivering some after-dinner remarks. "That sort of thing doesn't embarrass me," Mr. Pusey said afterward. "They're strenuous, but fun." He was in no mood a year later to describe the New Left as a fun thing.

For the most part, the S.D.S. had always got on pretty well with the Harvard administration. At Princeton, S.D.S. played touch football against the R.O.T.C. At Harvard, S.D.S. played softball against the College deans. When the administration found itself a man shy, the then head of S.D.S., Michael Ansara, obligingly stepped in and played shortstop for the deans' side, and combined on a few nice defensive maneuvers with the dean of the College, at third base, and the dean of freshmen, at second.

Ansara had always had good personal relations, moreover, with the R.O.T.C. men at Harvard. "We like a lot of the Rotcy people," he said at the end of 1967, "and we know they're just in it for the scholarship and loan money they get out of it. It's all right to take government money if you know how to handle it. I'd take all I could get, and use it for S.D.S. I see nothing wrong in using the resources of society to fight society." While Ansara was more or less commanding S.D.S.'s Harvard forces, S.D.S. never picked on R.O.T.C. "We don't want to alienate our Rotcy friends," he explained. A year later, he had been temporarily superseded, and S.D.S. began bombing R.O.T.C. without pause. Ultimately, early in the winter of 1969, the assault proved successful, despite the last-ditch attempt of the Naval R.O.T.C. unit at Harvard to repel marauders by means of a *Crimson* ad, couched in up-to-the-minute Pentagonese, that invited sophomores to a get-acquainted, free-beer party: "At the very least a sudsy confrontation while confirming or dispelling your suspicions is still a better bag than no suds at all."

The S.D.S., unimpressed that the 350 Harvard students enrolled in the R.O.T.C. program were continuing what was the longest-lived reserve officers training program on any American campus, was for having R.O.T.C. thrown off the premises entirely. The Faculty of Arts and Sciences voted instead, at first, merely to strip the program of its academic credit and the officers administering it of their professorial status, and to deny it further free use of Harvard buildings. Then the faculty, which in the frenetic spring of 1969 sometimes seemed to change its mind as giddily as a woman in a hat shop, voted to make R.O.T.C. extracurricular—about as stiff a verdict, the professors evidently thought, as could have been handed down by a court-martial, short of capital punishment. But then it turned out that, according to federal laws, R.O.T.C. *couldn't* be extracurricular, so the faculty decided to do away with it entirely after June 30, 1971. S.D.S.—at the small cost of alienating its few, if any, remaining Rotcy friends—had won a major battle.

Ansara had a mixed background—part Middle-East, part Harvard. His father, who for a while was executive secretary of the Syrian and Lebanese American Federation, was a Harvard College graduate, and also attended the Law School and the Graduate School of Arts and Sciences. The son could have gone to Amherst, but went to Harvard because he wanted to. "I suppose I'd have had many of the same gripes about *any* American university," he said, "but I felt it was important to come here. Still, I don't think I'll ever have the feelings about the place that most Harvard men have. I don't feel any great emotional attachment to the institution." The younger Ansara went to the Commonwealth School in Boston, a progressive private school founded and run by a son of Charles E. Merrill, who had himself founded Merrill Lynch, Pierce, Fenner & Smith. Both Commonwealth and Harvard have benefited substantially from Merrill money, which was derived from commissions on the sales of stocks of companies whose policies and practices are anathema to S.D.S. (Ansara married his headmaster's daughter, the Wall Street broker's granddaughter.)

Ansara began his involvement in the radical movement at an early age, picketing Woolworth's. At college, Ansara wanted to equip himself with the tools to study societies, so he concentrated in medieval history and literature, which some present-day students would consider an irrelevant field, but which seemed to him as good a starting place as any. In public, Ansara was a grim haranguer, a man who gave the impression that nothing would please him more than to have ivy-clad walls tumble at the impact of his voice; deans would wince when he reached for a bullhorn. In private, he was softspoken and affable, and would say things like "A university has to be a place where ideas are unshackled, but that doesn't mean you have to make it into a political haven for leftwingers."

*Dialogue during a demonstration against the Dow
Chemical Company:
Professor (scornfully): Like the Bastille!
Student (scathingly): Typical professorial remark!*

ix

ON THE EVE OF Harvard's 333rd academic year, in September,
1968, there was considerable apprehension in Cambridge about
what S.D.S. might be up to. At Commencement time, the previous June, some of its zealous members, cranking their mimeograph machines to the very end of the term, had distributed
tracts that said, "Harvard's most significant educational function
is, we believe, to train individuals to take their places in the elites
which benefit from, and to some extent control, the present
workings of our society. It is only because the American social
order is sustained by drastic inequalities of wealth and power
that Harvard can play such a role. And it is because such a social
order is so unjust—most brutally and blatantly in Vietnam and
the ghettos—that we cannot accept Harvard as it is."

This challenge having been flung, the University could not
help wondering nervously in what fashion these particular ac-
cepters of what Harvard thought it had to offer would address
themselves come fall to Harvard's unacceptability. Some University elders were convinced that the tactic would be to try to
block registration. But hardly anything happened at all. A few
more tracts attesting to Harvard's wickedness were handed out.
The contents, though, were familiar and stale except to freshmen,

for whom they had at least the appeal of novelty. A year earlier, S.D.S. had planned to pass out among freshmen what practically amounted to a book-length catalogue of its grievances, but had demonstrated that radicals can be as imperfect as liberals: the weighty indictment vanished after being given, for stencilling, to a girl who went instead to Africa.

That same academic year of 1967–68, notwithstanding, S.D.S. had climbed to what many people thought would surely be the peak of its Harvard militancy. Its members were no less concerned then than later about Vietnam and the ghettos, but the issue with which some of them wanted to confront Harvard had to do, rather, with coeducational living arrangements. Specifically, they wanted one wing of one Harvard house opened up for joint occupancy by men and women. "The good thing about this idea was that it was both radical enough and simple enough to make people think about other aspects of life at Harvard and how they could be changed," explained one of its originators. "Gosh, we didn't even talk about sex and all that stuff." They had a civil-disobedience gesture planned for November 5, 1967; they were going to announce that on that night they would deliberately violate Harvard's parietal rules, which prescribe the hours during which women may visit men's rooms. More than a year later, the rules hadn't been changed radically, but dozens of women were in full-time residence in Harvard houses. At a cocktail party in the spring of 1969, a student met Professor Robert Homans, the sociologist, and in characteristic no-beating-about-the-bush fashion asked, "What do I know about you?"

"Well, I'm chairman of the Homans Committee," the professor said.

"Which one is that again?"

"It's the Committee on the Houses."

"What have you decided about parietals?"

"We haven't even bothered to submit a report. And if we did, there wouldn't be room on the faculty docket for it."

"Well, what's your committee's attitude going to be about

coeducational living?"

"To tell you the truth, at this stage of the game we couldn't care less."

All S.D.S.'s coeducational-living plans went by the boards when, on October 25, the Dow Chemical Company sent a recruiter to Harvard. For years, Harvard had routinely welcomed visits by corporate interviewers, along with representatives of government agencies and other prospective employers. To serve undergraduates—graduating seniors, mainly—the College runs an Office for Graduate and Career Plans, which occupies a ramshackle building on a Cambridge side street and rates high in undergraduate eyes chiefly because it boasts the community's most comprehensive trove of out-of-town phone books. As far as careers were concerned, its activities had been negligible; graduate students were still eligible for draft deferments, and about 80 per cent of Harvard College seniors were going on to graduate schools. For that reason, most corporations—Dow included—had little interest in College seniors, who were largely unemployable. In the fall of 1967, the men Dow planned to talk to were mostly graduate students in chemistry.

But by that time, Dow was something special. Dow meant napalm. Few of the Harvard students who were to get involved in a protest against the manufacturers of the odious jelly were at first aware of the historical ironies of that particular confrontation. A distinguished Harvard professor of chemistry, Louis F. Fieser, had been napalm's chief progenitor during the Second World War (when it came to that, although hardly any members of the Harvard student body knew about it, James Bryant Conant had spent much of the *First* World War perfecting poison gas), and there had been, further, some remarks made in Washington, D.C., in May of 1954 by President Pusey. New to the presidency of Harvard, and buffeted by Joe McCarthy's windy blows at the place, Mr. Pusey, after reminding an audience at the National Press Club of Harvard's traditional responsibilities and attitudes, had gone on to emphasize the University's contributions to the war effort a decade earlier. He had called prideful attention to the contribution of the Harvard School of Public Health to the gas masks Jimmy Doolittle's raiders wore over Tokyo; he had alluded to the efforts of other elements of the University to refine radio-jamming and underwater sound-detection devices, and he had concluded, "Harvard scientists were in the forefront of . . . the application of chemistry to incendiary devices." How often in hindsight one might like to mute one's forefront boasts!

Harvard men, whatever their political stripe, like to be leaders, and by late October of 1967 there was nothing especially innovatory about demonstrating against Dow. Students at fifty-odd other institutions of higher learning had already done that. The main extracurricular event for October 25 at Harvard was to have been a poetry reading by James Dickey, who was expected to attract a large and responsive crowd of Harvard and Radcliffe undergraduates because some of his stuff was sexy. S.D.S. had no special advance plans for either Dow or Dickey. But on the 22nd of October, the march on the Pentagon occurred in Washington. Several busloads of Harvard and Radcliffe students went down, and at the last minute, Michael Ansara, who had decided to sit out the happening, hopped into a car and drove to the capital. What he saw there changed his mood, as it changed the mood of so many other students. He returned to Cambridge resolved more than ever that the way to attack what he perceived to be the ills of society was to attack his university. The Dow visit was a made-to-order launching pad.

As late as the 24th, however, Ansara and his associates in S.D.S. were uncertain what course to pursue. Should they stage a nonobstructive sit-in? Should they present themselves for interviews, and debate the Dow recruiter? Should they merely picket? The morning of the 25th began peacefully enough. The man Dow sent to Harvard was a thirty-seven-year-old organic chemist, Fred C. Leavitt, a Ph.D. from Syracuse who lived in Wellesley and had audited a few chemistry courses at Harvard.

He was his company's chief campus recruiter; he had spent the 23rd, uneventfully, at M.I.T. He had nothing to do with producing or distributing napalm.

Still, Leavitt symbolized the corporate enemy. On the 25th, he set up shop in Conant Hall, one of Harvard's chemistry buildings, and a handful of interviewees trickled in. So did a handful of S.D.S. members. So did the watchful Dean Watson, who talked to the radicals and said they could do whatever they wanted as long as they didn't obstruct the normal operations of the University. The crowd of protestors grew, and when Leavitt moved to another Chemistry building, Mallinckrodt Hall, they followed him. By now, they had begun asking him to cease interviewing and go away. He declined.

By noon, their ranks had swelled, and they had positioned themselves on the floor of the narrow corridor that led to the room he was in. They dispatched their own recruiters to the Yard, to summon more bodies to join them. Anticipating that the Harvard administration might react, and would do so by asking for their bursar's cards—the identification card that every Harvard undergraduate is issued and that he uses for, among other things, getting into libraries—they decided that their strength lay in unity. They collected bursar's cards; if any one of them was to be punished, they'd all suffer together. Outside Mallinckrodt, pickets carried the usual signs: "Napalm—Johnson's Baby Powder," and "Dow Shalt Not Kill." College administrators began to arrive in force, including Dean Glimp, who was the principal dean in Cambridge. His immediate superior, Dean Ford, was at an academic gathering in London.

Glimp had a lot of things on his mind that day. He had six students coming to his house for dinner. Scheduled for that evening at the University's Loeb Theatre, moreover, was the presentation by an experimental drama group of a show that, two worried members of the English department had just informed the dean, was quite likely to get the University in trouble with the local authorities. Featured in it was a rather graphic pantomime of a near-naked couple copulating; the producers, evidently worried themselves about that tableau, had somehow figured they would blunt its impact by casting two topless women in it, which to the professors only made matters worse. Glimp resolved that issue by telling the producers that, inasmuch as thay had put a lot of work into the show, they could perform it just once, before an audience composed only of invited friends.

The situation at Mallinckrodt was the stickiest, though. When Mr. Leavitt wouldn't leave, the students in the corridor—by now, there were a couple of hundred of them—decided to keep him prisoner. What if he should demand to be released? Would Harvard have to get him out by force? Would kidnapping be involved, and would the F.B.I. accordingly have to be summoned? The administrators hovering at the edges of the sit-in seriously debated hiring a helicopter, to lower a rope ladder outside the window of the room he was in. In the basement of Mallinckrodt, several members of the Harvard police, who were trying to keep out of sight lest they incense the demonstrators, were practicing linking arms and holding hands, in case they were asked to make a frontal assault on the students—a technique of which they were utterly ignorant.

Mr. Leavitt, happily, kept calm and didn't demand to be rescued. His sequestration was tolerable enough. His student captors shared with him the cookies and apples that other students sent in for them. Still, the administration was distraught, and for want of any better action to take on the spot, began collecting bursar's cards, which the students gladly handed over, in bulk. The administration, moreover, warned those students whose attention it could attract that by obstructing the Dow man's movements after they'd been told not to they were exposing themselves to retaliatory measures—perhaps even, for all anybody knew at that moment, severance of connection with the University. But this was mere speculation; all that anyone knew for sure was that the situation seemed to have got out of hand. "It was one of the blackest days in Harvard history," Dean Watson said afterward. "It was the most unpleasant day I'd ever spent—up to then. God, what a mess! I'd never seen Harvard students behave this way before." Mike Ansara's reflections were predictably dissimilar. "It was one of the most exciting days I ever spent at Harvard," he said.

There was one microphone and loudspeaker inside Mallinckrodt. Ansara held that captive, too. At about 5:30 in the afternoon, while James Dickey, just down the block, was reading his poetry to a fairly full and feisty house, Glimp decided to talk to the students in the corridor. (Many Harvard officials and faculty members drifted onto and out of the scene, among them Professor Fieser, the inventor of napalm, who seemed a bit put out that he was ignored.) Dean Glimp couldn't get to the microphone, but Ansara relayed his thoughts over it to the students, and in the midst of the turmoil Glimp realized admiringly that not only was the S.D.S. leader accurately paraphrasing his beseechments; he was actually editing and improving them as he passed them along.

At about 6:45, the students, some of them by now cramped, some hungry, some bored, took a vote and decided to let Leavitt go. (A number of reporters and photographers who had converged on the building also voted, and helped to swell the affirmative total.) Leavitt departed, in reasonably good cheer. "He was a nice guy," Ansara said later. "We were all relieved when we decided to let him go. And we only kept him a couple of hours more than he'd have stayed anyway if he'd put in a full working day." Ansara, for his part, intoned a few final threats against the university, but his star soon went temporarily into eclipse. He departed for England not long afterward, to do research on the C.I.A. for *Ramparts*, and when he next showed up at a Harvard S.D.S. rally, the following spring, outfitted in a hacking jacket and a beard, he was scarcely recognized by his erstwhile flock. There were those who thought—quite wrongly, as it turned out —that as a radical campus leader he was over the hill.

Dean Glimp, for his part, delayed going home long enough to

telephone Dean Ford in London. It was two in the morning there when Glimp got through. "We have a little problem here," he told Ford on waking him. "We had this Dow recruiter locked up for seven hours." Ford took the next plane home. He knew that in the Harvard scheme of things, whatever action was taken against the rebellious students would be taken by his faculty. (That was not the way of all universities. When Berkeley had its turmoil in 1964, its faculty stood around wringing their hands.) Meanwhile, some of the students who had imprisoned Leavitt voluntarily spent a couple of hours ridding the corridor of the litter that had accumulated during the vigil.

According to S.D.S., 450 undergraduates yielded up their bursar's cards that day. (Graduate students were involved, too, but they don't have bursar's cards.) According to the administration, the total was substantially lower. Thirty-four of the surrendered cards belonged to freshmen. Because the demonstration had come so early in their first term, the administration adjudged them youthful offenders and returned their cards in the mail.

At noon, on October 27, S.D.S. held a follow-up rally in the Yard, to collect more cards. It was a warm, sunny midday, and Harvard offered plenty of other enticements. Young men and women were lolling on the grassy banks of the Charles River, along the surface of which skittered single scullers in lonely, tonic contemplation. The labs and playing fields were crowded. Still, several hundred people assembled to hear speakers say, for instance, "It is not the purpose of a university to provide space for murderers to recruit other people to participate in their murders," and "We'd better start learning something: that this university doesn't teach us to begin to empathize with those problems that we don't immediately suffer from."

A few dissenters raised their voices, one of them pointing out that the trouble at Berkeley, whence so many demonstrations like the Harvard one had stemmed, had itself stemmed from the insistence of the students in California that recruiters of all sorts be allowed on campus, including recruiters for illegal and unpopular causes. The point was not pursued. More meetings were announced for the weekend ahead, though the organizers—evincing a practicality of which visionaries are often quite capable—took pains not to schedule any that conflicted with the Harvard-Dartmouth game. Eighty-six additional bursar's cards were collected, and a delegation of six young men and women marched with them purposefully up the steps of University Hall. Anticlimactically, they found the door locked, and had to march down and up another flight of steps. By then, they were wearing sheepish smiles, like boys and girls out trick-or-treating at Halloween.

Meanwhile, the Faculty of Arts and Sciences was preparing to meet in emergency session. The faculty was, understandably, divided. There were those whose instinctive reaction was to throw the rascals out. There were others—forty-seven of them—who hastened to sign an advertisement in the *Crimson* supporting the aroused students. The political scientist Stanley H. Hoffman spent much of the weekend composing a thoughtful and lucid memorandum to his colleagues in which he analyzed what had happened and advocated restraint. "A lot of my students were in on the Dow thing," he said later. "I knew these people, and I knew they were not fascist beasts of the left out to destroy the University."

Born in Vienna and raised in France, Professor Hoffman had been lured to Harvard by McGeorge Bundy when Bundy was dean of the Faculty of Arts and Sciences. One of the most poignant confrontations of the Harvard spring of 1968 was a debate on United States policy in Vietnam, with Bundy taking the government line and Hoffman the opposite; the two men are so fond of one another that it seemed almost painful for either to try to score a point at the other's expense. In his twelve years on the Harvard faculty, Hoffman had become one of its most widely admired and busiest members. ("I run around like a headless chicken," he said, and indeed he does somewhat resemble a wise fowl, with its head firmly on.) An undergraduate course he gives called "War" was one of the most popular around. ("It's a nice subject," he said, "although some of my students end up, I think, by mildly resenting the course. They somehow expect a remedy for war, and instead they get some very complicated lectures with no solutions.") Hoffman was not universally *liked* by the radicals—he would put them off by telling them things like "Sometimes a sense of tactics is indispensable, even for revolutionaries"—but they respected him, as did just about everybody else, including his faculty colleagues.

The faculty was scheduled to convene on Halloween night. Ordinarily, its sessions are held in its own room, on the top floor of University Hall. Seven hundred men and women are eligible to attend Arts and Sciences faculty meetings, but although the Faculty Room seats only 250 it is almost never filled at ordinary meetings. The meeting about the Dow demonstration was anything but ordinary, and it was held in a much larger auditorium. Four hundred and forty-three faculty members showed up, and so conscious were the presiding officials of the significance of the occasion that they assigned three individuals to keep minutes.

In the chair, President Pusey was edgy. When a visiting professor from Egypt, who had the right to attend but not, Mr. Pusey thought, to speak or vote, tried to get the floor, Mr. Pusey squelched him peremptorily. (They met again at a reception several days later. "Now, what was it you wanted to say?" Mr. Pusey asked graciously.) There was a good deal of argument pro and con, a few of those present demanding that a disciplinary precedent be set by harsh punishment, up to and including expulsions, a few others insisting that the students hadn't actually hurt anybody and should be let off scot-free.

The faculty showed no appetite for tasting blood. By a margin of more than five to one, it voted not to dismiss or suspend any of the students concerned, and to leave whatever milder form of punishment might be appropriate to the College's Administrative Board. "No one in an official connection with the University," Mr. Pusey said afterward, "has ever suggested that students should not have freedom to demonstrate in an orderly fashion or otherwise to express their views on these or other matters of concern to them. Indeed, they have been encouraged to do so. Objections arise only when they become so carried away by their conviction about the rightness of their cause and so impatient with civilized procedures that they seek to restrain the freedom of expression or movement of others who may not agree with them. This kind of conduct is simply unacceptable not only in a community devoted to intellectual endeavor but, I would assume, in any decent democratic society."

But as Mr. Pusey knew would be the case, not all members of the far-flung Harvard family reacted so temperately. For weeks afterward, his office was peppered with irate letters and telephone messages, the gist of which was pretty well summed up by one lady who yelled at the secretary luckless enough to answer her call, "Throw the bums out and make room for some good Americans." And the editors of the *Harvard Alumni Bulletin* concurrently braced themselves for a flood of letters from old grads that soon enough poured in, brimming with phrases like "I feel that it is useless to talk about raising another forty-eight million dollars until there is evidence of a complete housecleaning among the faculty and student body," and "Let us restore to Harvard some of the old Puritanical sense of what is right and what is wrong, with no compromise between the two."

There were also, though, letters like a joint one from two really old grads—Roger Baldwin '05 and Ernest Angell '11. These early stalwarts of the American Civil Liberties Union wrote to the *Bulletin*, "As citizens who happen to be ourselves strongly opposed to our military activities in Vietnam and who deplore the use there of napalm, we are sympathetic to the student protest against the war and this weapon; we would fully support any form of peaceful protest against the Dow presence on University property." But the student action, they went on, seemed to them "an invitation to anarchy in a democratic society—in effect a declaration that, if you feel sufficiently strongly on grounds of conscience, you are justified in using force to deny rights to others," and they added, "We should not be blinded to the confusion between the worth and high dignity of the motive and the lawlessness of the means." So, they concluded, the University's handling of the situation—"assuming," as the A.C.L.U. veterans would predictably say, "clear identification of the participants and a fair hearing accorded"—was fully justified. Whether or not S.D.S. would regard A.C.L.U. views as anything but old-hat liberal was, of course, another matter.

The Administrative Board considered 245 cases. One hundred and seventy-one students were let off with admonishments—a gentle, slap-on-the-wrist form of chastisement that caused no inconvenience to those thus sentenced. Seventy-four students were put on probation—all but three for the remainder of the year—and some of them, regarding that only slightly harsher penalty as a distinction, soon began wearing lapel buttons saying "On Pro and Proud of it." (Some students who hadn't been anywhere near Mallinckrodt and weren't on pro began wearing the buttons, too, to the resentment of those who had legitimately been rebuked.) What being on probation meant was that an individual couldn't play for Harvard in an intercollegiate game or hold office in an undergraduate organization, but nobody paid much attention to that; the *Crimson*, for instance, with the full knowledge of the College administration, appointed one probationer to a high editorial post; the paper tactfully observed the letter of the Harvard law by omitting his name from its masthead.

Most of the officers of S.D.S. were on probation; that organization straightfacedly submitted a new list of officers, all of them dummies, and the administration straightfacedly accepted it. One master of an undergraduate house was heard to remark enviously that his house harbored only the second biggest contingent of sinners and that if there had been a little more advance notice of the Dow demonstration he was sure his boys would have turned out in larger numbers and come in first. For weeks on end, the *Crimson* ran articles and letters about the stormy episode, among the latter one by a freshman who called attention to the construction in India by the Dow Chemical Company of a factory to produce a high-protein food derived from peanuts, to combat malnutrition. "On this basis," the writer said, "I accuse Dow of being a tool of the War against Starvation, and I accuse the University of complicity in this relationship; and I applaud the sit-in as an effective means of thwarting Dow's recruitment for this War."

Meanwhile, the original purpose of Mr. Leavitt's interviews had all but been forgotten. (Five Harvard graduate chemists, it turned out, had had further negotiations with the company.) Leavitt himself was not forgotten; a teaching fellow in the English Department invited him to a small dinner at Dunster House, with a dozen or so others; on a social basis, the evening went very nicely, but there was little in the way of substantive dialogue. However, when dinner was over Mr. Leavitt departed without a raised voice or an upraised hand encumbering him.

Love talk of the sixties—Harvard boy to Radcliffe
girl, holding hands during a student demonstration: "Solidarity is
not a moral cop-out."

WHAT BECAME KNOWN AT Harvard, as if it were a new and timely dance step, simply as "The Dow," was much discussed —now and then, even good-naturedly. Shortly after the Mallinck-rodt sit-in, Professor Wald was lecturing to his biology students on the polarization of light. To illustrate a point, he held up a piece of cellophane and, after an attention-getting pause, said roguishly, "I wouldn't dare come before this class with Saran Wrap." (Laughter and applause.)

In February, the Office for Graduate and Career Plans had a Chemicals and Drugs Day, in the course of which recruiters from various companies in those industries made themselves available for interviews. Dow was once again represented, though not by Mr. Leavitt. The Faculty of Arts and Sciences, petitioned by some students to ask the company to stay away, declined, but that only 150 faculty members even bothered to vote on the issue was indicative of its ebbing intensity. Some activist undergraduates, after a half-hearted attempt to storm the portals of Massachusetts Hall, the site of the president's office, let themselves be turned away by a single presidential aide. Then the students moved across the Yard to deans' territory, University Hall, where they trooped in unobstructed and sat on the floor. Dean Glimp and a few of his assistant deans sat down chattily with them, still another assistant dean passed coffee around, and the whole episode was so amiable and fraternal that it seemed less like a demonstration against Dow than a Radcliffe jolly-up.

Meanwhile, across the Charles River, the Graduate School of Business Administration had been taking its own cognizance of the Dow affair. Following the lead of the Harvard Law School, the Business School in large measure gives instruction by means of the case method: it presents a real-life situation to its students and asks them to cast themselves as corporate executives and to make managerial decisions. Scarcely had the clogged halls of Mallinckrodt been emptied and tidied when the late Professor George Albert Smith, Jr., for his fall-term course on "Business, Society, and the Individual," quietly sent a Business School researcher to Dow's headquarters at Midland, Michigan, where, with the company's cordial cooperation, he gathered material for an exhaustive case study of Dow's difficulties with napalm. Later, the president of the *Crimson* was one of twenty college editors who accepted a Dow invitation to visit Midland. On returning, he reported, "They were all pleasant people, these Dow executives, but they all firmly believe in the social value of the free market system, a belief not terribly current in Cambridge among my peers."

Professor Smith kept the mission under wraps not because he didn't want word to get around that the Business School was, in a sense, collaborating with Dow, but because he planned to spring that case on his students—as he did in January—for their final exam. After reading a thirty-six-page, single-spaced account about napalm, Dow, and the company's public image, the students were asked to answer, among other questions, "What is Dow's 'obligation' to the government, if any?" and "What criteria do you think Dow's top management should use in attempting to reconcile the interests of the several groups to which it has or which it can be argued it has obligations?" It was a four-hour test, and during a break at the halfway point Smith was pleased to hear one student tell another, "I can hardly wait to get back. It's the most exciting exam I've ever had."

About half the students in the course were critical of Dow, and half sympathetic to it. (For whatever significance it might have, the larger proportion of high grades was scored by the anti-Dow group.) Six weeks later, Dow made yet another recruiting visit to Harvard, to the Business School exclusively. This time it sent four interviewers, who over a two-day stretch talked to ninety-four graduate students, with no friction whatever. Across the river, S.D.S. was apparently unaware that the enemy had made a massive new attack on one of its exposed flanks.

During the big faculty meeting about The Dow, Professor Hoffman had urged his colleagues to endorse the formation of a student-faculty committee that could discuss matters like Harvard's attitude toward outside recruiters. In due course, a Student-Faculty Advisory Council was formed. It was composed of sixteen members of the Faculty of Arts and Sciences and twenty-four students. Dean Ford appointed the faculty representatives, Hoffman among them. The students were elected. Some undergraduates were suspicious of SFAC's mere existence. "Any time you get students on a committee you can bet it's powerless," said one of Harvard's most respected Negro undergraduates. (Not long afterward, he joined the board of the Urban League, probably without wishing to render it impotent.) The Council met faithfully throughout the remainder of the academic year, but though its meetings were public, it failed to become a magnetic attraction; the only time it drew a large audience was when President Pusey appeared before it. S.D.S. at once demanded equal time, and got it.

It is probably the fact that at Harvard, as elsewhere, the degree to which a student makes contact with a professor depends on the student's initiative, and that while most professors have to be approached, most Harvard students are innate approachers. "Harvard students have many outstanding qualities," Stanley Hoffman has said, "but shyness is not among them." Take the case of a freshman who, a couple of years ago, wrote an article about Harvard for a magazine. The magazine wanted some photographs, and this brought the freshman to the University's News Office, where he was introduced to one of its staff, Mrs. Fainsod. The freshman asked if she was related to Merle Fainsod, the eminent expert on Russia, who has been on the Harvard faculty since 1933 and had become a University Professor and also director of the University Library. Mrs. Fainsod said she was indeed; he was her husband. "Well, I read one of his books when I was a sophomore in high school," the freshman said, "and it wasn't bad at all." Mrs. Fainsod was relieved that her husband had passed muster.

Not even in classrooms are Harvard undergraduates fazed by the augustness of their instructors; a few days after George Wald won the Nobel Prize, a student walked into his lecture hall, took a center-front seat, and went straight to sleep. Professor Wald began to talk, stopped, and had the boy aroused. "All right, no blood drawn," the scientist told him, "but maybe you ought to wake up." The professor was apparently concerned that he had gone too far. "It's not nearly as bad as chewing gum in class," he added reassuringly.

Students hiss their professors with impunity, and some professors seem disappointed when a hiss-provoking statement gets no response. There are three standard kinds of hissing. When a professor chalks a notice of an exam on a blackboard, he gets hissed. William Alfred, thus excoriated, turns around and sticks his tongue out at his students, who laugh. A mood of scholarly camaraderie has been established. When a professor makes a pun, advertent or inadvertent (e.g., Ezra Vogel, the East Asian scholar, discussing the consumption of rice and potatoes in China today, says, "Well, I guess this gives you some of the flavor of . . ."), he gets hissed. When he says something controversial or contentious, he gets hissed. McGeorge Bundy was repeatedly hissed when he tried to explain the government's Vietnam stance to a Harvard audience. Bundy is a man who does not lightly take being hissed: "That interesting noise is not an argument," he retorted icily.

Sometimes students hiss at other students. After the assassination of Martin Luther King, Jr., there was a teach-in at Harvard. Professor Samuel Bowles, the economist, who is generally accounted one of the most progressive members of the faculty, had the floor, and was twice hissed by a black girl in the balcony. After the second time, he realized why. "You don't like my using 'Negro'?" he asked. "No," she shouted. " 'Black.' " She got hissed more loudly than Bowles had been. "If you've counted, I've used both words an equal number of times," he told her. That provoked laughter and restored equanimity.

MANY HARVARD STUDENTS, like those everywhere, think they should have more power than they do; some think they should even have a voice in granting tenure to professors, oblivious to their elders' argument that the students are only around for four years, while the tenured faculty is around for life. To what extent, the argument goes on, should a tenant be entitled to make permanent changes on the premises he rents? "Surely students can't be permitted to run this place," Dean Watson has said. "We may have to sweat blood, but we simply have to have the upper hand, or that'll be the end of this institution." Dean Ford, for his part, has said, "I don't see that the students have any right to have any power. They're here to be educated."

Harvard undergraduates have had crumbs of authority. The Fanny Peabody Professor of Music is a title conferred on the director of the Glee Club, and the members of the Club traditionally nominate the man for that post. The vast majority of Harvard undergraduates don't much want to run the University, but most of them do want a say in those aspects of it that affect their private, extracurricular lives. In the dining halls of the undergraduate houses, it was a longstanding rule that suit coats and ties would be worn. Nobody ever argued hard against this in the days when most students came from prep schools; coats and ties were part of their day-to-day attire. But public-school boys do not dress that way (nor do prep-school boys now, when they can get away with it), and for many of them it is unnatural and distasteful to wear dress-up clothes every day.

Not long ago, one undergraduate wrote his house master that he was going to defy the coat-and-tie rule because Harvard had "a ridiculous faith in the idea that external form is a meaningful measure of gentlemanliness," and added morosely that "The Harvard student is an uninformed, unfranchised member of a non-community which controls large areas of his life." The house master sighed, and from then on kept his eyes averted when the disgruntled student entered the dining room. For the most part, Harvard administrators try to be accommodating in these personal matters, but when it comes to what they construe to be the major business of the institution, they are less inclined to bend. "In educational matters, students are children of fashion," Martin Peretz says, "and the decisions in this area should be made by senior people."

Worldly Harvard junior to comparatively callow Harvard freshman: "You'll learn much more if you ignore all the recommended reading. Generally speaking, whatever Harvard says, don't do it."

xi

OF ABOUT 1,200 YOUNG MEN who become Harvard freshmen each autumn, 950 of them get quarters in the Yard, which in an orientation pamphlet they also get is described as "that oldest, noblest, richest of Harvard institutions." The Yard, a twenty-two-and-a-half-acre, largely brick-walled enclave with pleasant lawns crisscrossed by paths and shaded by stately elms, is the outgrowth of a modest cowyard where the first students to enter Harvard, in the fall of 1638, were grubbily boarded.

The Yard is the geographical center and symbolic heart of the University. Within it are a hodgepodge of buildings that figure importantly in Harvard life and Harvard history. It is an unwritten University rule that no one may trifle with the Yard, but most Harvard rules are broken with impunity. Thus no one complained, years ago, when the marvelously named professor of classics Evangelinus Apostolides Sophocles dug worms there for his pet chickens, even though nearly everyone knew he had named his clucking hens after the gossipy wives of his faculty colleagues. Thus no one complained, a year ago, when a newly arrived freshman once again spaded up the precious soil to plant bulbs whose flowers he hoped to enjoy if he survived until spring.

The oldest building in the Yard, Massachusetts Hall, constructed in 1720, is the oldest college building in the United States. President Nathan Pusey's office is in it, and his residence is also in the Yard. So is Holden Chapel (now the headquarters for the Harvard Glee Club and the Radcliffe Choral Society), a building doubly distinctive because, tiny though it is, it once harbored the entire Harvard Medical School, and because it bears on its gable a heraldic pun that graced the coat of arms of the family it was named after: *Teneo et teneor*—"I hold and I am Holden." Most of the buildings in the Yard are made of red brick, but the central one, University Hall, is a handsome Bulfinch structure of gray brick that, when it went up in 1814, provoked howls of dismay from alumni distrustful of architectural change. Harvard's present-day administrators are grateful for that furor, and cite it with relish when present-day alumni complain about the University's newfangled buildings.

At the west entrance of University Hall stands a statue of a seated John Harvard, done by Daniel Chester French in 1884. Nobody knows what John Harvard looked like; the sculptor used an unremembered graduate student as his model. There is very little indisputably known about the first Harvard, beyond that he was the son of an English butcher who died, along with four other children, in a 1625 plague; that he came to the United States in 1637 to serve as a Puritan minister; and that he died, at thirty, in 1638, of tuberculosis. He willed to the fledgling institution at Cambridge his library and just under eight hundred British pounds. There is some doubt that Harvard ever actually received John Harvard's monetary bequest. For his good intentions, though, the General Court of the Massachusetts Bay Colony named the new school after him; there had been no other private benefactor at all.

More recently, the decorativeness of the Yard has been enhanced by a Ch'ing-Dynasty marble dragon, presented to the University in 1936 by alumni living in China, at the time of Harvard's tercentenary; and by a bulky Henry Moore abstraction that, although it has been on display in the Yard for over three years, is still on probation. "I realize that the Yard is fairly sacrosanct, and we must be careful," a University art curator said when the piece was temporarily installed. "I don't want to encourage controversy."

The building alongside which the Moore has been emplaced is itself illustrative of Harvard's avoidance of controversy. It is called Lehman Hall, and it used to house Harvard's fiscal people. In 1963, they were moved elsewhere, and Lehman Hall was converted into the home base for Dudley House, a social center for undergraduates unaffiliated with any of the residential houses. Lehman Hall, however, has never been rechristened Dudley House. It might have been, but shortly after it was refurbished it was visited by Mrs. John L. Loeb, the wife of a recent Harvard benefactor whose gifts, running into the millions, *have* been received and have been very welcome. "I hope you're not planning to change the building's name," Mrs. Loeb, whose maiden name was Lehman, told her guide. Harvard decided it could live with the anomaly of having the same building known as Dudley House and Lehman Hall. Thanks to one of her husband's recent benefactions, Harvard will also soon be living with a library named exclusively after her.

John Harvard's own legacy to the institution was soon decimated. His library consisted of four hundred books. Harvard acquired them in 1642 and lost all but one of them on January 24, 1764, when a fire razed a building in the Yard called Harvard Hall. The General Court of Massachusetts—the Colony's legislature—had started Harvard, and the Court inadvertently destroyed its library. There was a smallpox epidemic in Boston that year, and the legislators crossed the Charles River to Cambridge and sat in Harvard Hall. A hearth fire got out of control. The building, containing the whole College library of five thousand books, as well as a museum—"a monument to the piety of our ancestors," according to the Boston *Gazette*—burned down in spite of the personal efforts of the Governor and members of the Court to save it. The book of John Harvard's that escaped—John

Downame's folio *Christian Warfare Against the Devill, World, and Flesh*—wasn't on the premises, having been charged out the previous October 14 to a student named Briggs, whose slowness in returning it enabled Harvard to retain at least one tangible link with its first patron. The library has been trying ever since to replace John Harvard's other 399 volumes, and so far has assembled 178 of them.

It would take a monstrous conflagration now to leave Harvard bookless. The University Library—libraries are partial to the use of the singular even for scattered collections—consists of ninety-eight libraries containing eight million books. Its annual budget runs to eight million dollars, in keeping with a curious pattern that also fits the sprawling New York Public Library: To operate a big library costs each year about a buck a book. Harvard's library is smaller than the New York Public Library (twelve million volumes) and also than the Library of Congress (fifteen million), but it is far and away the world's largest university library, and probably also the most valuable. Its contents are probably worth somewhere between eighty and a hundred million dollars.

The main library—fittingly enough, it is the dominant building in the Yard—is the Widener Library. It contains two and a half million volumes, arranged in ten stack levels, and it honors Harry Elkins Widener, the Philadelphian who went down on the *Titanic*. His mother gave Harvard the building, which was finished in 1914; a special room called the Treasure Room, near the main entrance, shelters Harry Widener's three thousand rare books and manuscripts. Undergraduates rarely go in there; they would rather explore another treasure room, called the "X Cage," a mysterious and largely inaccessible nook that is rumored to harbor Harvard's hottest pornography. Those few who have crossed its threshold have professed to be disappointed, one of them complaining that near as he could make out from a quick look-around the vaunted vault contained little more than a smattering of de Sade, a batch of *Playboy*s, both bound and unbound, and some documents issued during the Second World War by the Massachusetts Committee on Public Safety.

Dean Ford, whose speech sometimes reflects an attempt to bridge the Arts-and-Sciences areas over which he presides, has described Widener as "among the principal engines of our culture." A professor from nearby Boston University, on the other hand, perhaps a mite envious, not long ago referred to Widener as "that great tomb of knowledge." There is a certain rigidity, of course, to libraries, if not rigor mortis. Harvard, for instance, has its own classification system, which it has been using for practically as long as anyone can remember, and which seems somewhat moribund. Most books having to do with any part of the earth that used to be in the Ottoman Empire (books on contemporary Albanian economics, for example), are still classified under "OTT." Hungary is still under Austria; Korea, to the dismay of visiting Korean scholars, under Japan; Cyprus—how this galls Cyprian Turks!—under Modern Greece; and Ireland, doubly anachronistic, under the British Empire.

Tomblike Widener may appear to some, but to Harvard officials their main library is a precious living thing. Every now and then a malcontent student, unable to borrow a book he needs, takes a punch at a librarian. Harvard frowns on this, but it gets much more upset about mutilating books than mutilating book handlers. Each year, as a warning to its constituency, it displays in the main lobby of Widener an assortment of books and periodicals that have been ravaged, much in the same spirit that impels turnpikes to display mangled automobiles. In the Harvard ethic, to sully a library book is an abomination. Harvard professors will put up with a lot from students (and, the students would argue, vice versa), but when in the roiling wake of the April disturbance the rumor spread that undergraduates had it in mind to take over Widener, some of the oldest and stiffest professors moved with agility. They assigned themselves, for several nervous nights, to guard duty inside the library. The students made no move in that direction, and the professors soon learned that their chief problem was to stay awake. After they had run out of recondite intellectual games, they organized a competition to see who could find, around the huge library's acres of space, the most appealing graffiti. The winner was adjudged to be the unearther of an anonymous author who, coming across the scribbled phrase "My mother made me a homosexual," had appended, "If I gave her the wool, would she make me one, too?" Never had such raucous laughter bounced off Widener's marble walls as when, soon after this discovery, a professor assigned to the 4 A.M. shift turned up with an odd-looking knapsack slung over one shoulder. Someone asked him what it was. "My mother made it for me," he said innocently. Half a dozen professorial voices chorused "If we gave her the . . ." before they were drowned out by one of that period's few opportunities for unshackled hilarity.

The library world is a special one. Harvard's part of this world was notable, until his death in 1966, for the presence of an Honorary Curator of Paper Making and Allied Arts, who really made books. He manufactured his own paper, designed and cut and cast his own type, and printed and bound his books. He wrote them, too. The activities of the nearly nine hundred bibliophiles who man the Harvard library, not all of them quite *that* dedicated, are jointly supervised. There is a director of the University Library, a professor who occupies a chair endowed by the book-collector Carl H. Pforzheimer, Jr. The first Pforzheimer Professor was Paul H. Buck, the Pulitzer Prize historian, who still has an office in Widener, where he is now at work on, among other things, an intellectual history of Harvard. "It's hard to write about universities," he says. "Princeton historians know that the place has the reputation of being full of playboys, so they knock themselves out trying to imbue it with scholarly attributes. Harvard historians know it is thought of as austere and academic, so they try to show that the students there are capable of having a good time."

Buck was succeeded as director of the library and Pforzheimer Professor, in 1964, by Merle Fainsod, who had earlier been on the Library Committee of the Faculty of Arts and Sciences but considered himself otherwise unqualified for the post. "I don't know a damn thing about libraries except as a consumer," he said. Professor Fainsod brightened when he realized that his new responsibility entitled him to a reserved parking space in the Yard. He had been at Harvard for thirty-three years but had never enjoyed that privilege. (Clark Kerr once said, when he was at the University of California, that the alumni cared only about football, the students only about sex, and the faculty only about parking. This is true of Harvard, too. Many of the twenty-five hundred physicians affiliated in one way or another with the Harvard Medical School receive no pay for their teaching and don't care; what they do care about is getting a sticker that lets them park in the Medical School lot.)

The library is actually administered by a University librarian, who also rates a parking place. The incumbent is Douglas W. Bryant, a Stanford graduate who studied library science at Michigan. He came to Harvard in 1953 and became librarian in 1964. His main problem is one of selectivity. Not even counting Asia, some three hundred thousand books are now published annually. Harvard considers ten volumes for every one it adds to its shelves; it is harder for a book to get into the Harvard Library than for a boy to get into the College. There are so many books on earth that the most recent *World Bibliography of Bibliographies* listed 117,187 volumes of bibliography alone. Harvard not only tries to keep abreast of the incoming tide but to guess what kinds of books scholars will be wanting in the future. In the eighteen-nineties, when other libraries were mostly uninterested, it began to amass a comprehensive collection of Slavic literature. This was to prove invaluable not only for local scholars like Professor Fainsod but, as Russia became increasingly important on the international scene, for researchers from everywhere.

Often, again with an eye to the future, Harvard will buy more than one copy of a desired book. Books that are frequently used disintegrate fast, and Harvard prudently likes to have a second copy stashed away. "Most book dealers would give their eye teeth to get into our duplicate stacks," Bryant says. Sometimes Harvard will buy a whole collection, cull what it wants, sell the balance, and make a nice profit. (Among its recent good customers have been the Universities of Texas, Illinois, Toronto, and British Columbia, all of which have been expanding their libraries at a rapid clip.) Harvard has acquisitions men all over the world, on a retainer basis, and it has its own full-time acquisitions staff—specializing as a rule in regions or languages—who make periodic global forays. By 1960, two-thirds of the new books added to the library were in languages other than English. One cannot sustain a first-class library by sitting back and waiting for books to be delivered. To order a book from the government printer of Nigeria, for instance, does not mean that the book will arrive; the book world, like the political world, is sometimes underdeveloped. The home-based acquisitions staff includes one man, Dutch by birth and trained in Germany as a musicologist, who is fluent in sixteen languages. Then there is a tropical historian named Michael Cutter, whose areas include Southern Asia and Central Africa. It is a Harvard Library joke that the sun never sets on Mike Cutter.

The Harvard Library, like most libraries, welcomes gifts, but these are often a nuisance, since examining and cataloguing them can be a laborious and costly process. Vanity books and family genealogies are received with a public smile and a private shudder. One celebrated professor of Egyptology gave Harvard a whole trunkful of volumes. The library, considering itself a bit weak in that field at that moment, was about to celebrate when someone opened the trunk and found it crammed with detective stories, each of which the professor had meticulously graded, from A to F. Many gift books are sent by Harvard graduates, who sulk if on their next visit to the library an attendant can't find their book. Sometimes the librarians are astonished at what they *do* find. Escorting a visitor not long ago through a room in Widener crammed with periodicals—the Library gets twenty thousand of them routinely—a librarian came upon a heap of unbound copies of *Seventeen*. "I'm surprised we have it," the library man said. "We're not a public library, after all. Oh, well, I guess maybe it's social history. You can justify almost anything around here by saying it comes under social history."

Harvard men also often send Harvard their private papers. These are shunted off to the Harvard Archives, which occupy a corner of their own in Widener. For any kind of institution to maintain archives is relatively new. Harvard had some a couple of hundred years ago. They consisted mainly of personal files on students. But when New England towns that were recruiting ministers asked the College for a peek at these dossiers, Harvard demurred. Since no one else seemed interested in them, the Archives languished. In the middle of the nineteenth century, the administration began to save what seemed to be pertinent Harvardiana. In 1935, preparing to celebrate its three-hundredth anniversary, Harvard sent a librarian to Europe to see how some of the old universities there handled their archival material. By 1939, Harvard was ready formally to set up its Archives—thus blazing another trail in America. The United States government followed suit, establishing the National Archives in 1940.

The Harvard Archives are now the repository for the minutes of all meetings of the University's governing boards and standing faculty committees (101 of these, at last count); for important financial records; for official correspondence of all University officers; for all Harvard publications; and for any book the custodians hear of that has at least one chapter about the University. The Archives also files doctoral dissertations, which candidates for Harvard Ph.D.s have lately been turning out at the rate of nearly four hundred a year. As Harvard gets older and administratively more complicated, the Archives have begun to bulge; its present-day custodians have lately been weeding out some of the stuff that their predecessors accumulated over the years, such as a banjo that was reputed to be the first banjo strummed in the Harvard Banjo Club.

Many of the ninety-seven branches of the University library that are physically detached from Widener would on many campuses rate as good-sized libraries all by themselves. The Harvard Law School Library has a million volumes, among them copies of 80 per cent of the legal books written in English before 1601. The Harvard Business School Library has nearly five hundred volumes of letters and documents relating to business activities of the Medicis, along with the earliest description known (1494) of double-entry bookkeeping, and an 1848 first edition of the *Communist Manifesto*, which is not only not hidden away but unembarrassedly kept in a bright red box. Merely to catalog the library of the Museum of Comparative Zoology requires eight fat volumes. To accommodate the research needs of no more than two hundred professors and students in the field of anthropology, Harvard is spending a million dollars for a new home for the ninety thousand library items of the Peabody Museum of Archaeology and Ethnology. One of the latest of the eight dozen libraries, the Countway Library of the Medical School (which incorporates the old Boston Medical Library and subscribes to forty-five hundred medical journals), is so alluring an edifice that when a New York doctor not long ago went to Boston and planned to spend half an hour there he stayed five hours (and at that fell far short of seeing everything—missing, for example, an exhibit called "A Century of Harvard Dentistry"), even though it meant skipping a lunch at the Ritz with an attractive young woman. No higher compliment could be paid an attractive young library.

But the Widener, though now more than half a century old, is still *the* Harvard library. Since 1942, it has acquired two connecting adjuncts: the Lamont Library, a spacious undergraduate reading center, and the Houghton Library, the repository of most of Harvard's rare books. Long after Radcliffe became academically integrated with Harvard, Lamont remained a last male sanctuary. In 1966, girls were admitted, but they didn't seem to like it much: Harvard boys tended to read with their shoes off, and their feet smelled. The following year, Radcliffe unveiled a library of its own, the Hilles ("At last we've done something better for the students than they thought we could!" the president of Radcliffe exclaimed), and it proved to be magnetic for Harvard undergraduates, at least some of whom, before traipsing over, changed their socks. Hilles became so popular that just before exam time males had to be barred at peak hours to ensure the girls for whom the place had been built a fair shot at some floor space. Hilles had soft carpeting, and it was possible for a Harvard man to browse there not only in agreeable company but lying down. Hilles also had hi-fi music and a snack bar; a Harvard sophomore once brought a flush of pleasure to Radcliffe cheeks by declaring, "I'll never give money to a library without a snack bar."

The rare books in Houghton are an impressive lot, though in some areas other libraries have a quantitative edge. (Harvard has only sixteen first editions of *Paradise Lost*. The University of Illinois has seventy-four.) At last count, Houghton held some three million manuscripts. It has more Keats manuscripts than all the other libraries in the world together, along with some two-thirds of the poet's extant letters. It has twenty thousand letters to Ralph Waldo Emerson from eight thousand correspondents, along with Emerson's journals; opening a volume of these at random, one is apt to come across an appraisal of a piece of Emerson property by H. D. Thoreau. Harvard's rare-book custodians insist that they never acquire anything simply because it is the oldest or scarcest or smallest of its kind. Even so, they have a strong accumulative bent. "We are sometimes brought up short by the discovery that some obviously important work is inexplicably lacking in the Harvard Library," the director of Houghton, William H. Bond, has said. Mr. Bond is one of the few individuals in the educational field today who can report fearlessly and unapologetically that his shelves harbor *The Story of Little Black Sambo*, the recent acquisition of a first edition of which he revealed in a 1967 account of the Houghton's first twenty-five years of existence. Every item in the rare-book collection is supposed to serve some scholarly function. Thus a student interested in the pitfalls of creative writing can reflect on exhibits like the original manuscript of *Look Homeward, Angel* juxtaposed with a letter from Boni & Liveright rejecting it.

The Houghton has agents of its own scattered around the world who bid on its behalf when desirable items come onto the market, and sometimes it finds itself in fairly dramatic situations. In 1967, for instance, it had an unheralded visit from a mysterious European who disclosed that he had the original manuscript of the bulk of the *Codex Suprasliensis*—an eleventh-century work, written in the Cyrillic alphabet, that is perhaps of greater interest to Slavonic scholars than any other extant text. Nobody had thought it *was* extant; it had been in the Warsaw Library in 1944 when that building was burned to the ground, and scholars had ever since been mourning its supposed loss. But the man who came to Harvard had it all right; a professor of Slavic literature who was summoned to examine it went temporarily blind out of sheer excitement while establishing its authenticity. The circumstances by which it had fallen into the hands that held it were so cloaked in mystery, however, that Harvard decided not to try to buy it, though it would probably have had little trouble in rounding up the $350,000 its possessor sought. The Harvard library people were nonetheless concerned. The peddler of the *Codex* wanted a quick sale; otherwise, he hinted, he might break it up and divide it among various rare-book collectors at, say, two thousand dollars a page. Harvard felt that the entire manuscript should go, rather, to Poland. So a couple of Harvard librarians got in touch with a Polish-ham importer in New York, who bought it and, while the intermediaries from Cambridge stood by beaming, presented it to the Polish embassy in Washington. The grateful Polish government in turn presented Harvard with a photographic copy of the manuscript.

Along with being the director of Houghton, Mr. Bond also has a faculty appointment as professor of bibliography. He teaches a graduate course and tries to inculcate in his students one sage piece of advice: Wash your hands before handling rare books. To protect its manuscript copy of Pope's *Essay on Man* from students heedless of Professor Bond's admonition, the Houghton has had photostatic copies made for scholars who want to paw over it. Every Tuesday during the academic year, Bond lunches with his rare-book associates, and they start off in his office by drinking a toast in sherry to whatever literary luminaries had birthdays that day—Lady Gregory and Frank Norris one week, D'Annunzio and Edward Albee the next. The Houghton has attracted many generous patrons over the years. Amy Lowell ("Amy Lowell of Brookline," she is called at Harvard) not only bequeathed to Harvard most of her own library (it was very strong on Keats, Hardy, and Jane Austen) but an endowment that enables Houghton to buy forty thousand dollars' worth of other books a year. The rare-book people rarely discuss money, though, over lunch or anywhere else. "It isn't good to let our competitors know what our capabilities are," Bond told a visitor. The capabilities, like the collection, are prodigious.

Ninety-eight libraries notwithstanding, Harvard has been running out of shelf space, and this in spite of its having made some extra room in 1961 by giving all its cookbooks—fifteen hundred of them—to Radcliffe. In Houghton, rare books for which there is no other space are piled on radiators and window ledges; this keeps them off the floor and also reminds passersby that Harvard needs money for new shelves. Currently, a five-million-dollar library addition is in the planning stage. It will accommodate more than a million books, and is expected to meet the Widener's needs until the early nineteen-eighties. Harvard wanted to connect the new facilities to Widener, but there was precious little building space left in the Yard, unless its rustic flavor was to be diluted. So the University's planners decided to go underground, and to construct a four-story-deep catacomb.

Certain fund-raising problems at once became manifest. Harvard abounds with buildings that are testimonials to generosity.

(The first building given by an alumnus was a dormitory, Stoughton Hall, named after a jurist whose generosity was not all-encompassing; he also presided over the Salem witchcraft trials.) There are the Mallinckrodt Laboratories, named for the St. Louis chemist who gave Harvard four million dollars during his lifetime and left it more than twice that in his will. When the Harvard Business School embarked on its first big building-fund drive, in 1924, nearly all its money came from a single person, the banker George F. Baker. Its library is named after him (many of the other Business School buildings are named, at Baker's request, after secretaries of the Treasury), and, for reasons no one can now recall, the legend "George F. Baker Foundation" appears on that school's official letterhead. Philanthropists are especially fond of having libraries named after them. Arthur Houghton once said that he was better known for the rare-book library in the Yard than for all the glass Corning ever made.

The chief of Harvard's Planning Office, putting up a bold front, once said, "To serve Harvard is the hope of every architect." Maybe so, but the hope of many donors is, like that of architects, to have a glimpse of the fruits of their exertions. The chairman of the committee that has been raising funds for the underground library is Lammot duPont Copeland. When somebody asked him how he proposed interesting anybody in making a substantial contribution toward an invisible monument, he replied gamely that Harvard would find a way of solving that —perhaps, if necessary, by putting some sort of tombstone-like marker at ground level above the hidden shelves.

A Professor of Government: "It's hard to get through to students these days. They interpret everything you say as either a truism or sheer nonsense."

XII

THIRTY YEARS AGO, more than 20 per cent of Harvard freshmen were commuters. Today, only half a dozen of the twelve hundred of them live at home, and most of them live—as well as attend classes and go to libraries—in the Yard. Rephrasing an old saw, an upperclassman told a visitor, waving toward a freshman dorm, "If they're going to be miserable, they might as well have company." Harvard freshmen are really not all that miserable. For one thing, when they enter college they can generally count on four years before they're draftable. President Lowell used to say that the freshman year at Harvard was like a cold shower; it made men of boys. But these days many freshmen are quite worldly. Each is assigned, for academic guidance and moral support, to an advisor—usually a very junior faculty man. "A few years ago, when an advisee first came in, his palms would be sweating and he would lean forward intently and listen to what I told him," one advisor said recently. "By our third or fourth meeting, he'd be looking at his watch while I was talking and saying 'Uh huh, uh huh.' Now, I sometimes get those 'Uh huh's' at our first encounter."

While Harvard does not particularly coddle its freshmen (nor, when it comes to that, anyone else), it recognizes that they sometimes need special treatment. Their average age, after all, is only eighteen. One thing that it has been doing since 1960 is to offer a series of seminars exclusively for them. This program began when McGeorge Bundy was dean of the Faculty of Arts and Sciences. That faculty does not lightly allocate funds for innovations. For three years, accordingly, the fifty-thousand-dollar annual cost of the freshman-seminar program was, at Bundy's solicitation, underwritten by Edwin H. Land, the Polaroid man. Then the faculty decided the idea was sound and provided for the seminars out of its regular instructional budget.

Now, forty-two seminars are offered. They have become so popular that they are hugely oversubscribed, and this has led to difficulties. The program is announced to fledgling students with a great blaring of trumpets, but the most coveted of the seminars are so hard to get into that many freshmen perforce begin their Harvard years on a note of intellectual disappointment and frustration. Last year, 131 Harvard and Radcliffe freshmen vied for 12 places in a seminar called "Psychoanalytic View of Man," 144 students for 10 places in "Nature of Human Emotions," 140 for 15 in "The United States and the Cold War," and 104 for 14 in "Computergraphics." Bernard Malamud had 90 applications for a 10-place seminar in creative writing; he awarded one seat to a Radcliffe girl who, asked why she wanted to take the course, replied, in full, "I am a writer." According to George W. Goethals, a social relations professor who also serves as an assistant dean of the College, "This seminar program must be one of the most exciting things that ever happened at Harvard. No one else has had much of a chance at these kids, and you see the fruits of your own labor grow right in front of you, and it's unbelievable."

There were extracurricular seminars for freshmen, too, a couple of these conducted by an assistant dean who typified a fairly new breed of young Harvard administrator. He was James E. Thomas, a plumber's son from Virginia with the acronymic nickname "Jet." A Phi Beta Kappa graduate of William and Mary, he became a nuclear physicist and then an ordained Southern Baptist minister before deciding to aim at a Ph.D. in philosophy. While taking graduate courses in California a few years back, he lived with the Haight-Ashbury hippies. He dressed conservatively and had close-cropped hair; for a while, his West Coast hosts suspected him of being a narcotics agent. In Cambridge, he and some other young ministers set up a pad for homeless hippies, and when they got arrested he would go to court to bail them out, on such occasions donning clerical garb. "It is very effective around Boston," he says. "In a courtroom everybody calls you 'Father.' "

When Thomas first became associated with Harvard, as a proctor in a freshman dorm, he was, by Harvard standards, spectacularly uninformed. He had never heard of any private school, let alone a particular one, and when in undertaking to break the conversational ice with some boys under his wing whose school background he knew from reading about them, said, "Didn't you go to Cho-ate?" Later, he became a tutor in theology and philosophy for upperclassmen, and he organized two informal seminars for freshmen, one on radical theology and one on phenomenology and existentialism. He was assured by an old administration hand that even though the initial turnout was heartening, his students would never stick with him through a non-credit enterprise, but a couple of dozen did. The only assignment he ever gave was that at some point or another they should sit down and think for an hour. "They found it very difficult," he says. "Of course they did," countered a Radcliffe girl when she heard of the experiment. "Who in his right mind would want to waste an hour proving he can do what everyone knows he can do? It's taken for granted than anyone at Harvard can think."

Thomas achieved a wide celebrity when the S.D.S. took over University Hall in the spring of 1969 and ordered the regular occupants to leave. He probably had more affinity with most undergraduates than any other Harvard dean. He lived in the Yard. He was young, and a bachelor, and had no objection to being awakened at three or four in the morning by a worried student who wanted to talk about drugs or sex or suicide or anything else. He had an impeccable reputation for confidentiality. Nonetheless, he was the only Harvard administrator who was carried out bodily from University Hall. He had been commanded to depart by a student he knew. Thomas demurred. "This building is occupied," he was told. "But surely it's big enough for both of us to occupy," Thomas said. "Oh, come on, Jet," said the student, and hoisted him onto his shoulder. As Thomas was being carted off, another student walked behind him, solicitously picking up the things that fell out of his pockets. Thomas is slight and frail. Outside the building, a burly Maoist student threw a punch at him. "This is no time to hit me," Thomas remonstrated mildly. Other students intervened before he could be hurt.

The freshman year at Harvard is considered a tough one for graduates of public high schools, who are apt to come from small towns and to be bewildered by the freedom and variety of Cambridge life. The sophomore year is the tough year for prep-school boys, who often skate through their freshman year, finding it little different from, and sometimes less demanding than, their senior year at Andover or wherever. By the junior year at Harvard, in most instances, the public-school and private-school boys are running abreast. Regardless of a boy's background, if he stays at Harvard on anything like an even keel, by the time he finishes his fourth year of College he will not only have demonstrated signs of growth but have attained powers of discernment and detachment—an accomplishment, some Harvard elders insist, unique to Harvard—that enable him to observe and appreciate his own development. Professor William Alfred likes to cite an illustration of this. One of his freshman advisees stopped by to discuss a weighty problem—he had got a B-plus instead of an A-minus, or some such—while a senior was waiting in the next room to chat about an honors thesis. After the freshman left, the senior said to Alfred, "I couldn't help listening to what he was saying, and, my God, I just heard myself speaking as of three years ago."

There is very little homogeneity among Harvard undergraduates, unless it be that they are for the most part bright, stimulating, engaging, and unreceptive to telephone calls before noon, when they are apt to be asleep. By the same token, they are receptive to calls between midnight and four, when they are apt to be working, or, at any rate, conscious. Harvard itself makes few demands on them and gives them few guidelines. The College doesn't even make much effort to convene them. The only times a Harvard undergraduate class officially gets together are at the very start of the freshman year, for an indoctrination meeting (which many students are too confused to attend), and at the very end of the senior year, for graduation (which many students are too bored to attend). In between, they are supposed to be imaginative and self-reliant. The only thing they are supposed to do, really, is to do *something*—and to do it well. "We're quite serious here about excellence," says Professor George W. Goethals, who graduated from Harvard in 1943 and came back to serve both as a teacher and administrator. "Everybody realizes there's a wide choice of ways of demonstrating this—I call it a culture of alternatives—but whether it's in classwork, or dramatics, or athletics, or writing, it's excellence that counts. If you're in research, Harvard doesn't care what kind of research you do as long as it's good research."

After four undergraduate years, one senior concluded, "The way this place operates is that it stands ready to give you all the ingredients you want, but you have to make your own sundae. The range of activities and of people here is so amazing that at times I despaired of ever getting anything out of it. I'd pick up the *Crimson* in the morning and read about the speakers I'd like to hear that day and the political stuff I'd like to take part in, and then I'd realize I had an hour exam coming up and the *New Statesman* to read and then I'd get into a bull session on some philosophical problem and forget about the Marx Brothers film I wanted to see and this rock concert and that harpsichord recital and I'd somehow end up doing nothing." Harvard's intellectual standards are so high that some students think getting a B is a disgrace. "You're supposed to know everything here," an undergraduate complained. "If, say, in a Nat-Sci section some kid mentions casually that so-and-so is merely derivative of what's-his-name in Chicago, you may never have heard of either of them, but you don't dare admit it."

The brightness of some of the undergraduates is breathtaking. There was one a few years back who had formidable intellectual credentials (he had had a paper published in the *Journal of Symbolic Logic* when he was a high-school tenth-grader), but in college he never appeared to be doing any work. In his senior year, he had an honors thesis due, and his friends, worried that he might not graduate, offered to help him and said if he'd just scribble something down they'd get it typed and turn it in. He opened up a closet in his room, revealed a pile of handwritten manuscript, pulled out a few dozen pages, seemingly at random, and asked, "Will this do?" His friends put the stuff in presentable form, though most of it was beyond their comprehension, and, largely as a result of that paper, he graduated summa cum laude. "Nothing is beyond Harvard students," David Riesman has said. "You could hunt around at a place like Michigan and find a group of students equal to some of Harvard's best, but at no place other than Harvard will you find so much diverse idiosyncratic talent in a student body of manageable size."

Riesman is one of the most popular professors at Harvard. He has room in his undergraduate course on "Character and Social Structure in America" for 420 students; he usually gets 1,200 applications. He spends a lot of time with undergraduates—too much, some of his faculty colleagues think. He has more time to spend than most; when he came to Harvard it was agreed that he would only have to teach one half-course each year. It was not only that pleasant arrangement that persuaded him to move to Harvard from Chicago in the first place. The undergraduates were an important factor, too. He had a son at Harvard at the time, and the boy invited him to an orchestra rehearsal. The students involved had hired a conductor at their own expense, and the conductor was a demanding, Toscanini-like martinet who was whipping them through some difficult Stravinsky and beating their brains out when they made a mistake, and they were loving every tortured moment of it. "I thought this was simply extraordinary," Professor Riesman recalls. "At a school that specializes in music, like Oberlin, you might have expected to find something like that, but this thing I was watching didn't even have anything to do with the Harvard music department. It was just something the students wanted to do themselves."

Some students these days regard Riesman as a conservative (he believes, for instance, that people behave better the less sloppily they're dressed), and thus automatically suspect; others regard him as a useful agent provocateur, because he is always willing to lend a sympathetic ear to, and often also put an oar in for, new courses that they'd like to see added to the curriculum. He himself has made it a practice, over his Harvard years, to audit at least one course annually outside of his field. Now and then, he foregoes a course he would like to sit in on when the professor in charge of it indicates that to have Riesman among his students throughout a term might make him feel uneasy. Riesman, for his part, thought last year of auditing Dean Ford's course on German history, but gave up the notion because it made *him* feel uneasy. Not long ago, one of Riesman's brasher undergraduate acquaintances, who was familiar with his proclivities, asked the professor if he did the assigned reading in the courses he audited. "Do you do the reading in the courses you *take?*" Riesman replied, and the matter ended there.

"There are many ways of going to Harvard," says Professor Jerome Bruner, "and this is as true of the faculty as of the students. In the more than twenty-five years I've been here, I doubt that I've even met half the faculty. There will always be those who are perfectly content working the year round with a few gifted graduate students. They're happy where they are, and there's no reason—though these days it's hard to avoid—why they should be dragged into a student-faculty conference or a political rally. There are colleagues of mine for whom I have the greatest respect, but I haven't the foggiest notion what they're up to, and I suspect that a lot of them haven't any idea what I'm doing. But nearly all of us, faculty and students alike, do know one thing—that when you're at Harvard you're living in the middle of a rich pudding." When the *Crimson* sought to apostrophize one undergraduate violinist who had written the music for an undergraduate show, completed and performed an unfinished work of Mozart, and been a classical-music disc jockey on a local radio station, it said, in a variation of a current phrase that seemed appropriate, "he did his things (3)."

Once in the pudding, a student can indeed do almost anything he likes. One undergraduate in a new academic field called the Department of Environmental and Visual Studies spent nearly a year on a five-minute motion-picture documentary—a slow-motion examination of elderly people at the counter of a Harvard Square ice cream parlor; his fellow students acclaimed as a masterful touch his selection of a sound track, which was Muzak played backwards. For *his* sound track, another student in that field used President Nixon's Inaugural Address; the visual accompaniment, in the course of acquiring which the undergraduate and some of his actors got arrested for lewd and lascivious behavior, consisted in part of nude scenes. Still another student spent several months concocting an unusual sound track (he didn't bother with any pictures) on machine noises. He began with a buzzsaw and ended up with a flushing toilet and in between concentrated on a pinball machine at a short-order eating place. Pinball machines are very popular at Harvard, and the student captured twenty minutes' worth of action on Derby Day, the biggest, flashiest, and loudest machine in the joint. Halfway through, somebody turned on a jukebox, and he got contrapuntal effects beyond his wildest dreams.

Computers are playing an increasingly important part in education, and some Harvard students like to play with them in their spare time, as in another era they might have played squash. (Some, of course, do both.) Harvard has a big Computer Center, and all sorts of ancillary computer facilities, but even so these fall far short of meeting the demands for computer time. This is divided up into segments called "yen," and students fight for the yen like Japanese mendicants. One senior in the class of 1968 got six yen, but he was only technically an undergraduate; though he didn't yet have a college degree, he was lecturing graduate students in mathematics on complex variables. He was devoting his computer time to a rarefied aspect of cartography called conformal mapping, which had profound aerodynamical connotations, and he had trained a computer to recognize and respond to his handwriting.

Professor Edward M. Purcell, the Harvard physicist who won the Nobel Prize for research leading to the development of the nuclear magnetic resonance spectrometer, and has lately been dabbling in astrophysics, wangled a few yen himself. He would stop in at the Computer Center and find it swarming with sophomores he recognized from his undergraduate course. "After the computer kept putting me in my place by saying things to me like 'You can't take the square root of a minus,' I'd go up to these sophomores and practically say 'Sir, can you help me?'" Professor Purcell said, "and they generally could. Their way of life is a new one, and an insidious one, too. The students get hooked on the computer. Watching some of these guys wait for a printout is like watching a junkie wait for a fix."

Professor Purcell has been at Harvard since 1937. "I don't think I'm quite obsolete yet," he says, "though when I am I'll probably be the last one to recognize it. But I do sometimes wonder if the reason that I only teach undergraduates now is that I'm not smart enough to do anything else. When I tell students straight from high school these days that I don't understand some of the things they all seem to know, they laugh—fortunately, in a not unkindly manner."

It is pretty much the same in all the physical sciences. Undergraduates in chemistry have keys to the University's laboratories, and wander freely in and out throughout the day and night, nibbling at the facilities like kids in a candy store. ("Spin slowly; you'll be glad you did," a sign alongside one lab contraption ominously proclaims.) The labs are unattended, and Harvard's breakage is thus substantial, but the chemistry department figures that in these days of high personnel costs it's cheaper to pay repair bills than hire round-the-clock laboratory technicians. And it would be unthinkable to shut down the labs during the night. Who knows but what some inventive sophomore chemist might be inspired to fool around with an experiment at three or four in the morning?

The bulletin boards just inside the entrances to many Harvard buildings attest to the bewildering variety of choices that daily confront its citizenry. The one thing no member of the Harvard family in good standing ever does is look at the University's famous glass flowers; that is strictly for tourists—some two hundred thousand a year. The vestibule of Weld Hall, one of the freshman dorms in the Yard, has an enormous bulletin board, but it scarcely has room for all the notices about used bicycles, stereo sets, and trumpets for sale (Harvard students are always short of cash), about automobile rides wanted and offered, and about personal crises: the parents of a sixteen-year-old girl missing from her home in White Plains, New York, hope that anyone who knows anything of her whereabouts will get in touch with them at once.

Most of the notices, though, herald forthcoming events: a Cognitive Dissonance Talk-in, perhaps, at William James Hall; a lecture by Miss Indian America at the Radcliffe library; a colloquium sponsored by the Division of Engineering and Applied Sciences on the Two-Family Structure of Turbulent Wall-Layers; a colloquium sponsored by the Cambridge Entomological Club on Reproductive Diapause in Tropical Butterflies; a recital by an Israeli pianist sponsored by the Committee on Ethiopian Literacy; and so on and on until the eye blurs and the mind reels.

A high-school senior touring the Yard once paused in the lobby of Weld and, after a careful examination of its proclamations, said, "Gee, if I were at Harvard there'd be thirty-six things I could be doing tonight."

One best-selling author on a lecture tour spent an evening at Tulane, where he was lionized, and then moved on to Harvard, where he was one of a half dozen rival attractions and was all but ignored. A poetry reading by either Robert Lowell or Allen Ginsberg would create a cultural splash on most campuses; Harvard had them competing on the very same night. So, on another night, were David Rockefeller and McGeorge Bundy, somewhat to the consternation of President Pusey, who could and did put them both up at his house, but couldn't be in two audiences at once. (Mr. Pusey's own Sunday-afternoon teas for the faculty often clashed, when it came to that, with love-ins on the nearby Cambridge Common.) "My ambition is to live long enough to be around here with no responsibilities and have a chance to do everything," the president once said, but he knew as well as anyone that that would be physically impossible.

Nearly everybody at Harvard is overwhelmed by the pace of the place. "I'm too busy to be educated," said an undergraduate who had dipped deeply into the well of Harvard offerings. "I'm a desperate man," said a professor of sociology. "I seem to have so many things to do I have no time for reflection or for intellectual life." Some professors make eight-o'clock breakfast dates with visitors seeking appointments; it is the only time they can squeeze in. According to Professor Adam Yarmolinsky, "The demands on my time are greater than they've ever been. I have the same secretary I had in Washington, but in Cambridge I find myself forced to carry a pocket diary to keep up with myself. I have no time to read here. I'm busy five or six nights a week, and it isn't primarily social. A guy wanted to come up here from Washington to discuss something with me for two hours, and to my dismay I literally couldn't find two consecutive hours to give him."

Professor John Kenneth Galbraith, than whom it would seem offhand no Harvard professor could be busier, dissents. "The average university professor has a well-spaced life," he says, "and some professors are even unduly lazy." Galbraith, whose only faculty association since 1934, save for a brief Princeton flirtation, has been with Harvard, works quite hard, and in Cambridge he enjoys a special status. Some people think Harvard's academic year officially ends at the conclusion of its Commencement Day ceremonies. Others argue that it does not end until the conclusion of a party Galbraith gives later that same afternoon, and to which eminent recipients of honorary degrees would consider it a loss of face not to be invited. The Harvard Student Agencies, through which many students find part-time jobs, sends a lot of bartenders to private parties; it is characteristic of Galbraith's lofty standing in the local pecking order that in describing the intangible rewards to be derived from this work an Agencies booklet says, "Guests at a party often enjoy making conversation with their Harvard bartender, and these guests sometimes include people like Professor Galbraith, Senator Kennedy, and President Pusey."

Harvard has a news office that tries to keep up with the outside activities of the Harvard flock by assembling news clippings about them. "We don't even begin to collect Galbraith," one member of that office said. "We don't have the staff for it." In other areas of the University, he is regarded with mixed feelings. Some professors at the Harvard Business School, for instance, because of his liberal views on economics, look askance when he enters their Faculty Club, as if they had spotted a whore in a convent. Some professors in his own economics department think he has an unduly thin skin, and since he stands six feet eight inches, there is a lot of skin to stretch. When a distinguished M.I.T. economist reviewed Galbraith's *The New Industrial State* for a smallish publication, Galbraith got hold of proofs in advance, disliked what he saw, demanded equal space for rebuttal in the same issue that carried the review, and had his wish granted.

Galbraith is sometimes known around Harvard as "The Master," but there are overtones of irreverence in the phrase. Many students admire him, but say that they would admire him just as much if he were on some other faculty, since he is largely inaccessible to them. He spends every morning writing, seven days a week. In his spacious brick house on Francis Avenue, he has two studies—an upstairs one for whatever book he has in progress, and a downstairs one for lesser literary works. He will never make an appointment of any kind, when in Cambridge, before noon. Still, in marked contrast to those Harvard professors who profess never to have a spare moment, Galbraith would usually insist that he has plenty of excess time. He had because—although he was critical of the way the University is run, arguing that the men in charge of it were too remote from both faculty and students—until the events of April 9 he took hardly any part in University affairs outside of his immediate orbit.

Every Harvard faculty man's time is theoretically divided, like a gallon of whiskey, into fifths. (Graduate students working toward doctoral degrees may not teach for more than two-fifths of a year, and they get only two-fifths of what is advertised as their pay scale.) In theory, every faculty member with tenure is supposed to devote one-fifth of his time to non-academic university affairs—serving on committees, principally. Galbraith won't serve on committees. He used to be appointed to them, but the deans gave up when he never showed up at meetings. Like most faculty members, he is formally associated with an undergraduate residential house; he hardly knows where it is. He teaches one undergraduate course and one graduate seminar, but aside from that has almost no individual contact with students.

But—and, befitting the man, it is a big but—Galbraith has a good excuse for his unorthodoxy. Because he is who he is, the University makes demands on him that other professors cannot comprehend. No other Harvard man has ever been in such request as a guest speaker. Every house, every freshman dorm, every club, and every group more or less expects an appearance from him every year. There are the undergraduate Democrats, and the Democrats at the Law School. There are the doctors of the University Health Services, and the seminarians at the Divinity School, and if he fails also to visit Radcliffe (or several groups at Radcliffe) he is accused of discriminating against women. He calculates that he spends far more than one-fifth of his time making personal appearances.

Some Harvard professors nonetheless maintain that Galbraith consistently shirks his professorial duties. There is a story that circulates around Harvard—Galbraith himself has probably circulated it more than anyone else—to the effect that whenever word gets out that a senior professor hasn't been keeping up with his chores, the president's office checks to see where Galbraith has been. Because such an undercurrent of feeling exists, Galbraith is overly scrupulous about never missing a class, and considering the amount of traveling he does, he has to schedule himself with care. "If I didn't show up for a lecture," he says, "there would be a scandal approximating fornication in Harvard Square."

For all Harvard professors, keeping their commitments to their students is a serious business. Richard E. Neustadt was appointed by President Johnson, in 1968, to a six-man committee to plan an Urban Studies Center for the federal government. Professor Neustadt advised the White House that he couldn't make the first meeting because he had a class to teach. Professor Galbraith has nonetheless been absent from time to time. During the Kennedy administration, of course, he was long away, while serving as ambassador to India. Harvard has a rule that a faculty member must resign if he leaves for more than two years, unless there's a war on. Thus, Daniel Patrick Moynihan committed himself to only two years in the Nixon administration.

In the fall of 1962, Galbraith was in New Delhi and his two years were nearly up. Then China attacked the Indian border. Washington all but ignored the incident. The Kennedy administration was so preoccupied with Cuba at the time that during the first week of the China-India dustup, as Galbraith recalls it, he only got one cable from the State Department. But Harvard, delighted at having an excuse not to have to follow its rules of severance, quickly sized up the conflict as a full-fledged war and extended his leave of absence indefinitely.

Harvard has been less kindly disposed toward Galbraith's shorter leavetakings. Another rule the administration has is that a professor, no matter how towering a figure literally or figuratively, may not be away from the campus for more than a week, while school is in session, without formal permission from the president's office. Many senior professors resent this regulation and ignore it. If they are invited to chair a session of the Modern Language Association or to receive a gold medal for unearthing some fabulous tomb, and they plan to be gone a fortnight or so, they are damned if they are going to ask for a written excuse. That can be risky. Harvard is quite prepared to summon back to Cambridge from California a Nobel Prize winner who, though he has requested permission to be away longer than a week, has taken off without waiting for permission to be granted. Harvard once did just that. Galbraith, feeling himself to be a marked man, bends over backward, most of the time, to go through the irritating prescribed requirement, and since he suffers from a sinus allergy and believes that this can most quickly be alleviated at a chalet he has at Gstaad, in Switzerland, he not infrequently goes through the routine.

Once, he forgot. President Johnson had asked him to represent the United States at the funeral in India of Prime Minister Shastri. Galbraith stopped off at Gstaad on his way home, and, feeling that his sinuses were about to act up, decided to stay on a few extra days. He neglected to notify Harvard, which would probably have never caught on to his naughtiness had not Mrs. John F. Kennedy, followed by a corps of photographers, chosen to visit him for some skiing. In trying to protect his guest from the cameramen, Galbraith was himself repeatedly photographed, and when one of the pictures was published back home, someone in the President's office saw it. Galbraith at once got a message from Mr. Pusey, wondering when he was planning to come back to Cambridge, and he felt like a schoolboy caught smoking in the boiler room.

Undergraduate who is also a concert violinist with a heavy recital schedule: "Missing classes is a shame. Harvard professors are rather intelligent, and I lose that profitable experience."

xiii

IN THE OLD DAYS, Harvard College was unarguably the sun around which the whole University spun. The College, in part through restricted endowments, controlled most of Harvard's resources and ignored plaintive suggestions from the fledgling graduate schools that it more bountifully slice the Harvard pie. Today, the situation is radically different. There is never as much money around as any segment of the University wants, or says it needs, but each of the graduate schools is robustly endowed; and the dean of the College, having no faculty that he can call his own, is in a sense less powerful than the deans of the graduate schools.

Still and all, the forty-eight hundred men enrolled in Harvard College retain a special luster. It is the graduates of the College, rather than of the various graduate schools, who in later years seem to attain the greatest success in public affairs, business, and the arts. Professor Seymour E. Harris, the economist, who reached retirement age at Harvard in 1964 and is now at the University of California at La Jolla, once did some research on the college affiliations of other eminent American economists. The twenty-five men who he decided were the dominant scholars in that field, over a thirty-year stretch, had earned their advanced degrees at quite a number of places, but fifteen of them had spent their undergraduate years at Harvard. Filling in a questionnaire recently circulated by the *Harvard Alumni Bulletin*, one respondent wrote, "Harvard College and the Law School were the greatest experiences of my life. I loved the College; I appreciate the Law School."

President Pusey has tried to spread his attention and affection among all segments of Harvard. He has said, however, that if the University were ever to discriminate in favor of its graduate schools and at the expense of the College, he would consider that turn of events a personal defeat. To be in Harvard College, Mr. Pusey further asserted, was to be invited to sit at a table loaded with intellectual riches "beyond my powers to describe"—a table at which some of the diners, however, would refuse to eat, others would defiantly eat with their fingers, and still others would slop the food all over the place. When it comes to conventional steak-and-potatoes nourishment—macaroni-and-cheese, more likely—most of the upperclassmen in the College are nurtured in one of nine residential houses. The first one began operating in 1930, and the first eight of them were largely built with money contributed by Edward S. Harkness, a Yale man.

Some students, mostly seniors, have apartments of their own, and there is one group of sixty undergraduates who live thriftily and cooperatively in a couple of frame houses that the University owns and lets them occupy. Lately, this settlement has attracted a fairly militant clientele that seems to enjoy biting the hand that lets it feed itself so cheaply. When, for instance, a tutor sharing the premises, dismayed that the younger tenants kept breaking its windows with snowballs, said, "Don't throw snowballs," he precipitated a crisis. Instead of issuing a dictum, the students said, he should have called a meeting to discuss the pros and cons of snowball-throwing. "When it snows, I've *got* to go out and throw snowballs," one undergraduate argued. A compromise of sorts was reached: The tutor withdrew his command, and substituted for it a recommendation that thenceforth the students choose less frangible targets and strive for accuracy.

The majority of the residential houses are named for Harvard presidents (one who will probably never be thus honored, for obvious reasons, was Ebenezer R. Hoar), and over the years have acquired personalities of their own, usually a reflection of the tastes of the masters who preside over them. One house has the reputation of being an especially slapdash establishment. Its master for fourteen years was a professor who kept a home of his own a half hour away, so he wouldn't become totally immersed in house affairs, and who believed in a stewardship of benevolent negligence. He was once pleased to hear that when the mother of a boy under his wing asked her son what he thought of his house-master, the son said, "He leaves us alone."

Different masters have different styles. The professor of classics, John H. Finley, Jr., who was master of Eliot House for twenty-six years until he retired from that post in 1968, made a point of learning the name of every one of the four hundred or so students in his house. The task was not without its heartbreaks. Every now and then, after associating some such name as "George Washington Smith" with a particular sophomore, the conscientious master would triumphantly address the boy as "George," only to learn that since infancy he had never been called anything but "Wash." Professor Finley, moreover, hardly ever missed a house athletic contest; he liked to refer Homerically to the players on intramural teams as "these mute and glorious heroes." Each spring, he would spend a couple of hours writing a thoughtful character reference for every one of the 150 graduating seniors in his house.

Professor Finley was an especially notable Harvard buff, as well as an especially quotable one. He once compared being educated at Harvard to embracing the Statue of Liberty. "One never knows how far around that massive waist one's arm can travel," he said. On the lecture platform, he had an engaging knack of livening up the classics; he would compare a Greek chorus to a flock of sated gulls leaving a garbage dump, and, reflecting on Oedipus's rash behavior after having been warned against patricide by the Delphic oracle, he would say, "I should have thought Oedipus would have been a little bit leery about killing middle-aged men."

As a house master, Finley took the classical approach that the important things in life are those that bind men together, and he viewed Eliot House as his own extra-cohesive, long-lasting cement. To celebrate his twenty-fifth year at the helm of Eliot, old grads who had lived there came from all over to attend a testimonial dinner to him, in the course of which he observed, "One of the great pleasures of university life is the cheerful company of the young. It's a kind of conspiracy. You do your best to help them mature, and they do their best to keep you young. Happy arrangement." When he turned Eliot House over to a professor of English, Alan E. Heimert, Mr. Finley cried, "*Floreat domus de Eliot!*" and Mr. Heimert responded, "Following Master Finley will be like getting into the wake of the Queeen Elizabeth in a rowboat."

Each of the houses has its own faculty associates, the depth of whose association depends upon their inclinations; and its own tutors, some of them in residence. The contacts these older men have with the student residents are supposed to be one of the strengths of the house system, and sometimes they are. One of the weaknesses of the system, in recent years, has been the parietal rules governing the hours during which women may be in the rooms. As things stand now, there is never a stretch of more than twelve consecutive hours when women may *not* be, and on Saturdays the grace period lasts fourteen hours.

But the students resent any restrictions at all on their social lives. Yale has an open-house policy, and most of Harvard's undergraduates feel they deserve no less. They are in little danger of being punished if they break the existing regulations, but they resent being put in the position of having to cheat about something they'd like to be honest about. Adams House is especially popular among students of vigorous hospitality; it has the most entrances and exits of any house. Adams attracts intellectuals, too, and offers them printing classes and cheese- and wine-tasting rites. Eliot House has perennially attracted boys with socially impeccable backgrounds, and it perennially—there is no particular connection between the two—turns out the most Rhodes Scholars. The older house buildings were comfortable, Georgian-style complexes, never more than five stories high; the newest house, Mather House, has a twenty-one-story tower. Leverett and Quincy Houses are a blend of Georgian-walk-up and cement-block-elevator design. Dunster House has its own squash courts, and a composer in residence. Lowell House has long had an Anglophilic orientation. Every Monday night, after sherry with the master and his wife, some of the students dine at a high table (black tie optional) and flavor their fare with the house's master salt, a huge, solid-silver salt-cellar donated by an old grad and inscribed with a Biblical quotation that President A. Lawrence Lowell incorporated into his inaugural address—"Your old men shall dream dreams, your young men shall see visions."

Lowell House also has a set of strident tower bells that are tolled on Mondays while guests proceed from sherry to the high table, on Sundays just before lunch, on whatever day final exams end, and whenever Harvard wins a football game. They were tolled also during the funerals of the Kennedys and of Martin Luther King, Jr. The bells, originally from a monastery near Moscow, were a gift to the house from Charles R. Crane, of the plumbing family. The bells are so loud that they are something of a neighborhood nuisance. Whenever they start ringing the superintendent of Lowell House leaves his office, so he won't have to listen to angry mothers who phone in to complain that their babies have been awakened. But Lowell House men dote on them, and when there seemed once to be a possibility that the University might order them permanently stilled, the residents of the house, in what they judged to be a fitting tribute to a plumbing-business benefactor, synchronized their watches and flushed every toilet in the place simultaneously, thereby flooding the Harvard sewage system and bringing the Harvard administration to its knees.

Considering how recently it was that Harvard's undergraduates often went there for social as much as for academic reasons, it is surprising how small a role the College's eleven principal social clubs, most of which have their own imposing buildings, play in the contemporary scheme of things. Fewer than 10 per cent of the students now join these clubs; one that considers forty members a comfortable number at last count had only twenty-five rattling around in its spacious premises. "The nice thing about Harvard," one club member says, "is that everybody here is now a minority, including upper-class New England prep-school types like me. The only unifying force in the College is basic brain potential."

Belonging to a club can be pleasant for those who fancy a touch of the sybaritic life and can afford it; most of the clubs have billiard rooms, libraries, bars, kitchens, and stewards deferential to young gentlemen. The Phoenix, for instance, has lobster lunches every Friday in the spring, and black-tie dinners every Wednesday all year long. The Spee offers its members round-the-clock food service. Nearly all the clubs have springtime initiations that are lively and ritualistic, and that strike some observers of the youth scene as anachronistic. On spring nights along Mt. Auburn Street, where several of the clubhouses are located, one may see two young men in dinner jackets leading a third one, blindfolded, along the pavement, and spinning him around, perhaps to make him lose his bearings and think he is being escorted to an S.D.S. rally.

The ranks of the clubs are still largely, though no longer almost exclusively, filled with prep-school boys, who themselves are no longer what they used to be; nowadays, they treat the social whirl so offhandedly that when one of them gets an invitation to a deb party he is likely to post it on his club's bulletin board, on the theory that if the mother of a girl can't get one Harvard clubman at her party she'll probably settle for another. A few of the clubs have recently begun admitting Negroes; it was the Spee, the Kennedys' Harvard club, that broke this particular ice. Some of the clubs still want no part of Harvard's Negroes, and some of the Negroes want no part of the clubs. One black upperclassman was punched for a club a couple of years ago, but after going through some of the traditional preliminaries declined to join up. "I got bored with all their cocktails and platters of shrimp and dirty jokes," he said afterward. "I decided that these guys were interested in me only to reinforce their own impression of their own broadmindedness, so I said thank you but no thanks. They were amazed that somebody had turned them down. 'What do you mean, damn it,' one guy said. 'You'd be the second Negro in a final club at Harvard!' I left feeling nine feet tall, because I'd had a glimpse of what it was all about."

One white member, who was also an editor of the *Lampoon*, resigned from his club because of its discriminatory admissions policy. Later, he got involved in an extracurricular project; he spent two afternoons a week with some young Negro boys from a slum area just outside Harvard's borders. He would now and then take them to shoot pool on the top floor of the *Lampoon* building, a very clubby aerie that ordinarily non-members of the publication are forbidden to peek into, let alone try combination shots in. The black boys, unaware of the height of the social scale they had ascended but appreciative of the comforts to which they were exposed, began calling the place *their* club.

Some of the clubs have other than purely social *raisons d'être*. The Signet Society, among its alumni have been T. S. Eliot and Norman Mailer, thinks of itself as a haven for Harvard's more creative students. (One Negro who made the Signet said that its latter-day members think of themselves "as experiencing a continuous intellectual orgasm.") The Varsity Club, as its name implies, is the exclusive province of athletes, who outside of its muscle-swelled chambers do not rate especially high at Harvard, and are sometimes even regarded as social inferiors. So little weight do Harvard's athletes get to throw around, except while in competition, that their elders in Cambridge sometimes feel impelled to rally to their defense. David Riesman is among their up-holders and comforters. "I hate snobbery toward jocks," he says. "The jocks at Harvard are no threat to anybody. They don't even get the prettiest girls." Neither do their opposites—the bookish wonks. As one bright and pretty Radcliffe girl has put it, "The male wonk in Cambridge is unbelievably wonky. He is even wonkier than the female wonk."

For a place that downgrades its athletes, or at any rate doesn't put them on pedestals, Harvard does exceedingly well in intercol-legiate sports—all the more considering that its coaches are for-bidden to recruit (when they happen nonetheless to turn up at a high school to watch a promising hockey wing or lacrosse goalie in action, they are not recruiting, just visiting), and that the com-petitors themselves are often surprisingly relaxed in combat. There was a recent student, for instance, from a New England parochial school with an outstanding basketball team. Until he got adjusted to Harvard, he couldn't comprehend the place (and began to wish he had joined his high-school teammates at Holy Cross), because nobody on the basketball team seemed to care whether it won or lost.

This carefree attitude notwithstanding, Harvard's competi-tive record in sports has been exemplary. In the 1967–1968 aca-demic year, Harvard Varsity teams in seventeen sports won 141 events, lost 70, and tied 1, a better showing than that of any other Ivy League college; and it capped those performances by having fifteen men (including its crew) on the United States Olympic squad at Mexico City—a larger representation than any other American college of any kind could boast. The crew attracted a good deal of attention even before the Games began—six of its members issuing a statement supporting "our black teammates in their efforts to dramatize the injustices and inequities which per-meate our society."

On arriving in Mexico, they circulated copies of the statement among all the American athletes, and although the athletes didn't react perceptibly ("I don't see why the black athletes need the

Harvard crew to help them protest anything," one black American said), some United States officials were upset. They were leery of Harvard to begin with because a few crewmen had mustaches or beards or longish hair. Some people in Mexico City called them "the shaggies," but these people had clearly never been to Cambridge to see what really long Harvard hair looked like. The Harvard coach, Harry Parker, remained unperturbed. "All our guys are saying is that the blacks have a legitimate complaint and a right to express it," he said. What did worry Parker on the eve of the rowing events was that some of his men had been hit by intestinal or respiratory ailments. In their first race, the winner of which automatically qualified for the final, they finished a dismal next-to-last. They broke a rigging bolt, and their regular stroke, who had been sick, was all but unconscious during the last five hundred metres.

Two days later came Harvard's do-or-die moment, the repechage, out of which the first two finishers would progress to the finals. Parker shifted his men around, putting Steve Brooks at stroke, where he hadn't rowed before. Meanwhile, the university had rallied to the cause and dispatched Dean Glimp to Mexico to cheer its eight on. Mr. Glimp was a very conscientious dean. He hadn't ridden a bicycle for twenty years or so, but he borrowed one so he could follow his crew along the side of the two-thousand-meter rowing course during one of its workouts. In the repechage, Harvard again started off feebly. Glimp looked glum. During the first five hundred metres, he emitted strangled moans. During the second five hundred, as the boat continued to struggle, he lapsed into silence; he looked as if he would rather have been anywhere than where he was—even in his office in Cambridge, Indian-wrestling with S.D.S. But then Harvard began to move. Perhaps the oarsmen heard their faithful dean's wild shouts of "Atta go, Harvard! Way to go!" In any case, they put on a magnificent spurt, easily took the second place they needed, and came within a hair of beating out Czechoslovakia for first. Dean Glimp, trying to photograph his boys afterward, was so shaky he couldn't hold his camera steady.

There were seven finals in rowing, and of forty-three boats taking part in these events eighteen belonged to the United States and the two Germanys. The United States had an entry in every final, and the many Americans on hand were glowing with optimism, though a mite less for Harvard than for some of the shells in the smaller-boat races. Things got under way unpromisingly for the United States when the Americans finished fifth out of six in the first event—coxed fours—and as the long, hot day wore on, there was lots of heartbreak—lots, but not all, of it American. The fiancée of Great Britain's single-sculler watched in anguish as he came in last. "At least, he made the finals," she said. By the end of the penultimate race, the United States' haul for the day was just one silver medal and one bronze. Harvard was the last hope. As its shell approached the starting line, Mr. Glimp, who had given up smoking some weeks before, bummed a cigarette from the man beside him. (By mid-April, 1969, he was back to three packs a day.) The Dean was silent throughout the race; there was never a hint of anything to yell about. Harvard never got under way, and it finished an abject last. An onlooker said, "At least, they made the finals." As Mr. Glimp and his wife were walking mournfully toward the boathouse, to give what solace they could to the crew, they fell in with the manager of the Australian crew, who was feeling jovial, because his boat had come in second. He was carrying a large stuffed kangaroo with a baby kangaroo in its pouch. "Our mascot," he explained. Someone in the crowd suggested that perhaps Harvard should have had a mascot. "That's what *he* was," Mrs. Glimp said, looking compassionately at her downcast husband.

After the Dean had caught up with his students and murmured appropriate regrets, one of them took him aside. "Dean Glimp, I want you to know I've enjoyed my Harvard experience," he said. Glimp blinked. "So many people are saying things against colleges these days," the student went on, "that I just wanted to tell you I think Harvard's a wonderful place." Glimp was transformed from a bedraggled mascot into a beaming mentor.

Harvard coaches, unlike most of their fraternity, do not have to worry especially about compiling good performance records; it is part of the Harvard legend that a coach is never fired for the poor showing of one of his teams, although now and then a persistently unsuccessful or unlucky coach gets promoted to a different job. The easygoing Harvard atmosphere may be the only kind in which a varsity football coach could function after open-heart surgery—a sequence of events that has in fact occurred in the life of John Yovicsin, the Crimson incumbent. Yovicsin is an unusual football coach in several respects. He sometimes wears dark, conservative business suits at work. He has been likened to an abbreviated Galbraith, except that Yovicsin looks less rumpled and more scholarly.

Yovicsin has to put up with a ban on spring training, a resident constituency from which the most energetic of cheerleaders find it difficult to elicit loud hurrahs, and the sobering reflection that at least one Harvard president in this century has tried to abolish varsity football altogether. That happened in 1905, when East Coast football coaches were encouraging their players to maim their opponents. President Charles William Eliot was about to disown football when another president, Theodore Roosevelt, intervened. Summoning the coaches of Harvard, Yale, Penn, and Princeton to a secret conference at the White House (presidents of the United States had time for that sort of thing then), the Rough Rider obtained their promise to cut out the rough stuff. Roosevelt's timely intercession made it possible, among other things, for a Harvard alumnus in the class of 1902 to announce, sixty-five years after his graduation, that he had just been to his seventy-second consecutive Harvard-Yale game.

For undergraduates at Cambridge, the Harvard-Dartmouth game had until lately become the important fall sports event, but for alumni the Yale game never stopped being the big one. It has always been a special occasion. Only twice each year does the Locke-Ober Café in Boston open its storied men's grill to ladies—

on New Year's Eve and on the night of the Harvard-Yale game. The grip of this annual spectacle on Harvard affections was tightened on November 23, 1968, when Harvard and Yale both went on the field undefeated—the first time such circumstances had prevailed since 1909. The only difference was that while most people conceded that Harvard had a good team, everyone agreed that Yale had a very good team. The game was sold out weeks in advance. As a timely news picture, the Associated Press sent its clients a photograph of a pair of tickets. Harvard alumni who had graduated later than 1949 couldn't buy any. (Some of those who were shut out are still seething.) The Harvard Club of New York got four dollars a head for a closed-circuit television view of the spectacle. Undergraduates, who were entitled to two free tickets each, scalped them to alumni for hundreds of dollars a pair.

Most of the game itself, following most sportswriters' predictions, was hopelessly onesided. Yale jumped off to a 22–0 lead. The Yale spectators began humiliating the Harvard stands early in the first quarter, by waving handkerchiefs at them, and one group of spectators on the Yale side even held up—until the police confiscated it—a sign unlike anything that had ever previously been publicly exhibited at the Harvard Stadium. It said FUCK HARVARD. Maybe the Harvard team saw it. In any event, Yale was still comfortably ahead—29–13—with forty-two seconds to go. Even before that, hundreds of Harvard partisans had begun to drift out of the place, disconsolate.

Now, it was theoretically possible to score sixteen points and tie the game in forty-two seconds. Two touchdowns and two two-point conversions would do it. But as far as anyone knows this had never happened anywhere, and at the stadium that afternoon it can have occurred to few people that it could happen and to fewer still that it would. Some of the Yale coaches, in fact, had left their bench to get to the dressing-room and organize a victory celebration.

But of course it did happen—Harvard's second touchdown

coming at the very instant that the clock ran out. HARVARD BEATS YALE, 29–29 was the inspired headline a *Crimson* editor composed at the moment.

A fortnight later, the *Crimson* unprecedentedly reprinted a post-game editorial from the Yale *Daily News*, a tear-jerking eulogy addressed to the Old Blue team that ended, "Brian, Calvin, Bobby, Nick, Del, Bruce, Mike, Fran, Dick, Pat, Kyle, Ed, Fred, and all the others. You created something around this place which made everyone sit up and take notice, and you gave us all a bucket of pride. Thanks." Harvard was no less proud. President Pusey, who is fond of exclamatory sentences, alluded to the astonishing game in his annual report and said, "Here was at least one event in which all Harvard men could unite in enthusiasm and lifting of spirit!"

There were people who were in the stadium that day and saw the whole game and still don't believe it. An abject Harvard grad who had left the game disgusted at the end of the first half and had missed the climax on radio and then managed somehow also to miss all the television replays of the miraculous denouement wrote to the *Alumni Bulletin* inviting other Harvard men (provided they would send a self-addressed stamped envelope) to read an account he had written of his own debasement. In sending this out, he rubber-stamped his correspondents' envelopes with a large, bright-red DISASTER!

ATHLETICS ASIDE, there were, at last count, ninety-three undergraduate Harvard organizations registered with the dean of Students (thirty-one of them being joint Harvard-Radcliffe groups), as well as quite a few unregistered ones, among these one called Harvard-Radcliffe X, which purported to espouse pure anarchy. On registering with the dean, organizations are supposed to furnish him with a list of their officers; the originators of H-R X followed the letter of this law, if not exactly its spirit, by submitting some names that they had picked at random from the University directory.

Some of the organizations are small special-interest ones, consisting of a handful of devotees of, say, Celtic or cribbage. Others loom fairly large on the undergraduate scene. The Harvard Glee Club, for instance, has—accompanied by the Radcliffe Choral Society—made two round-the-world tours in the last decade. The second of these, in the summer of 1967, involved ninety-two people. Everybody who went along—even the tour physician—had to sing. The girls wore blue dresses while performing; crimson was ruled out because it would have clashed with the red hair of the assistant director of the Radcliffe contingent. The trip was so favorably regarded by the Harvard administration that it gave the Club's undergraduate manager a whole academic year off to go around the world alone and make advance arrangements. (His draft board didn't interfere his first time around because the State Department had evaluated the tour as an international cultural event in the national interest; and the second time around, the manager, on becoming violently ill from eating an Israeli cookie, learned to his delight that he suffered from a rare allergy, and would thus qualify for a medical deferment.)

Harvard had not always smiled on such expeditions. When the Glee Club wanted to go to the Far East in 1961, Mr. Pusey himself at first frowned on the notion, but his attitude changed, possibly because his daughter-in-law is a Chinese whom his son met when the Glee Club touched down at Taiwan. (Whatever his feelings may have been about other pieces of the Harvard mosaic, there was never any doubt that Mr. Pusey loved the Glee Club. When he listened to it, one could almost see his often-expressionless face soften; he would smile; he would lead the ensuing applause; it was patently a relief for him to bask in the Club's clear, harmonious, familiar chords, even when some of the men who enunciated them were wearing red, denunciatory armbands.) A Harvard blessing, however, does not always lead to Harvard backing. The 1967 trip cost $150,000, and the manager had to raise all the money himself, getting no more help from the University than if he had been a student taking a year off to be a chicken farmer. What was more, he had to check with the president's office before embarking on solicitations; Harvard's fund-raisers didn't want him draining off regular Harvard money, and would authorize him only to approach prospects with a demonstrable interest in the Glee Club. One airline offered him fifty thousand dollars if in its ads it could use a picture of the Cambridge singers in front of one of its planes; Harvard wouldn't let him accept that kind of money.

A few rules were prescribed for the trip. The participants were warned, for instance, that anyone "whose conduct reflects poorly on the good names of the groups" could be sent back to the United States, at his own expense. Much of the time, the traveling students were put up at local homes, and for the most part all went smoothly. In the Philippines, however, a Harvard boy staying at a house with a swimming pool invited a Radcliffe girl over for a dip one sultry night. He wasn't even dating her; they were just friends. It got to be late, and instead of trying to get back to her quarters, she stayed overnight, sleeping, alone, on a living-room couch. When the host discovered this the next morning, he raised such a fuss about what he regarded as a flagrant breach of decorum that to keep the peace the Glee Club reluctantly decided to send the innocent young couple home—the only time any such disciplinary action had been taken since the Club was founded, in 1858. The boy survived the experience, but the girl stopped singing.

Then there is the Harvard Band. To many alumni, the football team and the band *are* Harvard. To the younger alumni, that is. The band was not formed until 1910; before that, the halftime marching at Harvard football was provided by R.O.T.C. men, and the music by banjo and mandolin players. Relatively modern though the band thus is, it has acquired institutional status of its own, and somewhere around the year 2010, a Harvard statistician has estimated, it will publicly render "Ten Thousand Men of Harvard" for the ten-thousandth time.

The Harvard band is casual about marching. It has musical rehearsals three or four times a week during the football season, but it never practices its formations before Saturday mornings. "You cannot get a Harvard man concerned about whether his shoulder is absolutely in line with that of the guy next to him," the leader of the band has explained, "especially when he's ankle-deep in mud. To him, marching is not a relevant thing." Humor is. Inasmuch as the bandsmen consider their fellow undergraduates the primary audience for their halftime sallies, these in the last few years have had markedly sexual overtones. Lately, the band has somewhat tarnished its trumpet-bright reputation among alumni by presenting shows so ribald they can hardly be described in print, but few undergraduates seem offended, and most of them, indeed, are highly amused. The administration grits its teeth and tries to keep cool.

Most undergraduate organizations at Harvard are non-commercial. The student-run radio station, WHRB, sells advertising, but it is a non-profit corporation and it strives only to break even. Sixty per cent of its air time—except during crises, as when it furnished a first-rate and practically nonstop account of the April, 1969, S.D.S. rebellion—is devoted to classical music. Its commercials are sedate. It spurns raucous jingles, and it rewrites some standard commercials, eliminating phrases or noises that it deems excessively slambang. WHRB is chiefly known for its orgies. These—often to the disappointment of newcomers, who have heard of the Harvard Orgies and are expecting something different—are nonstop programs of recorded music, uninterrupted by commercials of any sort, that are put on during reading periods and examinations, a time when many students scarcely sleep at all. The orgies began when one boy connected with the station, his own exams finished, wandered into the studio and played all nine Beethoven symphonies in a row, pausing long enough only to change records. Subsequently, WHRB has had an eight-hour Duke Ellington orgy, a Wagner orgy (the whole Ring), and a Bach-and-Mozart orgy that lasted sixty hours.

Another commercially-oriented but non-profit organization is the Harvard Student Agencies, which in addition to farming out bartenders, supervises a host of potentially income-producing ventures, among these the sale of "survival kits"—food packages to succor oneself at orgy time. The Agencies' ambition is to encourage Harvard students to become entrepreneurs. Under its aegis, seven hundred students, working part-time for just about as long or little as they please, earn among them more than a quarter of a million dollars a year. They run charter flights, they cajole parents into sending their Harvard sons cakes on their birthdays, they publish books. One of these, a travel guide for students, had a section on travel in Red China. The Agencies' principal agency these days is something called an Information Gathering Service, which employs more than three hundred students, who for various clients engage in library research, make telephone surveys, or translate documents. (The Agencies could at last report furnish translations in thirty-five languages.) Students like this sort of work because they can get paid—at somewhere between $2.50 and $10 an hour, depending on the difficulty of the job and the degree of their skills—for doing the very thing they know how to do. All in all, the Agencies is involved in a couple of dozen business ventures, and since it got under way in 1957 it has experimented with another forty or so that were ultimately abandoned.

One that survived, and thrived, stemmed from the Agencies' purchase, in 1960, of two hundred old refrigerators, which were rented to students for forty dollars a year. By 1968, the appliances were so decrepit that the H.S.A. decided to reduce by 10 per cent its annual charge for them; at this welcome challenge to the rise in the national cost of living, so many additional students begged for refrigerators that an Agencies' operative had to rush to New York and acquire nearly two hundred more hand-me-downs.

Some of Harvard's undergraduate publications consistently make money. So do some graduate ones; the *Harvard Business Review*, put out by the Business School, has a circulation of over a hundred thousand and, not being allowed to show a profit at the end of each year, is sometimes hard-pressed to figure out ways to spend its income. A 1967 parody of *Playboy* published by the *Lampoon* netted more than $150,000. The *Lampoon* couldn't keep the money, either; so it went on an institutional spending spree, lavishly refurbishing its building and adding in magnum dimensions to its wine cellar. A parody of the *New York Times* the following year was less profitable but perhaps more effective. After the *Times* had been delivered to some of its regular Cambridge subscribers—among them President Pusey—early one March morning, *Lampoon* distributors substituted their fake for the genuine article, and a number of Harvard scholars were momentarily under the impression that, among other bizarre happenings, Castro had seized the American naval base at Guantanamo, researchers had discovered a link between asparagus tips and stomach cancer, and an earthquake had toppled the Parthenon.

The daily *Crimson*, traditionally but not very seriously the arch-enemy of the *Lampoon*, is the principal publication of the Harvard community. It is enterprising, lively, provocative, and determinedly critical of what it construes to be Harvard's flaws. In the fateful spring of 1969, its point of view often paralleled that of S.D.S. It saw no objection to having a professor accused of genocide in its columns until the possibility of a libel suit was raised. It was wildly inaccurate, and notably non-contrite. Running three letters of correction on one day, it complained that the university officials who'd written them were taking up too much space in the paper. The *Crimson* has described itself as pretentious, and its reporters as both cocky and sloppy. It is sometimes high-toned (discussing the effect of calendrical progressions on varsity schedules, it used the headline GREGORY DELAYS FOOTBALL SEASON), and sometimes larksome (reviewing the opening of a new restaurant in Harvard Square, as if it were a play or movie, it said, "The whole place has a precious air of olde fashioned Americanness"). The editors are argumentative; when they can't agree what side to take on an issue, they'll run one editorial representing the majority viewpoint, and tack on a dissenting editorial entitled "On the Other Hand." Not always, however. Just before the end of the academic year in 1969, the Crimson's editorial chairman, apparently pretty much on his own, proposed that the student body skip final exams, by way of "withdrawing our cooperation" from the University. He attracted practically no attention at all, either from his fellow campus journalists or any other students. Nobody at Harvard has yet seriously proposed that students urge their parents to withdraw cooperation by refusing to pay their tuition bills, or, when it comes to that, to withdraw cooperation with their children by refusing to pay the rest of their bills.

The Crimson editors are also social mentors. They give dinners for a handpicked group of senior Harvard people. In the fall of 1968, after President Pusey had been in office for fifteen years, he finally made the list. Mr. Pusey had often taken his lumps in the paper, but he read it, or at least glanced at it, with regularity, much in the spirit of an unathletic man whose doctor has prescribed two dozen pushups daily. He thought, though, that the Crimson had its limitations. "In a sense, it's unfortunate that the only means of communication we have in the University is an undergraduate paper," he said. At last report, Harvard was searching for alternate means.

Many graduate students hardly ever see the Crimson, but undergraduates find it useful not only for its news of Harvard life but for notices of course meetings and for what the paper itself sometimes cockily calls the "Harvard Crimson's Famous Classified Advertisements." These occupy a lot of space and cover a lot of ground. There are offerings of used potter's wheels and automobiles ("Great Sexy Jag"), offers of land in Brazil at $2.50 the acre, appeals for members to join a Harvard-Radcliffe unicycle club. Some of the classifieds, befitting Harvard advertisers, are couched in fancy language. A couple of Law School students looking for some Radcliffe roommates said, "No affairs. Platonic, isocratic, hereclitic, and epicureic contemplated." Some are written plain. An undergraduate who wanted forty-five dollars in cash for a fifty-dollar Brooks Brothers gift certificate explained, "Need bread, not clothes."

The *Crimson's* editors come as close as any Harvard students to being Big Men On Campus, though actually they are better known to the administration and the senior faculty members than to other students; and some of them work extraordinarily hard. One of the more recent of the paper's chief executives could be found there between 11:00 P.M. and 5:00 A.M. four or five nights a week. He hardly ever went to a class, but he won a Rhodes Scholarship notwithstanding. One of his equally diligent associates, asked why he and the others were willing to devote so much of their time and energy to a single extracurricular outlet, said, "It's really quite simple. I want to get to know these guys because the guys who are running the *Crimson* now are some day going to be running the country."

He had at least one precedent to go by; Franklin D. Roosevelt '04 was a *Crimson* editor in his day. And he was not alone in his viewpoint. For at just about the same time, His Excellency Lee Kuan Yew, who while prime minister of Singapore took a few weeks off to be a fellow of the Institute of Politics at Harvard, was telling some undergraduates there that one reason for his coming to Cambridge was to "meet people whose thinking will decide the mood of American leadership in the nineteen-seventies and eighties."

"The problem with an academic community is that as people get older they spend too much time with people less experienced than themselves. There is a great tendency, accordingly, for professors never to learn anything more. What they are and what they have is confirmed rather than enlarged."
—*Professor Arthur M. Schlesinger, Jr.*

xiv

A WORD THAT MAKES university administrators squirm these days, especially if it is chanted by students during a demonstration, is *paternalism*. Most dictionaries speak well of the word; most students do not. Yet though *paternalism* has acquired nasty connotations, no word better describes the attitude the Harvard administration long cherished and would probably like to cling to. Harvard is constantly aware that it is old and its undergraduates are young, and a jocose remark with overtones of seriousness has one administrator there, on being asked by another what to do with a particularly irritating student, reply, "Spank him and send him to bed without his tutor."

Years ago, recalcitrant students were sometimes disciplined by being "rusticated"—being told to go away for a while. Nowadays, Harvard, like other places with paternalistic leanings, is reluctant to sever students' connections; that would make them vulnerable to the draft. Most students who are asked to leave are later taken back. Only in extraordinary circumstances is a boy permanently expelled—a student, for instance, who got into a drunken fight and inflicted fatal injuries on a janitor who tried to break it up, and another who, having failed to win admission to the College on his own, attended under the name of a friend who'd been accepted but had gone elsewhere. The handful of students who were most severely punished after the 1969 disorder were "dismissed," but even they could return if two-thirds of the faculty approved.

The governing Corporation delegates disciplinary powers to the faculty, and as recently as 1869 the faculty—the one-fifth time rule notwithstanding—spent a good half of its time on breaches of discipline. In recent years, to its considerable relief, the faculty had in turn elected to delegate most of its responsibilities in this prickly area to an Administrative Board. (The faculty temporarily retrieved them in the spring of 1969.) The Ad Board, as it is called for short, has sixteen members, among them a clutch of deans and, for each residential house, a representative called a senior tutor, who plays a double and paradoxical role, serving both as an advocate for any student from his bailiwick who is being discussed and as a juror when his case is adjudged.

The economist and sometime fiction writer Richard T. Gill, who is now master of Leverett House, was for a while the senior tutor there, and had one experience the memory of which still makes him shiver. During a weekend when, as it happened, Gill's mother was visiting him, to see what his job was like, he was about to take her to lunch when he was summoned to the junior common room, where two eighteen-year-old identical girl twins had elected to have identical nervous breakdowns. Gill thought at first it was some kind of joke. The girls were yelling and screaming, and when his mother stuck her head inside the common-room door, the senior tutor said he'd be a bit late for lunch.

An hour or so later, the twins were still carrying on. The Harvard police and the Cambridge police had been summoned, and the twins, both of whom were adept at judo, had scored heavily against them. The girls were finally subdued by sheer force of numbers and carried out rolled up in non-identical rugs, while Gill's mother's eyebrows went further and further up.

(Throughout, a Harvard sophomore sat impassively in a corner of the common room, reading a magazine, and hardly batted an eye.) At one point in the tumultuous proceedings, Gill said to the girls, "You really have to tell me what you're doing here," and one of them asked who *he* was. "I am an officer of Harvard University," he said. "Big deal," said one of the girls. When Gill later faithfully reported this dialogue to his colleagues on the Ad Board, he at once became know as "Big Deal" himself—a nickname he had some difficulty shucking in an environment where memory is much respected.

Some colleges have undergraduates on their disciplinary boards. Until the spring of 1969, Harvard did not, and thought this was to the undergraduates' advantage; students tend to be harsh in their judgment of other students. In the last few years, the Ad Board has generally been quite gentle toward transgressors. In January, 1969, however, by a narrow eight-to-seven vote, the dean of the College abstaining (all seven of the minority votes were cast by senior tutors), it recommended suspension—by Harvard criteria, a stiff penalty—for seven students who had led a demonstration the Ad Board would not countenance, and who had been on probation for similar behavior the year before. The Faculty of Arts and Sciences had sought to convene several weeks earlier to consider a student demand that R.O.T.C. be abolished at Harvard, or at least be stripped of its standing as a full-fledged academic department, but more than a hundred students had gathered at the meeting place and had refused to leave, in calculated defiance of a longstanding Harvard rule that no one could attend faculty meetings except faculty members and, rarely, invited guests. But the faculty, which has always rubber-stamped the Ad Board's recommendations, in this instance overruled that body; it accepted the sentence of suspension, and in the same breath it suspended sentence. A few weeks after that, it decided to invite some undergraduates to its meetings thenceforth. How preposterous that would have seemed a decade earlier! How even more unlikely that, as it happened, the first undergraduate ever to speak up at a Harvard faculty meeting should be a girl! When, a few weeks after *that*, the S.D.S. took over University Hall, most of the administrators whom it tossed out of the building were members of the Ad Board.

To become a haven of leniency, Harvard has had to repeal or shrug off some powerfully restricting rules. There was one in 1655 that went:

No Scholler shall go out of his chamber without coate, gowne, or cloake, and every one, every where shall weare modest and sober habit, without strange ruffianlike or new-fangled fashions, without all lavish Dresse, or excess of apparel whatsoever; Nor shall any weare gold or silver, or such ornaments, except to whom upon just ground the President shall permit the same: Neither shall it bee law-full for any to weare long hair, locks or foretopps, nor to use curling, crisping, parting or powdering their haire.

As late as 1786, there were prescribed uniforms, a different one for each class. (Years afterward, James Russell Lowell of the class of 1838 was reprimanded by the president for wearing a brown coat on a Sunday.) The only vestige of a sartorial prescription is that students are expected to wear coats and ties in their house dining rooms. The rule is not enforced, although various house masters have tried. One of them said he didn't care how his students dressed at breakfast and lunch. "But dinner seems different," he said in a plaintive note on his house bulletin board.

Another master left a bunch of his own ties with the house superintendent, hoping that students who forgetfully approached the dining hall with open collars would grab one. Still another master decided that a tie stuffed into the breast pocket of a jacket could be considered the equivalent of one knotted around the neck. Most Harvard officials share the view of a psychiatrist on the faculty who observed not long ago that at a college it is a good thing to have rules and an equally good thing to ignore them. ("I hardly ever enforce a rule," says Professor Zeph Stewart, the master of Lowell House, who has a brother on the Supreme Court, "though I believe that the courts have held that colleges *can* make rules.") Thus, members of the Ad Board, passing the room of a student who they know smokes marijuana, are apt to hold their noses; how can you turn someone in if you can't smell the stuff? One student who was generally known to be on stronger drugs was suspended for a year, but not for that. He had been caught lying, which at Harvard is considered a very ungentlemanly thing to do, even for a gentleman on a trip.

Ignoring its rules had justifiably made Harvard think it could remain relatively tranquil in an era of academic tidal waves. "The deans and the faculty around here have learned the knack of keeping the pressure valves open enough so the pot never boils over," one undergraduate complained not long before the lid of the pot blew off. "Every time you want to hit out at Harvard, you find yourself punching a big fat feather pillow." Harvard was by no means lawless. "The one class I bothered to go to yesterday," the same student went on morosely, "I was asleep on the floor and somebody woke me up and told me to put my shoes on. I guess they must have some stupid old rule against sleeping in your socks." Most Harvard officials would not have bothered to enforce that one, either. They bent over so far backwards sometimes one could almost hear their spines crack. When an impoverished sophomore who wanted to play in a rock group asked for a student loan so he could buy a set of drums, he was at first flatly turned down; there was no category of loan for which he qualified. When he persisted, arguing that if his group got engagements he might make some money and be able to pay back the loan, Harvard capitulated. But, so as not to set a precedent, it invented a new category under which it straightfacedly filed his case—a long-term short-term loan.

There has seldom been a more poignant illustration of the

lengths to which Harvard will go in solicitousness than in its treatment of a student in the class of 1969 who had perhaps the most acute identity crisis of any undergraduate in Harvard's 333-year history. His name was John Harvard. Harvard has harbored few Harvards. The original John Harvard was never a student there. Not until the class of 1915 did a member of the patronymic family materialize—a distant relative, Lionel de Jersey Harvard, an Englishman who was killed in the First World War. (Lionel Hall, a freshman dormitory, honors his memory; it is the only University building that has a Christian name.) In the fall of 1965, a high-school senior from Andes, New York, a small town in the Catskills, applied for admission. He had become John Harvard by chance. His parents were religious, and wanted to give him a New Testament name; he could just as easily have been Matthew, Mark, or Luke Harvard. On his school record, he was admissible to the College, but Harvard did not accept him until it had checked and double-checked to make sure no one was playing a joke on it.

The September morning he arrived in Cambridge, he found a note at his dorm, asking him to report to the dean of freshmen before he did anything else. The dean wanted to let him know that the College appreciated the delicacy of his position, and would do everything it could to protect him against the consequences of his name. As a result, he got hardly any publicity. There were a few brief stories in the Boston papers, but, at the dean's request, the *Crimson* left him alone. He was so little known around the campus that a year and a half after he matriculated a high official of the College, asked how many students with the surname Harvard had ever gone there, replied, "Oh, we haven't had one for years, though we'd welcome a Harvard if he could get in."

Until John T. Harvard got used to being Harvard's John Harvard, he was a troubled young man. He used to worry overmuch about flunking out of the place; some newspaper would be bound to hear of it, and he could visualize the stories about John Harvard's failing to cope with Harvard. There were other aggravations: the hilarity when he enrolled in the Harvard Cooperative Society, the distrust the first time he tried to cash a check at the Harvard Trust Company. But he survived all right, abetted by a sympathetic administration (the University News Office never mentioned him to visiting journalists looking for local color), and came rather to enjoy his odd status. "There were even some good points to having my name," he said. "You see a girl on a bus and introduce yourself and you don't see her again for a whole year and then you call her and say 'This is John Harvard' and she remembers you. Of course, there were also the new students each year who'd spot your name in the Directory and couldn't resist calling you and saying 'Are you really John Harvard?' After a few exposures to that, I began answering my phone with 'John Harvard speaking,' to get it over with. When people ask me how I feel about how I'm named, I fluctuate in my response, but most of the time I figure it's something I have to live with and accept." There was one experience, though, that proved nomenclaturally too much for him—the time, during his sophomore year, when he was dating a Simmons College girl whose name was Radcliffe.

Harvard has aspired to be nice to everybody, regardless of his name. In the waiting room outside the office of the dean of the College is an old-fashioned glass cookie jar, vigilantly replenished. During the 1969 sit-in, it was removed to another part of the building, and all the cookies were consumed. (Under the moral code of the new revolutionaries, it is all right to appropriate food from the enemy without permission, but wrong to accept it if proffered. Thus, when late in April there was an all-night "study-in" at the Harvard Law School library, and the administration came around with coffee and doughnuts, the students who accepted them were charged with having been co-opted.) During the 1968 spring term, not long after some *Crimson* editors had dropped in there for one of their frequents chats with Dean Glimp, the paper ran (without dissent) an editorial in *favor* of paternalism—surely one of the wonders of present-day campus journalism. "Paternalism is not *always* a good administrative policy," the editorial went. "Some day the Ad Board's paternalism may become dangerous—but right now it looks better than any alternative." Some students were suspicious of the deferential kindness shown them (though certainly not the freshman who, seized with a writing block just before a paper was due, was saved by a couple of assistant deans, who all but wrote it for him); they wondered if the tender loving care they got might not be a kind of opiate administered to keep them calm. But others seemed to like it. What made them especially resentful when the police moved in, on April 9, was that by summoning the uncompromising outsiders the administration had betrayed these student's simple faith in the paternalism of the institution.

Harvard not only often demonstrates its concern for individual students—those, that is, to whose plight it is privy—but it periodically demonstrates an anonymous, catchall concern for Harvardmankind. Twice a year, the College runs what is known as its Exam Rescuing Service. If a student misses a mid-year or final exam without a valid excuse, he can be dunned $250—roughly, the tuition charge for a half-course. Exams last three hours. Morning exams begin at 9:15 and afternoon exams at 2:15. No one may be admitted later than 10:45 or 3:45. After that, he could conceivably get help from a friend who had breezed through in the first hour and a half and could help him do the same in the time remaining. The instant an exam starts, attendance is taken, absences are noted, and the names of the missing are phoned to the office of Robert Shenton, the University registrar. "I never can understand how anyone can sleep through an exam," Shenton says. "I was always up all night myself. But I guess students are more casual now."

His office isn't casual. Within forty minutes or so it has a list compiled of unexcused and inexplicable absences, broken down by houses and dormitories. When a morning exam is on, proctors and senior tutors call in at 10:00 sharp, and are given the names in their areas. The Rescuing Service is under way. A proctor will leave his room at 10:07, and, striding swiftly to a student's room, awaken the sleeping booby at 10:12. By 10:15 the student is both conscious enough and clothed enough to run out—often running his saviour down—and get to the scene of his exam by 10:20. He has thus missed only one third of the time allotted him, and is in no trouble; most Harvard students can easily knock off a C-minus in two-thirds of the time it might have taken them to get a more glittering mark. The most souls saved by the Rescuing Service on any single day was four; that day was all the more memorable because one of the four later sent the Registrar's Office a box of candy. It cost him a good deal less than $250.

At Harvard, as elsewhere, one can of course get out of taking an exam if one has a legitimate reason, and at exam time the doctors at the University Health Services have a lot of traffic. The U.H.S. is one of the few divisions of Harvard that deals with the entire University, and it is situated in the geographical heart of it, occupying several floors (one devoted to an infirmary) in Holyoke Center, a Harvard building that since 1961 has been an ornament of Harvard Square. The U.H.S. is not acquainted with every Harvard man. Physical exams used to be compulsory for undergraduates, but were dropped in 1965, partly because Harvard's doctors reasoned that the boys Harvard admits are likely to have grown up with their health pretty well supervised, and partly because there was a yearly saving of twenty-five thousand dollars involved. Annual check-ups are still de rigueur for undergraduates indulging in contact sports and for students in the Law and Medical schools. Law students are thought to need special stamina, and medical students get exposed to people with infectious diseases.

The U.H.S. is staffed by twelve full-time physicians, who are permitted to see private patients on the side, and it has practitioners in all the major specialties except urology, gynecology, and obstetrics. It is one of the few medical facilities around that has no difficulty recruiting attractive young nurses; even when it isn't exam time, seven hundred Harvard students stop by on an average day. Doctors find the U.H.S. medically interesting. Dr. Curtis Prout, the chief of medical services, saw one case of malaria (and failed to recognize it) in twenty years of private practice. In Harvard practice, he saw seven cases in a single year. Harvard Medical School students come by to have a look at diseases they might otherwise not glimpse—measles, mumps, chickenpox, and infectious mononucleosis, which has plagued college campuses for years and about which Dr. Prout is internationally recognized as an expert. (He has a hunch that this disease, which was once believed to be psychosomatic, especially at exam time, is actually a virus-transmitted ailment that hits college students hard because of their comparatively privileged upbringing. Few slum children get it when they're grown up; he suspects that most of them had it as kids.) Dr. Prout has other specialties; for more than twenty years, he had the honor of escorting the oldest alumnus who turned up on Commencement Day, and when the Harvard football team has a home game, he takes a portable resuscitator to the stadium.

So many Harvard people travel to so many remote, challenging, and unhygienic corners of the globe—there is always some anthropologist sharing a native's cave somewhere—that among Dr. Prout's associates at U.H.S. is one gastroenterologist who gives a non-credit course for prospective travelers, on self-medication. "What to do when the doctor never comes" is its theme. Dean Glimp got a gastroenterological briefing by the Health Services before he went to Mexico City to cheer on Harvard's Olympic crew, but deans can be as absent-minded as professors; while his wife was still unpacking, she heard a dread noise from the bathroom, and got there too late to stop her husband from downing a hefty swig of tap water.

For the most part, though, the administrators try to listen to what the doctors say to them. In recent years, the U.H.S. physicians have even had an impact on the curriculum. They have persuaded the Faculty of Arts and Sciences that there are students who should be exempt from language requirements because they suffer from strephosymbolia—an affliction that makes it difficult for some individuals, no matter how capable they may be in every other respect, to see the ends of written words in unfamiliar languages.

It may be indicative of campus trends that the director of the University Health Services, like his counterparts at Denver, Illinois, and the Austin branch of the University of Texas, is a psychiatrist. The Harvard incumbent is Dr. Dana L. Farnsworth, who in 1954 moved upriver from a similar job at M.I.T. He is also chairman of Harvard's University Committee on Environmental Health and Safety. (It does not do much, but its mere existence is reassuring.) Dr. Farnsworth is a man of firm views. He disapproves of boxing, considering it neither healthful nor safe, and soon after his arrival at Harvard persuaded the faculty to eliminate it as an authorized sport. (One of the weirder footnotes to the S.D.S. invasion of University Hall involved a student who, before Dean Glimp left the premises, insisted that he wanted to talk to him about boxing. Mr. Glimp was in no mood for such a dialogue at such a time, and what the student had in mind will probably never be known.) Dr. Farnsworth disapproves of messiness, too, but, being unable in these times to do much about *that*, confines himself to private reflections like "It depresses me to see how many people express their feelings by letting their personal appearance deteriorate."

Not long after coming to Harvard, Farnsworth was almost singlehandedly responsible for getting a grant from the National Institute of Mental Health for a ten-year study called "The College as a Social System and the Psychosocial Development of its Students." In 1959, a group of researchers, mostly psychologists and sociologists, were assembled by the University Health Services, given the name "Harvard Student Survey," and turned loose. They wanted to find out all anyone could about a specific group of students—their feelings about the faculty, their religious convictions, their dating habits, and so on—by interviewing them at regular intervals as they went through four years of college. Some members of the faculty at first objected to the survey. They were afraid that it might impose too heavy a burden on the student participants, and they were also afraid that if it succeeded some social scientist would propose a sequel called the Harvard Faculty Survey.

The classes that graduated in 1964 and 1965 were the ones scrutinized. (Earlier, a somewhat less comprehensive study had been made of the class of 1940, among whose members was John F. Kennedy. The results of this study comprise one of the few bits of Kennedyana that may never end up in his Memorial Library; although this will be at Harvard, the Health Services won't yield up its data because doing so might constitute a violation of confidentiality.) The findings of the survey are being prepared now for publication. One general conclusion the men in charge of it seem to have reached is that—opinions about the non-conformity of most college students to the contrary—the majority of Harvard undergraduates are really quite square when they enter college, and as each year goes by they get measurably squarer. If rebelliousness and squareness are antithetical, a breakdown by classes of the students arrested at University Hall in the spring of 1969 would seem to confirm the psychologists' conclusions. There were thirty-three freshmen, thirty-four sophomores, thirty-two juniors, and only sixteen seniors.

In addition to Dr. Farnsworth, the University Health Services has seven full-time psychiatrists on its staff, a varying number of part-time psychiatrists, and three psychologists, most of whom show a commendable concern for their own health. Every Tuesday afternoon they try to cripple each other at squash racquets. Since they toil in a world chiefly inhabited by academicians, they inevitably refer to these sweaty jousts as "cardiovascular seminars." Except while the seminars are under way, any Harvard student may walk into the Health Services at any time and get fifteen minutes of psychiatric help. More than five thousand such visits are made each year—some students naturally come more than once—but this does not necessarily mean that Harvard students are in greater need of psychotherapy than most persons. It may mean merely that they are more psychologically sophisticated, or that they come around because they know the psychiatrists are available.

Lately, the psychiatrists have had fewer and fewer visits. Some say this is because the students are getting healthier, others because students are finding Harvard less stressful than their predecessors did. Still others say that the reason is quite simple: students who are on drugs don't want to talk to the psychiatrists about it because they don't trust the doctors not to talk to anyone else. Nobody really knows. Nor does anyone at Harvard really know to what extent drugs are now used there. One thing is known. Every summer, the dean of freshmen asks parents of boys newly admitted to the College to send along, in confidence, any information about their sons that they think might help Harvard handle them. Two years ago, for the first time in Harvard's history, parents began reporting that their sons were on drugs.

Some presumably knowledgeable Harvard officials assert that 20 per cent of the students have tried drugs at least once. The figure seems low. To many—and quite possibly most—Harvard undergraduates (and to more than a few graduate students and faculty members), smoking marijuana has become as commonplace as drinking beer, and on the whole more pleasurable. Harvard Square, however, is not observably the milling hub of drug traffic that some romanticizers have claimed it to be. It is true that a few stores there peddle such wicked-sounding wares as whiskey-flavored chewing gum and Martini-flavored toothpicks, but the basic impression one gets from hanging around the area any length of time is that if there is any one kind of consumable to which the indigenes are addicted, it is ice-cream cones.

One not terribly scientific poll has been taken on drug usage. A student preparing a thesis for a social-relations course passed out questionnaires at mid-term registration time in the winter of 1968. He collected 1,940 filled-in forms. From these, he calculated that 50 per cent of Harvard freshmen from private schools, and 35 per cent from public schools, were acquainted with marijuana. Eleven per cent of the private-school boys and 7 per cent of those from public schools had tried something stronger. Eighty per cent of all undergraduates concentrating in social relations said they smoked pot; among scientists and mathematicians, only 20 per cent said they did. What it all comes down to is that at Harvard drug-users are apt to assert that everybody is on the stuff, which is untrue, and non-users that they are hardly aware of the presence of drugs, which is equally false.

Harvard became involuntarily prominent on the drug scene because of Timothy Leary, who spent two years and three months there between 1960 and 1963. He had no tenure. He was an academic nonentity—holding short-term appointments as a lecturer in clinical psychology. Nothing infuriates the Harvard administration more than to have him described, as he often is, as a "former Harvard professor." (A high-placed *Crimson* editor, less than a year after his graduation, called Leary a "former Harvard professor" in the *Village Voice*. It doesn't take long to forget what you learned at college.) Leary was fired, along with an associate, Richard Alpert, when they used undergraduates in drug experiments after they had promised they wouldn't. Leary had his revenge, in a way; he subsequently described a Harvard education as a "dangerous narcotic and addictive drug."

Leary's downfall at Harvard resulted in part from the *Crimson's* nagging coverage of his activities. The editor who dogged his heels was a versatile member of the class of 1963, Andrew T. Weil, who as an undergraduate had already demonstrated a flair for unconventionality by getting himself elected to the boards of both the *Crimson* and the *Lampoon*, which is analogous to achieving kinship with both Hatfields and McCoys. On entering Harvard, Weil wanted to be a writer and picked an unusual field of concentration—linguistics and psychology. He had to give that up because the heads of those departments weren't on speaking terms. Then he switched to the biological sciences, and after graduating from the College entered the Harvard Medical School. (He graduated from that in 1968 and became an intern in San Francisco.) As a second-year Medical School man, he led a student revolt against the curriculum; he was one of five men who, possibly to keep them out of their professors' hair, were given permission to teach themselves.

Earlier, as a college senior, Weil had studied botany under Richard Schultes and written a paper on the use of nutmeg as a narcotic. "I got a kick out of the Botanical Museum," Weil said. "It's so remote from the rest of the University that practically no one at Harvard seems to realize the people there knew a great deal about drugs before anyone else began thinking about them." Weil always seemed to find time to indulge in a variety of interests. He ranged the spectrum of the University more broadly than most individuals. While a senior in the medical school, he taught creative writing in the college, and for the Institute of Politics of the Kennedy School of Government he conducted a non-credit seminar on "Political Responsibilities of the Medical Profession." In connection with this, he arranged a debate on medical lobbying between the dean of the Harvard Medical School and the head of the legislative bureau of the American Medical Association.

In the summer of 1966, Weil presented a paper on nutmeg to a meeting of the National Institute of Mental Health. That research project got him to thinking how little recorded experimentation there was to be found on marijuana. Only three times, it appeared, had there been any truly scientific inquiry into its effects on human beings. One dated all the way back to 1933, and the most recent one was of 1946 vintage. Weil decided to put together the protocol for some experiments, but, being only a medical student, he needed a faculty sponsor. The choice was easy— Dr. Norman E. Zinberg, a psychiatrist who teaches an undergraduate course, "Medicine and Society," for the Faculty of Arts and Sciences (Weil had somehow also found time to serve as one of his section men) and who was well versed in drugs. Dr. Zinberg was delighted to join up. Some of the questions they hoped to find answers to were: Were people more easily distracted after they smoke pot? Did their blood-sugar levels actually change, as had often been contended? Were the pupils of their eyes enlarged, or could this perhaps be the result merely of smoking in a dim-lit room and staring fixedly at other people?

But while the dean of the Medical School, Robert H. Ebert, was sympathetic, his superiors in the Harvard hierarchy were far from happy about the prospect of getting involved in further drug experimentation. Leary had made Harvard leery. The University consulted its lawyers, who observed that it is illegal in Massachusetts to give anyone marijuana except, in certain circumstances, to relieve pain and suffering, and who wondered what would happen if, say, a human guinea pig got into an automobile accident a week after taking part in an experiment and blamed Harvard for whatever condition he was in. In a characteristically paternalistic gesture, at the same time that Harvard consulted its own lawyers, it offered to pay for the lawyers Weil had retained to argue his side of the matter.

While Harvard dragged its feet, Weil got Boston University to put an academic imprimatur on his project, and after protracted negotiations he also got the Federal Bureau of Narcotics to give him some marijuana its agents had confiscated. (There was always the ironic possibility, he reflected, that the pot he got had earlier been seized from Timothy Leary.) After that, the experiments went on without too much trouble; Weil's main difficulty was finding a particular sort of person around Cambridge whom he needed for his work—someone who had never smoked marijuana.

He finally rounded up nine such people. His findings were that non-marijuana-smokers were not notably affected by exposure to it (there was some distraction among them, but no marked changes in blood sugar or eyes) and that the drug was a "relatively mild intoxicant with minor, real, short-lived effects." Moreover, he checked up on the nine individuals who through him had their first taste of pot, and learned that six months after the experiment only two of them had touched the stuff again, and then just once apiece. Weil concluded, among other things, that "we need not fear the moral implications of giving naive persons their first marijuana experience, a factor that is very important to future research on the subject." The mimeograph machines of the public-relations office of the Harvard Medical School, which usually clank into action when anybody affiliated with that institution does anything of any consequence, were silent.

A retired dean, with something close to nostalgia: "In the old days, they never thought about students' rights. You pulled a guy in, told him he'd been caught doing something de flagrante, and threw him out, and there was no talk of his retaining outside counsel. We had riots, sure, but mostly they were about the Princeton game, and when you fired a guy there were no moral or political overtones."

XV

THE UNIVERSITY HEALTH SERVICES psychiatrists keep in close touch with another Harvard agency, called the Bureau of Study Counsel, which seeks to help students who find themselves in academic difficulties. Their woes, after all, may have emotional roots. The Bureau evolved in 1945 from a couple of older agencies: a Committee on the Use of English by the Students, which the faculty had established to improve the caliber of Harvard writing; and a Bureau of Supervisors, which the administration had paternalistically established to help students cram after, at the prodding of the *Crimson*, it had run private tutoring schools out of town. At the end of the Second World War, a psychologist, William G. Perry, Jr., was running these two outfits and a speed-reading program as well. The University incorporated all three into the Bureau of Study Counsel, and Perry has had charge of that ever since. "I've had a wonderful opportunity to look over students' shoulders as they try to get a liberal education," he says.

The psychiatrists also get together from time to time for

lunch with the Administrative Board and other officials, to discuss students in trouble. Not long ago, twenty-four busy Harvard men—the dean of the College, the dean of students, the University preacher, the chief of the University police, a half dozen psychiatrists, and assorted deans, tutors, and proctors—spent a two-hour lunch exclusively and compassionately discussing the case of a single student who had behaved so atrociously—among other campus capers, he had been caught with drugs, had been caught with girls at the wrong hours, and, worst of all, had been caught underlining library books—that there were ample grounds for booting him out unceremoniously. The forty-eight man-hours devoted to him at that meeting represented only a fraction of the time that some of the assembled men had spent on him altogether. One of the participants said afterward that as the session went on, a strange pattern of behavior began to emerge. The psychiatrists present, who didn't know the fellow, were for handling him firmly, and even toughly. The administrators present, who did know him, were for handling him gently. Perhaps, one of them had even suggested tentatively, his rebellious actions had been triggered by his house master's penchant for playing the bagpipes.

Finally the administrators, in whose hands the boy's fate ultimately lay, decided to adopt a wait-and-see attitude toward him. Maybe he would turn over a new leaf, they said, more in hope than expectation. At that, the senior psychiatrist present, Dr. Karl Binger, who had attained emeritus standing at Harvard, was moved to exclaim, "I don't know why it is, but on occasions like this psychiatrists seem to behave the way administrators are supposed to, and administrators behave like psychiatrists."

Over the years, the best attended of all Health Services lunches have been those during which the doctors discuss undergraduates' sex lives. The U.H.S. has fewer formal responsibilities in that area now than it used to; until 1935, it was in charge of a course on sex education that was compulsory for freshmen, who called it "Smut One." When the doctor who actually gave the course retired, his colleagues hastily retired the course. By then, they had just about decided that there was very little, in any event, that the faculty could teach the students about sex.

What the doctors say among themselves on that subject is, of course, discreetly guarded. It is known, though, that when one of them heard about a Radcliffe girl who promised a male instructor that she would do anything, *anything*, for a good mark, and the curious physician looked up her scholastic record, he found that she never seemed to get any grades except straight A's or straight D's. Not long ago, Dr. Prout spoke on Harvard health to a Harvard Club gathering in the south. There was a question period. The first question came from a woman who said she had heard about all the orgies and drug sessions in Cambridge; would he please expatiate on them. "I hear about them all the time myself," Dr. Prout replied, "but nobody ever invites me. Next question, please."

THE REVELATION in the winter of 1969 that Radcliffe would in the not too distant future cease to exist as a quasi-independent entity and become a full-fledged part of Harvard did not surprise many people around Cambridge. A few months earlier, Dr. George F. Berry had visited the place. The retired dean of the Harvard Medical School, he was looking into coeducation for Princeton, many of whose alumni seemed to view with horror that institution's losing its all-male status. There were, of course, some Harvard alumni, particularly the older ones, who had not yet even adjusted to the idea of girls in classrooms, let alone in dormitories or dining halls; but Dr. Berry was surprised in Cambridge to find hardly anyone of either sex who did not take coeducation matter-of-factly. He may not have discussed the matter with Professor John Finley, who had recently retired as master of Eliot House, an exclusively masculine—in theory, at least—residential complex. Musing on the likelihood of mixed living, Professor Finley said, "I'm not quite sure people want to have crystalline laughter falling like a waterfall down each

232

entry of the house at all hours. I should think it would be a little disturbing if you were taking advanced organic chemistry." But, these days, scratch an advanced organic chemist and you are apt to *find* a girl.

Before the merger talks, too, the relationship between Harvard men and women had been by no means mainly social, though when the two groups converged it was often for more than a meeting of minds. The girls are generally thought to be smarter than the boys, in part because there are fewer of them— only three hundred in each class. The disparity in numbers between the twelve hundred women and forty-eight hundred men in the total undergraduate population was one aspect of the merger that worried the Harvard Corporation when it addressed itself to that subject. The Corporation eventually took the position that, whatever happened, there were to be no fewer males than when the union went into effect. But then the problem at once arose: if admissions to the new bisexual Harvard were coordinated, how could the College maintain a ratio favorable to males without being liable to charges of violating the Civil Rights Act of 1964, which enjoins institutions from making sexual distinctions? Harvard's lawyers, who in the old days didn't have to bother themselves with that sort of thing, were at once asked to ascertain whether it was legally possible for the College to welcome women without immediately afterward being accused of spurning them.

Many of the Radcliffe girls are femmes formidables. Cambridge has it share of muggers and other threats to public safety, but one of the gravest dangers a visitor faces is being run down at night by a Radcliffe girl tearing along a sidewalk on a bicycle without lights. The girls can hold their own in tough company. At a cocktail party for Boston's professional football team, the Patriots, one of the players was moved to exclaim, "Women— you can't live with 'em and you can't live without 'em!" A Radcliffe girl turned a steely eye on him and said, "That's not original, but it is debatable." He collapsed as though clipped.

Some Radcliffe girls insist that they go to the spring under-graduate sprees at Fort Lauderdale not as frolickers but as sociological observers. Probably 80 per cent of the girls, not as sociological observers, date Harvard boys. The Harvard Dramatic Club has backstage lackeys who are called "Mini-techies"—Radcliffe freshmen who, according to a paper submitted in a social-relations course not long ago, are equally interested in building flats and building acquaintanceships, "both of which they usually accomplish, though often to their detriment." The report added, "No onus is connected with studying, provided one meets theatrical commitments."

For each new Harvard class, a *Register* is published; it reveals the hometown and school background of every freshman, and it also carries his picture. Among Radcliffe freshmen, it enjoys almost Biblical stature. The Radcliffe novitiates have a similar register. Some Harvard boys conduct ugliness contests from its pages—in only rare instances, happily, notifying the winners. Far less than 80 per cent of Harvard boys take out Radcliffe girls. For one thing, there aren't enough girls around. For another, as one of the girls has put it, "We don't build up their egos the way other girls do." The *Lampoon* once invented a campus organization called the Radcliffe Association for the Suppression of the Male Ego.

The cover of the official Radcliffe catalogue has its own viewpoint. A photograph on it shows the face of a fetching blonde, presumably a Radcliffe girl, and the back of the head of a boy, presumably a Harvard student. He is looking at her. She is looking over his shoulder. One Harvard definition of the typical Radcliffe girl has it that when she drops her glove, and you gallantly stoop to pick it up for her, she steps on your hand and says "That's mine."

Showing some visitors around the Yard, a Harvard senior passed one of the older buildings where classes are held, and remarked that a portion of the ceiling had not long before collapsed. "There were no casualties," he went on. "None of the hardheaded Cliffies would have noticed anyway." But then, with the beguiling inconsistency of the young, he said, "It is always a worthwhile experience taking out Radcliffe girls. They're enjoyable as people even when they're not as women. Their main trouble is that they often don't realize that Harvard boys are like anyone else and sometimes want to relax. One thing you can be sure of with a Radcliffe girl: she's bound to be intelligent. And if you run into one who's also modest, attractive, and feminine, you've got something rare."

Some Harvard boys, who see Radcliffe girls every day in class, carelessly dressed and without makeup, find it hard to think of them romantically. "We just accept them as boys," a *Crimson* editor put it, quickly editing himself and adding, "We just accept them as though they were boys." Harvard boys who feel that way consider Radcliffe girls daily working partners; their weekend dress-up girls are apt to come from Wellesley. Radcliffe girls, for their part, pity Wellesley girls. "I have no friends at Wellesley or Smith or any of those isolated places who are happy," a Radcliffe senior said. "They have this sickly feminine palship, as if they were endlessly playing girls' basketball. An all-female school is a place you go to during the week and pray to get away from over the weekend. The reason is simple enough. Women don't like women."

There are certain differences other than the obvious ones between most Radcliffe girls and most Harvard boys: a newsletter put out by the Radcliffe Union of Students, for instance, listed addresses of Navy men in Vietnam seeking pen pals. Radcliffe girls are much more serious, all in all, about their work. "Harvard people are always saying to me, 'Why are you so uptight about this paper or that exam?' " one Radcliffe senior said. " 'By the time you got to be a junior, for God's sake, you should have learned the ropes and been able to figure out a way to psych out.' " One way of spotting a gut course at Harvard, some of the boys contend, is to see how many girls sign up for it; the easier the course, as a rule, the fewer the girls in it. In class, the girls generally stay awake. One of them even went to Chapel daily until she married a Harvard boy.

It is illustrative of how radically Harvard has changed in its attitude toward women that there used to be a rule that they *couldn't* go to chapel. The bars were lowered because of the intransigence of Harvard's first full-time lady professor in Arts and Sciences, the British medieval historian Helen Maud Cam. (Earlier, the celebrated toxicologist Dr. Alice Hamilton, who observed her hundredth birthday in the winter of 1969, had been appointed an assistant professor at the Medical School.) On arriving at Cambridge in 1948 and turning up for morning services, Professor Cam was told she would have to sit behind a screen. She retorted that she had a faculty appointment as bona fide as any other professor's, and that she would brook no discrimination. At the end of the nineteenth century, Harvard was suspicious of ladies of all ages. Haverford, in the eighteen-eighties had a woman chairing its math department. It wanted her to take some graduate courses at Harvard, but President Eliot said no; it would be unsuitable to have women attending classes with men.

But even then chinks had begun developing in the dam of resistance. In 1879, a Society for the Collegiate Instruction of Women was founded in Cambridge. That was a memorable year for Harvard—being the year also that the University welcomed its first Chinese faculty member. A lawyer imported from China to teach a commercial language course, he was the first Chinese on any American faculty. He succumbed to the raw Occidental climate of New England in 1882, and Harvard was so discouraged it didn't add another Chinese to its ranks until 1921.

Radcliffe survived, quickly becoming known as the Harvard Annex, and, in 1894, as Radcliffe College—named in honor of the Englishwoman Lady Anne Radcliffe, an early benefactress of Harvard. The idea behind the new institution was that Harvard instructors could earn some extra money—this increment became known as "the Radcliffe mark-up"—by trudging the half mile or so to the girls' school and repeating certain courses there. President Eliot had no objection to his faculty's teaching women provided it was on separate premises; indeed, he used the mark-up as a recruiting inducement.

This emolument was paid only if a minimum number of students enrolled for a course. When one professor found himself a student shy, he had his wife enroll. It cost him a hundred dollars, but otherwise he'd have been out eight hundred. As soon as his wife had registered, he assured his legitimate students she'd never show up again, and she didn't. Some senior Harvard professors enjoyed teaching girls (others went along solely for the mark-up), among them Arthur M. Schlesinger, Sr., who kept telling them that American history had ignored the role in it of American women. After his death, Radcliffe honored his wife and him by establishing, appropriately, an Arthur and Elizabeth Schlesinger Library on the History of Women in America.

Other professors, however, deplored the intrusion of women, even while segregated, into their academic world. Whatever scholars may think of the Harvard library's classification system, it made sense that a treatise entitled *Harvard Attitudes Toward Radcliffe in the Early Years* was catalogued under "HUH." Barrett Wendell, who taught so many Harvard men to write decent English, was one of the most outspoken misogynists. In 1899, when Harvard announced that additional courses would be available to women, he wrote, "If the practice continue and increase, then, there seems a likelihood that Harvard may suddenly find itself committed to coeducation, somewhat as unwary men lay themselves open to actions for breach of promise." It was the Harvard tradition, Professor Wendell argued, that its environment should be "purely virile," and "a man who likes to teach women is in real danger of infatuation." He had a point there; a number of senior men on the Harvard faculty today have wives who used to be their students.

Coeducation finally arrived, informally, in 1943, and the relationship between Harvard and Radcliffe was formalized in 1946. Since 1963, Radcliffe girls have been getting Harvard degrees, and 88 per cent of the tuition that Radcliffe students pay goes straight into the Harvard Treasury. Radcliffe has no faculty of its own. All that it provides for its students is their room and board and a few fringe benefits like the extracurricular activities sponsored by its Office of Sports, Dance, and Recreation. It has its own governing board (with a generous sprinkling of Harvard governors on it), and it still has a separate charter (because of which it describes itself merely as being "closely associated with Harvard"), but it is, essentially, a college within Harvard University, and its president, Mrs. Mary I. Bunting, thinks of herself as a Harvard dean. "To me, Harvard has lots of parts," she says, "and Radcliffe functions as one of them."

A few of the old-timers on the Harvard faculty still have occasional misgivings about the sister institution. "I was asked to speak at a Phi Beta Kappa function, and I had a charming bawdy ditty I was going to sing," one professor said, "but I had to bowdlerize it when I discovered there were sixteen Phi Betes from Radcliffe present. It was quite inhibiting, and the antiseptic version really didn't go over at all. Too bad girls have to be so bright." President Pusey, though, thought that Radcliffe's close association with Harvard brought to Harvard a degree of social maturity that would not otherwise have been attained.

Radcliffe and Harvard had been getting closer all the time. They began to coordinate their admissions procedures in 1969 (Radcliffe appointed as its dean of admissions a man, who had formerly been director of the Harvard admissions office), and they would probably have long since coordinated their Commencements if Harvard had had space enough to accommodate all the parents and friends involved. Mr. Pusey used to dread the day when Radcliffe girls would ask for joint Commencements and he would be unable to think of any logical argument against it. The girls were bound to ask. They had become increasingly militant; there was a strange, old-fashioned suffragette quality to many of them, as if they thought that women still had to fight for their rights. They kept reminding everybody that women are as intelligent as men, though most people were perfectly willing to concede that the women may well be more intelligent. They went on hunger strikes, to protest Radcliffe's limitations on off-campus living; they put on a demonstration against the war in Vietnam during their 1968 Commencement; and some of the Negroes among them staged a 1969 sit-in that convinced Mrs. Bunting she should try to get more black students and a black admissions officer. Being female, the activists have also demonstrated in favor of Saturday-night milk and cookies.

Mrs. Bunting became president of Radcliffe in 1960, following a stint in Washington as an Atomic Energy Commissioner. A microbiologist by profession, she is a comfortable, genial woman with high ideals and a laudable desire to be everybody's friend. "She lunches with her girls and agrees with their views and they think she's given them the key to the fort when she was just trying to be nice," one of her older acquaintances says. "Then her governing board has to bail her out. Also, she thinks of Radcliffe as a hothouse for the forced propagation of professional females, instead of a place where intelligent women can get a background that will enable them, as ordinary human beings, to lead a broad intellectual life. Radcliffe always seems to be proudest of those of its graduates who enter and finish medical school." Ten percent of recent Radcliffe graduates have done just that, some of them conceivably influenced in their choice of careers by having played field hockey against the Harvard Medical School.

Mrs. Bunting, who worked for the National Science Foundation before going to the A.E.C., is unarguably interested in professional women. One of her proudest achievements is the establishment of a Radcliffe Institute, which spends a quarter of a million dollars annually to provide opportunities for forty or so middle-life resident ladies to take courses or write a book or compose a symphony—"mothers as part-time scholars," says an Institute brochure, "or other talented women whose plans are complicated by early marriage." The Institute scholars meet for lunch once a week (Radcliffe's endowment being only thirty million dollars, they bring their own sandwiches), and Radcliffe is proud of the intellectual interaction that flourishes among them. "Why, when Anne Sexton was at the Institute she got so fascinated with what a fellow scholar had to say about amber that she wrote a poem about amber," a Radcliffe official said. Each year, moreover, the Institute underwrites the advanced studies of a couple of dozen women doctors.

Mrs. Bunting's principal concern, naturally, has been with her twelve hundred undergraduates, and there has been no doubt in her mind where they stood with respect to Harvard. She is fond of recalling that at her investiture Mr. Pusey said he couldn't altogether comprehend the Harvard-Radcliffe relationship; he just knew that he liked it. What Mrs. Bunting liked was that whenever she herself would come out and say anything critical about her girls, Harvard boys would rise to their defense. "It's a very nice feeling of affection," she said. The girls defend the boys, too, or at any rate man the barricades alongside them. Nearly one third of the individuals arrested after the University Hall seizure were women. A Harvard senior said afterward, "There were more beautiful girls there than at any other Harvard function I've ever been to. One of them lent me a book to read. It was *Cuba: Anatomy of a Revolution*. The thing that worried me most about many of them was their ego-building. They seemed to spend half the time congratulating themselves on what they were doing."

HARVARD PROFESSORS are often academic gallivanters. Some seem to have a seminar in every port. But few of them are fickle. Returning to Cambridge after a few weeks as a guest lecturer at the California Institute of Technology, a senior Harvard scientist told a colleague, "It was all serene and ideal out there, but I kept thinking, what the hell is wrong with this place? Then I realized: It doesn't have Harvard Square." It is amazing in a way that the Square should have any grip on anyone's affections. It doesn't even have an honest name, to begin with, being an asymmetrical junction of thoroughfares embracing an island that contains a subway entrance and a newsstand. It is usually snarled with traffic, and often looks as though streetcleaners had boycotted it. Some of the stores that flank the streets that lead to it are seedy, and the principal characteristic of the personalities nostalgically associated with it is raffishness—a second-hand clothing-dealer, for instance, and an itinerant fruit-peddler who clinched his niche in history by translating the Harvard motto *Veritas* as "The hell with Yale."

Notwithstanding, the words *Harvard Square* have attained a certain radiance. Stores half a mile away from the Square profess to be located on it, and so does the Hotel Continental, which is across the Cambridge Common and invisible from Harvard Square. Actually, the hotel is closer to General Douglas MacArthur Square, a minor traffic island embellished by a statue not of MacArthur but of Senator Charles Sumner, and a spot of historical interest not because of General MacArthur but because General George Washington took command of the Continental Army a few yards away. Few members of the Harvard community ever glance at Sumner's statue, and fewer still are even aware that MacArthur Square exists. If some of them were, they'd probably picket it.

The Harvard Yard abuts Harvard Square, as do dozens of commercial establishments, ranging from banks to psychedelic-food shops to a drugstore with wall clocks that give the time for, among cities presumably of interest to Harvard patrons, Seattle, Moscow, Karachi, and Ngulu. A nearby typewriter store is prepared to sell machines that can handle Brazilian, Turkish, Hebrew, and Polish. The Crimson Travel Service advertises itself with the delightful slogan, "Please Go Away." The most prominent mart is the Harvard Cooperative Society, called for short the Coop. It has annual sales of twelve million dollars, most of these coming out of Harvard pockets. Harvard students are sometimes thought nowadays to spend more of their loose cash on phonograph records than on any other single commodity. (That may be one reason why they are partial to Dutch-treat dates.) When the Beatles' "Sergeant Pepper" album was released in 1966, at final-exam time, the Coop announced that a shipment would arrive on a Saturday. The albums came in a day early, and although there was no further announcement beyond a window placard that said IT'S HERE! hundreds of students—exams or no exams—soon lined up in impatient and expectant queues.

The Harvard Cooperative Society, the Harvard Trust Company, and the Harvard Square Theatre are all patronized by Harvard men. Few students, however, make much use of the Harvard Bar and Grill. That, at least, has a rightful claim to its name, being authentically on the Square. The University finds itself at odds with other establishments and institutions, some of them quite far-flung, that believe the use of the word *Harvard* will magically increase their sales. In 1891, the genuine Harvard was distressed by a real-estate development called Harvard Park on a mountain in Virginia.

The existence of businesses that few college graduates would be likely to think have anything to do with Harvard—in New York City, among others, the Harvard Shoe Repairing Shop and the Harvard Bed Frame Distributors—does not ruffle the University's composure. In 1969, though, it was upset enough by another New York outfit that was advertising in the *Wall Street Journal* and sounded as though it might have some link to Cambridge—the Harvard Executive Research Center—to get court injunction against it. The Center, which was run by a Harvard College graduate who had also gone to the Harvard Business School, inserted into its ads the self-defeating disclaimer "We are not connected with Harvard University." The Cambridge Harvard did nothing to discourage the use by a consistently winning trotting horse of the name "Harvard"; but if the horse had proved to be a second-rater, that might have been something else again.

On Friday and Saturday nights, Harvard Square is a rendezvous for high-school kids from nearby communities, some of them pseudo-Hell's-Angels types, who stand around and act tough and shout at passing cars. Now and then there is a fight. Hippies, too, have found the area congenial, especially in warm weather. Asked one time how many hippies there were at Harvard, a University psychiatrist said, "I don't think there are many, because it is part of the hippie philosophy *not* to be at Harvard." The chief of the Harvard police, asked another time whether many Harvard people turned up at hippie gatherings, said, "I don't think you'll find a gathering of any sort anywhere in the Eastern United States *without* a Harvard man in it."

The hippies have become especially attracted to an open plaza in front of Holyoke Center. A prominent feature of a meeting area in the penthouse of the Center is an abstract mural by Mark Rothko. Its drippy presence on the wall there drives some of the conservative elder Harvard statesmen who convene there right up the wall. Rothko, for his part, thought the Harvard atmosphere was thoroughly depressing. "After working in Cambridge for a few days and going to all those horrible Faculty Club lunches I found the air shuttle to New York didn't give me time enough to regain my composure," he says. "So I took to going back by train. I'd get on the sleeper with a bottle of Scotch and by the next morning I would just about have recovered from Harvard." A prominent feature of the plaza leading to Holyoke Center is a shady elm with a bench beneath it for footsore passersby. President Nathan Pusey has never shown himself to be especially fond of hippies, but he is fond of trees. "What a joy it has been to plant trees in Harvard Square, and rows of them along Dunster and Holyoke Streets!" he said in an exclamatory mood in one of his annual reports. Alas, how could he have forseen that his stately Holyoke Center tree would become a hippie haven!

The oasis where the hippies hang out is called Forbes Plaza. It is named after Edward Waldo Forbes, of the class of 1895. In the 1968 Commencement parade of alumni, he, at ninety-five, in the last year of his life, was the oldest marcher. (He was escorted by his son Elliot, the director of the Harvard Glee Club.) A grandson of Ralph Waldo Emerson, Forbes *père*, between 1909 and 1944, was director of Harvard's Fogg Art Museum, where he was a pioneer in research on forged paintings (Harvard's first-rate collection of fifty fakes, which are never exhibited but used for teaching, includes a splendid phony Van Gogh self-portrait), and where, according to a 1921 tribute paid him by President A. Lawrence Lowell, he "achieved the incredible."

Edward Forbes and his brother, W. Cameron Forbes, were both good to Harvard. Cameron Forbes held three important posts in his lifetime—governor general of the Philippines, United States ambassador to Japan, and coach of the Harvard Varsity Football Team. He was an unusual benefactor. He sent Harvard some wood from the Philippines out of which a huge round table was fashioned for the Faculty Room of the Faculty of Arts and Sciences, and he bequeathed a spacious house with several bizarre features. One was a cocktail bar with a ramp leading to it, so guests could approach on horseback. The University sold the property to a developer before it had made up its mind whether another—a large concavity in a Byzantine bathroom accessible only through a secret door—was a giant tub or a small swimming pool.

As for Edward Waldo Forbes, the hippies' plaza was named after him not for his curatorial distinction but for what Lowell called his "tenacity of purpose" in buying real estate. In 1911, he had cheaply purchased a five-acre farm and several odd lots just off Harvard Square, reckoning that the University, which had never shown much interest in or aptitude for picking up property, would some day need the land, possibly for student housing. Charles W. Eliot was president of Harvard then, and he didn't give much of a rap how students lived; he thought it was the function of the University to educate them, not to shelter them. In 1928, President Lowell, who believed that the way a student lived was very much a part of the educational process, decided to construct residential houses for undergraduates. Without the land that Forbes had prudently picked up seventeen years earlier,

Lowell might not have been able to build any suitably scaled houses within reasonable walking distances of the rest of the College.

Harvard began on 1½ acres of Cambridge farmland. Thanks to Forbes and others, it has considerably enlarged its holdings, but even so it now owns only 142 acres in Cambridge. They are worth about 50 million dollars, and the buildings on them (furnishings and equipment excluded) are worth another 250 million. Harvard has holdings outside the Boston area, but these largely represent gifts. Among them used to be a farm in England that the University sold in 1902 after renting it for 232 years, and among them still is Sutton's Island, off the Maine coast, with a house that faculty families may occupy rent-free, for two weeks during the summer. The University does suggest, though, that each tenant donate twenty-five or fifty dollars toward the upkeep of the island. The Harvard official in charge of the place is in Purchasing—mainly, it seems, because a predecessor in his office came from Maine.

Now, land-poor like so many other institutions, Harvard is building vertically. The residential houses of the Lowell era were five-story walk-ups. The newest residential house has a twenty-one-story tower. Harvard assembled the land for this house by buying dribs and drabs of property and leaving the buildings on them largely as they were until it was ready to demolish them. Many of the old buildings were decrepit apartments that the University rented out, since it wanted them to produce some income. In selecting occupants for these and similar accommodations elsewhere in Cambridge, the University would generally give preference to Harvard people, but it got so tired of their complaints—they would telephone President Pusey's office when the heat went off—that it retained a real-estate company to manage them.

Harvard has not been a happy landlord. Residents of Cambridge unaffiliated with the University have grumbled that because of the University's partiality toward its own constituency they can't find any place to live; others have grumbled that by neglecting maintenance on its properties the University has been acting like a slumlord. In January, 1969, a Radcliffe graduate who was continuing her studies at Harvard in anthropology was murdered in her apartment, in a Harvard-owned building a couple of blocks from Harvard Square. The other tenants said they had been trying for a long time to get the University to put proper locks on their doors (the victim apparently had had trouble locking hers), and they sued the University, unavailingly, for its alleged dereliction.

Harvard and Radcliffe and M.I.T. all together own less than 7 per cent of the land in Cambridge, but some of the other citizens of that community resent their owning anything, because when they acquire property it generally comes off the tax rolls. Tax-exempt though it is—its status dates back to 1650—Harvard has enough property that is used for commercial purposes so that it ranks as Cambridge's second largest taxpayer, being eclipsed only by the Cambridge Gas and Electric Company. Harvard has deliberately put itself in this position. When it built the Holyoke Center, it instructed its architects to design it so that the ground floor could be rented out to business enterprises. Moreover, in 1928, when it bought the property Edward Waldo Forbes had assembled, Harvard decided to give the city of Cambridge a break. The property was assessed at three million dollars, and to remove it from the tax rolls would have hurt the city badly. So Harvard volunteered to take only 20 per cent of the property off the rolls each year, and it further stipulated that on future properties it bought and removed from the rolls it would for twenty years following the acquisition pay the city an annual sum based on the time-of-purchase assessment and the time-of-purchase tax rate.

None of these placatory gestures has fully satisfied the city. Cambridge people tend to be distrustful of any move that Harvard makes concerning property. (So are some Harvard people. S.D.S., for instance, not long ago accused Harvard, with cloudy evidential support, of seeking to expand the Medical School by rendering poor blacks homeless.) A few years ago some Armenians bought a choice lot in a residential area. They planned to put up a church. A group of inhabitants of the area—among them, a couple of Harvard professors—tried to block the Armenians. The church people decided to avail themselves of a local statute that exempted tax-exempt organizations from zoning laws. In the legal proceedings that ensued, Harvard lawyers helped the newcomers. To protect the University in case it some day got into a similar squabble, the lawyers wanted to be sure that the Armenians handled the technicalities properly. But the aroused neighbors took the view that Harvard had chosen to side with a bunch of odd-worshiping foreigners in a showdown with some God-fearing Yankees.

A student conducting a guided tour of the campus:
"I guess the reason I love Harvard so much is the people."

XVI

WHILE A VISITOR IN RESIDENCE at one of the under-graduate houses, Lewis Mumford complimented Cambridge on its vitality and animation; there could be no finer place to live, he said, than within three-quarters of a mile of the Harvard Yard. Many members of the Harvard community live far beyond that radius and are less enamored of the city; indeed, more than 25 per cent of the tenured professors of the Faculty of Arts and Sciences revealed in a recent survey that they found Cambridge geographically unattractive. "The best you can say for it," one of them declared, "is that it has a certain gritty charm." Cambridge has a population of 160,000. Fifteen thousand residents of the city —one-fourth of its labor force—work for Harvard or M.I.T.

In the very best of worlds, town-gown relationships are rarely cozy, and in Cambridge they are often chilly. The two educational institutions used to hold an annual town-gown dinner, so their leaders could break bread and break ice with the community's leaders. At such a gathering in 1959, President Pusey compared Harvard's relationship to Cambridge to a marriage. "Harvard likes Cambridge, and I hope and believe that in her heart of hearts Cambridge likes Harvard," he said.

A marriage? One Cambridge politician has said of Harvard, "You feel you're living with a great big gentle giant who if he rolls over in bed will squash you." There have been no town-gown dinners for the last few years; nobody has had the heart for it, even in his heart of hearts. There is little unanimity in the feelings of the non-academic community toward the gentle giant. A Cambridge barber who one might think would have more reason than most these shaggy days to resent Harvard declared, "This long hair's ruining me, but I love these guys." A mayor of Cambridge, on the other hand, after a minor student riot, demanded a 9:30 curfew for Harvard undergraduates.

The municipal police get on reasonably well with some Harvard people (when the chief of the Cambridge force died, Harvard cops volunteered to direct traffic around the Square, so his men could attend the funeral), but not so well with others. A fire broke out not long ago in a Radcliffe dormitory, triggering a sprinkler system. As a group of girls sloshed out of their rooms, barefoot, a Cambridge cop who had gone to the scene said to them, according to the *Crimson*, "I bet this is the first time you've washed your feet in a week." Students of Harvard history thought there was a simple explanation for the brutality exhibited by some of the city policemen who broke up the University Hall occupation: they had been waiting for 333 years for somebody to invite them to hit Harvard heads.

In 1968, Harvard spent $3.5 million to have a street closed off and an underpass constructed at the north end of the Yard. The idea was to create a pedestrian mall that would link the Yard to graduate-school territory beyond it, and thus physically integrate components of the University. Moreover it was a dangerous street; twenty thousand cars passed along it every day during the same hours that twelve thousand students walked across it. An anti-intellectual taxi driver taking an out-of-town fare through the underpass told him, "They built this thing to keep Harvard boys from being run down because they're too stupid to look before they cross a street. Harvard boys are only good for shoplifting and demonstrating—that's all. Maybe one out of ten of 'em gets an education."

Harvard students sometimes punningly counter by referring

to Cambridge—which along with Harvard Square has other focal points called Central Square and Porter Square—as "a city of squares." There are more serious rifts. Cambridge has a so-so public-school system; Harvard has done little to try to improve it. Only in the last couple of years has the University's Graduate School of Education, which is concerned chiefly with turning out public-school educators and administrators, demonstrated much of a concern for the public schools in its own back yard.

For some years now, a bold-type footnote to the Harvard-Cambridge relationship has been provided by an articulate, prankish local politician named Alfred E. Vellucci, who has a love-hate rapport of awesome intensity with the University. A city councilman from East Cambridge, with a predominantly lower-income Italian-American constituency, Vellucci, who somehow also finds the time to work for the state tax department, has made much of proclaiming that Harvard is just about the worst thing ever to hit Cambridge. "Anybody who would bombard Harvard for two solid years could get elected to the Cambridge City Council on the strength of that alone," he has said at a relatively reflective moment. "When Harvard is for something, I'm against it, just because Harvard is for it." But he also says, "I love Harvard."

In truth, Harvard is his windmill. He'd probably be aghast if any of the anti-Harvard resolutions he is forever introducing to the council were passed. Once he proposed that Harvard move to New Hampshire, another time that it secede from Massachusetts and become an independent city-state. On being asked if there was any hostility behind still another proposal—that the Yard be converted into a bus-and-taxi terminal—he said not at all; why, he would try to get the new installation called the John Harvard Bus and Taxi Terminal. Mr. Vellucci thinks that Harvard's real-estate activities are making it impossible for Cambridge natives to find homes in Cambridge. Asked one time what land he favored Harvard's using for expansion, he said, "Let them tear down the football stadium. Why should they have to play here? They could use the Yale Bowl when nobody else is using it. It's only a hundred and fifty miles away."

Fortunately for Harvard, Vellucci hates Yale worse. He has been down on the New Haven institution ever since a scholar there put forth the hypothesis that America had been discovered by Leif Ericson instead of Christopher Columbus. Since then, Vellucci has been treating the Harvard varsity football team to a free Italian dinner every time it beats, or even ties, Yale. He dislikes Harvard Square. "They've turned it into a combat zone," he says, "with hippies and narcotics users and people of ill repute! Parents won't sent their children to Harvard Square! The great cry in every house of every Cambridge native is, 'Don't go to Harvard Square!'" Nonetheless, he recently proposed changing its name to Christopher Columbus Square, and for St. Patrick's day in 1969 did get it changed to Piazzo Leprechano.

The councilman gets on well enough with President Pusey, who has treated him gingerly. In 1965, Vellucci, then vice-mayor of Cambridge, visited Italy, and revealed he would be stopping by I Tatti, the Bernard Berenson villa at Florence that Berenson left to Harvard. Stopping in was hardly the phrase; Vellucci engaged a horse and carriage and made a flamboyant entrance. Harvard was ready for him. The university had alerted its caretakers at I Tatti to his arrival, and he was royally welcomed. Vellucci, unlike most other Cambridge councilmen, sometimes also attends Harvard Commencements, but he generally makes it clear that this is not to be construed as all-out endorsement of the University. Just before the 1968 graduation ceremonies he announced, characteristically, that he wouldn't be at all surprised if the bricks being used for some new Harvard sidewalks had been stolen from his East Cambridge district.

Harvard has lately indicated that if it cannot have a blissful marriage with Cambridge it would at least like a companionable friendship. For years, the University has prided itself that, unlike most other consequential educational institutions, it had only one vice-president. He is in charge of administration. In the winter of

1969, however, a faculty committee recommended that a second vice-president be appointed—this one to concentrate on external affairs. Mr. Pusey did not go quite that far. Since 1958, he had had a special assistant, Charles P. Whitlock, who tried to smooth outside relations, and among whose responsibilities was serving as Harvard liaison with Councilman Vellucci. "I think Al's very funny," Whitlock would say, wincing slightly. Responding, though, to the committee's feeling that external affairs needed extra attention, Pusey added a new assistant to his staff, to concentrate on Cambridge and free Whitlock for higher levels of government. The committee also urged Harvard to, among other things, do something about ameliorating the housing situation for all the citizens of Cambridge—Vellucci's disaffected constituents presumably among them. (One Italian-looking woman not long ago picketed Holyoke Center carrying a sandwich board that read, "Harvard wants to destroy our homes and build a parking lot.") Under pressure from S.D.S. and, indeed, from a good part of the student body, the Harvard administration announced in the late spring of 1969 that it would build eleven hundred housing units and would ask the federal government to furnish twenty million dollars for financing them—a kind of fiscal procedure that in ordinary times the University's money men would never have tolerated.

Whitlock, who joined the Harvard staff in 1945, teaches a course, under the social relations department, in group dynamics. On a national level, it was he who was most directly involved when, as happened in 1963, Harvard helped dissuade Congress from insisting that students had to sign an anti-Communist affidavit before they could get certain federal loans. On a state level, it was Whitlock who would arrange a Harvard job for a Massachusetts politician's nephew. For all they have been frayed, Harvard's bonds with the city of Cambridge are stronger these days than those that tie it to the Commonwealth of Massachusetts. It was not always so. In 1949, there were forty-six Harvard College graduates in the state legislature. In 1969, there were six.

For a Boston politician, nowadays, it may be a handicap to have gone to Harvard; he is apt to be better off if he can claim Boston College or Holy Cross as his alma mater. Harvard's principal ally in the Massachusetts State House these days is a liberal Republican, Mrs. Mary Newman, who has an academic orientation; her husband teaches psychology and she herself is a trustee of Swarthmore. She lives in Cambridge and not only doesn't play down her Harvard connections but whenever she campaigns has Harvard wives assist her. But she is not a legislative spokesman for the University. "Harvard talks to people at the top," she says. "It talks to the governor and it talks to the cardinal, but it never talks to me."

Harvard's talks with the Cardinal—Cardinal Cushing—have frequently proved fruitful. Mr. Whitlock tends to play these down, but another external-affairs man at the University has said: "Every time a bill comes along that threatens to take away our tax exemption, we yell to the cardinal, and he stops it cold. Several years ago, some guy reintroduced a bill that had been kicking around since Joe McCarthy's day. It would have given the state Board of Education the power to review the curricula of private institutions, and, if it wasn't satisfied, to take away their charters. There seemed to be a chance the bill might pass, so we used our big ammunition. We had Pusey call Cushing. The president began to explain his concern, and the cardinal said he'd take care of everything and asked for the number of the bill. The president gave it to him and went on trying to discuss the matter, but the cardinal brushed that aside and switched to pleasantries: How was Nate's health, how was Harvard's health, they must get together soon, and so on. Afterward, Mr. Pusey said he was afraid the cardinal hadn't understood him. But he had, all right. The day the bill came up for disposition, nobody voted for it—not even the guy who'd introduced it." When an anti-intellectual priest in Boston tried to block Harvard from acquiring some land there for an addition to the Medical School, the Cardinal squelched the priest.

Harvard manages sometimes to reciprocate in small ways for His Eminence's large favors. In 1959, it gave him an honorary degree. In 1968, another opportunity presented itself. The University has long insisted that its football stadium may not be used for non-Harvard events (it is afraid of compromising its tax exemption). This has brought upon Harvard the wrath of professional football fans in New England, there being no other suitable site around Boston for the Patriots to play their home games in. When, however, an exhibition game was proposed between that team and the Philadelphia Eagles, for the benefit of the Cardinal Cushing Fund, Harvard found it possible to waive its rule; it was doing so, a spokesman for the University's Department of Athletics explained, "in the interests of community relations."

Also in the interests of strengthening relations with the community—particularly the black community—Harvard has recently been paying increasing attention, as an institution, to urban problems that not too long ago were largely dependent on individuals for whatever Harvard attention they got. At last reckoning, the whole University was spending twelve million dollars a year on community-related projects, many of them only peripherally connected with the education of its own except, of course, in the participatory-democracy sense. Boston's Negro ghetto, over in Roxbury, has been the focus of the new concern —much newer for the University than for some of its students. Notable among these are the ones affiliated with Phillips Brooks House, an undergraduate social-welfare group. For years, Brooks House attracted genteel young philanthropists, many of whom salved their consciences by distributing holiday food baskets among the local poor, and fewer of whom put in a few additional worthy hours now and then as volunteers in settlement houses and the better-grade hospitals. But these institutions began to rely more and more on professionals and to care less and less about student volunteers. At the same time, the students began to look for new social-welfare outlets. One Harvard senior, for instance, said in 1968 that the most satisfying educational experience he had had in his four College years was helping the inmates of a nearby women's prison put out a newspaper.

The growing politicization of students, moreover, has affected their attitudes toward social welfare. Instead of providing services, they want to provide guidance to communities striving for self-improvement. Instead of plugging holes in a deficient environment, they want to support people trying to change that environment. "We have been asking ourselves questions like 'What good is it to give a Roxbury kid a book if there's no light in his house?' " a Brooks House student said. "To help us answer questions like that, we think Harvard should give us courses on subjects like 'The Role of the White Volunteer in the Black Community.' "

Harvard College has been trying to accommodate itself to such demands—though less rapidly than some of its affiliates would wish. Meanwhile, task forces from the Medical School and the Law School have been fanning out into Roxbury. Also, an Urban Field Service under the School of Design helped plan a park and a gymnasium there. Even the Harvard Business School, a traditionally self-centered and laissez-faire part of Harvard, has been stirring; its students and some of its faculty have been trying to help black businessmen operate successfully in West Roxbury, aided by a twenty-three-thousand-dollar grant from the Ford Foundation. In 1967, the Foundation gave Harvard and M.I.T. together an additional six million dollars earmarked for studies in urban affairs.

The two Cambridge institutions had had close urbanological ties for some time previously. Since 1959, they have run a Joint Center for Urban Studies. Its director, until he became a Nixon adviser, was Daniel Patrick Moynihan. The Joint Center rarely came to grips with any urgent municipal problems, and it wasn't particularly supposed to. Its main function was to dole out still additional Ford Foundation money for urban research, and some of this, in a time of crisis, was resolutely academic—research for instance, on thirteenth-century Muslim communities, and on nineteenth-century Irish migrations to London.

Aside from nurturing esoteric scholars, the Joint Center has been chiefly renowned for its weekly lunches, which, since it has no building of its own, it has had catered in a Unitarian church. (The church, abutting Harvard Square, is noteworthy because seven Harvard presidents are interred in its graveyard.) With Moynihan presiding, the lunches, though necessarily non-alcoholic in that setting, were lively affairs, and would attract scholars from all over the University—among them Harvey G. Cox, Jr., the author of *The Secular City* and the very worldly professor of divinity at the Harvard Divinity School. "Hey, guess what!" a member of the Joint Center staff told a friend after one such lunch. "Pat Moynihan got Harvey Cox into a church!"

Harvard and M.I.T. collaborate in other areas, as well they might be expected to. They jointly run something called the University Information Technology Corporation, a non-profit group set up to investigate, among other things, the potentialities of computers and television in education. Together, they run the Cambridge Electron Accelerator, which was built in 1957, at a cost of $11,500,000, by the Atomic Energy Commission. The A.E.C. pays for its $4,500,000 annual operating expenses, but otherwise leaves it pretty much alone; the scientists connected with it engage in non-governmental, non-classified research, and cheerfully welcome Soviet physicists who wish to inspect the installation. It is situated in Harvard territory, and its director is a Harvard professor, the physicist Karl Strauch, but the chairmanship of the faculty committee that supervises it alternates annually between Harvard and M.I.T. In its lobby, there is always one M.I.T. chair and one Harvard chair. In Professor Strauch's office, there are exactly four of each kind, and hanging on one wall, by way of stressing the duality of the place's sponsorship, is a two-handled shovel that the presidents of M.I.T. and Harvard used when ground was broken for it.

The same meticulousness is observed at the Joint Center for Urban Studies, where Moynihan, though on the Harvard faculty, always diplomatically sat in an M.I.T chair. Harvard people regard old-school chairs as some people regard old-school ties. Almost everyone at Harvard has a Harvard chair—an all-wood captain's chair with the College seal on it—in his room. So does the mayor of Cambridge. ("He asked for one for his home and I got it for him," says Mr. Pusey's external-affairs man. "It may have been a symbol of something.") So do many Harvard alumni, who buy them from the Coop, for thirty-nine dollars apiece, at the rate of a couple of thousand a year, even though they are almost universally conceded to be uncomfortable. In most Harvard offices, a visitor is offered a Harvard chair. It gets him out of there fast. The occupant of the office, on the other hand, is likely to be occupying something cushioned. One of the few big men on the Harvard campus—perhaps the only one—who would always sit in a Harvard chair himself was President Pusey.

MANY HARVARD PEOPLE find Cambridge delightful for the variety and spice of its social life. There is, to be sure, an academic pretentiousness to some of it. When the wife of a professor who moved to Cambridge after serving in the Kennedy administration told one of her husband's faculty colleagues that she missed the social life of Washington, he told her not to worry, she would find Cambridge equally exhilarating. "Where's the action?" she asked. By way of reply, he tapped his brain with his forefinger.

There is an inbred quality, moreover, to many Harvard gatherings; conversation at a faculty dinner party tends to resemble that at a faculty meeting. William Alfred wanted to entertain one evening for a lady who liked to knit and who made mistakes when she was irritated. Mr. Alfred invited some English-department associates to meet her. One of them made an inane literary remark, and the lady missed a stitch. A second professor said to the first, "That seems to be particularly Coleridgean," and her needle slipped again. "A point well taken," said the first, and the lady had to rip apart her work. The late Arthur M. Schlesinger,

257

Sr., and his namesake son and various gifted relatives have for most of the twentieth century been social lions on the Harvard scene; but when a Schlesinger went to a party otherwise attended almost exclusively by theoretical physicists, none of the scientific guests seemed to have heard of the name. It is characteristic of the Harvard community that long after Arthur Schlesinger, Jr., attained a full professorship and reached the age of fifty, around Cambridge he was still known as "Little Arthur."

But Harvard social life is by no means all shop talk, and to enjoy it to the hilt requires only the right connections, reasonably good manners, and durability. The wife of a professor transplanted from Berkeley said that in four years in California they hardly dined out at all, but that they had four dinner invitations their first week in Massachusetts. "The first year we were at Harvard we went out so much that my husband hardly had the strength to play squash," she said, "and for a while I was sure I had gout." Those deep in the social swim hardly have time to dry off between plunges. Jerome Bruner says, "You can dine out more amusingly in Cambridge than you can in New York," and the biologist James D. Watson says, throwing scientific caution to the winds, "Nowhere else in this country is social life so intellectually stimulating." The former diplomat Milton Katz, now professor of law at Harvard, says, "The great thing about living in Cambridge is that sooner or later you see everybody. I feel so sorry for people stuck in Princeton." Svetlana Alliluyeva lives in Princeton, but some of her reminiscences appeared in the *Atlantic* because its editor, Robert Manning, lives in Cambridge and ran into George F. Kennan, another Princeton denizen, at a party at the Cambridge home of Professor Merle Fainsod.

There are a bewildering number of social functions relating directly to Harvard affairs—lunches for Far East students, house masters' teas, receptions for groups galore. The consumption of sherry is staggering. (Some think it bad for the teeth—look at the British—but in a community devoted to the search for truth this remains speculative; the Harvard Dental School's chief researcher on the effects of beverages on teeth has not yet got around to sherry. In any event, it probably represents no real threat to health; academicians tend to outlive ordinary men.) One of the most agreeable sociable sects is the Society of Fellows. Harvard abounds with fellows. There are Nieman Fellows, in journalism; Danforth Fellows, in the Graduate School of Arts and Sciences; Bullard Fellows, in Forestry; Fellows of the Institute of Politics; and, most recently, Alfred North Whitehead Fellows for Advanced Studies in Education.

The most generally envied fellows are those who make up the elite Society of Fellows, which boasts a splendid wine cellar and is widely thought to command the services of the best cook in the area, a talented Frenchwoman whom it shares with Boston's venerable Club of Odd Volumes. The Society was founded by President Lowell, and it has its own suite of oak-paneled rooms in a corner of Eliot House. (In 1929, Lowell tried to get a foundation to endow the Society; when his efforts failed, he gave it more than a million dollars of his own money.) These fellows drink their sherry off the breakfast table that earlier belonged to Oliver Wendell Holmes' autocrat. They meet for dinner every Monday, and end their feasts, when sated with wines and champagne, with brandy and madeira served from a solid-silver cart that they wheel from place to place along a massive horseshoe-shaped table.

The membership is limited to twelve senior fellows—usually eminent professors—and a maximum of twenty-four junior fellows, who are allotted three all-expense-paid years at Harvard to pursue whatever scholarly bent they fancy. Their only obligation to the Society is to turn up for the Monday-night dinners. At these speeches are absolutely forbidden. Conversation is the big thing, and erudition prevails. A theoretical mathematician may hang intently on a discourse about American Indian dialects or may learn, as was once recalled by Federal Judge Charles E. Wyzanski, Jr., an ex-president of the Harvard Board of Overseers and the Society's only honorary senior fellow, "what Athenian potsherds show about election habits in fifth-century Greece." One night the learned men played a game. One fellow asked the others to write down the two numbers that logically followed "27-18-28-18-28-45-90-45." Nobody got the answer right, though most of those present knew it and were chagrined when the perpetrator of this stickler enlightened them. The missing digits, they realized, were "23," because what they had been given was a restatement of the start of a transcendental number in mathematics: 2.718281828459045 23.

A clubby rapport sometimes develops between the senior and junior fellows. When a senior, a classics professor, complained that his automobile kept being broken into, a junior, a physicist, obligingly rigged the car with an electronic alarm system guaranteed to frighten a tamperer out of his wits. (This was simple for the junior. His serious work had to do with building a radically new electron x-ray microscope.) Another junior fellow was engaged in analyzing the sleeping habits of monkeys, and would sometimes show up at fellows' dinners wearing a lapel button identifying him as a friend of the Japanese Monkey Center. He was Joel E. Cohen, a graduate student whose fields were biology and sociology and whose specialty within them was the investigation of theories of life processes.

A native of Michigan, Cohen decided at thirteen to be a mathematical biologist, and he was a largely self-taught math student throughout high school, since he rarely ran into a teacher capable of keeping up with him. He was also an accomplished musician—piano, oboe, and string bass. At the age of twelve, he had a composition for a brass quartet published. As a Harvard undergraduate, he composed the score for a musical show, wrote editorials for the *Crimson*, and graduated summa cum laude, thus becoming eligible for membership in a very exclusive, informal, undergraduate society, the Summa Club. The club has parties occasionally, but these aren't always a success, because some of the girls invited complain that the conversation is so abstract it's unintelligible. "Don't you ever talk about *people?*" one girl asked.

By 1968, Cohen, who was then twenty-three, had taken summer courses at several universities—Kansas, Michigan, Stanford, Chicago, Costa Rica, Emory, and Cambridge, England—and had been offered teaching jobs by several others—Yale, Princeton, M.I.T. and Wisconsin (Harvard was yet to be heard from)—but hadn't made up his mind what to do. He thought he might become a writer. Still, he found the interest far-flung places showed in him comforting. "I'm always glad to learn I can survive outside Harvard," he said.

Of two hundred-odd young men who have been junior fellows since the first ones were selected in 1933, forty-four are now tenured members of the Harvard faculty, and others hold distinguished posts elsewhere. The junior Schlesinger was a junior fellow when he really was fairly little. So were Paul A. Samuelson, the economist whom M.I.T. lured away from Harvard; Carl Kaysen, now director of the Institute for Advanced Study at Princeton, and McGeorge Bundy, who spent most of his three years collaborating on the memoirs of Henry L. Stimson.

Bundy first made an impact on Harvard in 1940, when he was a Yale undergraduate and, representing the literary Elizabethan Club in New Haven, spoke at an anniversary dinner of the literary Signet Society in Cambridge. It was President Lowell's belief that a Ph.D. was unnecessary for a real scholar (he had never earned a doctorate), and Bundy, like Schlesinger and many another junior fellow who later forged ahead, never bothered to get an advanced degree. This proved troublesome in 1951, when Professor Fainsod, then the head of the Harvard government department, wanted to offer Bundy a tenure appointment in that field. Several faculty members demurred; they sputtered that not only was Bundy bereft of suitable academic credentials, but as an undergraduate hadn't even studied government, having majored in mathematics. Fainsod finally took the matter directly up with President Conant, who capitulated, but not without having the last word. "It couldn't happen in Chemistry," he said.

Not only did it happen, but Bundy became dean of the Harvard Faculty of Arts and Sciences. He presided over faculty meetings, one professor recalled, like Orpheus taming the Furies; never had Harvard professors been exposed to so engaging a combination of flair, arrogance, wit, and grace. "Mac could talk for ten minutes and say nothing at all and people would lap it up," one survivor of the Bundy deanship says, "and he concocted a marvelous secret formula. Faculty meetings usually begin at four and end at six. Bundy came to realize that if he wanted the faculty to pass anything controversial, he should present it in the dullest possible fashion, and present it not before 5:45. Then, if anybody wanted to debate it, they'd be doing so on their own time." It was Bundy who is credited with once having said of the Harvard faculty, "They're literate, but they don't read."

Bundy was an innovator and a gambler. He would take chances on people and on courses. "Maybe he didn't work out too well when he was handling foreign policy in the White House," one of his former Cambridge associates says, "but he sure as hell was good for Harvard. Much of what Harvard is today is a reflection of his exuberance. We're especially aware now of the Bundy era, because once it ended we ran for the safe, high ground." Bundy's successor as dean, Franklin L. Ford, a phlegmatic, reflective pipe-smoker, was a respected educator in his own right, but even his most ardent admirers conceded that the two men were different. "Ford is every bit as capable as Bundy ever was of emitting smoke," one old Harvard hand said. "The only thing is that Franklin needs a pipe to do it."

One professor to another, waiting for a faculty meeting to start: "Economists shouldn't make value judgments."

xvii

ADDRESSING HIMSELF EARLY IN 1968 to the question of just what the president of a university does, Mr. Pusey, who was then starting his fifteenth year as president of Harvard, said that he should see to it "that the university continue quietly but steadfastly about its business, which, I take it, is not arrogantly to seek to tell the world what it should do in every immediate situation, but rather patiently to cultivate learning and constantly to seek to draw succeeding generations into responsibility for understanding, concern, and decency. Above all to inculcate respect for fact and regard for fairness—virtues fewer and fewer seem now to care for." He went on to cite three of his most esteemed abstractions: virtue, piety, and learning. "These are still the sorts of things about which a president has always to think," he said, "trying not to lose sight of them in the face of alarums, fashion, dispute, and all the rest." A year later, he may still have had them in sight, but if he did, hardly any one else at Harvard seemed also to be looking.

Mr. Pusey was the twenty-fourth president of Harvard. In the first 233 years of the long existence in which Harvard men take much pride and find much comfort, there were twenty presidents. For those two-and-a-third centuries, though, Harvard was really not much of a university. True, its Medical School had begun in 1782, its Divinity School in 1816, and its Law School a year after that. But these were frail and feeble appendages to the corpus of Harvard College, which itself was far from robust. It has only been in the century that started in 1869 that Harvard has flourished as an authentic university, and during that hundred-year stretch its course has been steered by only four men—Charles William Eliot, Abbott Lawrence Lowell, James Bryant Conant, and Nathan Marsh Pusey. If Mr. Pusey's helmsmanship had to be described succinctly, perhaps some words of his own would be most apt—words he uttered not long ago while clasping the hand of a bearded and beaded young radical on his own faculty to whom the president, clean-shaven as usual and wearing a vest, had just been introduced. "We try to maintain a balance," Mr. Pusey said.

There has been a curiously balanced and cyclical pattern to Harvard's progress since the end of the Civil War. Eliot, a professor of chemistry before his investiture as president, inherited an institution that was run as rigidly and unimaginatively as a grammar school. In the College, academic inquiry was stifled and ideas flowed sluggishly. The students spent much of their classroom time reciting lessons they had memorized the night before; the instructors impassively checked them out. Retentiveness was required and curiosity deemed intrusive. Eliot wanted to free the college from the grip of rote. He was even more worried about the pitiful condition of the graduate schools. When he asked, for instance, why oral instead of written exams were the custom at the Medical School, it was explained to him that many of its students were barely able to write. Eliot saw no reason why Harvard could not become an institution that was literate and that, more importantly, reshaped itself after the great European universities, where initiative and learning were not considered antithetical. As far back as 1825, a Harvard professor, George Ticknor, had returned from a visit to Göttingen urging that the principles and practices of *lehrfreiheit* be imported to Cambridge. But nobody had paid him much heed.

Eliot's ear was attuned to the echo of Ticknor's voice, and to other, fresher voices advocating that higher education in America be liberated from its self-forged chains. Eliot set about making Harvard a community of scholars pursuing their assorted scholastic bents on all levels under the protective umbrella of a university. He did not ignore the undergraduates, but he was especially sympathetic to the needs and wishes of graduate students. Under him, research came to be accepted as a normal—indeed, an essential—aspect of high intellectual activity in an academic setting.

The science-oriented Eliot reigned for forty years. The pendulum swung back toward undergraduates with the advent in 1909 of Lowell, who had been a professor of government. He was not opposed to the graduate schools, and they continued to grow during his administration, but he was oriented toward the humanities and partial to the College—so much so that, once having become a bachelor of arts, he had never bothered to try for any further degree, let alone a Ph.D.

His reign lasted twenty-four years, in the course of which Harvard put up most of its residential houses for undergraduates, and, altogether, more new buildings than had been constructed in all the University's previous history. Then the pendulum swung again. For to Conant, like Eliot, the Ph.D. represented all at once the home port of being educated and the launching pad to educating others. "Oh, my God, a chemist," one Harvard elder said to a faculty colleague on hearing of Conant's enthronement.

"But Eliot was a chemist," he was reminded.

"Yes," he said, "but not a good one."

Conant was an exceptional chemist, and for good measure had married the daughter of a Nobel-Prize-winning professor of chemistry at Harvard. Conant gave graduate-school study so high a priority that at one point he contemplated reducing the size of the College, so Harvard could concentrate on its more advanced students. He acquired the reputation of being indifferent about raising funds, most of which Harvard had traditionally solicited from alumni of the College. Conant has pointed out that he became president in 1933, not long after the bank holiday, that his term of office coincided not only with the depression but also with the Second World War, and that Harvard nonetheless reaped a hundred million dollars during his twenty-year stay. "The main thing I did was to keep the show running," he says.

Absent from the campus during much of the war, Conant finally left Harvard in 1953, when he became sixty—the earliest date at which he could retire as president emeritus rather than resign. He has been rather aloof from the University ever since. He thinks that two-year colleges are the wave of the future, although he concedes that there may be exceptions—Harvard perhaps among them. In 1968, when he was working on his memoirs, he told an acquaintance, "Nowadays, any institution of higher education represents a different world from the one I lived in at Cambridge. I consider my experience at Harvard almost irrelevant."

President Pusey was hardly a reincarnation of Lowell, but with his appointment the humanities were once more in the saddle, and the College once more had a friend at court. Pusey is not opposed to science—the number of scholars engaged purely in research has tripled during his administration—and is not unacquainted with the field. Early in the Second World War, married and the father of three, he was on the faculty at Wesleyan, which set up a special academic program for Navy and Marine pilots. The faculty was short-handed; for instructing the servicemen, availability counted more than experience. Pusey found himself teaching physics, which he hadn't thought about since high school; aviation medicine, which he had never given any thought; and the theory of flight, which he could approach with an open mind since he had never been on a plane. He managed more or less satisfactorily by following the practice of Harvard students a century earlier; he would bone up on a topic at night and the next day repeat what he'd learned. Basically, however, Pusey was, and is, a humanities man. As a Harvard undergraduate in the late nineteen-twenties, in the Stutz-Bearcat and bathtub-gin era, he had concentrated in English and Greek. (For a while,

Conrad Aiken was his tutor; extracurricularly, H. L. Mencken was his mentor.) He did get a Ph.D., from Harvard, in 1937; his doctoral dissertation was entitled "Athenian Law in the Fourth Century and Its Relationship to Chapter 42–69 of Aristotle's *Athenian Politics.*"

Pusey was born in Iowa in 1907. On reaching sixty-six, in 1973, he will be eligible for retirement. When he became president of Harvard, his origins struck some old New England hands as ludicrously quaint. One Boston dowager asked where he hailed from. Iowa, he said. She frowned; she had evidently never heard of the place. "You mean Ohio?" she asked. No, Pusey said, he meant Iowa—it was beyond Ohio. "Oh, well, God is everywhere," she said. Pusey had few personal contacts with undergraduates, but he was attentive to fellow Iowans. He engaged in a fairly protracted correspondence with one of them—it had to do with the pros and cons of remodeling a house dining room—and when the student at one point said that he felt he was outgunned in the exchange and wished he had Alexander Pope writing his letters for him, the President replied amiably that he knew just how his adversary felt; *he* wished he had Pope as *his* amanuensis.

Not only was Pusey raised in the midwest, but he attained his first administrative eminence, in 1944, as president of Lawrence College, in Appleton, Wisconsin. While in that post, he occasionally raided Harvard. He would travel to Cambridge unheralded, check in at a hotel, and cajole the secretaries of various academic departments into tipping him off to promising but little-known young teachers. He thus lured away several top-flight scholars for the Lawrence faculty. To his regret, when he became president of Harvard, they stayed at Lawrence. He became less aggressive as he grew older. He was basically a low-voltage man, with no desire to become a worldwide celebrity or to compete with those members of the Harvard faculty who enjoyed that *éclat*. He talked softly, and he looked bland. He had an uncommonly smooth-skinned face that was often nearly expressionless; it was said around Cambridge that he resembled a retouched photograph of himself. (Even more irreverent was another widely circulated description of him—that he looked like the back of a spoon.) Many of his students wouldn't recognize him if they bumped into him. "The president of Harvard can't be folksy. He can't do all the things he has to do and still maintain contact with the students," Mr. Pusey said. "What *really* worries me is that I don't have enough time to spend with the faculty. It was different at Lawrence. For five of the nine years I was president there, I even had time to teach."

Mr. Pusey was named president the year his class of 1928 was celebrating its twenty-fifth reunion. For an anniversary report, he had just written, of Lawrence, "I hope to be here for a long time to come." A man of striking conscientiousness, Mr. Pusey had no sooner accepted the Harvard post than he set about reading all the annual reports of his predecessors, which, fortunately, had been issued only since 1826. It took him most of that summer, but he was cheered to learn that every president of Harvard had had his share of troubles. "That kept me from taking anything for granted," Pusey said later, "and it helped to show me how Harvard had got the way it is." Although he would describe Harvard as an "adventure in education," he was not basically adventurous. Tranquillity appealed to him, and only a few weeks before Harvard erupted he had referred to the "exceptional good sense of Harvard men and women" as a chief factor contributing to its lack of turmoil theretofore. He had such horror of disruptiveness that people who knew him well were convinced that, should the situation at Harvard seem to him to have got hopelessly out of hand, he was quite prepared to close the place down, and, if necessary, to assume the responsibility for letting Harvard take a thousand and one years to provide a thousand years' worth of educational services. But he had a conciliatory bent, too. Just before delivering a Commencement Day address to Harvard alumni, he cut from the previously distributed text of it a reference to "the too obvious goals of so many of today's impatient revolutionaries."

Mr. Pusey was ceremonially installed as president on October 13, 1953, and in his acceptance speech expounded the global view he had of Harvard. "This community has never been a community unto itself alone," he said. "Today its relationships reach throughout the whole country and everywhere into the world." His horizons remained unlimited. Meetings of geographically confined organizations like the Associated Colleges of New England bored him, though he was too polite to show it. At the same time, he was as deeply convinced of the *sui generis* nature of Harvard as the narrowest-minded New Englander. He was overjoyed when an alumnus who for years had had the Massachusetts license plate "1636" yielded it up for Mr. Pusey's use. The president's wife, Anne, a Bryn Mawr graduate, has been a busy woman (she sometimes calls herself Harvard's "den mother"), but she has found time to knit Harvard sweaters—a maroon *H* on a white field—for selected Harvard children. Caroline Kennedy and her brother John have been among the recipients.

"Liberal education is my chief concern," Mr. Pusey said. His most important function, as he saw it, in expressing that concern was appointing the deans of Harvard's nine major faculties—Arts and Sciences, Law, Business Administration, Medicine, Public Health, Divinity, Design, Education, and Government. Every dean now at Harvard is a Pusey dean. "That's one of the ways I influence this place," the president said. Before one of his most recent choices, that of Derek C. Bok to be dean of the Law School (it may be indicative of the luster of a Harvard deanship that Bok preferred that job to the presidency of Stanford University), Pusey spent months pondering the recommendations of lawyers, professors of law, and even law students; but it was characteristic of Pusey's style that he had never met Bok, a full professor at the Harvard Law School, until he summoned him to his office and offered him the position.

Mr. Pusey considered his second most important obligation to be his participation in the choice of tenured appointments to the faculty. "Marshaling human talent is the main thrust of the president's job," he said. "That's why I don't have much time left for the students. They never do understand this, and you can't blame them." What the students really couldn't understand was why Mr. Pusey didn't try harder to *make* time. For the first two weeks after the April bust in 1969, he put in no public appearance at all at Harvard, and when he did expose himself it was at, of all places, the Business School. And before then he had seemingly failed to grasp the importance of the tactics that Mayor Lindsay of New York had found so useful for keeping his even larger and more complex constituency cool—simply walking around and mingling with it. If Mr. Pusey had restructured his time earlier, he might have had to spend less time later worrying about restructuring his university. On Commencement Day in 1969, after complimenting the graduating seniors on a sterling academic record (fifty-four summa cum laudes, honors of one sort or another for 70 per cent of the class) "despite distractions and diversions" (which, even for a mild man, was putting it mildly), he added, "We're sorry anything has occurred to make you unhappy." It sounded like a ski-lodge proprietor apologizing to his guests for bad snow conditions. But that was clearly not enough in 1969. What Harvard got, after the first fireworks, was compassion and regret. What it had perhaps needed all along was forcefulness and guidance. Mr. Pusey had in some ways seemed to be the ideal University administrator—reflective, intelligent, hard-working, and unassuming. He had appeared to think of himself as the captain of an all but self-steering ship. The trouble was that everybody at Harvard, himself included, thought of the place as the No. 1 educational institution, but nobody could figure out how it should retain that place in a time of anguish. What Harvard sorely needed, in the spring of 1969, was a leader who could show Harvard how to lead the way. Instead, it had a decent human being who could not thread his way safely between, in Harvard terms, an unimaginable Scylla and an inconceivable Charybdis—students who would burst into and seize a building, and administrators who would ask the police to throw them out.

Many of the students also could never understand Mr. Pusey's strong streak of religiosity. There can be few other presidents of lay institutions these days who refer to the earth as "this side of Heaven." He invokes the Deity as regularly as, though more delicately than, a Bible-belt congressman. Taking up Harvard's problems with the alumni in June, 1969, for instance, he said: "Organizational change may help, but by itself it will not do the job. The prior need today is for a reassertion of the confident, respectful, affirmative, and concerned attitude which has guided Harvard in the past and which, God willing, may do so now again with new vigor." Harvard has deep religious roots. Its first endowed chair was for a professor of divinity. Nearly half of the 543 graduates it turned out in the seventeenth century became ministers. Today, not even many of the graduates of the Harvard Divinity School become parish ministers, preferring social work or Biblical scholarship; the School, though, does still conduct an annual hymn-writing contest.

In the College's old alumni catalogues, every minister's name was italicized, and as late as 1834, one nickname for the College was "the Seminary." It was Harvard, notwithstanding, that in 1886 became the first major American university to do away with compulsory chapel. There are still daily morning services. These begin at 8:45, and the few classes scheduled for 8:00 must stop at 8:40, to give students in them a chance to get to chapel if they so desire. Chapel lasts no more than fifteen minutes, and nearly every morning there is a guest speaker, often a layman—a professor of nutrition at the Dental School, say—who can talk on any subject he cares to. He is firmly limited, however, to five minutes. After Richard E. Neustadt, the director of the Institute of Politics, had taken a turn, he declared, "I nearly died. I'll never do it again. I didn't even have time to tell a story I was reminded of just after I got started." Asked by a friend if he hadn't been embarrassed by the paucity of chapel-goers—eight boys and two girls, that particular morning—Neustadt quickly recovered. "You can't embarrass a Harvard professor," he said. "We'll open our mouths for anything."

An important part of any university president's job is fundraising. Mr. Pusey has been good at it. President Conant averaged five million dollars a year. Even allowing for prosperity and inflation, President Pusey's average of forty million a year has been a sterling comparative performance. In the 1967–68 academic year, he hit sixty-six million. Mr. Pusey laid his religious convictions on the line as soon as he moved into the president's office. His first major solicitation, in 1954, was on behalf of the Divinity School. A lot of Harvard people weren't even aware then that Harvard *had* a Divinity School, and Conant had thought of closing it down. Pusey persuaded John D. Rockefeller, Jr., to give a million dollars to shore it up. More recently, he has received another million and a half, for a Divinity School dormitory, from the philanthropist's widow and his son David, who is one of Pusey's closest friends. At the 1969 Commencement, it was with obvious pleasure that Mr. Pusey, conferring degrees on the Divinity School graduates, told them, "You are ready to advance the disciplines of faith in an age of radical change." Radical change, however, seemed to be what some Divinity School students were already committed to, just like students everywhere else at Harvard. Several of them, for instance, just a few weeks earlier, had gone into Boston to picket the office of Harvard's treasurer, oblivious of how hard Mr. Pusey had worked to raise money and pass it along to the treasurer on their school's behalf.

In Mr. Pusey's fifth year at Harvard, he generated a flap by asserting that Harvard had always been a Christian institution and that accordingly the Memorial Church could not be used for non-Christian weddings, confirmations, or funerals. There were so many protests so strongly expressed that he backtracked and opened up the church to all, saying that Harvard had become a secular university with, he felt constrained to add, a tradition of worship. In the spring of 1969, it was to become an assembly hall. Harvard's university preacher, Charles P. Price, is a far less flamboyant figure than Yale's William Sloane Coffin, Jr., but the Rev. Mr. Price opened up the church to any group that wanted to meet in it, and its thitherto unsullied floor was soon carpeted with cigarette butts, while casual blasphemies bounced off the marble walls on which are indelibly carved one thing that has not changed in this metamorphic academic era—the roster of names of those Harvard men (spanning three generations, from the class of 1904 through that of 1948) who died in the Second World War.

MR. PUSEY HIMSELF has been faithful to Harvard's religious tradition. He would usually conduct the first chapel service of each academic year, and when he was in Cambridge he would go to services in the Yard every Sunday. It sometimes distressed him that so few of the flock he shepherded followed his example. Still, 2 per cent of each of the last couple of senior classes have gone into theology—possibly influenced as much by their draft status as by burning faith.

Mr. Pusey suffered an especially sharp blow in the winter of 1968, when at his invitation Dr. Eugene Carson Blake, the secretary general of the World Council of Churches, flew to Cambridge from his headquarters in Geneva to share some of his thoughts with a Harvard audience. Dr. Blake drew a crowd of only forty. Ordinarily, that might not have been so bad—Harvard men are always too busy to attend all the events they'd like to— but it so happened that just twenty-four hours earlier the Maharishi Mahesh Yogi had been at Harvard, too. The whiskery guru had drawn a crowd of two thousand, and would have had a bigger one if latecomers had not been turned away for lack of room.

There were understandable reasons for the disparity in attendance. People in the news—Joan Baez, Stokely Carmichael, George C. Wallace, the Maharishi—are predictable campus magnets. Moreover, it meant little to most Harvard students that Dr. Blake was in a sense a part of their community, being a member of the Board of Overseers' Committee to Visit the Divinity School. What meant more was that the Maharishi had brought along Mia

Farrow. A university president has much to endure.

"Early in my administrative career at Harvard, somebody told me there were two things to steer clear of—religion and architecture," President Pusey said. "I've been over my head in both of them." For a man who is conservative in dress and manner, and for whom traditionalism rates almost as a virtue, he has had enlightened ideas about architecture. One of the University's landmarks is Memorial Hall, a gingerbread monument to Harvard men who died in the Civil War. Many people think it is an eyesore. "If it wasn't so majestic, I would have pulled it down," Henry James had a character say in *The Bostonians*.

Pusey loathed Memorial Hall. When it caught on fire in 1956, it was rumored he hoped it would burn to the ground, but only its clock tower was destroyed. He would not dare suggest razing the building, though. For many old grads, it was a symbol of continuity; just to look at it made them tingle with nostalgia. The president could and did have a good deal to say, however, about the design of the buildings that Harvard put up during his administration, and his choice of architects reflected his taste—among others, Philip Johnson, Minoru Yamasaki, Hugh Stubbins, Jean-Paul Carlhian, Walter Gropius, and José Luis Sert. Gropius and Sert both served as deans of Harvard's Graduate School of Design; more than most deans, they had a chance to restructure a university.

Pusey learned that in picking architects you can't please everybody. In the winter of 1968, he named John H. Andrews, who held a Master of Architecture degree from the Harvard Graduate School of Design, to design a new hall for that school. The editor of its principal publication examined the architect's sketches and criticized it as "a dramatic symbol of the tradition of purely subjective solution that American architects are still clinging to and which is no longer even remotely capable of dealing with today's environmental needs." When it came to providing a dramatic symbol for environmental needs at the time of the student strike that followed the April bust, the Design School, which normally has minimal contacts with the rest of the university, achieved quick and memorable prominence. Its students designed a clenched red fist that, by silk screen and stencil, they openhandedly imprinted on the clothing, or bare skin, of anyone who stopped by. In due course, at potentially serious consequences to the blood pressure of many old grads, the stark, angry symbol appeared on the cover of the *Harvard Alumni Bulletin.*

A few years earlier, Mr. Pusey had taken special pleasure in selecting Le Corbusier to design a visual-arts center; it was the only commission that architect had ever received in the United States. The building that ensued, an oddly shaped cement-block structure called Carpenter Hall, sparked considerable controversy back in the days when campus communities could get worked up about the shape of buildings. Some observers speculated that the contractors had misread the architect's plans and built it upside down. When Mr. Pusey took his Board of Overseers to look at it, one member suggested sourly that since the building presumably couldn't be removed perhaps it could at least be partly shrouded; he wanted to pass a hat around to collect money so ivy could be planted on it. Pusey, on the other hand, has argued that the building is "an extraordinary example of a man using his mind for an intelligent solution of a problem." To one critic who complained of the architect's stark, modern creation, the President replied, "Corbu, actually, is a sort of Puritan, who refuses to do anything just for the sake of prettiness. That Puritanism of his probably puts his building closer to the spirit of seventeenth-century Harvard than anything else we have around."

When Mr. Conant took over Harvard in 1933, he made it clear that the whole University was his province by relocating the presidential office. Since 1815, it had been in University Hall, which was also the administrative headquarters of the College. Mr. Conant moved to Massachusetts Hall, thereby downgrading University Hall from a White House to a state capital. Mr. Pusey, for all his attentiveness to the College, did not move back. He did not even remove from the president's office a portrait that Conant had hung of Benjamin Franklin, who had an honorary degree from Harvard but nonetheless kept saying uncharitable things about the place. "Franklin doesn't deserve to be there," Pusey said one day, looking up at the picture that had been looking down on him for fifteen years.

The ranking officer to remain in University Hall was another Franklin who Mr. Pusey thought had every right to be there (though there were, that April day, those students who obviously disagreed)—Franklin Ford, who has been dean of the Faculty of Arts and Sciences since 1961.

A midwesterner, like Pusey, Ford spent his undergraduate years at the University of Minnesota, where an uncle of his was a dean. As a dean himself at Harvard, Ford supervised a sixty-million-dollar budget and was responsible for 117 University entities, including an observatory, an arboretum, and the Department of Athletics—all of which Harvard arbitrarily lumps together under Arts and Sciences. Harvard grants its deans considerable autonomy and leeway. To the distress, and even anger, of many Harvard students, Mr. Pusey declined to commit the University, institutionally, to a stand on the Vietnam war. Mr. Ford, by contrast, joined a Harvard group that went to Washington late in 1967 to meet with President Johnson and express their personal misgivings about the government's policies. It clearly hurt him that Harvard students who regarded him, in his own words, as a running dog of the imperialists should apparently have forgotten that he was on their side; it struck him as particularly ironic that less than twenty-four hours before he was hustled out of his office he should have been attending a meeting of a local committee trying to stop the A.B.M.

Dean Ford described the invasion of University Hall as "sickening," and a few days later he himself was stricken with a circulatory ailment and forced to take a month off. On his return, there was a touch of tartness to some of his remarks. At a Phi Beta Kappa lunch, noticing that some of the students present had red armbands on, he mentioned the "continuing inventiveness of Harvard men in finding ways of wearing their school colors;" addressing the graduating seniors at their Class Day exercises, he said that he hoped the level of civility prevailing at that occasion suggested that decent manners had returned to Harvard. Speaking to alumni of the Graduate School of Arts and Sciences, he had some more reflective thoughts, on Harvard's past and future: "A central fact worth insisting on is that most free men, most of the time, support and sustain institutions not for what they make individuals do, but for what they permit individuals to do. . . . But let there be no mistake about two points, which no running fire of criticism can obscure, much less destroy. Harvard University is an institution, and its institutional structure, evolving constantly as it always has for three and a third centuries, will be sustained for what it permits scholars of all ages to do and protects them in doing. Second, Harvard University is dedicated to the broader definition of learning, a definition which is open and flexible as to content, but rigorous as to standards of accuracy and fairness. . . ." Fairness, since April 9, had been much on his mind.

Ford's office in University Hall was a step away from a massive, high-ceilinged chamber in which his Faculty of Arts and Sciences regularly met—a room that looks as though it belonged in the Capitol in Washington, and to which, until the students barged in, admittance had been even more restricted than to the floor of the Senate. Ford himself had once invited an outsider to sit in on a faculty meeting; then, appalled by his own temerity, he had held the invitation in abeyance until it could be approved by President Pusey. Until the spring of 1969, it almost went without saying, no student had entered the doors while the faculty was in session.

The Faculty Room is furnished with heavy, black leather chairs, and it is embellished with twenty-eight portraits, fifteen busts, and two plaques, commemorating Harvard dignitaries past and present, who have been depicted as if they'd never made a mistake in their lives. Artists have to be careful with Harvard subjects. In one of the undergraduate residential houses hangs a portrait of George Lyman Kittredge, the Shakespearean scholar. The fingers of one hand look peculiar. The artist had shown Kittredge holding a cigar, as he almost always did in life; the professor's family thought the cigar was undignified, however, and insisted that it be painted out.

A century ago the Faculty of Arts and Sciences consisted of twenty men, and they could meet around a single table. In 1969, there were over 700 of them, 375 with tenure. It has pleased Mr. Pusey that more endowed professorships were established during the first fifteen years of his regime than during all previous administrations together. The Faculty Room seats only 260, but this rarely causes any inconvenience. (After an examination of the room in the summer of 1968, a Cambridge building inspector had declared it unsafe for occupancy by more than 250.) At routine meetings of the group, the room is often barely half filled. Indeed, to achieve a quorum of 115, newly appointed instructors and assistant professors are all but ordered to put in an appearance. The sessions are usually dull. In a survey conducted among the group not long ago, of 225 tenured faculty members who evaluated faculty meetings, 9 found them needless, 46 pleasant, 95 interesting, 26 thought-provoking, 105 essential, and 85 boring. One professor who felt that students had gone too far in demanding the right to participate in the University's decision-making processes proposed that they should be punished by being *required* to attend faculty meetings.

There was always a certain somnolent majesty to these conclaves notwithstanding. The agenda, called a docket, would not be mimeographed but printed. Lady pourers were stationed at two urn-laden tables—one for coffee, one for tea. Sitting beneath a portrait of President Eliot, Mr. Pusey presided (as he was entitled to at the meetings of all other Harvard faculties), and the assembled professors, many of them men celebrated for their articulateness, would be strangely subdued. "It's the one place where I'm afraid to open my yap," said Edward M. Purcell, the ordinarily far from reticent physicist. There would be exceptions, inevitably. Professor Seymour Harris spent forty-two years on the Harvard faculty and not only liked to be heard but was more often than not the first man to speak up, whatever the subject on the agenda. After he left Cambridge, he ran into Mr. Pusey one day. "Gee, Seymour, we can hardly get things started now that you're not around," the president said.

At the faculty meetings, certain ritualistic formalities are observed. When a professor dies, a committee of his colleagues is designated to write a minute about him, and this obituary—which sometimes takes more than a year to prepare—is duly read aloud, and then released to the rest of the world through the University's *Gazette*, along with obits that have been delivered before other faculties. Some of the tributes are quite lively. In affectionate remembrance of one Medical School professor, for instance, his friends wrote, "No one will ever forget Sam's ability to mimic the sound and timing of a cardiac murmur."

In others, the authors sometimes seize the chance to make pertinent comments about the institution their departed colleague helped them serve. Thus, in reflecting on the life of Edwin G. Boring, the psychologist, whom a testimonial committee of five other psychologists memorialized as "Mr. Psychology," his chroniclers concluded, "His loyalty to Harvard was irrepressible, but for all its intensity, it was derivative and conditional. Harvard, he said, is an Institution of Learning, not an Educational Institution. The University ought therefore, he suggested, to declare itself for scholarship by dramatic action: adjourn all classes and place the institution at the unimpeded service of the scholar and the apprentice. A year's recess now and then would suffice to demonstrate that the creative life of the mind takes precedence over curriculum and credits. The march of the *zeitgeist*, which for Boring was the moving force of history, may yet see fit to rescue Harvard by the means he proposed."

Since 1942, it has also been Harvard practice for the president to award an honorary M.A. to every new faculty member who doesn't have some Harvard degree. "It's a strange custom," one

Yale man on the Harvard faculty has observed. "You're supposed to be naked around here until you're vested with a Harvard degree." For Mr. Pusey, however, this procedure had its uses. It enabled him to tell other professors something of a newcomer's background. It enabled the newcomer to stand up and be seen. Most of all, it reminded the assembled academicians how dependent Harvard had become on scholars elsewhere educated.

Some of the veteran members of the Harvard flock think that Harvard confers these honorary degrees for less elevated reasons: that they are either a form of decontamination, or an insinuation that Harvard believes other universities' degrees don't count, or an attempt by Harvard to swell the ranks of its alumni, so the recipients can be approached in the next fund-raising drive. One professor who switched to Harvard from the University of Chicago was unaware that he was eligible for a degree and skipped the meeting at which he was to be honored. When his name was called out, nobody stood up. "I'd have been there if I'd known about the deal, just to avoid embarrassing Pusey," the professor said later.

The sociologist Alex Inkeles, who merely had degrees from Cornell and Columbia when he joined the Harvard faculty in 1948, showed up for his initiation into the fraternity all right, but couldn't make up his mind over the next twenty years whether or not to mention the honorary degree in his curriculum vitae. "It seems presumptuous and embarrassing to list it, but not to list it would be in a way a rejection of the institution I work at," Inkeles says. "So I list it half the time. After all, it does lend reality to the notion that everybody on the faculty has an intimate connection with Mother Harvard, or is it 'Father'?" It is usually "Mother"; the Harvard view is that Harvard's sons are not conceived but whelped.

"In any good university, the faculty runs things and blames the administration when something goes wrong."
—David Riesman

xviii

MANY UNIVERSITIES HAVE a senate, composed of the members of all their faculties. Harvard has never had one, and that is just as well. On all its faculties together, there are five thousand persons, and its largest auditorium holds only twelve hundred. Harvard may or may not have a university-wide Faculty Council. There was one once. It convened while Eliot was president, to adopt a code governing the wearing of academic gowns. It met once under Conant, to discuss faculty pensions. Pusey professed never really to know whether or not a council still existed, and would as soon not have found out. If somebody had decided that there was a council, somebody else might have demanded that it meet, and the only large enough site that Harvard owned was the football stadium.

The students did use the stadium for meetings a couple of times while debating whether to strike in the spring of 1969. Nearly ten thousand people assembled there, and the sessions were remarkable, considering the circumstances, for their orderliness. Parliamentary procedures were pretty much observed, four-letter words were conspicuous by their absence, ideas were more frequently aired than epithets, and one outside observer, returning Harvard briefly to its leadership role, described the first stadium get-together as "a seminar in rebellion." Even the faculty was permitted to get in a word; Stanley Hoffman read a statement signed by over one hundred of his colleagues to the effect that they were eager to work with students to change and improve the university. "We as teachers strongly believe that our students must be heard," the statement went. "We as teachers also have a demand: it is that we work together in a rational atmosphere and compassionate spirit."

There is some mingling of all the Harvard faculties at the Faculty Club, where the lunchtime traffic is heavy. (Ever since the Second World War, the Club's menu has listed horse steak. Nobody ever seems to order it. Every so often, the dish is eliminated from the menu, but is soon restored at the behest of professors who never eat it but cherish its availability as part of the Harvard legend.) The Harvard faculties are powerful. The most powerful is the Faculty of Arts and Sciences. At Commencement time in 1969, the University News Office decided, just in case some students decided to make another march upon University Hall, to move out of its permanent offices there and into temporary quarters. The head of the News Office, William Pinkerton, an administrative officer directly responsible to President Pusey, made tentative arrangements to move to fairly confined and grubby premises that were under administrative control. There was an infinitely better spot available, but he didn't dare ask for it, because it was the domain of Modern Languages. But one of Pinkerton's assistants dared; her husband was a full professor in Arts and Sciences. She asked for the space and she got it.

The Faculty of Arts and Sciences used to be called "the immediate government." To become a tenured professor in its ranks was once the height of most American scholars' ambition, and many still think it an agreeable fate. Once a person achieves tenure, he is assured of a job until he retires. He may be dismissed only if he is convicted of a felony or is found guilty by the university of gross misconduct or gross neglect of duty or flagrant moral turpitude that reflects discredit on Harvard. "We had this professor here for years who was clearly insane," a member of the economics department told an acquaintance, "but since he was in the English department no one took any notice of it."

It is hard to be flagrant at Harvard. There was one senior professor who kept getting involved with young secretaries. It was an especially awkward situation because he was on the faculty of the Divinity School. He probably could have been dismissed, but instead he was transferred to Arts and Sciences, where greater leeway in personal conduct could be condoned. Whether or not a tenured professor is a bad teacher is irrelevant. A professor of economics told a visitor to Cambridge, "If I decided to devote the rest of my life to Chinese painting, nobody could do a thing about it." Less than 20 per cent of the younger teachers at Harvard ultimately achieve tenure there. This never bothered President Pusey. "Our *mission* is to send people out into the world," he would say. No matter how promising a scholar may seem, he cannot be offered tenure unless there is a vacancy in his department, and if after five years as an assistant professor he doesn't get promoted, he leaves. "Up or out" is the phrase.

Some men go out to other pastures and ultimately return. The chairman of the history department, H. Stuart Hughes, has shuttled in and out of the University. He got his Ph.D. from Harvard in 1940, but nobody asked him to stay around. He was invited back as an assistant professor in 1948. He was passed over for promotion to associate professor in 1952, and went to Stanford. Five years later, Harvard decided it really wanted him after all and offered him a full professorship. Some men leave and don't return. Harvard showed no enthusiasm for hanging onto Paul Samuelson when he was an assistant professor of economics. M.I.T. grabbed him, and he has stayed there. So many economists have drifted away from Harvard that they have inspired a small academic joke: "Does Harvard, M.I.T., or Yale have the best Harvard economics department?"

Because tenured professors are hard to get rid of, a university should be prudent before taking them on. Harvard likes to think that it usually is. It has turned down men for no reason other than that their wives were unbearable. Harvard can't be as choosy as it once was, however. "Anybody who's good enough for us to want is good enough for the place he's at to want to hang onto him even more," Dean Ford has said. Of three men offered in turn one particular post in the history department, the first, who was working in Peru, said he much preferred the climate there to Cambridge's; the second, in Germany, didn't want to give up the extra income he was earning as a consultant to the Volkswagen company; the third, in the United States, thought he'd been poorly treated by Harvard when he was a graduate student there, and was still resentful.

Like many other universities, Harvard has begun to offer inducements to people it sorely cherishes. Recruitment is tough all over nowadays. President Howard Johnson, of M.I.T., was told by one professor, "When there's a good Chinese restaurant within walking distance of my lab, get in touch with me again." A few months later, a Chinese restaurant providentially materialized at the edge of the M.I.T. campus. President Johnson at once phoned his man, and captured him. Harvard, for its part, landed a professor by casting before him some bait that its inquiries had established would be irresistible: the man's wife was an ardent tennis player, and Harvard offered him a house with a court.

A couple of years ago, the president of another university telephoned Oscar Handlin and wanted to know if he could recommend four first-rate people who might be interested in working on a new history program his institution was setting up. Handlin, who was then head of the Harvard history department and was having troubles of his own with its vacancies, said he couldn't think of anyone offhand. Not long afterward, he ran into the president, who reported smugly that he had his four first-raters. Handlin congratulated him and then asked how the president knew they were so good. "They have to be; we're paying them twenty-five thousand each," the president said. "He had a problem and didn't even know it," Handlin told a friend afterward.

Some universities will offer an especially sought-after professor thirty-five thousand dollars. Harvard will not. Its top pay for any man is twenty-eight thousand dollars, and it refuses to have any part of a so-called star system. Moreover, although Harvard offers some pleasant fringe benefits—a noncontributory retirement plan, for instance—it is sticky about others. Most universities, when one of their professors is asked to deliver a paper at a colloquium, will pay his expenses. They figure that it's good public relations. Harvard's contrary attitude, as summarized by one of its administrators, is, "If they want a guy from Harvard to dress up their meeting, let them pay for it."

Harvard professors, however, rarely have to make do with their salary. President Conant once said that any professor worth his salt ought to be able to double his earned income without impairing his work at the University. Today, at least 10 per cent of the members of the Harvard faculty earn more from books, articles, lectures, and consultancies than they earn from Harvard. Professor John T. Dunlop, of the economics department, is the very highly compensated impartial charman of a group that tries to settle labor disputes in the building industry; he has maintained a full-time office in Washington for twenty years. Professors at the Medical School have private practices. Professors at the Law School have clients.

Practically everybody connected with the Business School has lucrative outside connections. Professor James J. Healey gets forty-five thousand dollars a year for serving as the umpire of contract disputes between the Ford Motor Company and the United Auto Workers. Professor George A. Smith, Jr., served as a consultant to the Continental Oil Company for nearly twenty years. The Business School *likes* to have its professors get involved with real-life business situations. The professors, though, are supposed to get their dean's permission before they make commitments, and the work they do is supposed to do the School some good, or at any rate do it no harm. It is more or less the rule of thumb that they devote no more than one working day a week to moonlighting. For that one day, they are apt to get from three to five hundred dollars.

Vacancies in Harvard academic departments do not arise from anything as simple as death, retirement, or resignation. Rather, they crop up at prescribed intervals according to a formula that was devised some years ago by a Harvard mathematician of an actuarial bent. If a department is especially keen on trying to get a new man, however, and has no opening at the moment, it is allowed to borrow against some future vacancy. Only in this narrow, non-pecuniary instance does the Harvard administration, celebrated for its fiscal prudence, usually tolerate borrowing.

When a department wants to have a permanent appointment made, it asks the appropriate dean to ask the president to appoint an ad hoc committee to evaluate candidates. President Conant initiated this system. At least two professors from outside institutions are generally asked to serve on each committee; the president usually sits in himself. "It takes up an awful lot of my time, but it's given me marvelous insights into the development of knowledge," Mr. Pusey has said. "For one thing, I'm made aware of the thinking of important men in the various disciplines about where their disciplines are heading. A lot of this is guesswork, of course, but it's fascinating and at least it's enlightened guesswork. You simply can't plan on any rational basis for intellectual trends ten years ahead. That's one of the difficulties of running a place like Harvard. Who could have foreseen, for instance, that all the students who were passionately interested in government right after the war would turn into the students who felt the same way, a decade later, about Oriental religions? Who could have foreseen that theoretical physics would give way in popularity to biochemistry? Some of the committee meetings are anything but exciting, but over the years I've been privy to some tremendously interesting discussions of medical and legal curriculums, or, say, of mathematical logic. I would never have known about something like that except for the ad hoc committees, and the experts who serve on them are terribly considerate about finding ways to communicate with an ignorant man. Most college presidents would give anything to be present at some of these sessions. And, just think, it's my duty!"

Not only is Harvard meticulous about evaluating prospective faculty members; it is forever evaluating itself, sometimes seeming almost pathologically anxious about its motives and conduct. In the spring of 1967, Dean Ford asked six senior professors, with Mr. Dunlop as their chairman, to look into the worrisome manpower situation. The group was formally called the Committee on Recruitment and Retention of Faculty. To some of the men serving on it, it was known informally as the Committee to Keep Harvard from Going to Hell. The committee worked for a year, soliciting information not merely from its own community but also from ten outlying universities. A questionnaire that was distributed among all members of the Faculty of Arts and Sciences elicited some strange responses. One instructor declined to answer it. Instead, he sent along a note saying that Harvard was hopeless and its hopelessness could be summarized in four sentences: "Harvard is a factory. Harvard is a bureaucracy. Harvard is stingy. Harvard is illiberal."

Hoping for some expatiation, Professor Dunlop invited the fellow to lunch, but at the last minute the angry young man begged off. "I was sorry, because I wanted to find out whether he was mad at the university or the universe," Dunlop said afterward. "Also, I didn't like that business about the factory. I had a hunch he had never been inside a real factory, and I was going to say to him, 'I resent your disparaging factories.'"

The committee's report, issued in the spring of 1968, incorporated some statistics that indicated the difficulties Harvard faced in keeping its teaching staff up to snuff. Over a ten-year period, 86 of 203 scholars in the humanities and social sciences whom Harvard had hoped to recruit from other institutions had rebuffed its overtures, and in the natural sciences the picture was even gloomier—50 rejections out of 77 offers. "No university can hope to have a monopoly of the nation's talents, nor would it be in the national interest for any university to achieve such a concentra-

tion," the committee concluded. "The day is past, if it ever existed, in which an invitation to Harvard was all that was required
to bring a faculty member from another leading university." At
these bleak revelations, the *Crimson* ran an editorial commenting
on "the erosion of Harvard's eminence."

A considerable amount of Harvard power is concentrated in
the chairmen of the various academic departments, which have
been characterized by John P. Elder, the dean of the Graduate
School of Arts and Sciences, as "forty-five bastions of medieval
autonomy." His immediate superior, Dean Ford, has been thought
by some Harvard people to be, in one special context, the bravest
man in their midst, because each fall he would give a cocktail
party for all the bastiontenders. "What makes Franklin think the
heads of departments *like* each other?" said a man fresh from a recent such get-together. There is some backbiting within departments, too. At one departmental meeting not long ago, a professor
looked around the room thoughtfully and said to a colleague, "Is
there anyone here you'd have played with as a kid?"

It is the department heads who establish the patterns of instruction in their fields, and who, specifically, decide what courses
will be offered each term. Courses, that is, outside the area of general education, which draws on the various departments for instructors but has its own administrative set-up. Some professors
in each of the three broad areas into which Gen. Ed. is divided—
humanities, social sciences, and natural sciences—welcome a chance
to have a respite from the sometimes confining jurisdiction of their
own departments. "My humanities course is absolutely subversive
by the criteria of the English department," Professor Reuben
Brower said cheerfully not long ago. "The sciences aside, Harvard
has always had an historical approach to things, and that includes
literature. When I was asked to give a survey course on English
literature for Gen. Ed., I decided that there was no need to treat
the literary monuments in chronological order, and no reason to
cover everything. After all, who wants to read some of the minor
eighteenth-century poets, some of whom I teach about? When I

described what I proposed to do, or rather what I proposed to ignore, some of my colleagues blinked. Where were the landmarks?, they asked. Where were the Bible, Plato, and Shakespeare? I said that most people knew about them by the time they got to Harvard, and that anyway, what could be more general in education than to forget about landmarks and instead explain how a poem works or how a play is put together?"

Each department has its own recruitment policy. Chemistry rarely promotes young men from its own ranks. English and Classics more often do than don't. Recently, Classics made an exception, engaging a man from a midwest university. "We needed a papyrologist and didn't have one of our own," a professor explained. Two hundred years earlier, every Harvard instructor, like Miss Kantrowitz in the third grade, had been expected to, and did, teach every subject.

THE CATALOGUE OF the Faculty of Arts and Sciences lists 1,184 half courses and 166 full courses, not counting independent-study courses, a grab-bag category that covers work students do on their own. (One morose undergraduate got permission to inquire into "Inherent Discontent in Post-Industrial Civilization," which turned out to be little more than contemplation of his own despondency.) The statistics are misleading. Not every course listed is offered every year. If a professor is on sabbatical or simply chooses not to give his regular course, he doesn't have to. It is the responsibility of a department chairman to see to it that enough courses are given in his field to satisfy the needs of the students in it.

Some of the courses are quite special. At last report, several— Korean 102A (Intermediate Korean), Akkadian 233 (Advanced Akkadian), Hebrew 123A (Medieval Prose and Poetry), and Turkic 290 (Yakut)—had one student apiece. The professors in charge of courses like those are not abashed by the low enrollment figures. But if a man offers a lecture course on a general subject and only a couple of hundred students sign up for it, he may be mortified. One of the most popular courses among undergraduates has lately been Social Sciences 137 (the Legal Process), a course on law for men not planning to go to Law School. It has had an enrollment of nearly nine hundred and is taught by Professor Paul Freund, of the Law School. "I'm ashamed to talk about having so many students," Freund says. "It shouldn't happen at Harvard."

For all the variety of courses in the catalogue, thirty big lecture courses among them comprise more than half the classroom experience of all Harvard undergraduates, and this disturbs a lot of educators who consider the value of mass teaching to be, at best, moot. William Alfred, who presides over one of the bigger ones, says, "I don't consider that talking into a microphone to five hundred people is teaching. It's rather some kind of a performance."

Alfred is at least an engaging performer; he is quite likely to interrupt a discussion of classical Greek drama for a digression on Bulgarian curse words. There are some professors whose lectures are little more than paraphrases of their latest publications. Standing up and talking about material that is readily available in print embarrasses some men, but not others. One professor, asked if he didn't feel a bit uncomfortable, holding forth on a subject he had thoroughly covered in a book, said, "Oh, I'm not lecturing on that edition. I'm lecturing on the footnotes I'm collecting for the second edition." The proprietors of some of the old established lecture courses, however, hardly ever change their spiels; it is said of one professor that when he opens his notes, little bats fly out. And some of the younger men get nervous when they face a quizzical and sometimes nearly hostile Harvard audience. One lecturer gave up ten minutes before the end of his period, after telling his class, "Gee, and it sounded so *good* when I was preparing it last night."

And then there was the Harvard instructor in history—or could he be an apocryphal figure who has left his pitiable mark on campuses the world over?—who was being considered for promotion to assistant professor, and into his lecture hall six very senior professors solemnly marched, to observe him in action. The chap under scrutiny was talking away when he was all but drowned out by titters and then by unrestrained laughter. A wall panel behind him had been removed so the building could be rewired, and a workman's leg was dangling behind the instructor. Unawares, he kept on trying to talk, and he somehow got through what for him became a nightmare, but he was never the same man again. Ultimately, he gave up teaching and became a foundation administrator.

When it comes to selecting courses, the students are often bewildered by the choices confronting them, and they turn for help to a *Confidential Guide* issued each fall by the *Crimson*, which sells twenty-five hundred copies a year—mostly to freshmen, who are the most bewildered—at a $1.75 a copy. The *Guide* deals only with courses that have an enrollment of at least one hundred.

The Law School and the School of Education have similar guides. The Law School's, which bears the subtitle *Teachers as we see them—super stars, bumblers, minutiae minds, mumblers,* is apt to be severe in its judgments of professors: "getting old and has a tendency to ramble"; "a nice guy but the worst teacher I ever had at any level of my education"; "incredible HLS could allow this to go on." Professors at the School of Education get a somewhat better break; they are allowed to defend themselves immediately following their critics' comments: "I found my seminar group in general to be very intelligent and mature and am amazed at the idea that it should 'flounder and finally sink in its own independence.'"

The *Crimson's* booklet is often snide: ". . . undergraduates could absorb the subject matter more quickly and easily by reading Galbraith's book, and then inviting the great man to dinner." But for all its flaws, this *Guide* may be a better guide than a callow advisor who has been around only a couple of days himself, has barely had a chance to skim through the official course catalogue, and who may then say to a bewildered freshman, "Why don't you take HUM 2? They seem to have Dante and Milton in there, and you can't go wrong with those guys."

The perennial favorite of the undergraduate *Guide*'s publishers was the late Crane Brinton, the history professor in reference to whom this *Guide* once said that Harvard's history should be divided into two time eras, "B.B." and "A.B."—"Before Brinton" and "After Brinton." Urging all hands not to miss his History 134A (Intellectual History of Europe in the Eighteenth and Nineteenth Centuries) the *Guide* declared, "Take it because it *is* History, because it *is* Brinton, and because it *is* Harvard." History 134A also had the reputation of being a gut course. "You've all heard that this is a gut, and it is," Brinton would announce to his seven or eight hundred appreciative students at their first session together. It was all but impossible to get less than a C. It is hard to flunk anything at Harvard. During one faculty meeting, someone wondered how many "E's" were doled out each year in the whole College. No one present had any idea. A statistician left the room, and reported on returning that the total for the entire year before had been 231—about one-tenth of one per cent of all the grades handed out.

A possibly apocryphal story about Brinton had to do with the football player—Brinton was very popular with athletes—who discovered twenty-four hours before graduation that he lacked half a credit. He went to Professor Brinton, who, after a moment's reflection, said he guessed he had better enroll him in a course at once and move directly to the final exam. Brinton's half of the dialogue that allegedly followed went something like this: "Now, which of my two courses would you prefer? Do you know more about intellectual history or French history? . . . Ah, French. Question Number One: About when did the French Revolution take place? . . . Are you sure you mean the seventeenth century? . . . Ah, 'Some time in the eighteenth century?' Very good. . . . Question Number Two: What was the name of a strong fortress that was stormed during that Revolution? . . . Oh, come now, you know it; they have a holiday named after the place. . . . 'Bastille!' Splendid! All right, now; one last question: Who was Marat? . . . No, M-a-r-a-t. . . . Oh, dear, you've never heard of him? Well, never mind, you got two out of three, and that's passing."

It is hard to define just what a gut course is. A graduate student at Harvard once said that Sanskrit was a gut, provided one knew enough Greek. An undergraduate on the football team asserted that no course could be considered a gut if its prescribed reading list contained more than three books. By that yardstick, Professor Brinton easily passed muster. Announcing in a lecture one day that he was going to assign two books, and being greeted by a storm of friendly hisses, he said, "Well, one?" In his very last lecture, given two months before his death, he urged his students to read some back issues of *Punch* before an exam—"if it isn't too much trouble"—and reminisced about a young man who, trying to justify his having missed an exam entirely, had explained that he had a social obligation to get drunk the night before. "Permissive though I am," Professor Brinton said, "that was too much for me."

History 134A used to meet at nine in the morning. Students would bring along coffee and Danish, and the course got the nickname "Breakfast with Brinton." When its time was changed to eleven, it became "Brunch with Brinton." Professor Stanley Hoffman's course on "War" meets an hour later; it is called "Darkness at Noon." Harvard abounds with course nicknames. A gut course in geology, also very popular with athletes, is called "Rocks for Jocks." Pre-Civil-War American history is "Mint Juleps." The major lecture course on Chinese history is "Rice Paddies"; its counterpart on Mideast history is "Sand Dunes." The formal title "Psychopharmacological Search for Identity" was shortened to "Drugs 1." Professor Erik Erikson's course on "The Human Life Cycle" has *two* nicknames. His students call it "Womb to Tomb." He himself prefers "Bust to Dust."

A much talked-about course at Harvard in recent years has been Social Relations 120 (Analysis of Interpersonal Behavior), which also has a pair of aliases—"Sluts and Nuts" and "The Look-at-your-navel-in-a-group course." It is very popular. It can accommodate only 125 students, but has more than twice that number of applicants. Those who get in are put in five sections. Each meets three times a week, and the students freely discuss their own hang-ups—sex, religion, drugs, authority symbols, Vietnam, Harvard, whatever is bothering them—while other students peer at them through one-way-vision glass. The dialogue sometimes gets extremely personal. The people connected with the course are supposed to keep what they hear in it to themselves, and indeed take a sort of Hippocratic oath pledging themselves to reticence.

The oath is repeatedly violated. One Radcliffe girl had hardly left the class when word got out that she was furious at a Harvard boy because, whereas she wanted to be thought of as a mother image, he insisted that what she really wanted was to be a sex symbol. Around Cambridge, it is widely believed that Soc Rel 120 is an exercise in group psychotherapy; this dismays its sponsors, who are not physicians and who go out of their way to assert that they are simply trying to make their students realize that most of the functions and activities of society occur in group situations, and that the students, moreover, are merely engaging in advocacy of the kind of self-realization that was considered a significant aspect of education way back in Plato's day.

The syllabus for the course says, *inter alia*, "Improvement in general knowledge of human behavior is expected. Readings, papers, and examinations are utilized. But at the same time, you should take the course only if you are prepared to participate and try to improve your understanding of yourself as an individual person. . . . No student should take the course under the assumption that he will receive therapy. . . . Over the history of the course there have been no known instances of injury to emotional health. Nevertheless, no student who has reason to believe that he is not reasonably well-adjusted should enroll."

According to Professor Robert F. Bales, who has charge of the course (and who guards it vigilantly; it is the only official course at Harvard from which visitors are barred), "The members of our staff never maintain a therapeutic relationship to the students except when it might be needed temporarily as a cushion. It's a rugged kind of self-analytic procedure. Whereas in society it isn't polite to question other people's motives, in Soc Rel 120 it's expected. If people are silent in class, the possible reasons for that are discussed, and if people get embarrassed—well, we discuss *that*. Nearly everything that goes on is in one sense trivial. There is no definable task set for the students. All they do is talk. But when people reach the point in talking where they lay themselves on the line, it isn't trivial any longer. Taking the course can be a poetic, artistic, thrilling experience in the here and now."

Whatever people at Harvard may say about Social Relations 120, they hardly ever accuse it of being irrelevant. The students are increasingly requesting that the curriculum be amended to incorporate courses that relate to their driving interests—courses on, say, "Processes for Institutional Change." The kinds of courses that some of the more avant-garde students would like if they had a free hand in designing the curriculum were indicated by a syllabus produced by the proprietors of the Harvard New College—an informal, experimental, opportunistic, and short-lived academy that sprang into being while Harvard Old College was still suffering from its April convulsions. Among a couple of dozen course offerings were "Psychology of Modern Alienated Man," "Radicalism and the Music Drama," "The Limits of Rationality," "Legitimacy and Authority," "Elementary Yoga," "American Anti-War Literature," "Talking Straight," "Norman Mailer," and "Research and the American University." Some of the courses were conducted by undergraduates. Some were held out of doors on the Cambridge Common, which at just about the same time was proclaimed off limits to bicycle riders. For some Radcliffe girls concerned both about freedom of education and of movement it must have been hard to decide whether these changes in the Common represented a net plus or minus in values on the liberation scale.

As far as the conventional curriculum is concerned, the faculty has on the whole been receptive to student demands. It has resisted, so far, giving academic credit to students who drop out for half a year to take part in a political campaign (although some students would argue that this should be considered an independent-study project called, say, "The Social Aspects of Participatory Politics 62B"); it glumly contemplates the future day when it may have to argue with students who, desiring academic credit for their favorite pursuits, may beseech official academic sanction for *Crimson*-editing, Beer-drinking, or Goofing-off.

But with the elasticity that characterizes so much of Harvard, the faculty has cheerfully condoned "anti-courses"—sections of a course organized specifically to rebut the views of a professor in charge of it. A recent phenomenon was the emergence of the Harvard Education Project, which was organized by undergraduates in the fall of 1967 to take a long, hard look at the University. Its prime mover was Jeffrey L. Elman, a member of the class of 1969 from Los Angeles, who mustered five task forces to examine Harvard. "We wanted to articulate the things that are wrong about Harvard and plan an ideal university, and to establish a tradition that Harvard doesn't yet have—that of frankly radical self-examination," Elman said. He assembled a batch of material on which to base a syllabus for a course, and he decided to put one together in the fall of 1968. He got a foundation grant of fifty-five hundred dollars and planned to hire his own instructors. But as so many Harvard men had learned before him, Harvard proved resilient. The faculty decided to give his project its blessing, and an official new course was born—Social Relations 136 (Workshops on the University).

Thus Harvard students were enabled to scrutinize Harvard—punch and pummel it and belabor it if they chose—and to receive full academic credit for their efforts.

One graduate student to another in the elevator of the behavioral sciences center: "Get some undergraduate to help you. After all, how much scientific knowledge does it take to write down numbers while somebody spits chemical solutions into a pot?"

XIX

THE CHARLES RIVER, which flows sluggishly between Cambridge and Boston and curls through Harvard University, lends a pleasant note of rusticity to an institution that began in a cowyard and is increasingly being smothered in the embrace of megalopolis. On warm spring days, the gently sloping, grassy banks of the Charles are so comfortable—for reading, or thinking, or dozing, or cuddling—that the Harvard sponsors of militant rallies, even in these pulsing times, are hard-pressed to muster respectable turnouts.

The river—the crossing of which, by ferry and later by toll bridge, was a modest source of Harvard revenue for more than two centuries—is not broad. The Harvard stadium is on the Boston side of it, and many spectators proceed from the Cambridge side on foot. They usually take the Larz Anderson bridge, named after a Harvard College graduate who had died in the First World War. En route, homecoming alumni pass a memorial plaque informing them that the bridge is supposed to be "a lasting suggestion that they should devote their manhood developed by study and play on the banks of this river to the nation and its needs." Along with many Harvard athletic facilities, the Schools of Business Administration, Medicine, Dental Medicine, and Public Health lie across the Charles from the bulk of the University, and for this reason the narrow stream is sometimes figuratively described around Cambridge as "a very wide river." A professor at the Business School can usually pry a laugh from his students by remarking that he has two researchers at work in far-off places—one at Palm Springs, California, and the other at the Harvard Law School.

The once sharp lines of demarcation that isolated many of the components of the university from most of the others have lately become blurred. As at so many other citadels of higher education, at Harvard interdisciplinarianism has been on the upsurge. It used to take five years—the standard three at the first, the standard two at the second—for an individual who wanted degrees from the Law School and the Business School to go through both. Now, the two schools have started a joint four-year course. When the Medical School decided not long ago to request that people bequeath to it, at their death, such parts of their bodies as it could use, it boldly solicited the entire Faculty of Arts and Sciences. (Postmortem anatomical gifts to Harvard are just about the only ones, to date, that have not been declared tax-deductible.)

The gulf that used to separate the sciences and the humanities may be bridged, on a personal level, when a Nobel-Prize-winning biochemist asks a professor of classics to provide him with words of authentically Greek roots to describe his electromicroscopic discoveries. On an institutional level, an undergraduate course examining the role of engineers in the study of biological systems may be collaboratively conducted by the faculties of Medicine, Public Health, and Arts and Sciences. To study leadership in the economics of health, those three faculties are joined by still two others—those of Business and Government. A new doctoral program for the production of clinical psychologists is all at once under Medicine, Arts and Sciences, Education, and Divinity. Business students and medical students learn ethics from a Divinity School professor. (The late Samuel H. Miller, while dean of the

Divinity School, was a perennially popular lecturer at the Business School, partly because it was his ingratiating habit to remark that there seemed to be more religion taught on that campus than on his own.) An informal undergraduate seminar on urban Negro literature may be jointly supervised by a second-year student in the Divinity School and by a city planner in the School of Design. Even Harvard wives have lately been flirting faddishly with more than one discipline at a time, paying ten dollars an hour for the privilege of enrolling in an extracurricular study-and-exercise group that is supposed to relate psychoanalysis and physiotherapy and to lead them to the gates of a happy valley that its sponsors call psychophysical integration.

Much of the interdisciplinary activity at Harvard has centered about centers. No self-respecting university these days would be without its quota of centers, and Harvard is as amply endowed with them as with other riches. (The centers are largely supported by grants from the government or from foundations; McGeorge Bundy once called them the venture capital of the university.) Harvard has centers, to name just a few, for Cognitive Studies, Urban Studies, Population Studies, Research in Personality, Careers, American History, Environmental and Behavioral Biology, Environmental Design Studies, and the Far East. This last is a haven for experts from law, sociology, government, and economics. Under the Law School, a Center for the Advancement of Criminal Justice has lately got under way; under the School of Education, a Center for Educational Policy Research. The Medical School (in combination with other divisions) now operates a Center for Community Health and Medical Care, and in the summer of 1969 broke ground for a Laboratory of Human Reproduction and Reproductive Biology, which Harvard students call the Sex Center. It goes without saying that an Afro-American Studies Center is in the works—somewhat to the envy of Harvard scholars who have for years been bemoaning the absence of a Latin-American Studies Center. Latin-American students, however, do not constitute much of a threat to campus serenity, except, of course, in Latin America.

Some of the centers were supposed to be temporary establishments to foster certain research at a certain time; once in operation, though, they seem to hang on, like government agencies. When one of the earliest centers, for Russian Research, was set up in 1947, its sponsors wanted to call it the Russian Research Institute, but had to settle for "Center" because the University thought "Institute" had too entrenched a sound to it. That center is still going strong; the Harvard University Press alone, indeed, has already published fifty-nine books that have emanated from it.

The existence of all these centers is a boon to post-doctoral students, many of whom have run out of courses they can take and degrees they can study for. They can, though, get themselves a research grant and affiliate themselves with a handy center in their field. Harvard has a thousand post-doctorals around at almost any given time, and it welcomes them. Formidable in knowledge and intellect, they are attractive to professors, and there are few enough of them so they rarely get in anybody's way. Moreover, in an emergency they can always be pressed into service as teachers, though there is always the risk that by the time a man has reached the stage of post-doctoral research he is too wrapped up in his own rarefied pursuits to be able to communicate effectively with other human beings.

The principal graduate schools once functioned like feudal domains. Their deans were rival satraps who vaguely recognized the sovereignty of a president of Harvard and would now and then pay him ceremonial tribute. By way of illustrating some of the associations that deanship commonly conjures up in students' minds, the incumbent dean of the graduate School of Arts and Sciences, Professor John P. Elder, has three paintings on his office wall. One is of a school of philosophers. One is of a king. One is of a prison. Nowadays, deans are mellowing toward each other. Some of the old-guard officials of the University were astounded not long ago when a newly appointed dean of the Medical School, Dr. Robert H. Ebert, asked to have its teaching methods evaluated by the faculties of the Schools of Law, Business, and Education. On being asked if he might not have set a dangerous precedent, Dean Ebert replied cheerfully, "I guess I just didn't know any better."

The gesture was all the more arresting for the inclusion of the School of Education, which for many years had—along with the Dental School, a subsidiary of the Medical School with a student body of fifty—been thought of as a relative pariah among graduate schools. (It is a paradoxical truism of the academic world that the higher standing a university enjoys in education, the lower its regard for its own school of education.) Harvard's Graduate School of Education is now considered acceptable even at Harvard, but it has had to come a long way. Today, it is acquiring a six-million-dollar research center all its own, incorporating a new library; twenty years ago, the University was thinking of closing it down and its entire annual operating budget was $250,000.

The School of Education was launched in 1920, and for a long time its students were, by Harvard standards, country cousins— many of them being teachers from hick-town public schools who came to Cambridge to brush up on new trends in secondary-school education and who often, being of modest means, had to teach while studying. It was for that reason that many education courses were scheduled—as they still are—to meet only in the afternoon. Nowadays, the School of Education has a beefed-up faculty, many of whom are also affiliated with Arts and Sciences, and a more sophisticated student body; nearly one-third of the present crop of candidates for the basic degree of Master of Arts in Teaching made Phi Beta Kappa in college. Some of them even went to *Harvard* College. Even so, the School of Education is generally thought to be an un-Harvard-like part of Harvard. "They're very Joe Collegiate at Education," one part-time professor there recently observed. "They're not Harvard and they know it. My God, they even have beer parties."

The School of Education, snuggled in among Radcliffe's buildings, has the advantage at least of being on the Harvard side of the Charles River. Some students at the Business School, on the far shore, never cross the stream at all, and those who do often seem like tourists in Chinatown. Some of them *have* to cross the river; they live in Peabody Terrace, a Harvard-built residential complex for married graduate students. "I was walking through a Peabody hallway once," a student in the Graduate School of Arts and Sciences who also lives there said, "and damned if I didn't come across two guys having a heated conversation about which side of a refrigerator door the handle should be on to make it sell best. Two hours later, I passed by again and by then there were six of them, still discussing the same subject. That confirmed my original diagnosis that they could only be from the B School."

Let it not be thought that Business School students are without their carefree side. They have a newspaper of their own, the *HarBusNews*, and it puts out a *Collegiate Guide to Skiing in the East*. Eleven of them ran in the 1968 Boston Marathon, by far the most substantial contingent from any part of Harvard, and one of them finished eighty-fourth, well ahead of an assistant coach of the College's lacrosse team. The B-School boys, moreover, have a singing group of their own, called the Tycoons. It is an appropriate name; the average starting salary for those who finish the standard two-year course and get a Master of Business Administration degree is eleven thousand dollars. (Each year, currently, the School grants forty or so advanced Doctor of Business Administration degrees. The old term was Doctor of Commercial Science, but the degree was renamed when someone concluded that "D.C.S." sounded like the initials that might be used by a dentist who hadn't quite made it.) When outside critics suggest, as they sometimes do, that it's a pity the M.B.A.-holders don't have to begin a rung or two lower on the fiscal ladder, their dean stands ready with a rebuttal: "It is hard for us, as believers in free enterprise, to fight the laws of supply and demand."

The Business School had its near-pariah years, too. It started off, in 1908, on the Cambridge side of the river, but for quite a while had no buildings of its own, and had to operate out of cellars and attics. It did make a couple of dents on the community consciousness. In 1911, it established a Bureau of Research, and out of that came a nationally-adopted method of standardizing shoe sizes. Also, from one of its courses, "Administrative Practices," evolved a useful slang verb, "to adprac," roughly definable as "to make somebody do something you want him to do without his realizing he's being manipulated." But most Harvard professors sneered at the Business School notwithstanding: How could one take seriously, they argued, a school that taught graduate students neither a recognized profession nor an advanced art or science? Some of that attitude persists. "Our colleagues across the river," one Business School professor has observed stonily, "don't think it's academically respectable to study the real world." The Business School is so imitative of one important part of the real business world—the banking world—that at midday it bans drinking at its faculty club; if a bunch of Business School professors are giving a testimonial lunch to one of their colleagues and want to toast him in sherry, they have to cross the river and repair to the main faculty club.

In 1928, things began looking up for the Business School when, during the boom, it moved into its own quarters. Now, it has attained a sort of grudging respectability across the river, and, showing admirable interdisciplinary spirit, has for its own part been paying increasing attention to the role of the social sciences in commerce and industry. "We came to realize," one Business School professor explained solemnly, "that one of the great problems faced by business was that people had to work with other people." To the unconcealed envy of the rest of Harvard, the Business School, furthermore, has come up with some impressive fund-raising gimmicks. It gets more than seven hundred thousand dollars a year from some four hundred companies that, for a minimum annual fee of fifteen hundred dollars each, can call themselves "associates" of the School. There are also a handful of individual associates, among them Winthrop Aldrich and Supreme Court Justice Douglas.

The tangible rewards of the association are few—free copies of Business School publications and occasional invitations to seminars, where the associates can meet the dean of the School, George P. Baker, a tall, ruddy, immaculate, confidence-inspiring man who usually wears a vest. The associates, moreover, get favorably treated between January 20 and April 15 of each year, when students who expect to get their M.B.A. degrees in June are available for job interviews, to which the Business School attaches great importance. It sets aside an area for recruiting in its library, with stacks of corporate records near the interview booths, so the students can investigate the qualifications of the men investigating them. Over that twelve-week stretch, six hundred students take part in—perhaps, in view of the laws of supply and demand, *grant* should be the word—eight thousand interviews. The allotted space can comfortably accommodate only 375 corporations. Companies with associative standing get preference, all other things being equal; companies that get squeezed out have to do their recruiting by mail.

The Business School, not surprisingly, has a basically conservative orientation. Women were not tolerated as students until 1961, and miniskirts are still frowned on. A couple of girls who persisted in wearing them were banished from the students' dining hall. "There may be half a dozen beards here, but they're all pretty well trimmed," a guide told a recent visitor. In 1968, in a poll about Vietnam, half the B-School students who were eligible for the draft voted in *favor* of sending more troops there. Richard M. Nixon, who had only a passing acquaintance with the rest of the University, was the star attraction of the Business School's fiftieth-anniversary celebration in 1958. (Across the river, by stark contrast, Senator Eugene McCarthy could get a laugh from a largely Arts and Sciences audience merely by mentioning Nixon's name, and a double laugh by observing that the president had made a speech at General Beadle State College. It is quite possible that some of the students at the Business School *came* from General Beadle State.)

If the Business-School students tend to be straighter and squarer than most, so do their supervisors. Over at the College, not long before the S.D.S. eruption in the spring of 1969, a dean said, with equanimity, "Our tradition has been not to respond to hypothetical situations." At around the same time, at the Business School, where the possibility of demonstrations was all but engulfed by the improbability, the conservative administration was drawing up guidelines in case it had to respond to the same kind of hypothetical situation.

Most instruction is carried on by the case method, which can at first be upsetting for students from colleges where they were hardly ever asked, "What would you do in this situation?" The School has a collection of thirty thousand cases, all based on real-life business situations and all but a few containing real corporate names. From time to time, after the students have debated among themselves as to how a certain corporate problem might best be handled, an executive of the company in question will stop by and tell them how it actually was handled. Like other campuses, the Business School has senior professors who have acquired affectionate nicknames; until recently, a bulwark of the faculty was fondly known as "Mr. Retailing."

As students at the School are interested in retailing, so does retailing care for them. Jack I. Straus, the R. H. Macy man, is vice-chairman of the associates. Every year, Macy's, hoping to lure some newly-minted Harvard M.B.A.'s as junior executives, puts on a fashion show in a course called "Strategy Problems in Mass Distribution," complete with a slide projector, a deputation of hard-sell Macy executives—who in describing the store's board of directors make them sound like a cross between the Supreme Court and the Joint Chiefs of Staff—and a bevy of live models. Inasmuch as the class meets at 8:40 in the morning, this Harvard parade may be the earliest fashion show anywhere. At the most recent such strategy session, the forty male students who turned out for it hardly batted an eye as the models capered and swirled in front of them. It may have been the hour that made them unresponsive; it may have been the restrained behavior that even business seminarians deem proper; it may even have been that the indifference that theoretically afflicts all Harvard is contagious enough to reach across the river.

The Medical School is *really* detached, occupying a twelve-acre enclave in Boston, far from Harvard Square but within easy walking distance of four of the seven teaching hospitals with which it is affiliated—Peter Bent Brigham, Children's, Women's, and Beth Israel. That they are where they are was Harvard's doing. Peter Bent Brigham was a Boston restaurateur who died in 1877 and left $1,300,000 to accumulate for twenty-five years and then be used to build a hospital for the poor of Suffolk County. In 1902, his executors were glad to accept a Harvard proposal that the hospital—with, by then, a $4,338,137 legacy to draw on—go up alongside a new Medical School complex, particularly when Harvard offered to furnish the land, as in due course it did for the other three hospitals. Harvard's principal teaching hospital is Massachusetts General, in downtown Boston. With five affiliated hospitals, harboring five thousand beds among them, Harvard has rich clinical resources. It also has a complicated faculty. There is no single head of surgery, for instance, at the Harvard Medical School; instead, there is a council composed of the chiefs of surgery at its hospitals.

The twenty-five hundred doctors who are part- or full-time members of the faculty of the Medical School constitute half of the faculty of the entire University. Some of the physicians are specialists who may give a course—in cell biology, for instance—that lasts just a few days. Some work full-time at hospitals on research, do no teaching at all, and hardly ever visit the Medical School compound, where it is often said that a part-time professor is around part of the time and a full-time man is away all of the time. Not long ago, when Dean Ebert called a meeting of his faculty that was heavily attended (it had to do with rank and pay, matters that doctors take seriously), he remarked at the outset that, looking around the uncommonly crowded chamber, he felt like a minister on Easter Sunday. Some doctors are amazed to find themselves on the Harvard faculty. The Medical School has a further association with the McLean Hospital, a mental institution in Belmont. A few years ago, McLean hired a Belgian doctor to be its administrator. He didn't even know the place had any academic connection until he reached the United States and was handed an elaborate document proclaiming him a Lecturer in Psychiatry at Harvard University.

The Medical School is one of the toughest parts of Harvard to get into. The first two years of its standard four-year course involve a great deal of laboratory work, and there is lab space for only 125 students—less than one-tenth of those who apply. So the School can be choosy, and it is. "What we look for," its dean of admissions, Dr. Perry J. Culver, has said, "is a summa cum laude graduate of Harvard college who writes poetry, has taken a year off to tour Europe, and plays basketball." Of 110 graduates of Harvard College who recently applied for admission, only 26 made it. After the first two years, the School can accommodate additional students, and it then usually accepts transfers from two-year medical schools, like those at Dartmouth, Brown, Rutgers, South Dakota, and New Mexico—schools that have adequate science facilities but no teaching hospitals. At capacity, the Harvard Medical School can accommodate 570 prospective physicians; small as that number sounds, Harvard's is nonetheless the largest private medical school in the country.

Wherever the students come from and however long they stay, many of them have been trying to redefine the goals of their future profession. "I don't see many of them putting out shingles in the suburbs," Dean Ebert says. At heaven knows what consequences to the suburbs, the students, once they finish their internships, are now looking increasingly toward social service. This is fine with their dean. While the curriculum of the School is still largely geared to potential practitioners and thus has something of a built-in inflexibility, he has been working hard on his new centers and on community affairs in general—specifically, those of the black community of Roxbury. It is indicative of the direction the Medical School is moving in that one of the three Negroes on its faculty, Dr. Alonzo S. Yerby, who used to be commissioner of hospitals in New York City, was not long ago invested by Dean Ebert with the title of Associate Dean for Community Affairs. Not so long before *that*, many graduates of the Harvard Medical School would have thought of "community affairs" as the meetings of their county medical associations.

Fewer and fewer of the Law School's graduates, similarly, are doing what in the not so distant past many of them almost automatically did—going into the big, multi-named firms of New York and other litigious metropolises. Here supply and demand have also been in evidence. Recruiters from the better Wall Street firms once wouldn't talk to any Law School student whose average grades fall below a rather high level; now they will talk to any student who'll talk to them, and they are apt to offer him fifteen thousand dollars a year as starting pay. It used to be that the smaller Yale Law School—which admits 160 students a year as opposed to Harvard's 540—was the more idealistic and social-science-oriented of the two. Yale, the consensus was, taught law as it should be. Harvard, by contrast, had the reputation of being a practical sort of place that taught the law as it *is*. Its students were thought to have a trade-school attitude. They wanted to hitch up with a respectable firm when they graduated, and for the most part would have hesitated impairing their chances by making any move that could have struck the legal establishment as quixotic. Times change, and so do law students. A few months ago, some of those at Harvard picketed the recruiters of one august New York firm when they visited Cambridge, because among their clients was the Chase Manhattan Bank, among the sites of whose global operations is the Republic of South Africa.

There are still, of course, plenty of Law School students who aspire to become corporation lawyers and would be chary of picketing a fence. But there are hundreds more who while at Harvard are less concerned with courses on torts and contracts than

308

with local service programs like the Community Legal Assistance Office and the Voluntary Defenders. Ninety students, though they can scarcely expect to reap any short-range financial rewards from the experience, have enrolled in a course on Chinese law.

An old saw that has been passed along from one generation of Harvard Law students to another goes, "The first year they scare you, the second year they work you, and the third year they bore you." In all three years, and especially in the final year, what once counted most were grades. These were numerical and were computed to two decimal places. A man with an average of 72.49 might stand 109th in his class. A man with an average of 71.50 might stand 167th. The professors were as grimly serious about the marking system as the students; it was a Law School custom—a custom not observed in any other part of the University—that every professor had personally to grade every examination in his course. That meant that each member of the Law School faculty, regardless of his academic or jurisprudential eminence, had to set aside a three-week stretch twice annually to read exams. The professors still do that, but in 1968 they agreed to switch to letter grades, so now they are at least freed from grappling with abstruse mathematics. They may be freed from the alphabet, if some students get their wish and have all courses go on a pass-fail basis. In the minds of many Law School professors, though, grades still loom large. When a sixty-five-year-old lawyer was being considered by a Harvard Law faculty committee for an appointment as a visiting lecturer, more was made of how he had done at the Law School in the nineteen-twenties than of what he had done professionally over the next forty years.

The Law School is much zestier than it used to be, however. The Harvard Law School Forum, a student-run extracurricular group, sponsored a colloquium in 1968 that featured a soliloquy by Al Capp on dames. (Capp, who used to be a marvelously funny man, the engaging irrationality of whose comic-strip characters was a testimonial to his own disciplined rationality, moved to Brattle Street in Cambridge, a few years back, just off Harvard

Square, and has been acting strange ever since. Most recently, he has devoted a great deal of his non-vocational time to attacking Harvard, largely by means of false facts that represent quite a fabrication even for a man of his enormous inventive powers.)

In 1968, too, the dean of the Law School, Erwin N. Griswold, who was sixty-four, resigned to go to Washington as solicitor general. The professor eventually appointed to succeed him, Derek C. Bok, was thirty-seven. Another member of the Law faculty, Alan M. Dershowitz, had in 1964 become a full professor when he was only twenty-eight. A graduate of Brooklyn College, Dershowitz went on to Yale, where he ranked first in his class and was editor of the *Law Journal*. Following the customary pattern for men of that high standing, he clerked in Washington for a Supreme Court Justice—in his case, Arthur Goldberg. (Fifty per cent of all Supreme Court clerkships, in recent years, have gone to graduates of the Yale and Harvard law schools.) Professor Dershowitz's teaching typifies the evolutionary nature of legal education. His principal course, "The Prediction and Prevention of Harmful Conduct," relates to psychiatry and the law, and he gives it with a psychiatrist, Dr. Alan A. Stone. The two of them also preside over an interdisciplinary Law School seminar called "Psychoanalytic Theory and Legal Assumptions." Between them, they are trying to help bridge a communications gap that was recently deplored by the senior attending psychiatrist at the Bellevue Hospital prison ward. "Lawyers and psychiatrists just don't speak the same language," he said.

A College junior: "I'll go into the Peace Corps or VISTA between my undergraduate and graduate years. Then I'll get a Ph.D. and do some journalism. Then I'll spend some time as a labor organizer. When I'm thirty or so and can't be trusted any longer, I'll go into teaching."

XX

GRADUATE STUDENTS, who at Harvard outnumber undergraduates by two to one, are what give a university the right to call itself that. And whatever the quality of its undergraduates, its soundness depends in large measure on the caliber of the older students. They represent the continuity of scholarship; from their ranks, future educators will step forward, or be nudged. "There's nothing like a cynical graduate student for keeping you on your toes, by asking questions you can't answer," says Professor Karl Strauch, director of the Cambridge Electron Accelerator. Professor Strauch and some of his associates in Physics recently appeared in a half-hour documentary film, *People and Particles,* which showed faculty men and their graduate students not only working on a serious experiment (the effect of electron-positron pairs on each other at small distances) but also relaxing like just folks—attending a departmental picnic with hamburgers and touch football and folk songs and children underfoot. The film was made under the aegis of an undertaking called Harvard Project Physics, which, largely under the leadership of the molecular physicist, Professor Gerald Holton, began in 1963 to devise a new curriculum for secondary-school physics teaching. (One high-school student, asked for his opinion of *People and Particles* at a sneak preview said, astonishingly, that it was a lousy picture because the people in it smoked and drank.)

Important though the graduate students are, and larksome as some of them occasionally seem on film, many of them lead a fragmented, insecure life. They are all but untouched by the binding forces of the College—the residential houses, the athletics, the extracurricular activities that give most undergraduates whatever sense of belonging they feel. The students' reactions and experiences vary from field to field. Graduate sociologists have their own desks in the behavioral sciences building. Classicists can have tea once a week at Professor Mason Hammond's home. Biologists can have tea nearly every afternoon in Professor Carroll Williams' laboratory. English students, on the other hand, often seem to wander around as though they were lost, and one young woman who was in her fifth graduate year in government was unable to think offhand of the name of a single fellow student. A faculty committee investigating the Graduate School of Arts and Sciences proposed a non-residential social center as a high-priority morale-builder. The committee also thought there were too many students, and recommended that admissions be reduced by 20 per cent.

Many of the graduate students who attended other colleges were, during their own undergraduate days, Big Men on Campus. At Harvard, they are apt to be ignored and to think of themselves as very small, lonely acolytes in the cathedral of learning. "Even the *faculty's* more interesting than they are," one undergraduate says. The three thousand men and women enrolled in the Graduate School of Arts and Sciences are an intellectually select lot, chosen by an admissions process in which their academic records are all-important. Whether they are accepted depends chiefly on the appropriate academic department, and understandably so; those approved by a department not only study under it but also help teach the undergraduates taking the courses it offers.

Less than one-third of Harvard College graduates who aspire

to stick around Cambridge and get an M.A. or Ph.D. in Arts and Sciences realize their hopes. Less than two-thirds of the last group of applicants who were magna cum laude Harvard College graduates were admitted to the Graduate School. When a Harvard professor asked one time, of the administrators of this school, how in the world one of his best students could have been rejected, when the fellow had graduated magna cum laude from the College, the response was, "Ah, but it was a low magna." At least one summa cum laude graduate of the College has been spurned by the Graduate School.

Often there is a sound reason for rejecting these outstanding students; were they to stay at Harvard, they'd have pretty much the same professors they had as undergraduates. The professors wouldn't have much new to impart to them, but they might have a disconcertingly new attitude. "It can be a profound shock for a Harvard undergraduate returning here in G.S.A.S." one professor at Cambridge says. "Suddenly the faculty people who were his friends begin to look at him with a cold professional eye. He's no longer the gifted amateur. He's an apprentice pro, and he's judged accordingly. His footnotes are squeezed through a strainer, and he gets no sympathy whatever when a paper's turned in late." On the other hand, he may get some unique opportunities for exhibiting his scholarship. The students of one professor in the field of Russian studies have been putting out a magazine of their own called *Kritika*, a journal in which they review contemporary works of Russian history, and in a recent issue of which one of them was able triumphantly to call attention to some errata in the published errata of a Soviet author no one else had criticized before in English.

Students in the Graduate School of Arts and Sciences have been likened to high-class masons. Their principal *raison d'être*, it used to be thought by some of their supervisory professors, was to add a brick to the edifice of knowledge. Some of that feeling persists; there are graduate students, particularly in fields like history and literature, who believe that the way to get ahead in the academic world is to establish that one knows a little bit more about some tiny area of scholarship than anyone else around. A comparable protograduate quality, something that David Riesman calls precocious hyperprofessionalism, now crops up increasingly among undergradutes, too. Mr. Riesman was talking to an undergraduate once, an English major, who got onto the subject of novels of colonialism and held forth at enthralling length about *Heart of Darkness*. The professor asked if he was going to write his honors thesis about that book. Oh, no, the student said; much as he would like to, and keen as his interest was, the subject had been done to death; instead, he would write about some obscure Conrad novel that nobody cared much about, including himself.

To attain a scholarly state of grace, and sometimes also to avoid having to compete in the economic marketplace, some graduate students used to hang around universities as long as they could, inventing all sorts of strategems to defer getting their degrees. To circumvent such procrastination, Harvard now has a rule that no graduate student may enroll in Arts and Sciences for longer than five years. This rule is no more rigidly enforced than any other. One woman working toward a Ph.D. was, at last report, in her tenth year of residence. However, there were mitigating circumstances: she was also raising three children.

Harvard claims to have a six-to-one teacher-student ratio, but the figures need to be annotated; more than a thousand individuals characterized as teachers are themselves graduate students who work part-time as teaching fellows. A complaint frequently heard around Cambridge is that much of the instruction that undergraduates receive—especially in the sections of large lecture courses—comes, in fact, not from the august senior professors of whom the University is so proud, but from younger men and women of whom the hierarchs of the university have never heard. A concomitant complaint has it that while some teaching fellows are metronomically dependable and genuinely philanthropic, even providing coffee and doughnuts for their morning sections, others have a will-o'-the-wisp approach to their chores. One sophomore taking a humanities course had three different teaching fellows presiding over his section during a single half-term; the fellow who gave him his grade had laid eyes on him only three times.

It can be and has been contended, conversely, that the teaching fellows supply a useful leaven to the educational process. They are youngish themselves, and thus perhaps better attuned to the needs and wishes of undergraduates than many older men. They are apt to have a fresher and more adventurous approach to education than their elders. The argument is moot. "Are we gypping undergraduates by giving them teaching fellows in a section?" the very senior and much respected Professor Paul H. Buck recently said. "I doubt it. I was a much better teacher when I was young than I am now."

Even with such support to comfort them, the teaching fellows are far from universally happy. Their pay is frugal. They get about four thousand dollars a year, and if they are married their wives usually have to work—sometimes as teaching fellows themselves. (Harvard likes to claim that quality is its paramount consideration when it comes to hiring faculty people, but availability is sometimes also a factor. A woman who happens to be in Cambridge because her husband is there stands a much better chance of filling an instructional vacancy than a woman in Santa Fe, Honolulu, or even Providence.) For all their discontent, though, few of the fellows register loud gripes. In 1967, some of the bolder among them formed a group called the Teaching Fellows Federation, but when a rally was called so they could work shoulder-to-shoulder for, among other objectives, increased compensation, only seventy-five of them turned up; and when one of the sponsors of the meeting asked out of curiosity how many of them would be prepared to go on strike should that eventuality arise, only two hands were raised. Two years later, the result would doubtless have been strikingly different. After the April bust, eighty teaching fellows—nearly one tenth of that whole coterie— proclaimed themselves in sympathy with a package of demands that S.D.S. had presented to the administration.

If the graduates have had any single unifying characteristic, it would seem to be apathy. "A few of us in Biology went to a departmental meeting and one guy got up and explained how he was in a bind about the draft and asked what suggestions anybody had for him," a relatively unapathetic graduate student told an acquaintance. "Nobody said anything. So I got up and said, 'Hey, this guy just said he was in trouble and asked for help and nobody made a move. Did you *hear* him?' Then they heard, and tried to help. But first they had to be shocked into solidarity. The trouble with many of these people is that they've become so careerist in their thinking that they hardly ever talk about anything except what kind of paper this or that professor prefers. They hardly ever play with ideas. I went to a small, segregated, intellectually narrow college in the hills of Maryland, and I had more stimulating conversations my last three months there than my whole first year at Harvard. There are too many graduate students here who feel *guilty* if they creep out of the academic areas in which they're supposed to be acquiring skills. At the Law School, you can play touch football, and at the Business School they have a rugby team. In G.S.A.S., things like movies and music and social work and—yes, even sex and marriage—are regarded as diversions and fripperies. I've tried to get over some of that myself, but after four years here I still have the feeling that if I'm not sitting down and reading a book in my field I'm being terribly self-indulgent."

Some years back, a couple of visiting English academicians paid a call on the master of a Harvard residential house. He was not at home, and in his absence the Britishers were taken in tow by a fellow who chatted with them about Irish literature, a field in which he *was* at home. When the master showed up, the visitors remarked how graciously they'd been received by Professor Chamberlain. The master was puzzled. Then light dawned. "Oh, *Eddie*," he said. "He's our superintendent." "My God, you have to have a Ph. D. to be a janitor at Harvard," one of the Britishers remarked.

Not at all. Harvard doesn't care much whether its bona fide

faculty members have Ph.Ds. Fifteen per cent of those in Arts and Sciences *don't* have them. Within the last decade, the University has had a dean of the degree-conscious Graduate School of Education who never got beyond an A.B. himself, and a professor of vertebrate paleontology who never got a bachelor's degree. Erik Erikson holds the imposing title of Professor of Human Development, and conducts one seminar so advanced it is attended largely by other members of the Harvard faculty, but his own academic development never included college. To offset an Erikson, Harvard also has people around like Professor Harrison C. White, who, having earned a Ph.D. in theoretical physics at M.I.T. gamely plunged further into the doctoral thicket and emerged with a Ph.D. from Princeton in sociology.

Most of the graduate students in Arts and Sciences who plan to become teachers know, however, that they aren't likely to go far these days without a Ph.D. It is the cloak of scholarship without which, in the eyes of many prospective employers, they would stand naked; at most state teachers' colleges, one cannot be a professor without a doctorate. The candidates approach their oral exams full of dread and exhilaration, like younger students approaching fraternity initiations. One aspirant toward a Ph.D. in English claimed to have found the ideal preparatory routine: drink a stiff mixture of hot mustard and gin, lie on the floor for two hours—a stereo speaker at either ear—listening to the Mamas and the Papas, play three games of table tennis with your wife— she must let you win—and then take a steaming-hot bath. "Most of these people go into teaching," Oscar Handlin says, "and their Ph.D. is, in a sense, their certification. For ten years after they get it, whatever they do professionally may depend on the recommendations they got here while they were earning it. A candidate's dissertation gives the faculty a chance to learn about the qualities of his mind. And since most of these guys never write anything of consequence in their lives except their doctoral dissertation, it's important for them because it represents their only experience in scholarship."

317

H A R V A R D H A S a smattering of special students, too. Five thousand of them belong to Extension Studies, an offshoot of the University through which—in conjunction with other universities in the vicinity—courses are offered, at night and sometimes by television, to part-time students in the area. Outside the area—as far outside as the South Pole—they are offered by a variety of devices to sailors in the Navy submerged for long stretches on nuclear submarines or subjected to the rigors of Antarctic duty. The fees are modest. Although Extension Studies didn't begin until 1910, some of its costs are defrayed by the income from an 1836 bequest which stipulated that students benefiting from it should pay no more than the value of two bushels of wheat per term per course. So the basic charge per term per course in Extension Studies is a very reasonable five dollars. In 1960, Harvard began offering degrees in Extension Studies, thus affording a few tenacious individuals who had flunked out of the College thirty or forty years earlier a chance finally to obtain a real Harvard degree.

Then there are special students, fewer than a hundred a year, who are not candidates for any degree and want to sit in on regular daytime courses—perhaps students who are switching fields of concentration and want an extra year of study between college and graduate school, perhaps Negro graduates of small Southern colleges for whom an extra year seems desirable before they enter a competitive and largely white Northern graduate school, perhaps a retired businessman who wants to be able to discuss the new math with his sons. There are even special special students. A recent one was a Harvard College graduate of the class of 1937 who had become a corporation executive and was eager to bone up on the human aspects of business. He got a ten-week leave from his company and signed up for six courses and five seminars in history, economics, government, and sociology. He managed to carry that heavy workload by deferring all reading assignments until he returned to his regular job, when he'd have plenty of leisure time. He pronounced the experiment a huge success. "After only two weeks back at Harvard I was reading the *Times* with new insights," he said.

In almost every part of the University, moreover, one finds foreigners. Harvard has twenty-eight hundred students from abroad, and it has an International Office, to help them get visas, arrange transportation, and cope with alien-registration and income-tax problems. The University, much as if it were the United Nations, also runs a hospitality program on the visitors' behalf. Its solicitousness is reciprocated; recently, the director of the International Office, David Henry, was invited to judge a beauty contest put on by a Chinese students' group. Mr. Henry generally has more serious problems to preoccupy him. Harvard, like many another university, has welcomed quite a few foreign professors and researchers. Most of these tended to come from the British Isles and Northern Europe, and people from that area used to get preferential treatment under the immigration laws. But in 1965 Congress passed a new law that was to take effect on July 1, 1968, and that limited the admission of individuals with "distinguished skills," the category that usually fitted scholars, to seventeen thousand a year. Whoever filed an application first got admitted first. A good many scholars from Southern Europe and Asia, who followed immigration regulations closely, hastened to file; few Northern Europeans did. It didn't occur to many of them (or to the American universities that would eventually be yearning for them) that they should. As a result, it may now take an Englishman two or three years to get a visa that allows him to work in the United States. Several department chairmen at Harvard are indignant about this nasty turn of affairs. "Get the law changed," one of them told Mr. Henry. "It's in the Harvard tradition to seek the best man no matter where he is in the world, and I don't see why some petty bureaucratic detail should be permitted to keep us from the advancement of truth."

Concerned as the University now must be about getting some foreigners into the country, it is also concerned about getting some others out. Harvard scholars frequently go abroad (Professor Edward S. Mason, the founder of an Overseas Advisory Service at the University, averaged a trip to Pakistan every year for fifteen years, to help that country's economic planners), but in nearly every instance they return home. It is not always so with citizens of other lands. They come to an American university, sometimes under a grant their struggling government can barely afford, and then after being educated, theoretically to help their compatriots, they decide not to go back after all and instead to settle, if they can, in the United States. Harvard has one African on the scene who is in his eleventh year of graduate work. His government hopes he will come home and lend it a hand, but at the rate he is pursuing his studies he may just about make it back in time for retirement.

To try to maintain a fairly orderly flow of international traffic —specifically, to keep scholars moving in two directions—Mr. Henry was instrumental in 1960 in setting up something called the African Scholarship Program of American Universities, or ASPAU. The idea was that high-school graduates from Africa would do their college work and a couple of years of graduate work in the United States—their expenses partly underwritten by their own countries and partly by America—and would then agree to return home and teach for at least two years. More recently, Mr. Henry and his ASPAU associates have formed a counterpart organization for Latin-American countries, called LASPAU, under whose aegis students are brought to this country after finishing their first two years of college. They, too, have to promise to go home and teach. Five hundred of them are now in the United States. Harvard, which has half a dozen, had a hard time persuading one of them to come north. He was a Bolivian who'd been elected head of student government at his home university. Among the perquisites off that job were a car and a chauffeur, and he hated to give them up. Latin Americans, it would seem, have carried student power to enviable lengths.

T H E   M O S T un-Harvard-like academic subdivision of the University, all things considered, is its Summer School. The Harvard

Summer School has neither an alumni organization nor a fund-raising office. (It would, of course, make little sense to have the one without the other.) It does have a social director, who supervises afternoon punchbowl parties. The Summer School dates back to 1870, when it was established as a private enterprise of some faculty members. The prime movers were two professors of botany, Asa Gray and Alexander Agassiz, who believed that summer was the best time of year to teach their subject, especially in New England, and who acquired an island in Buzzard's Bay for their warm-weather students. (After a while, Harvard gave up the island, and it became a leper colony.) The first students were nearly all professional schoolteachers, but in 1890 the Harvard Faculty of Arts and Sciences decided that summer courses could count for credit, and undergraduates began to enroll.

Today, of forty-eight hundred students in the Summer School, around one-quarter are Harvard and Radcliffe undergraduates. Schoolteachers still comprise a large proportion of the enrollment. Some of the students are real veterans of the academic wars; one minister has been faithfully returning every July since 1924. For the past two summers, as part of a national undertaking called the Intensive Summer Studies Program, the student body has also included sixty or seventy young southern Negroes and some teachers from the black universities they went to. The Summer School is by all odds the easiest part of Harvard to get admitted to, and that is fine with the University; Harvard *wants* to open up its facilities, off-season, to people who might not otherwise be exposed to them. Some alumni think this open-door policy goes too far; it particularly nettles them to walk through the Yard in July and August and see girls' laundry flapping from the windows of dormitories to which during other months it is at certain hours a punishable offense to invite a girl even if she keeps her clothes on.

Some members of the Faculty of Arts and Sciences tend to act snobbish toward the Summer School (what they think of summer sessions at the Business School beggars description), but others welcome it as a source of a second income; they can earn 20 per cent of their regular salary by teaching there. As a result, nearly half the Summer School faculty comes from Harvard. But as if to emphasize that the Summer School, while *at* Harvard, is only marginally *of* Harvard, the University insists that it have its own admissions office, deans, and registrar, and charges it twenty thousand dollars a year rent for space it occupies in a Harvard building. The riverbanks it gets to use for free.

Graffiti: "Yeah, but if we end the war, then how do we end society?"

XXi

IN 1963, AFTER TEN YEARS as president of Harvard, Mr. Pusey wrote that the university had just been through a "troubled decade." By the troubled year of 1968, he had come to reflect on that bygone decade as halcyon, and wished he had saved his "troubled" for a span that really deserved it. "I used up my capital too early," he said.

Adjectival capital is about the only sort that Harvard presidents permit themselves to dip into at any time. Harvard's formidable resources are, in Harvard's words, "carefully husbanded," and while the University's official motto is the naked *Veritas*, some observers of Harvard's fiscal policies have suggested that a more descriptive Latin motto might be *Pecunia non olet*—loosely, "Don't spend it; keep it." At Harvard, New England thrift and prudence have reached full flower, and faculty members sometimes ruefully assert that it is easier to get a new atom-smasher or electron microscope than to get a room painted.

When President Eliot took over, in 1869, Harvard's endowment funds totalled $2.5 million. At the start of the Lowell era, in 1909, the figure was 22.5 million; at Conant's inauguration, in 1933, 126 million; at the dawn of Pusey's first decade, 360 million. Today, thanks to careful husbanding of stocks and bonds and wall paint, Harvard's endowment funds have a market value of well over a billion dollars. Considering that the endowment funds of

323

all independent universities, colleges, and schools in America amount to twelve billion dollars, and that there are only 180 institutions with endowments higher than five million, Harvard is relatively well fixed.

Rich as Harvard seems in the envious eyes of academicians elsewhere, though, it has been feeling poorer and poorer lately, and not without reason. The cost of education has risen more swiftly in America than that of any other services except perhaps hospital care and funerals. Harvard's annual operating expenses came to fifty million dollars in 1958. In 1968, they went past one hundred and fifty million; by 1978, if they continue to accelerate at the present rate, they'll reach a third of a billion. The income from a mere billion dollars is, in Harvard eyes, not an overstuffed cushion but a slender and ever more bending reed. "How fast we must run even to stand still!" President Pusey lamented in a recent report to his constituency.

Until 1920, Harvard was so comparatively uncomplicated a place to run that President Lowell kept all the University's budgetary data in a single desk drawer. Now, Harvard—which Pusey has called "a kind of federation of semi-autonomous institutions" —has fifty-four principal budgetary segments and twenty-six hundred sub-segments. The fiscal rallying cry, an old English variation of an old Danish homily on self-sufficiency, is "Every tub on its own bottom." What this means is that every dean or department chairman is responsible for keeping his own tub or sub-tub (the latter being a Harvard term, not a British or Danish one) on an even keel. Specifically, he must not show a deficit. A practical navigator, appropriately, initiated this policy—*the* practical navigator, Nathaniel Bowditch, who in the eighteen-twenties found Harvard's money-handling slipshod, and raised such a fuss that the incumbent president, John T. Kirkland, resigned. (Kirkland's own finances were shipshape; he had married a Cabot.)

Ever since Bowditch made Kirkland walk the plank, Harvard's administrators have been partial to nautical jargon. All but forty million dollars of Harvard's money, which is the amount of its restricted funds, is invested as an entity, but each budgetary director knows precisely his stake in the kitty and the limits—unless he can raise some money on his own—of his expenditures. When in 1948 the Harvard Medical School naughtily spent more than it was supposed to spend, it got a dressing-down from President Conant and a flat order to slash its budget by 10 per cent the following year.

The university is not entirely callous, however, in dealing with its subordinate, or insubordinate, divisions. If one of its graduate schools or centers gets into financial trouble, the University may step in and lend a hand, but in such instances it operates only as a banker would, and it charges interest. Thus, when the Graduate School of Education found itself five thousand dollars in the hole one year, the University graciously bailed it out, though it charged 5⅔ per cent interest, which was slightly above the going bank rate. The University has—except in very special circumstances—refused to borrow money from outside. Its rationale is that, owning some four hundred million dollars' worth of government bonds, it is already a substantial lender, and why both a borrower and lender be? Moreover, being tax-exempt, it would not be able to write off any interest it paid as a tax deduction.

Sometimes, though, Harvard borrows from itself. A few years ago the University put up a ten-million-dollar apartment complex, to house married graduate students. A fund-raising drive had produced five million dollars that was earmarked for this project, but where was the other five to come from? The University treasurer ruled that this money could be taken out of unrestricted funds, but only if each of the graduate schools whose students used the new premises repaid the money—with interest, of course—proportionate to its share of usage. The whole transaction made for tangled internal bookkeeping, but the every-tub-on-its-own-bottom principle remained inviolate.

More recently, the University was preparing to construct a central cooling plant, which would pipe cold water into a number of buildings occupied by diverse tubs. The installation would cost around fourteen million, and the users of the buildings that were cooled would be charged a percentage of the cost, with the usual interest. But among the buildings to be chilled was Harvard's computer center. Eighty percent of its facilities were used for government-sponsored research projects, and 80 per cent of its overhead was accordingly charged to those projects. But what of the 80 per cent of the interest on the cooling-plant cost? The government had a rule that interest payments could not be charged to research projects. At last reports, Harvard administrators were still wrestling with that thorny problem—the kind of problem that they would probably be glad to turn over to any student-power advocates who could come up with a satisfactory, suitably prudent solution.

Harvard's penchant for decentralization may make for cumbersome accounting, but can be advantageous when it comes to the other half of a tub-captain's fiscal concern—raising money for his own operation. If a Harvard alumnus is sore at the University because, say, a Law School professor has denounced the John Birch Society, or a Business School student has assaulted an S.D.S. orator, he can always be reminded of the semi-autonomy of, say, the Divinity School or the Dental School, and be asked to contribute to one of them. Harvard federalism can and does lead to embarrassing situations: The day a fund-raiser for one graduate school was making a pitch for a large gift from a wholesale drug company, a professor from another school turned up in Washington at a Senate-committee hearing and scolded the entire drug industry for its pricing practices.

Harvard deans, like nearly all university presidents, spend a good deal of their time as high-class mendicants. While Francis Keppel, later President Kennedy's commissioner of education, was dean of the Harvard Graduate School of Education, he flew to Washington in quest of a federal handout. Stopping in the airport lunch counter for a cup of coffee, he spotted six more Harvard deans, all on similar missions. "You don't stomp on another Harvard dean's toes in a Ford Foundation elevator," Keppel said not long ago. "That isn't nice. But you have to get out there and fight for yourself." One major foundation, bewildered by an apparently uncoordinated assault on its resources by a clutch of Harvard hands, sent its chief administrator to Cambridge, to inquire of President Pusey which of Harvard's ever-hungry children he deemed the most important to be nurtured. "They're all important," Pusey said.

HARVARD'S principal governing board used to meet in Boston, and its treasurer is still located there. Geographically, things have been worse. In 1775, when John Hancock was the treasurer, he went off to Philadelphia one day, taking most of the University's ledgers with him, and it was two years before Harvard got them back. Since 1967, Harvard's treasurer has been George F. Bennett, an executive of the State Street Research and Management Corporation, which is an affiliate of the State Street Investment Trust, which is very big in Boston finance. The State Street-Harvard relationship dates back to the late nineteen-twenties, when Charles Francis Adams was the University's treasurer and decided to do something that by Harvard standards had never previously been considered tolerable—to invest in common stocks.

The man who advised Harvard on what stocks to buy was Paul C. Cabot, a State Street official who himself became treasurer of the University in 1948 and on reaching seventy in 1967 was succeeded by Bennett, his State Street deputy. A salty patrician with a rough tongue and an uninhibited manner, Cabot has been described by some of his friends as Brahmin Fo'castle. He was the epitome of prudence. He had warm enough feelings for Yale, which gave him an honorary degree, but he could not refrain from mentioning to people who discussed Harvard finances with him that around 1930 Yale's endowment was only fifteen million dollars less than Harvard's, and that thirty-odd years later, partly because Yale dipped into capital, the gap was half a billion.

Cabot had a knack not only of hoarding capital, but of hiding income. It had long been Harvard practice for the administration to disclose to its several tubs, before they submit their annual budgets, what rate of return they can expect on their share of the big endowment. Cabot thought it risky to guarantee a rate of return before the returns were in, so he began tucking odd millions away until he had accumulated a reserve equivalent to 30-odd millions, or a whole year's probable income on the endowment funds. He continued on that squirrel-like course so determinedly that by the time he retired Harvard had a rainy-day cache of more than 60 million dollars of undistributed income—which itself now generates an extra 2.5 million or so in income annually. Harvard, in other words, could convert all its holdings into cash and tuck the money under a mattress for two years without feeling any pinch.

Of late, there has been much agitation over Harvard's investment practices. There are those who argue—the two years' hidden income aside—that Harvard has been overcautious in its investment policies, and that, substantial as its funds now are, they could have been even greater if their custodians hadn't been so conservative. What others attack as conservatism, however, the custodians defend as prudence. Harvard's branch of S.D.S. has been grumbling, for its part, that the University's unrestricted endowment funds have been invested in stocks and bonds of, among a host of corporations, the Mississippi Power & Light Company, which has not publicly condemned segregation, and the Chase Manhattan Bank, with its South African connections. Harvard's stake in these two companies together comes to 0.25 per cent of its endowment. It could thus be argued both that this $2.5 million could readily be reinvested, to placate the students, or that the sum involved is too trifling to affect domestic or foreign policy. In any event, it would be hard to invest a billion dollars nowadays in any companies that some students would not find offensive.

Some of Harvard's Negro students feel, for *their* part, that the University should take some of its endowment—a hundred million dollars is the amount they generally propose—and reinvest it in

Roxbury, the principal Boston ghetto. And Harvard's fiscal policies have come in for criticism from other sources, too. A recent gadfly was a most unlikely one—Harvard classmate of Nathan Pusey, chief fund-raiser for the class of 1928 for twenty-five years, trustee of and counsel to Radcliffe. He was Robert I. Hunneman, a Boston lawyer who filed a bill in the Massachusetts legislature (a prerogative of any citizen of that state) which would have required tax-exempt institutions to handle their investments on a market-value basis, or face the loss of their exemption. Harvard had long used a modified book-value basis, and it was Hunneman's contention, in brief, that this method unfairly discriminated in favor of contemporary contributors to the endowment and against those now long gone. The embattled Hunneman believed that Harvard's generations of supporters, could they know what their beneficiary was up to, would spin in their many weathered graves. By the winter of 1969, Hunneman's bill hadn't got anywhere, but his crusade had. Harvard, hardly batting an institutional eye, shifted to an evaluation basis more or less in conformity with Hunneman's notions.

"American universities are constantly on the verge of insolvency. They are forced to live from hand to mouth; teachers are underpaid; equipment does not keep pace with modern demands; as educational institutions they will be unable to keep up to standard. And Harvard is no exception." The words could be used today, but they appeared in a 1919 brochure of the Harvard Endowment Fund. Over the years, Harvard men have unflaggingly been begging other Harvard men to give money to Harvard, and the response, by and large, has been touching. (The general public is not excluded, and at the start of the nineteenth century, indeed, it enthusiastically bought tickets in a couple of Harvard lotteries, with first prizes reaching twenty thousand dollars, which would just about pay for four years at Harvard today.) Harvard not only has far and away the largest endowment in the nation; it consistently leads all other educational institutions in raising new money, and over the past decade has been favored with four hundred million dollars in gifts.

Most of this has been in the form of capital funds, but Harvard does all right in annual giving, too. The Harvard College Fund, which has charge of that, is one of the few departments of the University that is permitted its own bank account, but it is characteristic of Harvard prudence that the account is for deposit only. The Fund's yearly take is now well above the three-million-dollar mark. Yale's total is over four million, but Yale lumps together gifts from college alumni and graduate-school alumni; since 1948, Harvard has had separate fund drives for the College and for each of its schools. The College Fund, which seemed the most likely to be affected by alumni reactions to the events of April, 1969, suffered a 20-per-cent loss in the number of contributors, but in money received its total went up a hundred thousand dollars over 1968's $3.3 million.

Until fairly recently, Harvard College used a soft-sell approach to its alumni. Its chief pitchman was David McCord, who would nudge them gently with light essays and poems that barely mentioned anything as crass as money. In 1969, the Fund resurrected some McCord verses—"Is that you, John Harvard?"/ I said to his statue./ "Aye—that's me," said John,/ "And after you're gone."—and sent them out to its mailing list with the simple statement, "If you believe that John Harvard will be here after we all are gone, and if you believe that he represents the best that is in mankind, then you don't really need any more news about Harvard this troubled spring." The Harvard Graduate Society for Advanced Study and Research fell back on the poet, too, with the addendum, "We submit that Harvard itself is not the property of any single generation of students; it is the product of many years of searching and change, by many people."

When McCord retired, in 1962, Harvard awarded him its first doctorate of humane letters and—since administrators, unlike professors, do not attain emeritus standing—conferred on him the resonant title of Honorary Curator of the Farnsworth Room and the George Edward Woodbury Poetry Room. These are adjuncts of the main library, where McCord for many years had had an office, and out of which, at about the same time he attained honorary curatorial distinction, he was, because of a need for offices for active-duty men, unceremoniously evicted. Harvard's fund-raisers are tougher nowadays, and in casual conversation use non-poetic words like "hard-nosed."

Not long ago, Harvard calmly estimated its current needs for additional capital funds at $250 million, half of this to implement plans that were considered urgent. True, dollars are cheap these days, but even so, that was a lot of money. Most other universities are currently also dreaming grandiose dreams, and as in so many other aspects of education, Harvard has been the bellwether that has made them resolute. The new era in large-scale university fund-raising probably dawned in 1958, when Harvard embarked on a two-year capital-funds drive called a Program for Harvard College. Totting up the College's requirements, President Pusey and his associates arrived at a figure of $100 million. But they got scared off by professional fund-raisers, who guessed that 45 million was about the most that a drive could realistically be expected to net. One project that was dropped, accordingly, was for a new undergraduate science program. It was revived in 1967, with a $49-million goal, and was given a whacking boost when a single contributor came through with 12.5 million. Officially, he was anonymous, but around Cambridge everybody assumed he was Edwin H. Land, the inventor and businessman, who had dropped out of science and everything else at Harvard while an undergraduate to concentrate on Polaroid. He ended up all right academically, too. In 1969, the Harvard chapter of Phi Beta Kappa made him an honorary member.

When the 1958 Program was launched, Mr. Pusey hedgingly set its goal at "somewhere under one hundred million." Pressed by his chief solicitors to be more specific, he eventually settled for the figure of 82.5 million. For a while, the drive lagged. There were pleasant surprises. Buttonholing prospects in San Francisco, Mr. Pusey dined almost by chance with a pear-orchard proprietor, Alfred St. Vrain Carpenter. Pusey had a nasty head cold and thought the evening had gone poorly. The next morning, notwithstanding, Carpenter and his wife pledged a million dollars toward the construction of a visual arts building.

Despite such bonanzas, Harvard was beginning to run scared, and the scaredest man of all was the coordinator of the drive, James R. Reynolds, whose official title was Assistant to the President for Development and who kept in his office one of Harvard's most precious rosters—the names of fifteen hundred of its alumni who were deemed its most promising benefactors. (Carpenter's name hadn't even been on the list.) In the winter of 1959, Reynolds told Roy E. Larsen, the *Time* executive and a faithful Harvard patron, that he didn't see where the rest of the money was coming from. "I'll tell you where," Larsen said. "Most of it is going to come from people who've already given." He was right. One man, for instance, who initially gave the Program eight hundred thousand dollars because he wanted to have about a 1-percent share in fulfilling Harvard's goal, later decided to be a 2-percent participant. The drive was supposed to terminate at the end of 1959, and that fall Harvard was still five million dollars short. It ultimately got that amount from thirty-five men, all but two of whom had given previously, and none of whom eventually gave less than one hundred thousand.

Among the thirty-five was Harold S. Vanderbilt, who came through just after Christmas. When President Pusey, who had been spending the holidays in the Caribbean with David Rockefeller, who was also in the elite group, returned to his office on January 2, Reynolds suggested that he phone Vanderbilt to thank him. During their conversation, Pusey also praised Vanderbilt's generosity to Vanderbilt University, and mentioned something he'd heard the chancellor of that institution say at an educators' conference. "He said Harvard was doing a wonderful job," Pusey told Vanderbilt. "He said, 'Harvard's carrying the banner for all of us.'"

"He *did?*" Vanderbilt replied. "That rather changes my view of things."

A couple of hours later, Vanderbilt called a Pusey lieutenant, asked how much was still needed to put the drive over the top, and on learning that the sum was 2.5 million, promptly made a further pledge in that amount.

Counting additional gifts that dribbled in and some interest that was earned on Program contributions before they were spent, the total ultimately reached 103 million. Other universities were heartened. Princeton, for instance, soon announced a drive for fifty-three million. Shortly after its inception, Paul Cabot had some business in New York. Arriving in the city early one morning after a restless train ride, he decided to take a nap, and went to the Knickerbocker Club, where he had a room reserved. The room wasn't quite ready, so he wandered into the bar, which was deserted at that hour, and settled himself on a couch for a snooze. He was dozing off when some Princeton men walked in and began talking about their fund drive. One expressed doubts that Princeton could raise fifty-three million. "We shouldn't have any trouble," Cabot recalls another saying, "if that drunken son of a bitch stretched out over there can raise eighty-two and a half."

OVER THE YEARS, Harvard has received many odd benefactions. A great-grandson of General Artemus Ward, who didn't get on well with George Washington, gave the University more than a million dollars on condition that it put up and maintain a statue of his ancestor in Washington, D. C. The University has had bestowed on it a Stradivarius violin that it sold for seventy-five thousand dollars, and a warehouse receipt for 205 pounds of grain sorghum. Harvard disposed of that for thirty-five hundred dollars, but the donor was miffed; he thought the University should have got a hundredth of a cent more per pound than it did. In 1924, Henry Clay Frick gave Harvard a partial interest in some coal-oil and mineral rights in Whitley County, Kentucky. Harvard still carries this on its books as a one-dollar donation—the same value that it ascribes to various dry wells and to securities that have no clearly ascertainable market value and that it refuses to assess at more than a dollar until they're actually sold.

Harvard has profited handsomely from being willed wine cellars and postage stamps (it has in custody one collection that was appraised at sixteen thousand dollars when it arrived in 1963 and that by its donor's decree must be kept until 2013), and it once grew several thousand dollars richer from selling the pornography alone in a library it inherited. On the death of a midwestern admirer, Harvard learned that he had set up a ten-thousand-dollar trust fund, with his pet cat as the immediate beneficiary and Harvard as the residuary legatee. Harvard had to take care of the cat as long as it lived, and over the three years that the animal survived its master its upkeep slightly exceeded the income from the trust, so that eventually Harvard got only $9,931.80. Another man set up a trust in 1962 under the terms of which Harvard would eventually come into his estate, but only after the deaths of himself, his four children, their nine children, and a few random relatives. He advised Harvard that he expected them all to be out of its way by the year 2045.

"Harvard will take any bloody thing that's given," Paul Cabot has said. He was being a mite hyperbolic. Every so often, Harvard politely declines a gift that strikes it as excessively frivolous or restrictive. The University turned down the offer of a man who wanted to endow a chair to be devoted exclusively to lectures against careers for women, and it was equally cool to a woman who wanted to establish a chair of musical therapeutics, in the Medical School, for "the application of music to medical cases as a treatment." Harvard did just recently, though, welcome a five-thousand-dollar gift to the Medical School from one of its alumni who stipulated that the income from it go to a student who had distinguished himself by contributing to extracurricular fun and who was characterized by "medical unproductivity and scholastically idle diversion." If nobody filled that particular bill, the donor decreed, the money should go to the medical student deemed least likely to succeed.

334

When Harvard knows in advance that people are planning to mention it in their wills, it tries to persuade them not to make the terms of their bequests too specific, and it has a lawyer on full-time duty in the treasurer's office to help smooth out potentially prickly clauses. One will Harvard did not get a chance to look over in advance was the 1880 testament of a doctor that ran to ninety-five handwritten pages, most of them brimming with philanthropic references to the University, but in sum so complex that Harvard has almost found it more trouble than it was worth to comply with that benefactor's picayune desires.

Prizes can be a headache. People like to have their names attached to prizes. But college students are no longer eager to compete for the award of a ten-dollar book bearing some unknown benefactor's bookplate, and faculty members resent serving on prize committees. Sometimes, after years have gone by with nobody even trying for a prize, and with income piling up that a donor has stipulated can be used for no other purpose, Harvard seeks relief in court. It received a bequest of $25,000 in 1941, for instance, the income from which was to be used in the Department of English as an annual prize "to be awarded to the student writing the most understanding essay on the True Spirit of Book-Collecting." During the next eleven years, the prize, which by 1969 was worth $2,045, was awarded only once. In 1954, at Harvard's petition, a court decided that the income could be used for the purchase of books for the English department, with priority to be given to books on book-collecting.

There have been literally thousands of gifts for scholarships. To list those for Harvard College alone requires a catalogue two hundred pages long. A half dozen of these are limited to descendants of particular families. When boys apply for one of them, Harvard demands unassailable proof of relationship, and if there is any uncertainty about eligibility it insists that the candidate hire a genealogist and submit a family tree. One scholarship was confined to boys born in Marblehead. Harvard had been having trouble with that one, and was much relieved not long ago when the

Marblehead hospital closed and merged with a hospital in nearby Salem; you *couldn't* be born in Marblehead any longer. Or so Harvard thought until a lawyer pointed out that there was nothing to prevent anyone's being born in a street or a park.

Other scholarship funds can be doled out only to a Greek student, an Exeter graduate, a debater, a South Carolinian, a member of the Harvard Band, a prospective career diplomat, a Boston newsboy, a future specialist in applied astronomy, an Iowan (this one was set up by the Chicago, Burlington & Quincy Railroad, and Nathan Pusey has been among its beneficiaries), a graduate of Gadsden High School, in Alabama, and a graduate of the Boston Latin School—preferably one named O'Hare. There is also a slight advantage, in applying for Harvard aid, to bearing the surname Anderson, Baxendale, Borden, Downer, Haven, Hudson, Murphy, or Thayer. Some of the donors of scholarships merely expressed preferences—for, among many other donees, a boy from the West End of Boston or the Fiji Islands; for a Protestant Christian student of New England stock studying the humanities, a New Mexican boy of Spanish-American descent, an aspiring minister with leanings toward dissent, a piano player, an orphan, a son of a widow living west of the Appalachians, a son of a member of Battery A, 247th Field Artillery, and a son or daughter of an employee of Godfrey L. Cabot, Inc.

Four times annually, the University puts out a booklet entitled *Gifts to Harvard,* a publication of considerable girth in spite of the fact that as a rule it omits mention of any gift under a thousand dollars. (This is also the cut-off figure that determines whether or not a donor gets a personal letter of thanks from President Pusey.) In a random quarter of the year, one can ascertain from this publication that George Bennett has contributed a thousand toward the Treasurer's Award in Track (given to the outstanding performer when Harvard and Yale meet at Cambridge; at New Haven, in alternate years, the Charles S. Gage Award, endowed by a Yale man, is up for grabs), that the Grocery Manufacturers of America, Inc., have bestowed $30,000 on the Business School for general research, and the Coca-Cola Company $12,500 to the Medical School for research and testing in its Department of Nutrition. A persistent patron like David Rockefeller may turn up in a single quarterly record several times—$5,000, for instance, for the Harvard Graduate Society for Advanced Study and Research, 2,500 toward a twenty-fifth anniversary gift fund for the Master of Rockefeller's Harvard residential house; 5,060 to Phillips Brooks House, 19,000 more to the Divinity School for a summer program involving Negroes, and, of course, the 1.5 million he and his stepmother gave not long ago for a Divinity School dormitory.

The biggest book of all these annals of Harvard bounty is one called "Endowment Funds of Harvard University," which is so big it is printed in two volumes totalling more than seven hundred pages. Harvard now administers 3,224 separate endowment funds. One of the most recent to be set up honors the late Mark De-Wolfe Howe, the professor of law. The sponsors of this fund originally wanted it to be used to support student activities in civil-rights movements. But Harvard demurred; it thinks both to the past and the future. The University officials who handle endowment funds recalled that their predecessors had once been obliged to go to court to change the provisions of an endowment established to support student activities in the Abolitionist movement; the movement had ceased to exist. How could Harvard be sure that there would *be* a civil-rights movement a hundred years hence, or whenever? University officials spent six months mulling over the Howe endowment, and eventually arrived at what they called "a satisfactory position for flexibility." Professor Howe, happily, had been as interested in Anglo-American history as he was in civil rights. So it was agreed that the money raised in his memory could be used for research and study in both areas.

In the two-volume roster are recorded all of Harvard's endowments for professorial chairs and for lectureships (it costs six hundred thousand these days to endow a full professorship), including a lectureship on Indo-Muslim culture bestowed on Harvard by A. K. Ozai-Durrani, who was born in an Afghan nomad tribe and ultimately invented Minute Rice. This catalogue of gifts ranges from princely ones—a fund of more than fifteen million dollars, for instance, from the late Gordon McKay, the shoe-machinery inventor, for stipends in engineering and science—to $1,143 donated in 1903 by a group of ladies for furnishing band music to promote the dignity and beauty of public ceremonies.

Then there is the Thomas Hollis Fund of 1721, which, in addition to underwriting Harvard's first endowed professorship, set aside ten pounds a year for the Treasurer, to compensate him for his trouble in maintaining separate accounts for such funds. (The income thus sequestered for the Treasurer now amounts to $39.59 a year, but Harvard does not give him this as a bonus; instead it charges that much of his compensation to the Hollis Fund.) Another early-eighteenth-century benefactor established the Thomas Cotton Fund, the income of which was supposed to supplement the then meager salary of the president of Harvard. (*That* fund now throws off $11.90 a year. The treasurer's office would insist when asked that it was sending Mr. Pusey an extra check for slightly less than one dollar every month; Mr. Pusey contended that he had never laid eyes on this windfall.) Some funds, inevitably, have strings attached. The Louise E. Bettens Fund, set up in 1917 by a son of that lady, supports Phillips Brooks House, which is required to keep a portrait of Mrs. Bettens and another son in a third-floor room in perpetuity. There is also a Ford Foundation Forgivable Loan Fund, surely just about the nicest kind of loan fund anybody could imagine.

In a time of tumult, one can leaf through these two fat volumes, their pages a stately testimonial to loyalty and largesse, and come away with a restored sense of the permanency of Harvard. For what institution could fail, or even falter, with underpinnings like the Huntington Frothingham Wolcott Fund to sustain it?

Slightly over one third of Harvard's more than 150 million annual operating expenses is contributed by the federal government. The impact of Washington on private higher education naturally concerns Harvard, but not as much as it concerns other places. Harvard's chief concern is to maintain its academic freedom under whatever pressures it may be placed, and it is serenely aware that it managed to do that during the first 150 years of its existence while receiving subsidies from the government of Massachusetts. An expert on relations between government and higher education, Dean Price of the Kennedy School of Government, holds that a university is safe from imperiling its freedom as long as it receives whatever government support it accepts from a variety of sources, no single one of which can hope to have much leverage.

In that respect, Harvard would seem to be fairly immune from bureaucratic infection. It has 1,076 contracts with 42 federal agencies. (As a result, the General Accounting Office keeps three auditors on permanent station in Cambridge.) Nearly every part of the University is involved to some degree or other with government funds, though the Divinity School has come close to a clean slate, obtaining only .2 per cent of its budget from federal sources. The Medical School, by contrast, because of the vast scope, complexity, and importance of its research projects, gets more than two-thirds of all its funds from Washington—for that school alone, twenty-five million a year. Between April and June of 1968, the Medical and Dental schools together received 145 federal grants totalling $10,405,622 and ranging in size from $128 to $1,621,000.

Harvard looks upon all federal money as soft money, and it is the only institution of higher learning in America that—except in one or two very special cases—won't use federal funds to pay the salary of any tenured employee. "Harvard has an obligation to keep its distance from the federal government," Mr. Pusey has said. Another reason for its circumspection is that federal grants are often made on an annual basis and may be discontinued at the whim of Congress; Harvard feels that it also has an obligation to recompense anybody on whom it confers a career appointment out of funds it generates itself. If Harvard never got another penny from the government, it could carry on, though its research would of course be vastly diminished.

Other places, however, might face disaster. Eighty-five per cent of M.I.T.'s budget, and 65 per cent of Princeton's, are federally funded. According to Mr. Pusey, "We're the only one that has maintained our detachment." Moreover, since 1945, Harvard has had a policy of refusing, as an institution, to accept any government grants during peacetime (Korea and Vietnam were not counted as wars) for classified research. Professors and research associates may while at Harvard negotiate as individuals for classified research grants, but, in theory, while preoccupied with them they are not wearing their Harvard hats.

Individual professors initiate most government-research projects, classified or unclassified. "The academic is the new entrepreneur," a Harvard psychologist said recently. He himself had been working for ten years under a government grant, and a colleague of his, working under the same auspices, had even got the government to pay for tickets to professional basketball and hockey games. (There was academic justification; he was giving a course in which his students were seeking to observe and analyze the differences between two groups who habituate the Boston Garden —the fans of the Celtics, who are perennial winners, and of the Bruins, who perennially lose.) Sometimes the new entrepreneurs are so persuasive when they go to Washington that they end up with more money than they can use. When a senior professor at Harvard remonstrated with a younger man, pointing out to him that he could probably do a better research job with half the money he'd been allotted, the younger man replied, "But then I wouldn't feel so prestigious."

Lately, Congress has shown signs of beginning to appreciate the pork-barrel potentialities of higher education, and it seems likely that a good deal of federal money that has been drifting toward places like Harvard, M.I.T., and Berkeley will be drained off into small two-year colleges in all sorts of remote constituencies. This prospect has worried the presidents of the larger institutions, not least among them Mr. Pusey. Harvard may be theoretically self-sufficient today, but if the cost of higher education continues to soar, Harvard and all other places are going to need federal help in some form or other, and they would hate to have to battle for it through Congress with the hinterlands. But they are prepared to if they must, and it has been Mr. Pusey's belief that the time has come for them—perhaps operating through the Association of American Universities—to install a lobbyist of their own in Washington to protect themselves against the grasping upstarts.

A Harvard overseer: "Some people get periodically worked up about so-called power figures like me, but to tell the truth, I sometimes wish we had more real authority than we do. Everybody at Harvard seems to understand that the basic premise is that the place is run for the faculty and the students, and when the chips are down the faculty will call the tune."

xxii

I N J U N E, 1964, the Division of Research Grants of the National Institutes of Health asked Harvard for an organization chart. Harvard was thrown into a spin. Components of the University had had organization charts. The Medical School—a complex structure itself, involving relations with all sorts of hospitals and clinics—had had one, though its usefulness was dubious; a doctor arriving there was handed a copy, to help him learn his way around, and after glancing at it said, "My goodness, this is interesting, but I'm sure it doesn't apply to me," and threw it away.

But the University as a whole had never had any such chart, although President Conant had once asked for one; the man assigned to the task had thrown up his hands when his best effort resembled a diagram of an elaborate football play, with reverses and laterals and ends running around and guards pulling out of the line and maybe too many men on the field. Indeed, many of the officials of what one Harvard dean has called "this enigmatic sanctuary of learning" seem to pride themselves on being unable to comprehend how it is run or even held together.

Some of Harvard's administrative procedures seemed so bizarre that one Admissions man, appalled at the difficulty of selecting a freshman class, once suggested that any person should be admitted who could fill out the required forms on registration day without having to ask for guidance. Once, a graduate-school dean, hoping to establish some order within his own internal chaos, hired an efficiency expert, straight out of the business world, who quit after two months, saying he could be of little use because he had been trying to relate that graduate school to the University and it was impossible to figure out how the University worked.

Thus, steeped in a tradition of confusion, Harvard was hard-pressed to accede to the N.I.H. request. The dilemma was finally resolved by Harvard's solitary vice-president, L. Gard Wiggins, who holds the place together administratively, to the degree that it can be called cohesive; it is said by some of his associates that he finds it possible to do so because he went to Columbia. Wiggins sent the N.I.H. a copy of the University catalogue, a 1,367-page tome, and invited the agency, since nobody else deemed a Harvard organization chart essential, to make up its own.

At God knows what cost to taxpayers and what diminution of funds that might otherwise have been channeled into more fruitful research, the N.I.H. plunged gamely into the Harvard thicket and came up with a chart—though that the adventure may have been at best quixotic was suggested by the inclusion, on a chain of boxes radiating from the box marked "President," of two squares helplessly labeled "Other."

One puzzling aspect of the organization of Harvard is that in some respects it is autocratic—the top echelon of the University approves the expenditure of practically every penny—and in some democratic—most faculty recruitment is initiated at the grass roots, down in the scattered academic departments. A truly illustrative chart, some Harvard people think, would have to be three-dimensional, and others have proposed that the whole matter should have been turned over to James D. Watson, the Harvard biologist who helped make graphic the double-helical structure of DNA. This would probably not be a good idea, because

Professor Watson, like other Harvard academic luminaries, has never got on particularly well with the administration, and were he to tackle an organization chart he might conceivably omit entirely someone like, say, the president of the University.

Amid all the current talk about restructuring universities, it has been argued that Harvard will be a particularly tough one to do over, because it was never logically structured to begin with. A one-time dean of the College, reflecting on how the place functions, has said, "It's a kind of anarchy. It's really not run by anybody. It just goes on." Exaggerated, but in a sense true. It could be argued that it would be ridiculous to try to put everybody at Harvard into tidy little categories, because what in the world would one do with somebody like Edward T. Wilcox, an administrator in charge of General Studies part of the time, and of Freshman Seminars part of the time, and of the Committee on Educational Policy part of the time, and a man who cannot even be pinpointed physically, inasmuch as he operates out of two detached offices and is often at the one when he is sought at the other? (On a shelf of one of his offices he has something called an "Artistic Efficiency Sorter," but it has never been removed from the carton it came in.) The fact is that Harvard is frequently in flux, as a good university probably ought to be; its Professor Gerald Holton, the molecular physicist, calls it kaleidoscopic and likens it to the earth before life was created, with a lot of ultraviolet radiation and molecules floating around in space. The organization of Harvard cannot be wholly capricious, though; a mere assistant dean in the University's administrative hierarchy was not long ago tapped to be administrative vice-president of the Ford Foundation.

At Harvard, it is hard to tell at any given moment just who the power people are. Professors, for instance, no matter how steadily their wisdom may illuminate the outside world, flicker like candles on campus, where their influence may depend on their popularity, and where their popularity may rise and fall as sharply as the ratings of a television show. It has been suggested by, among others, Mr. Pusey that the permanent locus of Harvard power rests with what the president has described fondly as its "little old ladies"—a dozen or so women in secretarial or junior-administrative slots who have held their jobs for many years and know where to find things. Mr. Pusey himself served one year both as president and as acting dean of the Faculty of Arts and Sciences. It was an abrasive period, in the course of which he was vigorously and sometimes almost viciously attacked by the *Crimson*, but the only time he could recall having then lost his composure was when the little old lady in the Dean's office took ill and left him on his own.

There is a little old lady in the Law School, and another in Public Health, and one dean has a little old lady who has been around so long and seems to have him so firmly in hand that some students are convinced she must have been his nanny, and others that she still is. To many an undergraduate, the most important person at Harvard—the spider, as it were, in the center of the whole inexplicable web—is not the president nor the dean of the College nor the master of any house, but, rather, the little old lady who zealously guards the portals of the dean of students.

The little old ladies, of course, know better. They know that nearly every organization this side of anarchy has an ultimate repository of authority and responsibility. Harvard has two such governing entities, a Board of Overseers and a Corporation, reflecting the circumstance that it was a joint creation of church and state. ("Harvard operates on an intangible system of separation of powers," the *Crimson* has said.) The basic difference between the boards is that the Corporation initiates and the overseers approve, or nearly always approve. In 1869, they turned down the Corporation's decision that Charles W. Eliot be given a tenure appointment as professor of chemistry, on the ground that he was too young; three months later, the Corporation made him president, and the overseers capitulated.

Until the nineteen-thirties, the two groups, by way of emphasizing their shared sovereignty, had separate addresses and separate secretaries. Now they share a secretary, who sometimes in the course of handling official communications between them corresponds with himself. The Corporation, a self-perpetuating body and the oldest corporation in the Western Hemisphere, derives its powers from a 1650 charter granted to the president and fellows of Harvard College by the royal governor of the Massachusetts Bay Colony. Harvard University is thus organizationally subservient to Harvard College.

The Corporation is composed of five fellows, the president, and the treasurer, and it is a hardworking body. Except for the summer months, it meets every other week throughout the year. "We're not expected to permit anything to interfere," one fellow said recently. This oldest corporation convenes, appropriately, in Massachusetts Hall, the oldest building (1720) on any college campus in the country, where it has a newish room (1938) directly above President Pusey's office. The meeting room is also directly below a chamber occupied by College freshmen, and once or twice in the last thirty years inquisitive undergraduates have had themselves lowered by ropes to peek inside at their august elders. The last one down was dangled headfirst and quickly asked to be pulled back; he was getting a headache, he reputedly declared, and anyway things looked pretty dull inside.

The Corporation has had little to do with the faculty or the students. It hasn't wanted to. It has delegated all its administrative, educational, and disciplinary powers to others. Its one link to the rest of the University is the president. When one fellow was asked by an acquaintance in 1968 how he felt about the surge of activism that had lately roiled all campuses, he replied cheerfully, "Thank the Lord, that's the deans' problem, and not mine. At the Corporation level you can sit back and watch." That was what troubled many students when S.D.S. threw the deans out of their offices; the Corporation might be watching, but it was invisible. There have been slight changes. On April 13, 1969, the Corporation exchanged views face to face with five undergraduates. Indeed, one would be foolish to state flatly that in the near future an undergraduate might not be a fellow of the Corporation. Radcliffe has a somewhat similar governing board, called a Council, and two members of the Harvard Corporation sit on it. At a time when the Council was debating admitting students to its deliberations (as it subsequently did), a Radcliffe girl innocently asked a Corporation member, the Boston lawyer Francis H. Burr, if there were any Harvard students on the Corporation. "I thought Burr was going to have a stroke," an onlooker later reported, "and he was the youngest fellow." But that was a long time ago—way back in 1968.

In Harvard's early days, most of the fellows were professors and tutors who, in effect, governed themselves. More recently, the Corporation has been made up mostly of Boston bankers, lawyers, doctors, and businessmen, with a Cabot or a Lowell or both frequently among them. (It may be a measure of change at Harvard that now the Corporation has neither.) By and large the men have been politically and economically conservative, and socially enlightened—this last, to be sure, in an old-fashioned liberal way. Finances are their main Harvard concern, and their scrutiny is unremitting. Some years ago, a loyal old grad presented Harvard with a set of Russian church bells, which were installed in the tower of Lowell House. The Corporation decreed that the bells should be rung once a month, and it appropriated funds for a bell-ringer. Then the Second World War broke out, and the bells fell silent. After the war, Lowell House got a new master, and he wrote the Corporation asking for a renewal of its bell-ringing allocation. The answer was no; the donor of the bells had died in the interim, and there was no further need to placate that particular patron.

To be a fellow of Harvard College is such a distinction, at least in Harvard eyes, that vacancies are filled only after the utmost scrutiny. It was more than a year before the last vacancy was filled, in the spring of 1968. The Corporation then welcomed to its select ranks a forty-four-year-old Cleveland lawyer, Hugh Calkins. He was a midwesterner largely by adoption. He had been born just outside of Boston and had gone to Exeter before distinguishing himself as a magna cum laude graduate of both Harvard College, in 1945, and Harvard Law School. He was president of the *Crimson* and president of the *Law Review*. In 1956, by chance, another Harvard law man had asked Calkins for some advice about his life. Calkins had recommended that the chap leave Washington, where he was doing able work but was hardly known, and move to some place like Cleveland, where he could become a big frog in a comparatively little pond and, like as not, become well enough recognized to be chosen for the Harvard Corporation. Calkins's friend never acted on the advice, but Calkins did himself.

Calkins further distinguished himself in Cambridge, after the April agonies, by actually seeking opportunities to talk with students. He went on television. He offered to debate an S.D.S. spokesman, but the organization didn't want to tangle with him. When he felt that he had been misquoted, Calkins ambled down to the *Crimson* office and asked to borrow a typewriter so he could peck out a rebuttal. In the eyes of the militant left he committed what, for a member of the hated Harvard Corporation, was an unforgivable crime: he behaved like a decent human being.

Until 1948, no fellow had lived farther away from Cambridge than New York City, and every one, with the single exception of the redoubtable Nathaniel Bowditch, had been a Harvard College graduate. That year, in a sense paving the way for Calkins of Cleveland, Harvard had chosen as a new fellow William L. Marbury, a lawyer from then far-off Baltimore. True, Marbury had gone to Harvard Law School, but he was not Harvard College; he had spent his undergraduate years at the University of Virginia and was, moreover, the son of a Princeton man. On top of all that, he was a close friend of Alger Hiss and had been Hiss's first counsel during the Whittaker Chambers business. Marbury had worked for the War Department, with Secretary Henry L. Stimson and Undersecretary Robert P. Patterson, and Stimson had introduced him to President Conant, who had been devoting more of his time to the atomic bomb than to Harvard.

When Marbury was proposed as a fellow, by Grenville Clark, Conant thought it a splendid suggestion. There were several fellows, though, who bridled when the president, on being asked why they shouldn't elect another Bostonian, replied that he had looked around Boston and couldn't find anybody suitable. Marbury's nomination was argued back and forth among the fellows for months. It was all done so secretly that the news didn't even leak to Paul Buck, on whom Conant had conferred the title Provost so he could be the senior University administrator while the president was unavailable. One morning, Buck got a phone call from Leverett Saltonstall, then the president of the Board of Overseers. "Tell me what you know about the Marbury case," Saltonstall said. Buck thought he was referring to *Marbury* v. *Madison*, and referred him to a Law School professor.

Marbury was finally elected—it was widely believed that if he hadn't been, Conant would have resigned—and the day before his first Corporation meeting, Grenville Clark tendered him a lunch at the Somerset Club in Boston, to introduce him to various Harvard elder statesmen. One of them, in a welcoming speech, disclosed that in that old-world club, the night before, he'd observed three venerable alumni in a grumbling huddle. One of them had finally exploded, "By God, the place has gone to hell! First those radical undergraduates pick as marshals of the senior class a Roman Catholic, a Jew, and a Negro. And what's even worse, they say this Marbury isn't even a Harvard man!"

Twenty years later, Marbury was the senior fellow, and was beginning to look like a Harvard man. He had commuted faithfully between Baltimore and Cambridge practically every other Monday in the interim, except when he had to represent a client before the Supreme Court, and for the most part he had enjoyed it. "It's been an absolutely fascinating experience," he said. "To sit here and listen and watch the thing go by is just wonderful. That's why the Corporation takes its work seriously." Most students didn't take the Corporation seriously—few of them, indeed, gave it a moment's thought—until Harvard erupted, at which time many thoughtful members of the campus community began to wonder if it was a good idea to have so much power—even power unexercised—concentrated in the hands of a small, self-perpetuating, and peripheral group of men. It pleased the militant students, moreover, to have an enemy with such a delightfully wicked name; Marbury and the other fellows, though, would have been a target for disgruntled students' slings and arrows even if they'd been collectively known as, say, Supervisors of Democratic Study.

The Honorable and Reverend Board of Overseers, as the Corporation's alter ego has been formally called since it was appointed by the General Court—the legislature—of the Massachusetts Bay Colony in 1637, is a larger group, thirty strong, with the president and the treasurer sitting in ex officio. At its inception, the Board consisted of six magistrates and six ministers—thus the "Honorable and Reverend." After the formation of the United States, with Harvard specifically mentioned in the Massachusetts constitution and receiving an annual state subsidy, the governor and lieutenant governor were always on the board, and this practice continued until 1865. Until eight years before that, most Harvard examinations were oral, and the overseers presided over them. They could still attend Ph.D. orals, if they chose to, but they don't.

Five new overseers are elected by mail vote each year, for six-year terms, and all alumni of the University may vote save those who hold Corporation appointments. Nominations are usually made by a committee of alumni, but any Harvard man may get on the ballot—Norman Mailer,' 43 did in 1969—if two hundred eligible voters petition on his behalf. Overseers are usually successful graduates well into their thirties or older (their last two presidents have been David Rockefeller and C. Douglas Dillon), but one of the most radical and articulate members of the class of 1968, Henry Norr, announced on the eve of his graduation that he was planning to run in 1969, so that his generation's viewpoint could be aired, and the *Crimson* acclaimed his candidacy. (While Norr generally had few kind words for Harvard or any other institution of higher learning, he did once say, "The universities may not necessarily be the bastions of fairness and freedom, but they do seem to be better than the world outside.") Overseers' elections are usually popularity contests. John F. Kennedy, however, failed to make the board the first time he ran, in 1955; he was nominated again in 1957 and won. Robert Kennedy ran in 1967, and was defeated, too. The candidate who received the largest number of votes in 1968 was Andrew Brimmer, the first Negro governor of the Federal Reserve Board, who almost certainly benefited from the national impulse to identify with black Americans.

The overseers, who constitute a Harvard House of Lords, meet seven times a year, including the Monday after the Yale game, so they can have themselves a fine three-day Harvard weekend. Their meetings last all day. No drinks are served at lunch, not even sherry, on the theory that you can't oversee through half-closed lids. In May, though, when they have a two-day meeting, this Spartan rule is eased, and at that time they are further regaled when the president gives a dinner for them and the Corporation. Mr. Pusey added a fillip to these banquets by having the governing boards shrilly welcomed into his house by his son James, a bagpiper, playing "Fair Harvard" on his pipes. The quorum for an overseers' meeting is nine, but, considering that most overseers are men with many interests, attendance is surprisingly high; as a rule, some twenty-five of them show up for each session.

The overseers have three standing committees (one of them a Committee on Committee Assignments) and forty-one visiting committees, which implement the implications of the word *overseer*. There is a committee to visit just about every nook and cranny of the Harvard establishment, from Middle Eastern Civilizations to Kitchens and Dining Rooms. The visiting committees are not only a useful device for getting overseers interested in the detailed operations of one or more parts of the University, but for luring other people—more often than not high-income people—into the Harvard orbit. The first large gift to the University's forty-nine-million-dollar Program for Science fund-raising campaign was a three-million-dollar contribution from a member of the Committee to Visit the Chemistry Department. Each committee (except the kitchen committee, which consists largely of mothers of Harvard students) has an overseer as chairman, but at last count there were 742 non-overseers serving on them, too, some of whom weren't even Harvard alumni. The investment banker Sidney J. Weinberg, for instance, who never got beyond public school, was one of seventy-three members of what is understandably the largest overseers' committee of all, the Committee on University Resources.

As in Congress, committee appointments are based largely on seniority. When Walter D. Edmonds first joined the board, he was made head of the Harvard Forest Committee. Toward the end of his term, the author took over the Committee to Visit the English Department. When a committee visits, it usually has a dinner. Edmonds assembled his English group one year at the Signet Society, the undergraduate literary club, and laid in a few bottles of whiskey. The consumption was so brisk he had to send out for more. He happened to mention to a friend on the Corporation later that he had spent seventy dollars for refreshments that evening. Soon afterward, the Corporation, which is not entirely unbending, voted solemnly to reimburse Edmonds and other hosts in similar fixes, on the ground that it was a proper function of the University to support all overseer activities.

John P. Marquand and John Mason Brown have been on the English committee, too, such bibliophiles as Donald Hyde and Arthur Houghton on the library committee, and Robert Kennedy and Arthur Schlesinger, Jr., on the government committee. David Rockefeller has been on the economics committee for twenty years. (That committee, concluding that instruction in economics at Harvard was too theoretical and political and insufficiently oriented toward business, brought about the establishment of a chair in the economics of enterprise; the professor occupying it bears allegiance both to the economics department and the business school. The committee has also ferried a few Harvard economists to New York annually to talk to businessmen and bankers, who have traditionally been wary of the economics taught at Harvard.) The Committee on Harvard College boasts among its members the presidents of Williams, Cornell, and Boston College, and the headmaster of Andover. Several men serve on more than one committee. Carlton P. Fuller, for example, a retired Polaroid executive, is a visitor to the Divinity School and the physics department, as well as president of the Harvard Glee Club Foundation. Complimented one time on the diversity of his Harvard interests, Fuller, who was then seventy, replied, with New England diffidence, "My real interest is mountaineering."

The functions of a Harvard visiting committee, like those of many an honorific group, are often pro forma. One visiting committee, though, vigilantly protective of its appointed ward, became embroiled in a nightmarish opera bouffe that racked Harvard for more than twenty years and that, before its denouement, was to occupy more of the time of the University's governing boards than any other single issue in Harvard's entire three-odd centuries of existence. The object of this wrangling was a part of the University that hardly seemed cast for a disputative role—the Arnold Arboretum, a quiet grove of trees and bushes that is not even physically close to any other part of the University, but instead occupies a 265-acre tract in the Jamaica Plain section of Boston.

The Arboretum was once described by one of its aficionados as "the Great Pioneer Tree Institution of the American Continent," but few Harvard students know that it exists, and few of those who know care. Nonetheless, because of this remote and tranquil garden, a fellow resigned from the Corporation, some of Harvard's most faithful supporters hauled it into court, the President was accused of playing fast and loose with trust funds, and the sundered Corporation felt obliged, for the first time in its

Olympian history, to issue a statement of self-justification to the *Harvard Alumni Bulletin*. The whole debate was almost withering enough to shrivel Harvard's ivy.

The trouble began in 1872, when a merchant named James Arnold died and willed to Harvard some land and a trust fund for the establishment of an arboretum that "should contain, as far as is practicable, all the trees, shrubs, and herbaceous plants, either indigenous or exotic, which can be raised in the open air." The president and fellows and three trustees handling Arnold's estate agreed, among other things, to spend his money "for the promotion of Agricultural or Horticultural improvements or other Philosophical or Philanthropic purposes at their discretion." Harvard was fortunate in that it had already been given a tract of land, alongside Arnold's, by a Roxbury merchant named Benjamin Bussey, in whose memory a school for plant geneticists was subsequently established. The Commonwealth of Massachusetts took over the Bussey Institution in 1963; before that, it had turned out forty-one scientists, fourteen of whom became members of the National Academy of Arts and Sciences.

The Arnold Arboretum became, and still is, one of the world's most esteemed examples of its genre. Its next-door neighbor used to be a non-Harvard forest called Joyce Kilmer Park, which is now the site of an old-folks' home and contains but a solitary tree. The Arboretum was from the start so popular a park that in 1882 the city of Boston cast covetous eyes on it. Harvard gave Boston title to the property, and the city then leased it back to the Corporation for a thousand years at a dollar a year, with options to renew the lease in perpetuity, a further thousand years at a time, at the same rent. Boston agreed to maintain the roads and benches inside the place, and Harvard to let the public in free of charge during daylight hours.

Nowadays, on spring weekends, when the Arboretum is ablaze with crab apples, azaleas, forsythia, or lilacs (there was an annual Lilac Sunday until the weather turned fickle and nobody could predict when the blooms would be full), fifty thousand people are apt to stroll through its serene groves. In theory, Harvard has sole jurisdiction over the grounds after sunset, but neither Boston nor the University agreed in 1882 to fence the place. Lovers accordingly find its lawns accommodating on warm nights, and the neighborhood kids—many of them from the Roxbury ghetto—drift in and out at all hours. If they feel like angling for goldfish in an Arboretum pond, they may fashion a rod out of the handiest branch, heedless of the fact that the mutilated tree may be the only one of its kind on the continent.

Soon after the Arboretum began, it came into the loving custody of a botanist named Charles S. Sargent, who presided over it with single-minded devotion from 1873 to his death in 1927. He quickly increased its staff, adding to it a professor of forest pathology and cytology, and also a propagator. The Arboretum's library, one of the world's foremost in its field, began when Sargent donated his personal library to the Arboretum. Sixty-five hundred different species and varieties grow on the grounds; Sargent sent expeditions all over the world to collect them, and he often went afield himself. He hoped to amass plants from every corner of the globe, and he succeeded, with the exception of Madagascar, New Caledonia, and New Guinea. He tried vainly to get eucalyptus and citrus trees to withstand the harsh New England winters, but prevailed—on his fourteenth try—with a cedar of Lebanon. One of his successors had equally good luck with a Chinese redwood.

Asia was Sargent's special field of interest. He built up a celebrated *bonsai* collection of Japanese dwarf plants, which are kept in a treasure room; some are well over a hundred years old. In 1892, foraging through Asia, Sargent brought back from Japan alone a thousand additions to the Arboretum's herbarium. His successors were Asia-minded, too; they got the last apple tree out of China before the Communist takeover in 1949. At the end of the Korean War, when the United Nations wanted to help rehabilitate South Korea by providing seedlings to cross with its native oaks, the Arboretum, which had Korean oaks and about seventy-five other species, varieties, and cultivars of oak, hospitably took in a Korean dendrologist who spent a year crossing oaks and astounding his American colleagues by the agility he displayed in climbing trees and wrestling precious acorns away from squirrels. More recently, the Arboretum has helped the United States Department of Defense by studying and propagating a plant called *upa upa*, whose poisonous juices the Vietcong have smeared on bamboo spikes to impale enemy feet.

A number of activities at Harvard are sustained by special groups of patrons—the Friends of Harvard Hockey, for instance, and the Friends of the Fogg Art Museum. There are Friends of Track, Crew, and the Harvard Forest. No portion of the University could muster an aggregation of supporters more amicable and open-handed than the Friends of the Arboretum whom Sargent steadily recruited, among them a man who earmarked his contribution for the scientific and empirical improvement of the beach plum. The Arboretum's endowment grew and grew; it had reached one million dollars at Sargent's death in 1927, and in tribute to his memory his Friends collected another quarter of a million. He himself may ultimately prove to be the Arboretum's most lavish benefactor. In his will, he left twenty thousand dollars for the institution's library, and an additional ten thousand for general purposes. The latter sum was to be lazily disbursed. He stipulated that its income be capitalized for one hundred years, and that the income of half of the principal that had accumulated by the year 2027 be similarly handled for another century. At 4.5 per cent compound interest, someone at Harvard has computed, the second half of the principal alone will, by 2127, amount to thirty-four million dollars.

The Arnold Arboretum is just a tiny fraction of the biological sciences that altogether constitute a tiny fraction of the University. In recent years, Harvard has numbered among its shining scholarly lights such men as, to mention just a few, Elso S. Barghoorn, the paleobotanist, who after examining some South African rocks found fossilized evidence of microscopic bacterial life more than three billion years old—the oldest known life on earth; Carroll M. Williams, the biologist, who isolated an insect hormone that can keep insects in a cocoon stage forever, so they never grow up and lay eggs, and the applications of which could some day conceivably make insecticides obsolete; Paul C. Mangelsdorf, the plant geneticist, who recently retired after a career marked by his development of a rustproof wheat and a protein-rich corn; and, of course, James D. Watson, the DNA man.

In 1944, there was a feeling at the University that the activities of its biologists and botanists were insufficiently coordinated, and a wood anatomist named Irving Widmer Bailey agreed to take a year off to study the "total botanical situation." Bailey, who died in 1967 at eighty-three, was a gentle, quiet scientist, and Harvard was his whole life. His father, an astronomer, had been on the staff of the University's Observatory; he himself had gone to Harvard College and after graduating in 1907 had never left the place. In the nineteen-twenties, though confined by the limitations of optical microscopes, Bailey had done dramatic research on cotton hairs (they grew in rings, he concluded, like trees), and he lived long enough to have his radical surmise confirmed by infinitely more probing and revealing electron microscopes.

Bailey submitted his report on the total botanical situation in June, 1945. Among other things, he found the Arboretum's main building at Jamaica Plain overcrowded, and something of a fire hazard; its rare books had already been removed for safekeeping to Cambridge. His chief recommendation was that most of the Arboretum's remaining library and most of its 600,000 dried specimens of herbs also be moved to Cambridge and merged there with the library and herbarium (principally 175,000 dried ferns) of the Gray Herbarium. Bailey had other suggestions, some involving the consolidation of Arboretum funds with other biological-science funds. His proposals were routinely approved by the administration, by his colleagues in Botany, and, finally, by the Corporation; in presenting the matter to the fellows, President Conant told them not to bother to read the Bailey report, since everybody whom it could conceivably affect had already endorsed it.

But soon all botanical hell broke loose. The word began to get around among people who cared about Harvard trees and shrubs —and how many of them there were staggered Harvard—that the University was callously dismembering the Arboretum. Those who felt that way argued that the Arboretum was an all but autonomous entity, that people who had contributed to it would not have done so had they thought it to be merely another subdivision of Harvard, and that the Corporation, as trustee for the Arboretum's endowment, had no business arbitrarily separating its library and dried herbs from its living trees. Soon, professors who had approved the Bailey report were recanting, notable among them Oakes Ames, the orchidologist, who for a while had been head of the Arboretum himself. Then the Visiting Committee for the Arboretum, of which Mrs. Grenville Clark was a staunch and articulate member, got aroused. So did her husband, who resigned from the Corporation in 1950, after nineteen years' service, when his fellow fellows declined to adopt a compromise he proposed. The Board of Overseers appointed a special investigating committee, a Committee on Biological Sciences. Walter D. Edmonds had by then attained enough seniority as an overseer to be chairman. He got so involved in biological sciences that he had to abandon writing entirely for three months.

Eventually, Edmonds's committee, after consulting lawyers and being satisfied that the trustees of the Arnold endowment were acting in good faith, came out for moving the books and herbs to Cambridge. That was in 1950, five years after the submission of the Bailey report, and it would be almost another three years—in the course of which more and more lawyers joined the battle—before the Corporation acted. In January, 1953, in the interests of "fruitful [could the pun have been intentional?] and harmonious cooperation between the Arboretum and other parts of the University," it decided to remove the "main body of the library and herbarium" of the Arboretum to a new herbarium building in Cambridge and to leave behind "a working library and herbarium."

The decision had been made, and the new building went up, but the battle was far from over. Some members of the Visiting Committee asked the attorney general of Massachusetts to declare that Harvard had been derelict in its handling of the trust; such a declaration would have brought the matter to court. The attorney general begged off. Then, the opponents of the move to Cambridge formed a militant organization—militant, at least, by garden-club standards—called the Association for the Arnold Arboretum. Among *its* members, who eventually numbered 1,150, were the stalwart Boston names of Mrs. Charles Francis Adams, Mrs. Ellery Sedgwick, Endicott Peabody (he had not yet been elected governor and could take sides), three Cabots (no Lowells, but one Saltonstall); Mr. and Mrs. Grenville Clark and Mr. and Mrs. Grenville Clark, Jr.; and such other formidable personages as Henry F. duPont, of the Winterthur Gardens in Delaware; Mr. and Mrs. Robert Woods Bliss, who had already given Harvard Dumbarton Oaks, their home in Washington; Dr. F. A. Bartlett, the tree surgeon; the superintendent of parks of Spokane, Washington; the director of the Brooklyn Botanic Gardens, the president of the Federated Garden Clubs of Maryland, the acting president of the Marblehead Garden Club, the director of a Pennsylvania wildflower preserve, the president of the Tacoma Rhododendron Society, the Horticultural editor of *American Home*, the curator of the Montreal Garden Club, and the presidents of the Garden Club of America and the National Council of Federated Garden Clubs.

These were adversaries to be reckoned with in any contest, as tough in their horticultural way as S.D.S. in its way, and the more they fulminated (at one time some of them suggested that Harvard planned to plough up the Arboretum for a hospital site), the more Harvard reacted. "They said such awful things about us," McGeorge Bundy recalled years afterward, "that the zest of battle arose in our veins and everybody went to war." Bundy himself was subjected to considerable sniping when he expressed amazement one time that anybody could make such a fuss about a bunch of dried leaves and twigs. His predecessor as dean of the Faculty of Arts and Sciences, Paul Buck, had been subjected to such harassment at one Beacon Hill dinner party that he had said to his hostess, "If you regard me as a thief, why do you want me in your house?"

In due course, Massachusetts elected a new attorney general. This one sided with the Association and in 1954 presented the case to the Supreme Judicial Court of Massachusetts. Meanwhile, Conant had retired and Pusey, who was an amateur orchidologist but tried to maintain a sense of balance about the plant world, too, had inherited the by now nine-year-old mess. Early in 1954, moreover, Harvard appointed a new director of the Arboretum, Richard A. Howard, who, standing six feet five inches, has an innate compassion for trees. Professor Howard, a specialist in West Indian mountaintop vegetation, currently teaches two courses at Harvard: Biology 209 (The Phylogeny of Flowering Plants), and Biology 310 (Dendrology and Plant Systematics)—the latter limited to graduate students. During the war, he struck a blow for plants, when the Army unfairly thought that one of them was responsible for an outbreak of dermatitis among troops in New Guinea who hung their towels on bushes. Howard managed to pin the blame where it belonged, on an untidy, hair-shedding caterpillar.

Howard had a solid Harvard background, having earned a Ph.D. in Cambridge and been elected a junior fellow of the Society of Fellows. Notwithstanding, after four years as an assistant professor, he had been passed over for tenure, and had left Harvard to become head of the Department of Botany at the University of Connecticut. Six months later, Harvard asked him back to take charge of the beleaguered Arboretum. (One of the first things he did in 1954 was to ascertain whether the rent had been paid to Boston. It had—well into the twenty-first century.) In June, 1954, Harvard instructed Professor Howard to evacuate to

Cambridge 600,000 of the Arboretum's 675,000 herbarium specimens, and all but seven thousand of its forty-nine thousand bound volumes.

There was an immediate outbreak of apoplexy among some of the Associates. The Arboretum, they lamented, had ceased to exist "as a separate independent institution." William Marbury all but risked his life by endeavoring to explain the University's position to a Baltimore garden club. There was opposition at home, too, principally from a botanist named Ivan M. Johnston, who had been at Harvard since 1922 and could identify a dried plant from across a room. Despite that prodigious knack, he had never earned a full professorship, and was feeling put upon. When moving day came around, Johnston refused to take part. He sat stubbornly at his microscope in Jamaica Plain while truckloads of specimens were trundled past him, and until his death soon afterward he would have nothing to do with any research in Cambridge. Nobody chided him; he had tenure; he was exercising his academic freedom.

The conflict dragged on. It was not until 1961, sixteen years after Professor Bailey's report, that the Supreme Judicial Court appointed a master to hold hearings and determine, as well as any one could, the relevant facts of the tangled case. He held hearings for six months, and submitted *his* report in June, 1963. In the midst of this, the Arboretum, which had been periodically buffeted by hurricanes, was struck by philanthropic lightning. Many of its regular benefactors had been sitting on their hands, while not wringing them. In 1962, a Boston octogenarian named Martha Dana Mercer, whose very name was unknown to most people at the Arboretum, died. She had evidently been taken to the Jamaica Plain institution a girl, and had fond memories of it. She left one-third of her estate to the Boston Museum of Fine Arts, one-third to the Boston Symphony, and the other third to the Arboretum—each third producing an income of two hundred thousand dollars a year.

The Supreme Court finally got around to the case in the fall

of 1965, and rendered its verdict in June, 1967—a decision uphold-
ing Harvard by a narrow 3–2 vote. The Court enjoined Harvard
to take certain placatory steps. The new herbarium building was
to be called the University Herbaria; there had to be a plaque in
the lobby attesting to the participation of the Arboretum in this
joint venture; and each book in the merged library that had come
from Jamaica Plain was to bear a bookplate identifying it as an
Arboretum book. Professor Howard wrote a conciliatory letter
to every individual who had been arrayed in battle against the
University. About one-third of the recipients agreed to let bygones be bygones. Another one-third never replied. The rest were
noncommittal.

Inside the Herbaria today, there are reminders of the scuffle.
A portrait of Professor Irving Bailey, his trusty optical microscope at hand, hangs in the main foyer. The place of honor was
originally occupied by a portrait of Linnaeus. The Bailey painting
was finished in the spring of 1967, and at his family's request it
was exhibited in the lobby at Commencement time, so his returning students could see it. Then, suddenly, just before the Court
decision, Bailey died, unaware that after twenty-two years of turmoil and unhappiness his viewpoint would be vindicated. The administrators of the Herbaria haven't yet been able to bring themselves to restore Linnaeus.

Further along in the building are two bas reliefs. One of them,
by Saint-Gaudens, is a profile study of Asa Gray, the botanist
after whom the old Gray Herbarium was named. It was a renowned enough work of art so that visitors to Cambridge who
didn't care a fig for herbs would go to the Gray Herbarium just
to look at it. Naturally, when the new herbarium—later herbaria
—was constructed in 1954, Harvard transplanted the celebrated
bas relief. But with the fate of the Arboretum still moot, the University didn't want to take a chance on further nettling any of its
adversaries. So it commissioned a companion bas relief of Charles
Sargent, exactly the same size, and also in profile, except that
Gray had been done staring in one direction, and Sargent was de-

picted staring in the other. The new bas relief, moreover, was treated with patina to make it look the same age as the old one. Then the two portraits were displayed, a few inches apart, nose to nose, eyeball to eyeball. Knowledgeable botanists consider this an odd juxtaposition, inasmuch as for most of their professional lives Professors Gray and Sargent, though equally heroic figures in the Harvard plant world, were barely on speaking terms.

The Arnold Arboretum still thrives. "The vegetation of the world is too big for any one institution to master," Professor Howard told a visitor to the Jamaica Plain area not long ago. "We have a damn good working organization here for the kind of horticulture the world needs at this particular time." By way of demonstrating this, the Arboretum has lately held a series of "Meet the Staff" lectures—one topic being "Climbing Plants, Stranglers, and Whoa-Vines." Professor Howard commutes contentedly between his living plants at the Arboretum and his dried ones in Cambridge. One spring day in 1966, he had the satisfaction of being out at Jamaica Plain when the National Park Service proclaimed the Arboretum a National Historic Site. It was also the day, fittingly, of the annual formal inspection of the unique establishment by the members of the Board of Overseer's Committee to Visit the Arnold Arboretum.

"The academic year 1967–68 will surely prove to have been one of the most difficult in the history of higher education in America." — *Nathan M. Pusey, before he got hit by 1968–69.*

xxiii

HARVARD CAME OUT OF THE Arboretum battle bleeding, but not too badly wounded. Many of the people whom it had estranged were, after all, only women, and of course Mrs. Mercer's legacy compensated for the defection of a lot of them. Harvard was lucky. It hates to alienate its sons. There are 130,000 living Harvard alumni, 50,000 of whom went to Harvard College, and probably no more than a thousand or two belong to garden clubs. Many Harvard men—whom one bygone Harvard president wanted to be known as "Harvardinates"—have done quite well in the post-academic world. "The names of its famous graduates ring like iron bells across the history of the Republic," Archibald MacLeish wrote clangingly in 1941. Forty-seven per cent of the trustees of all art museums in America went to Harvard; 9 per cent of the college's living alumni are listed in *Who's Who in America,* and 6 per cent of the authors in *Bartlett's Familiar Quotations* have a Harvard connection. ("Harvard men are itchingly literate," an anthologist of Harvard writing observed in 1931.)

Most people take it for granted that most Harvard men will do all right, but President Pusey always liked to be reassured that the products Harvard turned out were up to snuff. "When I go around to different cities to speak to alumni," he said, "it's heartening to find evidence of what Harvard is. Looking through a directory of Harvard alumni doesn't mean a thing; you have to meet flesh-and-blood people. I like to *think* that our alumni are conspicuous on school boards and are running hospitals and that kind of thing, and when I go out, I find that they *are*."

Like the University itself, the alumni are decentralized. The various graduate schools have separate alumni publications, associations, and fund-raising offices. (The most recent group is the Harvard Extension Alumni Association.) All Harvard men, however, are loosely linked by a body called the Associated Harvard Alumni. It has no membership dues, and it is almost impossible not to belong to it. Anyone who has spent as much as six weeks in a course of study at Harvard that could have led to a degree is automatically a member. People who try to sever whatever connections they once had with Harvard (one old grad, for instance, now hates the place because he hates his son-in-law, who also went there) are nonetheless listed in the catchall alumni directory, but their addresses are thoughtfully omitted, to save them, for one thing, from getting fund-raising letters from Harvard that might throw them into ungovernable rages. The only sure way of cutting all one's ties with the University is to return mail from it marked "Deceased," but that could lead to an embarrassing item in an alumni bulletin.

There are also, however, twenty-five thousand alumni who have taken the trouble to join one of the ninety-six Harvard Clubs in the United States or one of the thirty-seven abroad. Only the Boston and New York clubs have clubhouses. The New York one has a Committee on University Relations, which sponsors symposia on subjects like "The New Student and the Old University," and in the early spring of 1969 it horrified some of its older members by letting a *Crimson* photographer, and a female one at that, spend a lunch hour wandering around parts of its premises from which, at that time of day, members' wives with signing privileges are firmly barred. In the late spring, the Club's executive committee horrified some members of all ages, or at any rate disappointed them, by sending President Pusey a telegram in which it unequivocally endorsed his handling of the University Hall affair. (The club also, with a nod to the gentlemanly past, runs black-tie, brandy-and-cigars, prizefight evenings in its main hall.) The University has nothing to do with the admissions procedures of Harvard Clubs, which are fairly relaxed; as a rule, bad manners is the main ground for exclusion. An applicant for membership in the Boston club was turned down because, during a visit to its dining room while his application was pending, he threw a glass of water in his wife's face.

The old grads who care about Harvard are kept informed about it principally by the *Harvard Alumni Bulletin*, the only self-sustaining alumni publication in the country. Most institutions send their alumni publications to everybody, free; the *Bulletin* charges for subscriptions, like any other commercial magazine, and has a paid circulation of eighteen thousand—one-third of the living alumni of the College. The *Bulletin* takes Harvard men's accomplishments and activities pretty much in stride. One of the big news stories of the winter of 1968 was handled tersely in notes about the class of 1948: "Robert F. Kennedy has announced his candidacy for the Presidency of the United States." For a while, the *Bulletin* published notes about Radcliffe alumnae, but it discontinued the practice, partly because of lack of space and partly because some of its male readers fumed. "Unforgettable Part of the Harvard Scene: Radcliffe Girls in the Classrooms," ran the text of a recent *Bulletin* ad. "Unforgettable, too . . . the rich and creamy quality of Whiting's Milk." The *Bulletin* itself solicits orders for bronze bookends that are small-scale replicas of the statue of John Harvard in the center of the Yard; fifty-five dollars a pair, and conceivably the ideal gift for the Harvard man who has everything else.

The *Bulletin* used to be a fairly stodgy journal, thus no doubt reflecting the stuffiness of many of its readers. Lately, Harvard men have changed, and so has the magazine. It is trying to become known simply as *Harvard*, and it has turned frisky. Whereas in

1967 its entire description of the scatological *Why Are We in Vietnam?*, written by Norman Mailer, was "An Alaskan bear-hunting expedition is turned into a reflection of America today," in 1968 its coverage of a Harvard football game consisted of a parody, by an undergraduate, of Mailer's *The Armies of the Night*. Soon after that, the magazine devoted its cover to a picture of Timothy Leary. Making a survey among alumni, it asked them questions like "Did you go to Harvard because: You really wanted to? Your father wanted you to? He wouldn't pay your tuition at Princeton? You were turned down by Annapolis? Yale? Some other place? Uncle Sam sent you? It just seemed inevitable? It was there?" Throughout 1969, the magazine gleefully continued to outrage some of its readers, going so far, in an attempt to give faithful coverage to the events of early April, as to reprint in its columns some of the four-letter words that were inevitably a part of the hectic episode. At Commencement a few weeks afterward, the president-presumptive of the Associated Harvard Alumni bravely described the magazine as "unusual and provocative." Despite its determined independence from the Harvard administration, the *Bulletin* does not rate high with the *Crimson;* in puckish recognition of the suspicion it has engendered, the magazine took an ad in the newspaper toward the end of the 1968–69 academic year calling itself the "Corporation Press" and soliciting subscriptions.

Thanks to sheer durability, Harvard has had more opportunities than most universities to reconvene its old grads, but it moves slowly. It didn't even celebrate its 100th and 150th anniversaries. A 200th anniversary was deemed something to make a mild fuss over, and in 1836, accordingly, nearly fourteen hundred celebrants gathered in Cambridge and banqueted for six and a half hours, immersed in a sea of toasts. They were exposed for the first time to "Fair Harvard," which has been the University's anthem ever since. The lyrics were written by Samuel Gilman, a member of the class of 1811. As an undergraduate, he had been punished for absence from prayer and not returning library books, but he had reformed and become a Unitarian minister in Charleston, South Carolina. The words he wrote for the bicentennial gathering were not only a tribute to Harvard but an attack on religious orthodoxy—"Let not moss-covered error moor thee at its side, as the world on truth's current glides by." More than a century later, in a booklet issued to newly arriving freshmen, the Reverend Mr. Gilman's admonitory *not* was transposed to a *the;* a few students who didn't realize that this was a typographical error seized on the phrase as evidence of Harvard's failure to keep up with the times.

Among the principal celebrants of Harvard's 250th birthday, in 1886, were President Cleveland, James Russell Lowell, and the senior Oliver Wendell Holmes. There was a torchlight procession, and some light entertainment, including an historical skit in which six Harvard professors of yore went about flogging a young instructor—the point of which apparently was to show that Harvard had grown up. The biggest celebration Harvard ever had marked its tercentenary, in 1936; it lasted ten months. An outdoor theatre with nearly fifteen thousand seats occupied the Yard for an entire academic year. Five hundred and forty-seven scholars, representing 530 institutions all over the world, came to Cambridge to pay their respects, and so did President Franklin Roosevelt and ten thousand other alumni. At the final session, on September 18, 1936, the Harvard assembly was not terminated but, with Harvard's casual attitude toward the passage of time, was merely adjourned to September 18, 2036. On that day, barring some cataclysm, ten thousand men of Harvard almost surely will turn up.

In ordinary years, Commencement time, of course, is reunion time. Harvard's principal reunions are those of the college classes that graduated twenty-five and fifty years earlier. Radical politics was much on everyone's mind at the time of the 1969 Commencement, but nobody paid any attention to a returning member of the class of 1919, Lawrence Dennis, whose extremist credentials were gilt-edged. The chances were that few undergraduates who glanced at his name tag would have had the slightest awareness that this gentle-looking elder citizen shuffling around with a cane had once been head of the fascist movement in America.

There are people who stoutly assert that a Harvard twenty-fifth reunion is the world's best party, as well as one of the longest-lasting. It goes on for four days, and there are reasonably authenticated cases of boys who have decided to go to Harvard because they had such a good time at their fathers' twenty-fifths that they wanted to repeat the experience on their own. The usual attendance is close to two thousand—classmates, wives, and children. The party costs $250,000, four-fifths of which the University underwrites. This is largely a paper subsidy, covering payments for rent and food that one part of the University pays to another; Harvard's actual cash outlay for twenty-fifth reunions comes to only ninety thousand dollars, or a mere eleven dollars per person per day. (The total bill for liquor, despite persistent rumors to the contrary, is a mere eleven thousand dollars.) Over the twenty-five years, though, most classes have already enriched Harvard by something like $1.5 million, and for 1968 alone the reunion class of 1943 was credited with $850,000; the reunion is the University's way of saying "Thank you, and come again."

The twenty-fifth reunion is taken so seriously at Harvard that it has a separate office, with a staff of two young women who work on arrangements the year round. (Both incumbents are Harvard daughters and attended their fathers' twenty-fifths.) The big reunions are beautifully organized: The principal fund-raisers in a class are apt to end up, as if by the sheerest coincidence, rooming spang alongside the class's best-heeled prospects. The busy reunion office provides all comers with free wastebaskets, ashtrays, raincoats, and soap, but this doesn't cost as much as it might; some companies are glad to have their products in the hands of so elite a group. (The soap is easy; Neil McElroy, the chairman of Procter and Gamble, is also chairman of the giant Committee on University Resources.) The program doesn't change much from year to year, but there have been variations.

369

The class of 1937 wrote and produced an original show. Leonard Bernstein conducted a Boston Pops recital for his class of 1939. Pete Seeger sang for his 1940 classmates (and was such a hit that the next year the class of 1941 hired him for a reprise). For the twenty-fifth of the class of 1943, convening as it did the spring after the Boston Red Sox won the American League pennant, Harvard arranged for nine hundred class sons and daughters to take in a night game at Fenway Park. The class of 1944 cross-examined itself, by means of a reunion questionnaire, on hot Harvard issues. Seventy-six per cent of the returning classmates who responded thought that Harvard students should be able to take R.O.T.C. if they wished, with 60 per cent opposed to their getting academic credit for it; 90 per cent condemned the forcible occupation of University Hall, and 58 per cent approved of Mr. Pusey's summoning the police; 86 per cent thought students should have a say in organizing the curriculum, but 68 per cent thought they shouldn't in selecting the faculty; and 54 per cent—an encouragingly open-minded showing for men teetering on the edge of grandfatherhood—approved of the notion of having undergraduate members of the Corporation.

The reunions are held concurrent with Harvard's chief annual ceremony, its Commencement. People who go to this ritual just once or twice find it impressive; the English writer Marcus Cunliffe once appraised it in *Encounter* as both solemn and debonair. (Harvard officers use both "festival rites" and "tribal rites" to describe the exercises.) People who go perennially tend to be less awed, and sometimes even bored. Ex-president Conant, for instance, told an acquaintance in the spring of 1968, "I have no desire ever again to see a Commencement procession of *any* institution." (During Harvard Commencements, the president of Harvard customarily sits in the president's chair, an eighteenth-century Tudor throne that is elaborately carved but not very comfortable.) In Harvard's Commencement program, vestiges of its ancient ties to the state are evident. The sheriff of Middlesex County is an important figure, and so is the governor of Massachusetts, the latter traditionally being escorted by a troop of mounted lancers. The order of precedence in the procession is inflexible. Nobody can remember now just why, but the trustees of the Charity of Edward Hopkins—the eighteenth-century benefactor whose wife was born a Yale—rate very high. They get to sit on the platform, and in the procession they march just behind the Phi Beta Kappa orator and the poet, and ahead of clergymen.

The Commencement ceremonies are organized and run by the University marshal, who is to Harvard what the chief of protocol is to the rest of the United States. As the Office of Protocol has its Blair House in Washington, so does the University marshal's office have its Dana-Palmer House in Cambridge, where V.I.P.s can be lodged. The Marshal used to do little more than walk at the head of academic processions, but now he is occupied much of the year with foreign visitors. During a single week not long ago, Harvard played host to the prime ministers of Singapore and Tonga, and the ambassadors to the United States from Russia and Rumania. Each consequential visitor has a program arranged to suit his presumed tastes. The prime minister of Tonga was introduced to some Harvard oceanographers.

All told, Harvard welcomes nearly a thousand foreign visitors a year. Mr. Pusey, it is tacitly understood, has time to see only those who are at least of cabinet rank or are important religious figures. The University marshal gets the rest. Since 1965, he has been William G. Anderson, a member of the class of 1939, a yachtsman, and, by his own account, a professional loafer until he took the Harvard job. He had spent most of his time handling family investments. In 1964, he ran his class's twenty-fifth reunion. He applied himself to that responsibility so vigorously that he embarrassed the young women in the year-round office; no other chairman had ever come in day after day and sat around licking stamps. Anderson couldn't help it. "I fell in love with Harvard College," he explains. In due course, Pusey decided that such uncommon love should be requited, and offered Anderson the marshal's job. Anderson didn't know all that much about Harvard, enamored though he was, so he betook himself to a Caribbean island, where he spent three weeks with no companions other than Samuel Eliot Morison's Harvard histories and three gallons of rum.

Returning to Cambridge to assume his new duties, he found a directive from Pusey: "Please shorten Commencement by half an hour." Nobody had managed to do that for a hundred years or more, but Anderson was game. He began studying old orders of march, and suddenly reflected, as he was pacing through the Yard, stopwatch in hand, that all of Harvard's twenty-five hundred degree candidates customarily walked to their seats in succession. At Yale, he remembered having heard, different contingents of candidates walked in simultaneously from different directions. "We'll do it too!" he cried aloud, startling several Radcliffe girls on their way to a Choral Society rehearsal.

Anderson enjoys his ceremonial position. "The deans are very sweet to me," he says. "They always ask me over when they're laying a cornerstone." Among his perquisites are to lead every formal Harvard procession, carrying a gold-tipped marshal's baton and, although he holds only a B.S. degree, to wear resplendent red robes that are ordinarily reserved for doctors of philosophy. "I don't seat dinners State-Department-protocol-wise," he says. "I seat them academic-wise."

Commencement Day is the only day of the year on which the Harvard Yard is closed to the general public, which might otherwise conceivably try to horn in on the chicken salad and beer that the University serves free that noon to all homecoming alumni. The ceremonies are held out of doors; Harvard rents fifteen thousand folding chairs for the occasion and usually fills most of them. Rain is ordinarily no problem. "It never rains," said the *Crimson* tersely and traditionally on Commencement Day in 1968. It had not rained on the big day since 1922, and although Harvard had long had a contingency plan for bad weather, there was no one around who could recall its being carried out.

In 1968, at 8:00 A.M. on Commencement Day, huddled under

an umbrella, Anderson—who among other duties serves on one of Harvard's most charmingly named committees, the Committee on the Happy Observance of Commencement—unhappily decided to move the ceremonies into Sanders Theatre, which has only twelve hundred seats and could accommodate only a fraction of the graduates and their proud families. "But my son's a summa!" cried an anguished mother as a Harvard cop politely but firmly barred her from the theatre. So many people got mad that day that Harvard resolved never again to have an indoor Commencement, rain or shine, and to make the best of any future soggy situation by resorting to closed-circuit television and raincoats.

A feature of every Commencement Day everywhere, of course, is the awarding of honorary degrees. Harvard's go way back. George Washington got one on April 3, 1776, while the University was temporarily located at Concord, having moved to makeshift quarters there because of the fighting around Cambridge. (Rich Harvard was so broke then—to save firewood money that year, it had cancelled its fall vacation and extended its winter vacation by one week—that it also gave a degree to a man who had in effect bought it the day before, for three hundred dollars.) Thirteen other United States presidents have received honorary Harvard degrees; Grover Cleveland turned down an LL.D. on the peculiar ground that he didn't know enough about law to deserve one. Harry S. Truman never got one, and it has been a running *Crimson* gag for some years that Harvard was about to repair that omission. On the eve of Commencement in 1969, the paper had him leaving Kansas City for Boston by a chartered Ozark Airlines plane; it concluded an extra that it put out halfway through Commencement Day with "For the 25th time since he became president in 1945, Harry S. Truman failed to receive an honorary degree from Harvard." Mayor John Lindsay did get one, which was unusual, because he was in the middle of a primary battle for renomination, and Harvard has traditionally shied away from conferring honorary degrees on individuals campaigning for office. One high Democratic politician who was singled out was Stewart Udall, the former Secretary of the Interior; he proceeded to make Harvard history, in the course of a prepared Commencement address, by blurting out, "History will judge you and I. . . . "

The recipients of honorary degrees are chosen in December by a three-man committee of the fellows, and after being passed on by the Corporation and approved by the overseers in January are invited to Cambridge the following June. (Mayor Lindsay was tapped before it occurred to anybody he might *be* in a primary.) Since 1886, it has been Harvard's policy never to confer an honorary degree unless the recipient shows up in person. It made an exception once after that for an unavoidably absent president of Yale (but not for President McKinley), and for Ernie Pyle, who was killed in 1945 between his selection and Commencement Day. Generals George C. Marshall and Douglas MacArthur were both awarded open-ended degrees in 1946; that is, they were notifed that they would be honored whenever they could come. Marshall turned up in 1947, at which time he expounded the Marshall Plan. MacArthur never did materialize and never got his honorary degree.

Harvard presidents customarily write the accompanying citations themselves. "It's kind of fun," Pusey has said. He would often get some help from an aide-de-camp, William Bentinck-Smith, an author and bibliophile who also raises pedigreed sheep (his wife knits sweaters from the wool from the fleece) and has what is reputed to be the world's finest—if not its only—collection of sheep art. Bentinck-Smith's most heroic and in a sense most tragic Harvard experience came in the spring of 1968, when he interrupted his search for felicitous citation phrases to block the doorway of Massachusetts Hall, which some S.D.S. demonstrators seemed of a mind to invade. Bentinck-Smith stood them off alone, but he had to endure the indignity of being addressed by their ringleaders, who apparently didn't grasp the niceties of hyphenization, as "Mr. Smith."

For many years, the citations were in Latin. The President

would write them in English, and a senior classics professor—Mason Hammond, chairman of the University Committee on Seals, Arms, and Diplomas, was the last one—would translate them. E. B. White was the unwitting cause of the abandonment of Latin, in 1954. Pusey acclaimed him as the "sidewalk superintendent of our times," and Professor Hammond complained that there was no Ciceronian equivalent of the phrase. Pusey decided to skip the Latin and, while he was at it, decreed that thenceforth all Harvard diplomas would be written in English unless a recipient specifically requested Latin. To Mr. Pusey's astonishment, he found himself at once under fire. Professor Hammond, for one, thought it made sense not to have diplomas couched in a language that most graduates could not comprehend; a great many undergraduates, though, complained that they didn't like to see Harvard go modern. More modern, to be precise; up to 1829, the president of Harvard and the governor of Massachusetts had always been expected to converse in Latin when they met on formal occasions.

The 1968 Commencement was special in many ways. The graduating college class had matriculated two months before John Kennedy was killed. In the spring of its senior year, it had endured the assassinations of Martin Luther King and Robert Kennedy. Earlier in the year, the seniors had invited King to be the principal speaker during their Class Day—observed the day before Commencement. Class Day had usually been a larksome occasion, but in 1968 the atmosphere was sombre. Mrs. King spoke instead of her husband. The Ivy Orator, who is selected for his comicality, got a laugh with an anti-S.D.S. joke and poked mild fun at Phillips Brooks House (it ministered to starving people, he said, by teaching them ceramics), but the main thrust of his oration was that it was not a year to be funny. The Class Orator was the radical Henry Norr, who in addition to urging everybody to vote for him for overseer the next year (he didn't make it) solicited signatures for draft-resistance petitions. The following day, Norr was among a handful of students who tried to interrupt the Shah of Iran, one of that year's crop of honorary-degree recipients; the audience was treated to the strange spectacle of Harvard men in caps and gowns being shoved around by older Harvard men in top hats, tail coats, and striped pants. At Class Day in 1968, the traditional odist had struck what was for Harvard an odd editorial note: "Fair Harvard, your sons are unsure of themselves. . . . " A year later, his successor started off once more with uncertainty —"Fair Harvard, your sons are assembled again/ To assess the proud words of the past/ In a spirit beclouded by doubts of their worth/ To the world where our lot has been cast"—but ended with what, considering the time and the place, was comparative optimism—"May our spirits be turned from all doubts to the hope/ Growing up from the spending of zeal;/ May the lessons we learned here be turned to make peace,/ To bind up, to renew and to heal."

While he was expressing those irenic sentiments, an S.D.S. girl was distributing literature calling for a mass walkout during the Commencement exercises the next morning. It was inconceivable that the June that followed the April of 1969 would be completely tranquil, and a number of demonstrations had been foreseen. "If you burn your diplomas," the 1969 Class Orator told his fellow seniors with mock seriousness, "have them photostated first." But if any diplomas were destroyed, the flames went unobserved, and the walkout that did take place was unimpressive. It was President Pusey, a man so widely thought to be unbending, who saved the day. He bent. Literally minutes before the Commencement exercises got under way, he yielded to the entreaties of the marshals of the graduating class and to the intercession of Judge Charles E. Wyzanski, Jr., a former president of the Board of Overseers, and allotted S.D.S. five minutes' time at the very outset of the ceremonies.

S.D.S. was taken aback. The spokesman who stepped forward on its behalf apparently did not wish to chance improvising a speech, so for the most part he merely read from one of the tracts that the group's mimeographers had been turning out: "Harvard is used by the very rich to attack the very poor. . . . David

Rockefeller [who was seated on the platform with other dignitaries] needs R.O.T.C. to protect his empire. . . .This Commencement is an atrocity. It is an obscenity." When the S.D.S. representative, already past his allotted time, called Mr. Pusey a liar, the audience almost drowned him out with boos and hoots, and a moment later a half dozen of his own classmates moved in on him and escorted him away from the microphone.

The unscheduled speaker had been so inept and churlish—he was probably also understandably nervous—that a good many students who had had every intention of walking out stayed in their places; they didn't want to seem to be endorsing his remarks. Only a hundred or so individuals—perhaps thirty or forty seniors among them—actually departed, thus missing a golden opportunity to boo Mr. Rockefeller, who, as they did not know, would be awarded an honorary degree a few minutes later.

While the anticlimactic walkout was under way, a senior named Dean P. A. Nicastro (who was subsequently misidentified *as* a dean) began delivering an address in Latin—"*Gratissimi te primum salutamus, Nathan Marsh Pusey, praeses huius universitatis. . . .*" As far as maintaining the peace that morning was concerned, it was just as well that there were only a handful of people present who, like Mr. Pusey, were fluent in the classics, because the sound effects Nicastro was proving over the loudspeaker system for the radicals' exodus were inflammatory. In translation, they went, "Most gratefully do we salute you first and foremost, Nathan Marsh Pusey, president of the University. Undaunted in the cause of truth, you recently defended Harvard against anarchy and demagoguery, while not a few teachers and students went astray. . . . Hail also, most judicious fellows and overseers. Without you and without your guiding presence this university cannot be sound, nor free, nor vigorous." Quite a few students who had decided not to burn their diplomas might have been moved, had their Latin been less rusty, to try to burn Nicastro.

The students who departed also missed a beautiful chance to

witness the discomfiture of some of the older members of the audience, who walked serenely into a baited trap. A Law School student elicited warm applause from them by starting off his remarks with some ringing words about law and order, and then revealed that he was quoting Adolf Hitler.

Neither in 1968 nor 1969 was Commencement exactly a happy occasion at Harvard. Disaffection ran high among both graduating classes. Yet each of the classes, in turn, pledged more money to the Harvard College Fund than had any seniors before them. And it was worth remembering that during the Class Day ceremonies in 1968 one of the loudest student ovations had been accorded to Professor John Finley, notorious for his advocacy of old-fashioned virtues and verities. One might have thought that this gentle classicist would typify much that the rebellious generation was supposed to find distasteful and irrelevant. But here was Finley unreservedly applauding the brash young Norr's declaration of his candidacy for overseer, and here was Norr, in his turn, vigorously clapping after Finley had concluded some graceful, eloquent remarks about "our beloved Harvard" with the soft testimonial: "Fair Harvard—she has been that to us in both senses of the word, more than we deserve." As long as most people at Harvard could continue to applaud fairness, Harvard probably had not much to fear.

Guest at 1969 Commencement, discussing Harvard's future with an assistant professor: "You sound optimistic."

Assistant professor: "That's because I'm taking a sabbatical next year."

Index

379